Capitalism and Democracy in Central and Eastern Europe

Assessing the Legacy of Communist Rule

This volume presents a shared effort to apply a general historical-institutionalist approach to the problem of assessing institutional change in the wake of communism's collapse in Europe. It brings together a number of leading senior and junior scholars with outstanding reputations as specialists in postcommunism and comparative politics to address central theoretical and empirical issues involved in the study of postcommunism. The authors address such questions as how historical "legacies" of the communist regime should be defined, how their impact can be measured in methodologically rigorous ways, and how the effects of temporal and spatial context can be taken into account in empirical research on the region. Taken as a whole, the volume makes an important contribution to the literature by utilizing the comparative historical method to study key problems of world politics.

Grzegorz Ekiert is Professor of Government, Chair of the Committee on Degrees in Social Studies at Harvard University, Senior Scholar at the Harvard Academy for International and Area Studies, and Senior Research Associate at the Center for European Studies. His previous work includes *The State against Society: Political Crises and Their Aftermath in East Central Europe* (1996) and *Rebellious Civil Society: Popular Protest and Democratic Consolidation in Poland* (1999, with Jan Kubik).

Stephen E. Hanson is the Boeing International Professor in the Department of Political Science at the University of Washington and the Director of the Russian, East European, and Central Asian Studies (REECAS) Program of the Jackson School of International Studies. He is the author of *Time and Revolution: Marxism and the Design of Soviet Institutions* (1997) and a coauthor of *Postcommunism and the Theory of Democracy* (2001).

Capitalism and Democracy in Central and Eastern Europe

Assessing the Legacy of Communist Rule

Edited by

GRZEGORZ EKIERT
Harvard University

STEPHEN E. HANSON
University of Washington

PUBLISHED BY THE PRESS SYNDICATE OF THE UNIVERSITY OF CAMBRIDGE
The Pitt Building, Trumpington Street, Cambridge, United Kingdom

CAMBRIDGE UNIVERSITY PRESS
The Edinburgh Building, Cambridge CB2 2RU, UK
40 West 20th Street, New York, NY 10011-4211, USA
477 Williamstown Road, Port Melbourne, VIC 3207, Australia
Ruiz de Alarcón 13, 28014 Madrid, Spain
Dock House, The Waterfront, Cape Town 8001, South Africa

http://www.cambridge.org

First published 2003

Printed in the United States of America

Typeface Sabon 10/12 pt. *System* LaTeX 2ε [TB]

A catalog record for this book is available from the British Library.

Library of Congress Cataloging in Publication data available

ISBN 0 521 82295 5 hardback
ISBN 0 521 52985 9 paperback

To Igo Bagnowski

To Hobart and Adele Hanson

Contents

About the Contributors

Phineas Baxandall taught at the Budapest University of Economic Sciences (1990–91) and received his Ph.D. in Political Science from MIT. He has published articles in *East European Politics and Societies, Journal of Socio-Economics*, and *West European Politics* and has contributed chapters to a number of edited volumes on the welfare state. His recent research has been on ideology and the "new economy," and a comparative political economy of work time. His book *Constructing Unemployment: The Political Economy of Joblessness in East and West* is forthcoming from Ashgate Press. He is a lecturer at Harvard's Committee on Degrees in Social Studies.

Grzegorz Ekiert is Professor of Government and Chair of the Committee on Degrees in Social Studies at Harvard University. His teaching and research interests focus on comparative politics, regime change and democratization, social movements, and East European politics and societies. His previous work includes *The State against Society: Political Crises and Their Aftermath in East Central Europe* (Princeton University Press, 1996) and *Rebellious Civil Society: Popular Protest and Democratic Consolidation in Poland* with Jan Kubik (University of Michigan Press, 1999).

Anna Grzymała-Busse is Assistant Professor of Political Science at Yale University. Her research focuses on political parties, the state, and institutional transformation and has been published in *East European Politics and Societies, Politics and Society, Comparative Politics*, and *Comparative Political Studies*, as well as in edited volumes. Her book on communist legacies and their impact on successor party performance is titled *Redeeming the Communist Past: The Regeneration of Communist Successor Parties in East Central Europe* (Cambridge University Press, 2002).

Stephen E. Hanson, Boeing International Professor in the Department of Political Science at the University of Washington, is the Director of the

Russian, East European, and Central Asian Studies (REECAS) Program of the Jackson School of International Studies. His teaching and research interests focus on comparative politics, ideology, political parties, democratic transition and consolidation, and postcommunist politics. He is the author of *Time and Revolution: Marxism and the Design of Soviet Institutions* (University of North Carolina Press, 1997), winner of the 1998 Wayne S. Vucinich book award from the American Association for the Advancement of Slavic Studies, and a coauthor of *Postcommunism and the Theory of Democracy* (Princeton University Press, 2001).

Tomasz Inglot is Associate Professor of Political Science and Douglas R. Moore Research Lecturer at Minnesota State University–Mankato. He received his Ph.D. from the University of Wisconsin–Madison and is a recipient of Fulbright, IREX, and other research grants. He specializes in the politics of social policy in postcommunist countries and has published several articles on this subject. He is currently working on a book titled *Historical Legacies, Institutions and the Emergence of Modern Welfare States in East Central Europe.*

Juliet Johnson is Associate Professor of Political Science at McGill University. Her current research explores international influences on central bank development in postcommunist states. She is the author of *A Fistful of Rubles: The Rise and Fall of the Russian Banking System* (Cornell University Press, 2000) and has published articles on postcommunist political economy in *Comparative Politics*, *Post-Soviet Affairs*, *Europe-Asia Studies*, *Problems of Post-Communism*, and *Communist and Post-Communist Studies*, among others. She has been a Research Fellow at the Brookings Institution and a National Fellow at the Hoover Institution. She received her Ph.D. in Politics from Princeton University in 1997.

Herbert Kitschelt is Professor of Political Science at Duke University, specializing in European political systems, comparative public policy, political economy, and twentieth-century European social theory. He is the author of three books in German about industrial policy formation and technology controversies. He has also written several books on European parties: *Logics of Party Formation: The Structure and Strategy of Belgian and West German Ecology Parties* (Cornell University Press, 1989), *Beyond the European Left* (Duke University Press, 1990), and *The Transformation of European Social Democracy* (Cambridge University Press, 1994). For his book *The Radical Right in Western Europe: A Comparative Analysis* (University of Michigan Press, 1995), he received the American Political Science Association's Woodrow Wilson Foundation Award. He is also the coauthor of *Post-Communist Party Systems: Competition, Representation, and Inter-Party Cooperation* (Cambridge University Press, 1999). His scholarly articles have appeared in a number of American, Belgian, British, French, and German journals. He held a joint appointment as Professor of Political Science at Humboldt University in Berlin, Germany, from 1993 to 1996.

Jeffrey S. Kopstein is Associate Professor of Political Science at the University of Toronto, specializing in comparative and European politics. He is the author of *The Politics of Economic Decline in East Germany, 1945–1989* (University of North Carolina Press, 1997) and coeditor of *Comparative Politics: Interests, Identities, and Institutions in a Changing Global Order* (Cambridge University Press, 2000) and has written numerous articles on postcommunist Europe. He is currently working on a book comparing the recent political experiences of Hungary, Slovakia, Ukraine, and Kyrgyzstan. Kopstein has also begun a new project (with Jason Wittenberg) on the voting patterns of ethnic majorities and minorities in interwar Eastern Europe.

Jan Kubik is Associate Professor of Political Science and Director of the Center for Russian, Central, and East European Studies at Rutgers University. He received his B.A. and M.A. from the Jagiellonian University in Krakow and his Ph.D. from Columbia University. His work is focused mostly on postcommunist transformations in Eastern Europe and revolves around the relationship between culture and power and contentious politics. His publications include *The Power of Symbols against the Symbols of Power: The Rise of Solidarity and the Fall of State Socialism in Poland* (Pennsylvania State University Press, 1994), which received an award from the Polish Studies Association, and (with Grzegorz Ekiert) *Rebellious Civil Society: Popular Protest and Democratic Consolidation in Poland, 1989–1993* (University of Michigan Press, 1999), which won the 2000 Orbis Book Prize from the American Association for the Advancement of Slavic Studies.

Paul Pierson is Professor of Government at Harvard, teaching courses on comparative public policy and social theory. He is the author of *Dismantling the Welfare State? The Politics of Retrenchment in Britain and the United States* (Cambridge University Press, 1994), coeditor of *European Social Policy between Fragmentation and Integration* (Brookings Institution, 1995), and editor of *The New Politics of the Welfare State* (Oxford University Press, 2001). His articles have appeared in such journals as *Comparative Political Studies, Governance, Politics and Society, Studies in American Political Development,* and *World Politics,* as well as numerous edited volumes. He has just completed a book on the role of historical analysis in social sciences: *Politics in Time: History, Institutions, and Social Analysis* (Princeton University Press, forthcoming)

David A. Reilly is Assistant Professor of Political Science and Director of the Global Affairs Program at Niagara University. His research evaluates the relationship between globalization and democratization. He is currently working on a book titled *The Diffusion of Political Ideas: Stocks and Flows in Democratizing Countries.*

Allison Stanger is Associate Professor of Political Science and Director of the Rohatyn Center for International Affairs at Middlebury College. She is the coeditor and cotranslator (with Michael Kraus) of *Irreconcilable Differences? Explaining Czechoslovakia's Dissolution* (Rowman and Littlefield, 2000; foreword by Václav Havel). In academic year 2001–2, she was Visiting Associate Professor of Government at Harvard University and a Visiting Scholar at the Minda de Gunzburg Center for European Studies.

Acknowledgments

This volume is based on the conference "Postcommunist Transitions a Decade Later: How Far East Can Western Europe Go?" which took place at the Minda de Gunzburg Center for European Studies at Harvard University in the fall of 1999. The conference was supported by the Program for the Study of Germany and Europe at the CES through a grant from the government of the Federal Republic of Germany, with additional funding from the European Union Center at Harvard University. The conference brought together a diverse group of scholars specializing in East European affairs as well as students of democratic transitions and comparative politics in general. All chapters in this volume benefited enormously from our lively exchanges and debates during the conference. Accordingly, the authors would like to thank all the participants and especially the following moderators and discussants: Valerie Bunce, Daniel Chirot, Ellen Comisso, Stephen Holmes, Ken Jowitt, Gail Kligman, Jacques Rupnik, Roman Szporluk, David Stark, Vladimir Tismaneanu, and Jan Zielonka. We would also like to thank paper presenters Cecilia Chessa, Arista Cirtautas, M. Steven Fish, Mitchell Orenstein, Vesna Pusic, Ákos Róna-Tas, and Jason Wittenberg. Finally, special thanks are due to Abby Collins and Lisa Eschenbach for their efforts to make this conference a success.

Portions of two of the chapters of this volume have appeared elsewhere in print: Jeffrey S. Kopstein and David A. Reilly, Geographic Diffusion and the Transformation of the Postcommunist World, *World Politics* 53(1) (October 2000): 1–36; and Juliet Johnson, Path Contingency in Postcommunist Transformations, *Comparative Politics* 33(3) (March 2000): 253–74. We are grateful to the publishers for permission to use this material.

Acknowledgements

Introduction

Grzegorz Ekiert and Stephen E. Hanson

> For the peoples of Central Europe, the past, to use Faulkner's phrase, "is never dead. It's not even past."
>
> Jacques Rupnik, 1989: 36

> Whatever the results of the current turmoil in Eastern Europe, one thing is clear: the new institutional patterns will be shaped by the "inheritance" and legacy of forty years of Leninist rule.
>
> Ken Jowitt, 1992: 285

> Post-communism ... deserves its name. Its character is an uneasy mixture of elements of the past and of the different visions of the future that are on offer.
>
> George Schöpflin, 2000: 169

> Social structures, types, and attitudes are coins that do not readily melt. Once they are formed they persist, possibly for centuries, and since different structures and types display different degrees of ability to survive, we almost always find that actual group and national behavior more or less departs from what we should expect it to be if we tried to infer it from the dominant forms of the productive process.
>
> Joseph Schumpeter, 1947: 12–13

The collapse of the East European communist regimes and the ensuing end of five decades of Cold War in Europe has often been described as a revenge of history. The dramatic unraveling of party-states, centrally planned economies, and the Soviet-centered international regime was as consequential as it was unanticipated. From East Berlin to Murmansk and from Gdańsk to Tirana, massive political, economic, and social transformations, described by Jowitt (1992) as the "Leninist extinction," repudiated and fundamentally reshaped inherited institutional structures that had been in place for most of the century. This "great transformation" was testimony not only to the failure of communist policies but also to the fact that societies shaped by their particular histories, cultures, and geographic locations ultimately failed to succumb to the most brutal and persistent efforts at unification and homogenization implemented by communist rulers. Various old and new countries and regions of Central and Eastern Europe, despite decades of communist *uravnilovka*, have been able to reassert links to precommunist identities and, in view of many observers, "return" to their specific historical trajectories interrupted by communist rule.

From this perspective, it should not be surprising that postcommunist political and economic transformations and regionwide experiments with democracy and the market economy have produced such starkly contrasting outcomes. Despite seemingly similar domestic challenges and global pressures, parallel elite goals and policies, and common communist experiences, the region has reemerged as a mosaic of rapidly diverging societies. This diversity of outcomes has its source not only in the legacies of the past, but also in choices made by strategically located actors in various critical moments of the unfolding processes of change, as well as in the modalities of transitional politics and institutional characteristics of the postcommunist period. The remarkable diversity of outcomes across Eurasia since the collapse of the Soviet bloc has even led Jacques Rupnik (1999: 57) to conclude that "ten years after the collapse of the Soviet empire, one thing is clear: the word 'postcommunism' has lost its relevance. The fact that Hungary and Albania, or the Czech Republic and Belarus, or Poland and Kazakhstan shared a communist past explains very little about the paths that they have taken since."

Yet from a different perspective, this declaration of the "postpostcommunist" period appears premature. Indeed, the most extreme contrasts to be found among the countries of the region mask continuing similarities among those that made up the core of the former USSR – especially Russia, Belarus, and Ukraine, but including other areas particularly burdened by the aftereffects of Stalinist planning and repression, such as Romania and northern Kazakhstan. Over a wide swath of Central Eurasia, more than a decade after the Soviet collapse former apparatchiki continued to hold sway over local political machines inherited from the Leninist past; collective farmers continued to labor inefficiently under the eye of longtime rural bosses; and millions of blue-collar workers continued to maintain at least formal job affiliations with the massive, polluting industrial dinosaurs of the Stalinist era. In these countries, new liberal and market institutions functioned poorly or not at all, corruption was endemic, and civil society seemed unable to recover from its suppression under one-party rule (Hanson and Kopstein, 1997; Howard, 1999; Fish, 2001; Tismaneanu, 1999). In short, the "Leninist legacy" described by Jowitt (1992) appeared, unfortunately, as burdensome as ever.

Thus the key paradox presented by the experience of the first decade of postcommunism is that the "Leninist legacy" mattered both *less* and *more* than scholars originally expected. On the Central European periphery of the former Soviet bloc, the constraints of past forms of communist standardization have seemingly been cast aside, and diverse new paths of development have emerged that cannot be explained simply in terms of the aftereffects of Leninist rule. In the core of the former USSR, however, the initial expectations of neoliberal institutionalists of a rapid "transition to democracy and the market" have been thwarted precisely by the largely unanticipated tenacity of old socioeconomic structures and the obstacles these have posed to successful liberal state and market building.

The post-1989 experiences of the region thus raise a number of questions and puzzles at the very heart of historical-institutional political analysis. How can we explain the divergence of political and economic trajectories across postcommunist Europe? Can we legitimately maintain the notion of a single region for countries that emerged from the former Soviet bloc – and if so, in what sense? How distinctive are postcommunist societies, and what are the sources of their most important differences? What are the relevant dimensions of postcommunist uniformity and diversity? Why do democracy and capitalism seem to be firmly established in some parts of the region but not others? Is a specific type or form of East European democracy and capitalism emerging? Are elite policies, institutional choices, modalities of transformation politics, international influences, or historical legacies most important in explaining divergent outcomes? Are there factors that have explanatory power in some cases but are not relevant in others? Do we have adequate methodological and analytical tools to provide convincing answers to such questions? Which of the established methodological approaches generates more fruitful questions and puzzles and offers more promising research strategies?

This volume is designed primarily as a contribution to the debate on explaining the diverging trajectories of postcommunist transformations. Its contributors have conducted extensive empirical research in the region, employ diverse research strategies, and offer various answers to the above questions. The theme that unites all chapters, however, is the emphasis on *legacies of the past* and mechanisms through which they shape the initial outcomes of East European transitions. This shared focus has broad theoretical and methodological implications. According to Kitschelt et al. (1999: 11), "legacy explanations claim that resource endowments and institutions that precede the choice of democratic institutions have a distinct impact on the observable political process under the new democratic regime. Moreover, such explanations claim that democratic institutions themselves depend on legacies, because they are endogenously chosen by political actors emerging from the old pre-democratic systems." The need for a historical approach to the study of postcommunist transformations has also been aptly articulated by David

Stark (1992: 2), who argues that "the economic and political institutions that must be reconstructed on the ruins of state socialism cannot simply be chosen from among the economists' designs like selecting wares from the supermarket or choosing the winning blueprints in an architectural competition." Similarly, the evolutionary approaches developed to account for the collapse of state socialism and various paths of transformation across the region emphasize the role of historical continuities (see, e.g., Staniszkis, 1991; 1999; Poznański, 1995; 1996). The issue of historical continuities and legacies of the past is also highlighted by ethnographers and anthropologists studying postcommunist transformations, who explore microlevel responses to macrolevel changes and focus on how the past frames various strategies of adaptation (see, e.g., Burawoy and Verdery, 1999; Berdhal, Bunzl, and Lampland, 2000).

Our objective, however, is to go beyond general reaffirmation of the utility of historical analysis for understanding postcommunist transformations. This volume attempts to develop a far more specific and theoretically precise understanding of the nature and causal role of legacies than has been typical of the literature to date. So far there is no consensus among scholars concerning how legacies should be defined, what types of legacies have more explanatory power, and through what mechanisms legacies shape current outcomes. A glance at the prevailing conceptualization of legacies reveals several distinct understandings. Crawford and Lijphart (1995: 179) specify six fundamental legacies – the history of "backwardness," the absence of a successor elite, weak party systems, interrupted nation building, the persistence of old institutions, and the legacy of the command economy – that may affect postcommunist transformations. Barany and Volgyes (1995) distinguished among physical and environmental, economic, societal, and political legacies of communism. Hanson (1995) identified four components of the Leninist legacy – ideological, political, socioeconomic, and cultural – that may have different impacts and varying capacities to persist. Other scholars have defined legacies in terms of inherited sociopolitical cleavages or core conflicts (see, e.g., Ekiert and Kubik, 1999; Seleny, 1999); prevailing attitudes inimical to liberal values such as intolerance, mistrust of authority, hostility to competition, excessive welfare and distributional expectations, and so on (see, e.g., Jowitt, 1992; Koralewicz and Ziółkowski, 1990; Kolarska-Bobińska, 1994; McDaniel, 1996; Simon, 1998; Rose, Mishler, and Haerpfer, 1998; Zagórski and Strzeszewski, 2000); the persistence of formal institutions, social organizations, or industrial structures constructed under the old regime that inhibit the formation of new states, democratic accountability, market-oriented behavior, and horizontal social linkages (see, e.g., Linz and Stepan, 1996; Jowitt, 1992; Burawoy and Krotov, 1992; Ekiert and Kubik, 1999; Bunce, 1999); policy legacies constraining the choices of economic and political actors (see, e.g., Campbell, 1996; Vujacic, 1996);

inherited informal rules and networks[1] (see, e.g., Walder, 1995; Stark and Bruszt, 1998; Lebedeva, 1998; Böröcz, 2000; McDermott, 2002); the formal or informal resources at the disposal of collective actors (see, e.g., Eyal, Szelényi, and Townsley, 1998; Ekiert and Kubik, 1999; Grabher and Stark, 1997; Grzymała-Busse, 2001); the inheritance of past institutions defining and sometimes aggravating contemporary forms of national or ethnic identity (Suny, 1993; Brubaker, 1996); and the persistence of old elites, social hierarchies, and social structures (Wasilewski, 1995; Szelényi, Treiman, and Wnuk-Lipiński, 1995).

In most of these analyses, the boundaries between precommunist and communist legacies are not clear. Indeed, the former are rarely systematically investigated, and there is a marked ambiguity about the nature of their impact.[2] The precommunist history of ethnic conflicts and divisions in the region, for example, is frequently invoked to explain the occurrence and intensity of ethnic strife in the postcommunist context, but the causal mechanisms linking the former to the latter are usually left unspecified. In fact, the view linking the current resurgence of ethnic conflicts to old hatreds and divisions has two components. One refers to the history of ethnic and national conflicts in the region. Another describes the impact of communist rule on suppressing of what Shlomo Avineri (1992: 31) has called "the demons of hate and anger that fuel ethnic strife."

Legacy explanations usually highlight *the burden of the past*, understood as a set of factors likely to impede the formation of modern democratic polities and market economies in the postcommunist context. Like the concept of "centuries-old ethnic conflicts" used to explain the intensity of ethnic politics throughout the region, the notion of "Leninist legacies" thus also tends to have a distinctively negative connotation. In Grabher and Stark's words (1997: 4), "legacies indicate institutional pathologies contaminated with the deficiencies of the old regime obstructing the process of transformations: the future cannot be realized because the past cannot be overcome. The legacies of state socialism block the promising road to free market." The positive impact of some of the legacies of state socialism, however, should not be overlooked (see Ekiert, Chapter 3 in this volume), especially when one compares the experiences of postcommunism with other cases of postauthoritarian transformations burdened by massive social problems (see, e.g., Greskovits, 1998). The same point may apply to some of the region's

[1] North (1990: 91) emphasizes the importance of informal constraints, arguing that "although wholesale change in the formal rules may take place, at the same time there will be many informal constraints that have great survival tenacity because they still resolve basic exchange problems among participants, be they social, political, or economic."

[2] For attempts to capture the impact of precommunist legacies on specific dimensions of transition, see, for example, Vujacic (1996); Walicki (2000); Nadelsky (2001).

precommunist social and institutional legacies (see Kitschelt, Chapter 2 in this volume).

In our view, before the plausibility of explanations based on the notion of legacies can be fully assessed, clarification of such key definitional and conceptual issues is necessary. This task, however, turns out to be far more complex than is often appreciated in the literature. Indeed, to develop a more precise theoretical understanding of institutional and cultural legacies of the past and their specific effects on political, economic, and social outcomes, we are forced to confront some of the most fundamental theoretical problems of social science – in particular, the problem of theorizing the nature of the temporal and spatial contexts of social change. We are not alone, however, in this effort to reassess such critical issues of comparative historical analysis. By focusing on this specific set of regional experiences, we hope to contribute to the growing body of literature reassessing historical institutionalism and advocating a systematic and disciplined approach to the problem of historical causation (see, e.g., Steinmo, Thelen, and Longstreth, 1992; McDonald, 1996; Goldstone, 1998; Thelen, 1999; Pierson, 2000; Mahoney, 1999; Mahoney and Rueschemeyer, 2003).

This volume is accordingly organized around three major themes. In the first part of the book, we present two contrasting theoretical essays that attempt to reassess the nature of historical legacies in East Europe by rethinking social science approaches to the analysis of institutional change – in the postcommunist region and more generally. In Chapter 1, Grzegorz Ekiert and Stephen E. Hanson argue that the temporal and spatial contexts within which institutional change in the region is taking place can be usefully categorized in terms of a distinction among structural, institutional, and interactional levels of analysis. In Chapter 2, Herbert Kitschelt presents a methodological critique of causal arguments that rely on overly "deep" structural continuities in East European history as well as those that present an overly "shallow" testing of short-term variables affecting institutional outcomes, and argues for a middle-range approach to understanding the causal effects of historical legacies.

The second part of the volume presents a general overview of empirical trends during the first decade of postcommunism in Eastern Europe and assesses the key historical and geographical factors that help to explain the diversity of postcommunist outcomes to date. In Chapter 3, Grzegorz Ekiert argues that the distinctive and varied features of state socialism in different parts of the former Soviet bloc have generated path-dependent effects that have constrained the institutionalization of democracy and capitalism in some subregions while facilitating them in others; thus contemporary Eastern Europe cannot be understood except with reference to developments in the communist and precommunist past. In Chapter 4, Jeffrey Kopstein and David Reilly argue that the initial outcomes of transition have been decisively affected by the geographical positioning of various regimes, because postcommunist institutions have unavoidably been shaped by cross-border flows of norms, resources, and institutions from neighboring countries. In particular, they show that geographic proximity to Western Europe has been a crucial determinant of success in postcommunist democratization and marketization. Thus, whereas Ekiert's essay emphasizes the importance of the historical context of postcommunist transitions, Kopstein and Reilly tend to highlight the importance of the spatial context.

The third part of the volume includes a series of comparative case studies that attempt to isolate the concrete processes and mechanisms through which legacies of the past have affected efforts to build democratic and capitalist institutions in postcommunist Europe. In Chapter 5, Anna Grzymała-Busse examines efforts to reform communist successor parties in Poland, the Czech Republic, Slovakia, and Hungary, arguing that the reasons for communist party regeneration lie neither in electoral nostalgia for the Leninist past nor in favorable political institutions, but rather in the degree to which communist party elites acquired "portable skills" based on the organizational practices of these communist parties while in power. In Chapter 6, Allison Stanger investigates the relationship between communism's institutional legacy and early constitutional decisions in postcommunist Poland, Hungary, and the former Czechoslovakia; she argues that the initial reluctance of postcommunist Central Europe's democratizers to scuttle communism's constitutional framework and the obstacles to further institutional reform that arose as revolutionary gains were locked in demonstrate two different variants of path dependence – the former with its origins in inherited informal rules of conduct, the latter stemming from the new formal rules of the game. In Chapter 7, Tomasz Inglot compares and contrasts efforts to reform social security systems in Poland and Hungary, arguing that they both display far more institutional continuity with the communist and precommunist past than is generally recognized by analysts; indeed, these systems can be understood as two distinct variants of a new postcommunist "entitlement state" that builds on inherited patterns to create a viable safety net for the prolonged and difficult period of market reform and democratization. In Chapter 8, Phineas Baxandall looks at the different ways in which the communist-era "unemployment taboo" has eroded in East Central Europe and the former Soviet Union, arguing that this legacy of state socialism has endured only where enterprises are still run in ways typical of the Leninist past; elsewhere, the combination of widespread informal labor markets and distinctive postcommunist norms of "entrepreneurship" have tended to undermine efforts to hold the state to old promises of full employment. In Chapter 9, Juliet Johnson looks at the development of the Russian commercial banking system since the collapse of the USSR, arguing that institutional "design failure" in this sphere has been the product of an interaction among policy choices, institutional legacies, state capacity, and policy sequencing – a process she terms one of "path contingency." In Chapter 10, Jan Kubik explores the complex problem of how to theorize about the causal effects of "cultural" legacies on institutional change. Building on recent developments in cultural theory, Kubik argues that cultural legacies of state socialism should be understood as both "discourses about the past" proposed by contemporary cultural-political entrepreneurs and as "syndromes of attitudes" built upon actors' past experiences. Through a comparative analysis of conceptions of national identity in Poland and Russia in both the communist and postcommunist periods, Kubik shows that postcommunist cultures vary in terms of the degree to which socialist and nationalist discourses are welded together to generate debilitating political polarization.

In the Epilogue, Paul Pierson ties together the findings from these theoretical and empirical studies, showing how an effort to be rigorous about the impact of Leninist and pre-Leninist legacies on contemporary institutional change in Eastern Europe contributes to emerging theoretical trends in the political science literature on comparative historical institutionalism.

References

Avineri, Shlomo. 1992. Comments on Nationalism and Democracy. *Journal of Democracy* 3(4): 28–31.

Barany, Zoltan, and Ivan Volgyes, eds. 1995. *The Legacies of Communism in Eastern Europe.* Baltimore: Johns Hopkins University Press.

Berdahl, Daphne, Matti Bunzl, and Martha Lampland, eds. 2000. *Altering States: Ethnographies of Transition in Eastern Europe and the Former Soviet Union.* Ann Arbor: University of Michigan Press.

Böröcz, József. 2000. Informality Rules. *East European Politics and Societies* 14(2): 348–80.

Brubaker, Rogers. 1996. *Nationalism Reframed: Nationhood and the National Question in the New Europe.* Cambridge: Cambridge University Press.

Bunce, Valerie. 1999. *Subversive Institutions: The Design and the Destruction of Socialism and the State.* Cambridge: Cambridge University Press.

Burawoy, Michael, and Pavel Krotov. 1992. The Soviet Transition from Socialism to Capitalism. *American Sociological Review* 57: 1, 16–38.

Burawoy, Michael, and Katherine Verdery, eds. 1999. *Uncertain Transitions: Ethnographies of Change in the Post Socialist World.* Lanham, Md.: Rowman and Littlefield.

Campbell, John L. 1996. An Institutional Analysis of Fiscal Reforms in Postcommunist Europe. *Theory and Society* 25: 45–82.

Crawford, Beverly, and Arend Lijphart, eds. 1997. *Liberalization and Leninist Legacies: Comparative Perspectives on Democratic Transitions.* Berkeley: International and Area Studies, University of California.

Ekiert, Grzegorz, and Jan Kubik. 1999. *Rebellious Civil Society.* Ann Arbor: University of Michigan Press.

Eyal, Gil, Iván Szelényi, and Eleanor Townsley. 1998. *Making Capitalism without Capitalists: Class Formation and Elite Struggles in Post-Communist Central Europe.* London: Verso.

Fish, M. Steven. 2001. The Dynamics of Democratic Erosion. In Richard Anderson Jr., M. Steven Fish, Stephen E. Hanson, and Philip Roeder, *Postcommunism and the Theory of Democracy*, pp. 54–95. Princeton: Princeton University Press.

Goldstone, Jack. 1998. Initial Conditions, General Laws, Path Dependence and Explanation in Historical Sociology. *American Journal of Sociology* 104(3): 829–45.

Grabher, Gernot, and David Stark, eds. 1997. *Restructuring Networks in Post-Socialism: Legacies, Linkages, and Localities.* Oxford: Oxford University Press.

Greskovits, Bela. 1998. *The Political Economy of Protest and Patience: East European and Latin American Transformations Compared.* Budapest: Central European University Press.

Grzymała-Busse, Anna. 2002. *Redeeming the Communist Past: The Regeneration of Communist Successor Parties in East Central Europe.* Cambridge: Cambridge University Press.

Hanson, Stephen E. 1995. The Leninist Legacy and Institutional Change. *Comparative Political Studies* 28(2): 306–14.

Hanson, Stephen E., and Jeffrey S. Kopstein. 1997. The Weimar/Russia Comparison. *Post-Soviet Affairs* 13(3): 252–81.

Howard, Marc. 1999. Demobilized Societies: Understanding the Weakness of Civil Society in Post-Communist Europe. Ph.D. dissertation, University of California, Berkeley.

Jowitt, Ken. 1992. *New World Disorder: The Leninist Extinction.* Berkeley: University of California Press.

Kitschelt, Herbert, Zdenka Mansfeldova, Radosław Markowski, and Gábor Tóka. 1999. *Post-Communist Party Systems: Competition, Representation, and Inter-Party Cooperation.* Cambridge: Cambridge University Press.

Kolarska-Bobińska, Lena. 1994. *Aspirations, Values and Interests: Poland 1989–1994.* Warsaw: IFiS.

Koralewicz, Jadwiga, and Marek Ziółkowski. 1990. *Mentalność Polaków.* Poznań: Nakom.

Lebedeva, Alena. 1998. *Russia's Economy of Favors: Blat, Networking, and Informal Exchange.* Cambridge: Cambridge University Press.

Linz, Juan, and Alfred Stepan. 1996. *Problems of Democratic Transition and Consolidation: Southern Europe, South America, and Post-Communist Europe.* Baltimore: Johns Hopkins University Press.

Mahoney, James. 1999. Nominal, Ordinal, and Narrative Appraisal in Macrocausal Analysis. *American Journal of Sociology* 104(4): 1154–96.

Mahoney, James, and Dietrich Rueschemeyer, eds. 2003. *Comparative Historical Analysis.* Cambridge: Cambridge University Press.

McDaniel, Tim. 1996. *The Agony of the Russian Idea.* Princeton: Princeton University Press.

McDermott, Gerald. 2002. *Embedded Politics: Industrial Networks and Institutional Change in Postcommunism.* Ann Arbor: University of Michigan Press.

McDonald, Terrance, ed. 1996. *The Historic Turn in the Human Sciences.* Ann Arbor: University of Michigan Press.

Nadelsky, Nadya. 2001. The Wartime Slovak State: A Case Study in the Relationship between Ethnic Nationalism and Authoritarian Patterns of Governance. *Nations and Nationalities* 7(2): 215–34.

North, Douglass Cecil. 1990. *Institutions, Institutional Change, and Economic Performance*. Cambridge: Cambridge University Press.

Pierson, Paul. 2000. Increasing Returns, Path Dependence, and the Study of Politics. *American Political Science Review* 94(2): 251–67.

Poznański, Kazimierz, ed. 1995. *The Evolutionary Transition to Capitalism*. Boulder, Colo.: Westview.

1996. *Poland's Protracted Transition: Institutional Change and Economic Growth*. Cambridge: Cambridge University Press.

Rose, Richard, William Mishler, and Christian Haerpfer. 1998. *Democracy and Its Alternatives*. Baltimore: Johns Hopkins University Press.

Rupnik, Jacques. 1989. *The Other Europe*. New York: Pantheon Books.

1999. The Postcommunist Divide. *Journal of Democracy* 10(1): 57–62.

Schöpflin, George. 2000. *Nations, Identity, Power*. New York: New York University Press.

Schumpeter, Joseph. 1947. *Capitalism, Socialism, and Democracy*. New York: Harper and Bros.

Seleny, Anna. 1999. Old Rationalities and New Democracies: Compromise and Confrontation in Hungary and Poland. *World Politics* 51(4): 484–519.

Simon, János. 1998. Popular Conceptions of Democracy in Postcommunist Europe. In Samuel H. Barnes and János Simon, eds., *The Postcommunist Citizen*, pp. 79–116. Budapest: Erasmus Foundation and IPS of HAS.

Staniszkis, Jadwiga. 1991. *The Dynamics of Breakthrough in Eastern Europe*. Berkeley: University of California Press.

1999. *Post-Communism: The Emerging Enigma*. Warsaw: ISP PAN.

Stark, David. 1992. Introduction. *East European Politics and Societies* 6(1): 1–3.

Stark, David, and László Bruszt. 1998. *Postsocialist Pathways: Transforming Politics and Property in East Central Europe*. Cambridge: Cambridge University Press.

Steinmo, Sven, Kathleen Thelen, and Frank Longstreth, eds. 1992. *Structuring Politics: Historical Institutionalism in Comparative Perspective*. Cambridge: Cambridge University Press.

Suny, Ronald. 1993. *The Revenge of the Past: Nationalism, Revolution, and the Collapse of the Soviet Union*. Stanford, Calif.: Stanford University Press.

Szelényi, Iván, Don Treiman, and Edmund Wnuk-Lipiński. 1995. *Elity w Polsce, w Rosjiina Węgrzech*. Warsaw: Instytut Studió w Politycznych PAN.

Thelen, Kathleen. 1999. Historical Institutionalism in Comparative Politics. *Annual Review of Political Science* 2: 369–404.

Tismaneanu, Vladimir. 1999. The First Post-Communist Decade. *Romanian Journal of Society and Politics* 1(1): 5–15.

Vujacic, Veljko. 1996. Historical Legacies, Nationalist Mobilization, and Political Outcomes in Russia and Serbia: A Weberian View. *Theory and Society* 25: 763–801.

Walder, Andrew, ed. 1995. *The Waning of the Communist State*. Berkeley: University of California Press.

Walicki, Andrzej. 2000. The Troubling Legacy of Roman Dmowski. *East European Politics and Societies* 14(1): 12–46.

Wasilewski, Jacek. 1995. The Crystallization of the Post-Communist and Post-Solidarity Political Elite. In Edmund Wnuk-Lipiński, ed., *After Communism*, pp. 117–33. Warszawa: ISP PAN.

Zagórski, Krzysztof, and Michał Strzeszewski, eds. 2000. *Nowa rzeczywistość. Oceny i opinie* 1989–1999. Warsaw: Dialog.

PART I

POSTCOMMUNIST TRANSFORMATIONS AND THE ROLE OF HISTORICAL LEGACIES

1

Time, Space, and Institutional Change in Central and Eastern Europe

Grzegorz Ekiert and Stephen E. Hanson

The momentous political and economic transitions that followed the events of 1989 have moved East European studies into the mainstream of social science research. For decades the field was relatively marginalized, focused as it was on the specific institutional and developmental tendencies of communist politics and societies. It developed its own context-specific analytical approaches and particular empirical concerns. Communist studies always maintained a dialogue with other parts of comparative politics, to be sure, but only in recent years did the field open up, rapidly expanding its range of theoretical and substantive topics. This change was reinforced by the emergence in Eastern Europe of procedural democracy and market institutions, long at the center of comparative politics research. The fundamental concerns of Western-based social sciences, with their focus on the architecture and processes shaping developed democratic regimes and mature market economies, suddenly became crucial for understanding and explaining East European developments. At the same time, democratic transitions and market reforms taking place in the region opened opportunities for comparative investigation across regional boundaries and for research projects encompassing postcommunist and other countries outside the developed West experiencing political and economic transformations.

This opening of the field, enthusiastically welcomed by many students of East European politics, has created exciting opportunities to reinvigorate scholarly reflection on the region and has generated unprecedented amounts of new research and analysis. It has also motivated researchers with different backgrounds and regional specialties to contribute to, and often to initiate, fruitful scholarly debates. At the same time, however, the inclusion of East European cases in the political economy and democratic transition paradigms removed old disciplinary boundaries, blurred the theoretical identity of the field, and produced many dilemmas that mirror the problems facing contemporary political science and other social sciences. These include patterns of excessive specialization and segmentation taking place along disciplinary, methodological, theoretical, and substantive lines as well as pressures for nomothetization – that is, efforts to generate parsimonious models and universalizable findings – characteristic of mainstream economics and a growing part of political science research. Such developments have generated exciting theoretical debates on numerous substantive issues such as constitution design, formation of party systems, electoral politics, economic reforms, and performance of democratic institutions. But they also renewed often acrimonious disputes on the relationship between comparative politics and regional studies (see Bernhard, 2000; Hall and Tarrow, 1998; Bates, 1997; Johnson, 1997; Lustick, 1997; Bunce, 1995a; Schmitter and Karl, 1994).

There is no denying that regional studies in the past frequently suffered from an excessive focus on unique developments and outcomes and from a tendency to employ simple narrative strategies to depict the complexities of specific historical places and times. In short, they frequently succumbed to the "particularist fallacy" (Rueschemeyer, Stephens, and Stephens, 1992: 28) and renounced the possibility of achieving more-generalizable and systematic knowledge applicable beyond a single case. At the same time, contemporary comparative politics increasingly suffers from the "universalistic fallacy" (O'Donnell, 1979) in its drive to develop parsimonious models and to search for context-independent causal regularities. This pressure to exclude temporal and spatial context in social science inquiry has become increasingly present in East European studies. Many research projects, for example, treat all twenty-seven countries that emerged in the region as a universe of identical cases; various cross-regional comparisons dilute the importance of contextual factors specific to various countries and regions even further. This situation is highly ironic: the most contextualized and historicized field in the social sciences has become the playground of relentlessly ahistorical and decontextualized research.

Thus postcommunist studies have been drawn inexorably into the multifaceted debate about the respective roles of area knowledge and general theory in comparative politics. It should be noted that at the heart of this debate is the issue of contextualization and limits of generalizable knowledge in social science. Seen this way, the debate is, indeed, a very old one. In his recent visitation of the issue, Strohmayer (1997: 280) reminds us that "[t]he central problem that has haunted the social sciences since the late nineteenth and early twentieth century was the question of how to reconcile analytically the Kantian a priori of space and time with their very own and socially constituted object of analysis." Windelband's distinction between idiographic and nomothetic sciences, trade-offs between the variable-oriented approach and the case-oriented approach (Ragin, 1987), and the contrast between the "variable paradigm" and "contextualist paradigm" (Abbott, 1997) are all improvisations on the same theme. Positions in this debate range from asserting irreconcilable differences between the contrasting approaches based on fundamental ontological and epistemological premises to efforts aimed at minimizing these differences, or a search for methodological innovations capable of bridging them (Ragin, 1987, 1999; King, Keohane, and Verba, 1994).

It is our conviction that scholars studying the communist and postcommunist region are in an ideal position to contribute in an empirically compelling and systematic fashion to these long-standing debates about the nature of social science inquiry and the ontological status of social and political phenomena. The historical experience of common subjugation to Leninist and Stalinist attempts at institutional and ideological standardization, followed by the remarkably rapid "return to diversity" in Eastern Europe after 1989,[1] itself demonstrates that institutional transformations sometimes take a generally similar form across time and space, but sometimes depend upon specific "conjunctures" leading to divergent outcomes in particular historical and geographic contexts. Scholars looking for general features of commonality in postcommunist societies, then, will always find them; so will observers looking for unique features of particular cases. What we apparently lack is a consensual analytic framework in which the general and the specific features of the postcommunist institutional environment can be integrated within a single research program capable of accommodating a wide range of substantive concerns and generating cumulative knowledge.

The way forward, we believe, is to theorize – much more explicitly than has been typical of comparative social theory in recent decades – about the nature of temporal and spatial contexts themselves and the causal relations between them and specific, observable outcomes. Only by better understanding the particular levels of analysis at which different scholars approach problems of understanding social change, and how these levels of analysis are implicitly dependent upon different understandings of the nature of time and space, will scholars be able to link the general theoretical formulations of the most abstract "nomothetic" social science to the insights of scholars conducting highly contextualized research on particular cases.

In this chapter, we sketch the basic theoretical elements of a research program that can transcend some unproductive controversies and provide the foundation for a more compelling and methodologically sound approach to analyzing the effects of Leninist and pre-Leninist legacies and explaining the variety of postcommunisms. In our view, this approach must combine sensitivity to contextual factors and multiple causes with an effort to produce generalizable knowledge. Our substantive focus is on theorizing "dual contextuality" – temporal and spatial. We argue that attention to this double context can generate a much better understanding of postcommunist transformations and their initial outcomes across the region. The study of

[1] This expression is borrowed from the title of the brilliant political history of modern Eastern Europe written by Joseph Rothschild (1993).

institutional change in the former communist region (and elsewhere) requires systematic reflection about the status of our generalizations and the nature of the causal inferences we propose. Distinguishing clearly among different levels of analysis can help to reconcile theoretical arguments designed to apply in all places and at all times with specific insights uncovered through careful tracing of social developments in very particular geographic and temporal contexts. The purpose of this chapter is to explore various ways in which temporal and spatial contexts should be taken into account in examinations of institutional change and its initial outcomes in postcommunist Europe – a task with which all the contributors to this volume are deeply engaged.

Levels of Analysis in Postcommunist Studies

How can analysts move beyond a counterproductive oscillation between acontextual variable testing and atheoretical narrative description? What, exactly, would a "disciplined contextual" approach to comparative study of communism and postcommunism look like in practice? How can we theoretically account for the impact of communism – as well as other historical legacies and geographic influences – on the course of postcommunist institutional change? In temporal terms, how can we understand the overlapping influences of precommunist social and cultural legacies, the effects of Leninist rule, and the role of agency in the postcommunist period, particularly since these three factors appear often to interact or reinforce one another? In spatial terms, how do we distinguish among the regional continuities that have been characteristic of East Europe for centuries, political and economic regional patterns imposed by Moscow in the period of Soviet rule, and the influence of postcommunist efforts to reorient the spatial linkages of "Western," "Central," and "Eastern" Europe?

In order to provide a systematic account of causal patterns shaping postcommunist transformations, we should assess carefully the scope of our generalizations and the sorts of explanatory accounts or strategies to be utilized. We should also distinguish the impact of specific temporal and spatial contexts, as well as the various mechanisms through which that impact is actualized, on the range of outcomes emerging in Eastern Europe. Such an effort can be guided by the analytical framework outlined in Table 1.1, which distinguishes among "structural," "institutional," and "interactional" levels of analysis for investigation of the temporal and spatial contexts within which social and political change takes place and suggests specific mechanisms operating at these different levels.

The application of this analytical framework, it should be emphasized, is not in principle limited to the problem of understanding the legacy of communist rule or of accounting for the processes of change taking place in the Eastern European region; it can be used to disentangle the various levels of temporal and spatial patterning in a wide variety of social settings. Reference to these levels of analysis helps to clarify important theoretical distinctions among three different types of temporal "path dependence" that are often used interchangably in the comparative politics literature: (1) the necessarily contextualized study of innovations and policy outcomes, as well as other interactive economic and political processes, that through specific dynamics generate increasing returns (Pierson, 2000), and of contingent events that set in motion "reactive sequences" of historical development (Mahoney, 2000); (2) the study of more general "institutional legacies" that shape a wide range of policy domains and tend to be much more uniform and predictable in their effects across space and time (Jowitt, 1992; Esping-Andersen, 1990; Linz and Stepan, 1996: 55–66); and (3) the persistent influence of historical and cultural legacies inherited from the more distant past that shape the choices and behavior of political and social actors (Putnam, 1993; Huntington, 1996). In terms of spatial context, the framework allows analysts to distinguish among: (1) the local spatial dynamics of informal networks of personal communication and interaction that transcend formal boundaries and facilitate processes of diffusion and imitation; (2) the formal structuring of space through the political construction and enforcement of boundaries generating specific political and/or economic "cores" relative to which neighboring, less powerful or developed regions are defined as "peripheral" (Berend and Ránki, 1982); and (3) the enduring geographical features that produce more-fundamental environmental constraints on social, economic, and institutional development.

In terms of the theoretical framework suggested in Table 1.1, "Leninism"[2] represents a taxonomical categorization at the institutional level of analysis: a powerful institutional patterning of time and space, such that its features were intuitively understood as constraining by actors both within and outside of the Leninist regime-world. Leninism, in short, was a "regime type" comparable in its global impact with other regime types such as liberal capitalism, fascism, and feudalism. The consistent institutional features of the Leninist regime's organization of political space and regulation of social time make comparisons among Leninist regimes theoretically rewarding, allowing scholars to "hold constant" many important variables while assessing the impact of others (Bunce, 1999). When we speak of "Leninist legacies," then, we refer to the specific impacts on postcommunist societies of the

[2] We distinguish between "Leninism," which we use to designate the formal institutions characteristic of countries ruled by communist parties of the Marxist-Leninist type, and "state socialism," by which we mean the overall patterns of informal social action that typically emerged in response to Leninist domination. Where other designations for the period of Soviet hegemony and its aftermath are used in this chapter – such as communism, postcommunism, socialism, and postsocialism – we do so simply as a shorthand way of referring to these countries that has become a part of "ordinary language," both in the region and in the field.

TABLE 1.1. *The Three Levels of Temporal and Spatial Context*

Level of Analysis	Temporal Context	Spatial Context
Structural level	Structural time: The *longue durée*; historical patterns of economic and cultural reproduction	Structural space: Natural geography, physical environment, and demographic patterns
Institutional level	Institutional time: Regularized patterns of social action enforced by institutional characteristics of particular regimes	Institutional space: Political construction of formal national and international boundaries and jurisdictions
Interactional level	Interactional time: Contingent events, choices, and decisions engendering processes of increasing returns/reactive sequences	Interactional space: Informal personal networks; spatial patterns of interpersonal communication and interaction

particular forms of institutional standardization that were characteristic (in ideal-typical terms) of all countries in the communist world. But the social order generated under the period of communist rule cannot be identified solely with the formal institutions of Leninism. Each Leninist regime generated institutional innovations and produced distinctive and widespread informal social relationships or cultural patterns that, while not themselves necessarily included among Leninism's formal definitional features, are broadly characteristic of those countries where Leninism was enforced (see, e.g., Baxandall, Chapter 8 in this volume, on the state socialist "unemployment taboo"). These we refer to as legacies of state socialism.

As is indicated by the framework presented here, however, there is no need for comparative historical research in the postcommunist era to limit itself to the study of Leninist or state socialist legacies alone. At a more general level of analysis, scholars can explore the mechanisms of reproduction of long-term temporal and spatial patterns, such as the reinforcement of East Europe's "semiperipheral" economic status in the modern period, and of long-term historical legacies, such as the influences of inherited religious traditions or patterns of foreign domination and state formation in different parts of the region (see, e.g., Szücs, 1988; Berend, 1986; Chirot, 1989; Stokes, 1997; Janos, 1995; 2000). Lasting socioeconomic, political, and cultural[3] patterns at this level of analysis – what Braudel has termed the *longue durée* – may be generated by long-term developments and underlying causal factors that have

[3] In many ways, Bourdieu's (1977; 1998) concept of "habitus" attempts to capture this long-term cultural dimension of social reality.

influenced pre-Leninist, Leninist, and post-Leninist regimes in similar ways. Such research may, in fact, sometimes uncover deeper constraints on social, cultural, and institutional change that severely limit the range of possible regime types and economic institutions that may be built in the region and influence their institutional performance. At the same time, such research is very demanding methodologically because causal mechanisms at this level of analysis are highly uncertain and difficult to link to observable outcomes (see Kitschelt, Chapter 2 in this volume).

Table 1.1 also helps us to identify the kinds of insights likely to be obtained from research at a more contextually specific level of analysis – one that emphasizes how the empirically diverse historical patterns of development within formally Leninist regimes, as well as the contingent spatial diffusion of institutions and innovations across Eastern Europe, have influenced institutional change in communist and postcommunist societies. At this level, highly contextualized studies of the impact of watershed events, critical junctures, or turning points (see Collier and Collier, 1991; Ekiert, 1996; Abbott, 1997b) allow analysts to trace the contingent temporal sequences by which similar initial starting points may generate divergent outcomes in later periods (Róna-Tas, 1997). In the same way, analysts may explore the complex and ambiguous nature of spatial linkages – often quite unconstrained by formal political boundaries – that are generated by informal social networks of communication and interaction (Stark and Bruszt, 1998). This "interactional" level of analysis – that is, one that emphasizes the concrete historical and spatial context within which particular social actors in postcommunist Europe "interact" – should not be interpreted as a residual category to be invoked whenever structural and institutional explanations fail. Rather, it is precisely at this level of analysis that the causal mechanisms generating new, distinctive institutional outcomes within the region can be initially traced and their potential effects on the broader structural environment discerned.

In the sections that follow, we outline how research on political, social, economic, and cultural change in Eastern Europe can be reinterpreted and synthesized in terms of the three levels of structural, institutional, and interactional time and space outlined here.

How Temporal Context Matters

How to evaluate the impact of the "Leninist legacy" on postcommunist politics and societies has proved to be a contentious problem for analysts (Jowitt, 1992; Crawford and Lijphart, 1995). Scholars working within what Crawford and Lijphart have termed the "imperatives of liberalization" approach have generally focused on the role of institutional choices, international pressures, and elite strategies in the successful liberal reforms in East Central Europe as proof that Leninist legacies can easily be cast aside. Others, mostly specialists on East European politics, see the communist period as largely conditioning the postcommunist present and tend to study countries further east (and south) where liberalization and marketization efforts have been inconsistent and often frustrated. An overview of political, social, and economic developments in the entire postcommunist region, however, clearly invalidates both extreme perspectives and forces us to search for theoretical understandings of how historical and institutional legacies of Leninism and state socialism matter more in some places than in others, how they interact with more-distant historical patterns, and what kinds of legacies are most enduring and pervasive.

Traditionally, historical approaches to social, political, and economic development tended to concentrate on a very abstract conceptual level in showing how history matters. Theorists operating at this "structural" level of analysis attempt to demonstrate that social life reveals patterns and uniformities operating in a very wide range of historical and institutional contexts. Here we find the grand social scientific theories of "social development" that purport to provide underlying accounts of the basic structure of human history in toto, beginning with Marx and Durkheim, and extending in contemporary times to theorists like Olson (1981), Wallerstein (1991b), and Fukuyama (1992). Frequently, of course, grand theories of history tend to embrace quite unscientific forms of historical teleology, in which favored ways of organizing social life are said to have a "natural" tendency to win out against all competitors. Yet one need not embrace any particular vision of the "end of history" to appreciate the genuine insights into empirical long-term social patterns of reproduction and change in human social history arrived at by these scholars and their disciples.

For understanding social change in postcommunist Europe and Eurasia, such structural theories concerning the impact of long-term historical patterns can be quite enlightening. From the perspective of the *longue durée*, the Leninist period can be seen to fit within a much longer-term pattern of responses to the development of technological and social innovations in Northwest Europe throughout the European semiperiphery and periphery – a dynamic dating at least back to the 1500s (Wallerstein, 1974; Mann, 1986). As Berend (1986: 344) observed, during the communist period "political Eastern Europe had, for the most part, become identical with historical Eastern Europe." Indeed, the "problem of backwardness" has been seen as an enduring constraint on political and economic development in Eastern Europe by a wide range of scholars both within and outside the region (Gerschenkron, 1965; Chirot, 1989; Janos, 2000). According to Rupnik (1989: 13), "the original paradox of Central European politics is the incongruity between its endorsement of Western civilization, political ideas and institutions, and the reality of the area's social and economic development, as well as the complexities of its ethnic puzzle." Underdeveloped agrarian economies, the weakness of urban centers, the absence of an indigenous, independent bourgeoisie outside the core areas of the Industrial Revolution, and the need to compete militarily with advanced capitalist powers have seemed to necessitate the adoption of coercive, "top-down," statist developmental strategies (Tilly, 1990) – whether under monarchy, fascist dictatorship, or communism. The adoption of such strategies, however, has tended to reinforce the role of the state, limiting both individual liberties and the potential for autonomous economic innovation. Statism, in Rothschild's (1993: 21) words, "is a trait of continuity from the interwar period to contemporary East Central Europe." Thus short-term "leaps forward" in economic development have generated longer-term economic crises – ironically reinforcing the peripheral economic status of the region (Berend, 1996). For the more economically distressed areas of the postcommunist world, the potential for another repetition of this tragic cycle is all too real – as illustrated, for example, by President Putin's calls to "rebuild the strong state" in Russia as a way of spurring economic growth (Holmes, 2001; see also Verdery, 1996: 209–16). For the more successful postcommunist marketizers, fortunately, it appears – for contextual reasons that will be dealt with later – that this vicious cycle might finally have been broken. It is worth pointing out, however, that the economic gap between postcommunist economic successes such as Poland and Hungary and the richer members of the European Union remains quite significant – indeed, it is much greater than before 1939 (Greskovits, 2000; Sachs and Warner, 1996).

The long-term historical patterns of national identity formation are similarly important in understanding developments taking place in the region. Here, too, the historical problem of relationships with the "developed" West has played a fundamental role. As Gellner (1983) and Greenfeld (1992) have argued, the sort of "civic" nationalism pioneered in Britain and the United States was greatly facilitated by the fact that these countries could achieve a distinct high status through their self-perception as "leaders" of world progress toward liberal, individualistic norms. For later nation builders further east, national identity was often "constructed" precisely in opposition to the British and American models. Having to compete against these wealthy and powerful "civic" nations generated a sort of *ressentiment* nationalism that upheld the superiority of emotion, community, and hierarchy to reason, individualism, and representative democracy. In this respect, too, one sees commonalities among feudal, fascist, and communist ideologies developed in the region – and at least in some countries, contemporary ideologues spin "fantasies of salvation" emphasizing similar antiliberal themes (Tismaneanu, 1998; Ramet, 1999).

Admittedly, though, it is very difficult to establish precise mechanisms generating the social reproduction of such phenomena as developmental statism and ideological *ressentiment* over the course of centuries through a series of diverse regime types (Kiser and Hechter, 1998). At the structural level of analysis, it is certainly useful to think about continuities in the precommunist, communist, and postcommunist historical context of East

Europe that are reflective of general patterns in European history and produce general constraints limiting the range of possible choices for postcommunist collective actors. Research designed to uncover patterns of "deep" causation faces significant methodological difficulties, however; the reconstruction of causal mechanisms over such long time spans is highly uncertain and the empirical evidence is difficult to master. For these reasons, most comparative research into the impact of the historical context on trajectories of transformation in the region is likely to focus instead on the institutional level of analysis, pursuing what Sartori termed the "middle range" level of generalization (Sartori, 1970) and identifying more readily accessible causal mechanisms. At this level we deal with the specific legacies of Leninism and state socialism and the patterns of their impact and breakdown across the postcommunist world.

We have claimed that Leninist legacies are a specific part of the inheritance of postcommunist societies. To understand their precise role and impact, however, we must first define what "Leninism" is. In this regard, it is one of the great ironies of social scientific history that mainstream approaches in the field of communist studies – despite its initial emphasis on the "unique" aspects of its subject matter – have had difficulty developing a consensual understanding of the precise definitional features the Leninist institutional order. As a result, scholars today have little guidance in identifying the key institutional features of Leninist-type regimes in order to chart their effects on post-Leninist change. This is a serious theoretical problem, because a practically infinite number of possible aspects of the communist (and precommunist) past could in principle exert some influence over later historical developments; simply showing that elements of the past still "matter" tells us little about whether Leninist rule per se has identifiable general effects on post-Leninist social development.

In retrospect, neither the totalitarian model nor the modernization paradigm ever adequately set out theoretical criteria for determining just how to tell when "Leninism" had ended and a qualitatively new type of regime had begun (Hanson, 1995a). Totalitarian theory did set out a list of features characteristic of full-blown "totalitarianism" (Friedrich and Brzezinski, 1956), but its advocates neither specified which of these features were definitionally central nor how many of them could disappear before the designation became theoretically inapplicable. Once the period of high Stalinism ended, then, scholars in this school were forced to generate a whole series of ad hoc concepts with shifting and vague empirical referents – such as "totalitarianism without terror" (Kassof, 1964) or "oligarchic petrification" (Brzezinski, 1969) – in order to make sense of institutional changes in Soviet-type societies. Modernization theory, meanwhile, focused on the ways in which Soviet-type societies were similar to "modern" industrial and urbanized societies in the capitalist West; thus scholars in this tradition spent very little effort identifying continuing distinctive features of the Leninist regime type.

As Breslauer (1992) points out, many modernization theorists, too, fell into the trap of analyzing each change of leadership as a qualitatively new sort of "regime" – each more "modern" than the last.

There was, however, an alternative theoretical tradition in the field of communist studies that did tackle the problem of taxonomical categorization relatively successfully, a tradition we might term the "comparative sociological" approach. Scholars in this camp rejected both the argument of the totalitarian school that Leninism was "sui generis" and hence impossible to compare with other regimes, as well as the assumptions of most modernization theorists that "Soviet-type systems" were essentially similar to other "developed modern societies." Instead, they endeavored to utilize comparative analysis precisely in order to shed light on the unique features of the Leninist regime type (see Bunce, 1999: 21–25; Comisso, 1991; Ekiert, 1991).

Within the comparative sociological tradition, two main lines of analysis were explored that, in retrospect, appear to be ultimately complementary. The first was the Weberian school associated with such figures as Rigby, Tucker, and Jowitt, which focused on the problem of identifying Leninism's distinct type of institutional legitimation and the informal elite and social practices it generated. The second was the historical-institutional approach developed by a diverse group of sociologists, anthropologists, political scientists, and economists, including such scholars as Szelényi, Kornai, Staniszkis, Stark, Comisso, Bunce, and Verdery. The historical-institutional school tended to focus not so much on the institutional norms of Leninist politics and Stalinist economics but rather on the broader patterns of state-society relations that developed within Leninist polities – patterns that could be usefully understood as characteristic of "state socialism." David Stark and Victor Nee summarized the common convictions shared by this school as follows:

> [S]tate socialism represents a distinctive social formation that has its own institutional logic and dynamics of development.... The institutional perspective insists, first, that theories explaining processes and outcomes in state socialism must take into account the institutional arrangements specific to state socialism. Second, rather than an exclusive focus on party and state elites, the new institutional perspective opens up society and economy and their relationship to the state as arenas of research. Thus subordinate groups, popular culture, social networks, markets, entrepreneurship, organizational innovations, political coalitions, local-level administration, and the new forms of interest representation become subjects of study. (1989: 30)

Together, these two schools developed an understanding of the Leninist regime type that allows us to pinpoint its key political, economic, and social features in comparative theoretical perspective.

Taking Weber's own political sociology as their starting point, the first group of scholars began their analysis of communist systems by interpreting them in terms of Weber's three types of legitimate domination (Weber,

1968). They interpreted Lenin's leadership as an example of "charismatic domination" in Weberian terms – that is, rule by a leader seen as exemplary and extraordinary by his followers and obeyed by them for that reason. Analysts in this school then logically interpreted later institutional developments within Soviet-type societies in terms of Weber's theory of the inevitable routinization of charisma, although debates continued as to whether this routinization in Leninist regimes was in a more modern (Tucker, 1971), clientelistic (Rigby, 1990), or "neo-traditional" (Jowitt, 1992) direction. Despite these disagreements, all these scholars understood that Leninist institutions reflected the avowedly ideological starting point of Communist Party elites who built them – making the role of formal Marxist-Leninist ideology itself in political discourse one of the key identifying features of Leninist rule in comparative perspective.

Jowitt's distinctive and most important contribution, however, was to identify Leninist party institutions as representative as a *new* taxonomical type in Weberian terms – as a form of "charismatic impersonalism" combining charismatic and rational-legal organizational elements into a relatively coherent institutional amalgam (Jowitt, 1992). The second large-scale institutional standardizing project in Soviet-type societies was the formal enforcement of "planned heroism" in the Stalinist economy (Hanson, 1997), which was designed to synthesize heroism and efficiency in everyday productive labor. In retrospect, these taxonomical criteria have proved to be enormously useful in marking the historical and geographic dividing lines between Leninist and post-Leninist regimes.

Specifying the key institutional features of charismatic impersonalism in Leninist politics and Stalinist economics in this way provides a much clearer starting point for comparative analysis of the effects of Leninist (and Stalinist) legacies on postcommunist societies. Attempts to institutionalize Marxism-Leninism as a hegemonic ideological discourse, the "leading role" of Leninist parties, and obligatory "planned heroism" in industry and agriculture constitute the three most important features of the standardizing project carried out by communist elites in the postwar period (Bunce, 1999: 130). If "communism" was ever really a coherent theoretical category, it was due to the remarkable (if bloody) success of this attempt in much of Eurasia for several decades. Understanding Leninism in comparative sociological terms – that is, as a distinct set of charismatically impersonal institutions generating distinctive formal and informal socioeconomic responses – helps greatly to clarify just how the postcommunist world does, and does not, differ from other new democracies and "emerging markets" elsewhere.

From this point of view, one can understand the legacies of Leninism as reflecting the sequential decay and disintegration of charismatic impersonalism as expressed in Marxist-Leninist ideology, Leninist party rule, and Stalinist economic planning. In general, these institutions have broken down throughout the Leninist world in the same order in which they were originally established, a pattern that reflects the increasing difficulty facing individuals deciding to abandon them (Hanson, 1995b). Marxist-Leninist ideology, of course, was nearly costless to abandon; indeed, in most of the Leninist world, cynicism about this world view had become so widespread that the few remaining "true believers" after 1989 sounded simply ridiculous. The ideological vacuum this rapid collapse left in its wake, however, has not easily been filled in the years since, and a general public cynicism regarding professions of ideological faith throughout the postcommunist world has been one of the most distinctive legacies of the Leninist past. Affiliation with Leninist parties, by contrast, was not so painless to disavow; the monopolization of public life under the one-party system meant that personal allegiances to other former party officials were often still crucial for personal advancement in the postcommunist period, especially in small towns and rural regions where political competition was weakest (McAuley, 1997). Indeed, the organizational core of many postcommunist political parties can be traced to affiliations developed within the Leninist regime. Finally, abandonment of one's position within the factories and collective farms established under the Stalinist planning system has proved to be the most painful individual choice of all. Stalinist socioeconomic institutions, built around the ideal of "planned heroism" and with little if any historical promotion of Western norms of efficiency, left older workers and managers with few valuable skills enabling them to compete effectively in a genuinely competitive market context. Thus, regions of the former Soviet bloc that were heavily industrialized and/or collectivized in the postwar period have proved exceedingly difficult to reform.

The legacies of state socialism, by contrast with the previously discussed legacies of Leninism, have not all been so negative in their implications for reform in postcommunist societies. Indeed, many of the sociological impacts of Leninist development emphasized by the historical-institutional school have been undeniably beneficial for contemporary efforts at reintegration with the liberal capitalist world. Most obvious, perhaps – but still worth emphasizing – postcommunist Europe is no longer bound to a backward agricultural economy and peasant-dominated social structure. The high levels of urbanization and education attained in almost every Leninist country after World War II have clearly facilitated both democratic reform and marketization in Eastern Europe and the former Soviet Union since 1989; generally speaking, urban and educated citizens tend to be more supportive of liberal values and policies than those in smaller towns and villages or with less schooling. To this extent, at least, conventional modernization theories of communism had a point – even if they missed the ways in which the charismatic component of the Leninist project imparted a distinctive and deleterious structure to the kinds of industries and cities built in the Soviet period.

The legacy of nomenklatura rule, by contrast, has been rather more mixed in its effects. On the one hand, the widespread trend toward "nomenklatura privatization" throughout the Soviet bloc under Gorbachev's leadership has left a bitter taste among those who were not initially so well placed to benefit from the initial redistribution of party and state assets. What Staniszkis has described as "political capitalism" is clearly a legacy of the declining years of state socialism (Staniszkis, 1991; Solnick, 1998). On the other hand, as Eyal, Szelényi, and Townsley (1998) have shown, former nomenklatura status does not automatically translate into elite status in the postcommunist period; those who relied most on their connections within former communist party circles, in fact, have ended up in a decidedly inferior position relative to those who moved quickly into various forms of open and/or covert entrepreneurship. More broadly, it seems clear that training in the Leninist party bureaucracy did impart some skills that were transferable to the postcommunist environment; particularly where Leninism itself was superimposed upon countries with previous legacies of rational-legal bureaucratic proceduralism, the period of Soviet domination did not uproot and perhaps even reinforced the professional norms of civil servants (Kitschelt et al., 1999). In part for this reason, splits between ideological dogmatists and more Western-oriented technocrats developed in most East European countries quite early in the communist era – and such divisions continue to influence the dynamics of postcommunist politics today (Grzymała-Busse, 2002).

A final general sociological legacy of state socialism – its generation of widespread informal networks in the "second economy" (Böröcz, 2000; Róna-Tas, 1998; Stark and Bruszt, 1998; Grossman, 1990; Walder, 1986) – has had perhaps the most important impact on postcommunist institutional change. In the core countries of the former USSR, in fact, some analysts estimate that well over half of GDP now takes place in the informal sector (Shama, 1996). Even more than in Soviet times, perhaps, ordinary people rely on *blat* (connections) to get through daily life (Ledevena, 1998) rather than depending on formal salaries or government transfer payments, which have often been delayed for months at a time. The widespread growth of the post-Soviet "*mafiya*," too, has its roots firmly in the Stalinist economy; indeed, problems of economic corruption, asset stripping, capital flight, and so on were evident well before the final collapse of the USSR (Handelman, 1995). Even in East Central Europe, where formal liberalization and marketization have been vastly more successful, personal networks inherited from the Leninist period still play a vital role in economic life. Indeed, the sorts of "recombinant property" studied by Stark and Bruszt (1998) emerged directly out of the hybrid market economy that developed through economic reforms such as the Hungarian New Economic Mechanism.

This brings us to the problem of temporal context at the interactional level of analysis. If the "history of Leninism" does exert some common influence on the postcommunist region considered broadly – thus helping to explain the failures of neo-institutional engineering in at least some parts of the region after 1989 – we must still find a way to account for the remarkably diverse trajectories of historical change in the postcommunist period, emphasized in the Introduction to this volume. Indeed, at this more contextualized level of analysis, it becomes clear that the types of communist takeovers; the degrees of enforcement and institutionalization of Marxist ideology, Leninist party rule, and Stalinist economics; modalities of transition to a post-totalitarian regime; and modes of deconstruction in the final years of state socialism varied widely across the region. After all, the efforts to standardize Leninist institutions in Eastern and Central Europe after World War II met with extremely high levels of social resistance. Crisis points involving Soviet military intervention in Hungary in 1956 and Czechoslovakia in 1968, and the Soviet-supported imposition of martial law in Poland in 1981, can be seen as "critical junctures" leading to profoundly changed relationships between regime and society (Ekiert, 1996). Efforts to reimpose Leninist party rule in Hungary and Poland, in particular, involved compromises about the enforcement of economic Stalinism that opened up social space for the articulation and institutionalization of various counterhegemonic political and cultural projects. In the case of Poland, formal party rule itself was reestablished only through a decisive shift toward military hegemony that fundamentally undermined the legitimation of the Polish United Workers' Party (PUWP) as a "Leninist," charismatically impersonal institution. These diverging institutional outcomes of regime crises set in motion paths of institutional development in the three cases whose effects can be seen up to the present day.

In this respect, a more contextual approach to the analysis of "path dependence" in comparative politics holds much promise for understanding the long-term impact of specific events occurring at "critical junctures" during the Leninist period (Collier and Collier, 1991; Pierson, 2000a). Indeed, the main point of the classic analysis of economic path dependence developed by such scholars as Paul David is to show how seemingly "random" events at one point in time may generate long-term economic trajectories that are inexplicable in terms of static equilibrium models (David, 1985). Increasing returns processes represent "narratives" whose outcomes could not in principle have been predicted at either the structural or institutional levels of analysis; one might "rerun" history and get completely different outcomes based upon different event sequences (Gould, 1989). The analytical advantage of studying such contextually embedded processes is the capacity to identify with great precision the initial events, reactive sequences, and causal mechanisms producing institutional change. Analysis at the highest level of generality (looking at "problems of backwardness") or even the medium level of generality (looking at specific "institutional legacies") will often overlook the significance of contingent temporal sequences of this type.

For analysts of postcommunist change in particular, much of the most fruitful research is likely to occur at this highly contextual level. The quite rapid collapse of formal Leninist institutions has certainly left identifiable legacies in common to much of the region, but it has also cleared social space for innovations and articulations of identity not fully predictable from the starting point of the communist breakdown.[4] If we follow Staniszkis (1995) in distinguishing among the various modes of imposition of Leninist rule, the different forms of de-Stalinization, and the diverging modes of exit from communism in various Eastern European countries, we may gain a more precise understanding of the specific ways in which history provides very different resources for, and constraints on, political and economic development in different places. Moreover, it is at this highly contextualized level of analysis that the quite specific historical experiences of different postcommunist countries may be relevant to future outcomes. To the extent that contemporary political science promotes only highly abstract, "nomothetic" theories of democratization, marketization, and state formation that are valid among all postcommunist countries (and beyond), the "chaotic" but consequential outcomes of particular event sequences taking place in Eastern Europe are likely to be altogether missed.

How Spatial Context Matters

A review of any set of economic, political, or social indicators for Eastern Europe reveals a clear pattern of spatial distribution. Countries that are situated closer to the West have consistently higher scores and ranks in various indexes designed to measure the progress of political and economic transformations, quality of democracy and market institutions, macroeconomic indicators, and so on. Such scores tend to decline the further east the country lies. This spatial pattern reflects a hierarchy of subregions across Eastern Europe that differ significantly in their efforts at consolidating democracy and building a market economy (see, e.g., EBRD, 2000: 27). Moreover, such differences among subregions within Eastern Europe not only tend to persist, but even grow larger with every passing year. In the forefront of regional development are the countries of East Central Europe (the Czech Republic, Hungary, Poland, Slovenia, and Slovakia). They have established solid institutions of procedural democracy, overcome the transitional recession, and resumed economic growth much sooner; in addition, their governments have pursued relatively consistent reformist policies, and their institutional transformations are most advanced (see Ekiert, Chapter 3 in this volume). East Central Europe is followed in descending order by the Baltic republics (Estonia, Latvia, Lithuania), which have emerged as the most successful

[4] This is why it is possible for Jowitt to insist simultaneously that the "Leninist legacy" is likely to shape events in Eastern Europe for years to come, and to describe the region as a "Genesis environment" in which truly unprecedented forms of social and institutional development may occur (Jowitt, 1992).

part of the former Soviet Union; Southeastern Europe or the Balkan region (Romania, Bulgaria, Albania, Croatia, Macedonia, Serbia, and Bosnia and Herzegovina); the European part of the former Soviet Union (Russia, Ukraine, Belarus); and finally the Caucasus and Central Asian states. Not only do the general scores decline when one moves from west to east, the data also show that the further east the region is located, the greater intraregional variation seems to be, with some countries departing significantly from subregional trends and averages.

How can the emergence and persistence of such spatial patterns be explained? Can geographical location be considered an independent explanatory factor influencing the initial political and economic outcomes of postcommunist transformations? Do the existing spatial patterns merely reflect other more important factors at work, such as institutional choices or historical and cultural legacies? How should the impact of geographical location and the spatial context be conceptualized, and what are the mechanisms reproducing spatial patterns? Finally and more generally, what is the relationship between history and location or temporal sequences and spatial patterns? These are important questions with profound theoretical and methodological implications. They cannot and should not be ignored or dismissed, especially in the context of comparative theorizing and research. Large-scale regional transformations in general and East European developments in particular offer a unique opportunity to investigate these issues and develop at least tentative answers to these questions.

A review of research on postcommunist transformations supports Lynn's claim that "very few commentators have taken geography into account when theorizing the process of post-socialist change" (Lynn, 1999: 824). This evident omission has both theoretical and methodological sources. In terms of the theoretical dimension, the importance of spatial patterns has been underestimated or even ignored in mainstream social science for a long time. Interest in and concerns with the impact of geography were too often associated with a morally suspect geographic determinism and traditional cultural diffusion models that assumed the cultural superiority of the West and a unidirectional evolutionary path of social development. Methodologically, established professional norms put the construction of "universal" explanatory models at the center of social science inquiry. Spatial complexities were seen as excess detail, the removal of which was often justified in the name of parsimony. Kitschelt (Chapter 2 in this volume) points to such methodological constraints in explaining the outcomes of postcommunist transformations, claiming that "it is not easy to determine the causal mechanism that underlies the indisputable correlation between geography and political regime form."[5]

[5] Kitschelt argues that a causal relationship between proximity to the West and political regime form, if it exists, should be mediated by the volume of trade and the level of foreign direct

Given the seeming empirical correlation between location and initial outcomes in Eastern Europe, however, we should begin to pay more attention to the research done in other disciplines that take space and spatial patterns seriously. Political scientists are often not familiar with current developments within the field of human geography as they look for theoretical inspiration from other more "successful" disciplines. Lynn (1999: 826), however, makes a convincing argument that analytical approaches developed in the "new regional geography" have implications for "the way the specificity of transition is understood as being modified within the generality of social change and the particularity of place. The most effective approaches will situate social action and social change within particular space-time settings and particular localities and recognize that these are constitutive rather than passive."

The impact of geography, like that of history, can be conceptualized at three distinct levels of analysis. At the most encompassing level, geography can be understood as a set of underlying natural or structural factors, including climate, topography, resource endowment, population density, migration patterns, patterns of trade and spatial patterns of production, and distance from economic centers. Such structural factors shape social practices in many important ways and create powerful constraints and opportunities for political and economic development. The idea that various characteristics of peoples and countries grew out of their geographical situation has had influential supporters in Western social philosophy, history, and social science. Some of them advocated an extreme form of geographical determinism, but the majority saw geography as one among many important factors shaping social behavior, economic progress, and political institutions. Bodin, Montesquieu, and Herder are commonly considered the founding fathers of an approach in which geographical factors are conceptualized as major forces in shaping the ways of life and destinies of various peoples. More recently, Fernand Braudel (1981–84), William McNeill (1974), and E. L. Jones (1981) have investigated the impact of geography and climate on the

investment (FDI). In his analysis, however, closer geographic distance shows only a moderate effect on variance in trade and in FDI. This prompts him to focus on temporal rather than spatial causation and to test the impact of historical legacies on the variation of political regime forms that emerged in the region. On closer inspection, Kitschelt's dismissal of spatial explanation in East European context may be premature. The weak statistical relationships he discovers are more the result of the problematic nature of his initial assumption about the mediating role of trade and FDI as well as other more specific measurement and analysis problems. In contrast, Kopstein and Reilly, in Chapter 4 of this volume, insist that their "spatial dependence" explanation shows a considerable impact of geographic location on outcomes of postcommunist transformations. They argue that specific locations provide opportunities for greater and more effective diffusion of norms, resources, and institutions that are critical in building democracy and a market economy. In short, spatial proximity to the West shapes the direction and outcomes of transformations through processes of diffusion. Their work opens up new ways of mapping postcommunist transformation and should be followed by more research to explore the multiple channels, mechanisms, and contents of diffusion.

trajectory of European economic development. According to these interpretations, various geographical advantages of Europe (temperate climate, coastal trade, navigable rivers, etc.) were key factors in explaining the emergence of Europe as a center of global capitalism. While the role of various geographic advantages may decline over time as a result of technological changes, spatial patterns shaped by geography have a tendency to persist. In short, geographic advantages often provide an auspicious context for generating long-term political and economic developments leading to higher economic growth and more-liberal political regimes.

In a recent paper, Gallup, Sachs, and Mellinger (1999) revisited the relationship between physical geography and macroeconomic growth. They concluded that location and climate have large effects on level of income and growth and are a factor in the choice of economic policies. Other economists, including Paul Krugman (1991; 1995) and Anthony Venables and Nuno Limao (1999), have investigated the highly differentiated spatial organization of production, emphasizing the role of agglomeration economies, transport costs, and product differentiation. Current research on the role of geographical factors shows that location still matters, despite all the technological advances that have transformed the ways in which goods are produced, transported, traded, and consumed. By extension, as research on the relationship between levels of economic development and types of political regime implies, location has a measurable impact on the form of political regimes.

From this point of view, the countries of Central Europe, by virtue of their proximity to the West, location on the crossroads of major continental trade routes, and well-developed transportation networks should have an obvious advantage. This advantage may even compensate for otherwise inhibiting features such as landlocked location in the cases of Hungary, Slovakia, and the Czech Republic (see Gallup et al., 1999). By contrast, the geographical positioning of many post-Soviet countries continues to be highly disadvantageous. Russia, like most of the other former Soviet republics, lacks easy access to established shipping and trade routes; many of its largest cities lie thousands of miles away from centers of world trade and capital. Moreover, the country is burdened by a largely Arctic climate that necessitates enormously expensive investments in housing, utilities, and transportation infrastructure to enable economic exploitation of many of its most valuable raw materials (Lynch, 2002). The inhospitable natural environment in much of the former Soviet Union has been exacerbated further by the massive pollution of air, water, and land resources generated by the Stalinist model of industrialization (Feshbach and Friendly, 1992). In addition, Stalinism contributed in numerous ways to a contemporary demographic crisis that threatens to have devastating long-term consequences for Russian society (Feshbach, 2001). The institutional effects of Leninism have thus in this respect become part of the structural spatial environment constraining contemporary efforts to integrate into global capitalism.

Clearly, however, structural and natural spatial contexts alone do not predetermine political and economic outcomes in postcommunist Europe. Indeed, at the second, institutional level of analysis, social space can be seen to a significant degree as a politically constructed phenomenon. Boundaries dividing space, from this perspective, are created and maintained by political, economic, and cultural actors, and the resulting regional differentiations profoundly shape economic, political, and social developments. Geopolitical factors based on the international division of economic, military, and political power define territorially dependent susceptibility to conquest, predation, and economic exploitation and impose powerful boundaries across geographical spaces. Geopolitics has framed the destiny of East European countries throughout their modern history in many fundamental ways. As Rothschild (1993: 263) has argued, "It has become conventional to regard East Central Europe as the object, target, and victim of the power thrusts and power projections of others – be they Ottomans, Germans, Russians, or 'the West.' And there is much truth in that perception." Eastern Central Europe was the battleground of contending empires in the eighteenth and nineteenth centuries and was again completely reshaped through the turmoil following the First World War and the Soviet revolution. Countries of the region had faced profound geopolitical instability and German and Russian irredentist pressures during the interwar period; they were politically, economically, and socially destroyed during the Second World War. The region emerged from the war under Soviet domination and endured one more period of dramatic territorial, political, social, and economic transformations.

The term "captive nations" was coined to describe the geopolitical reality of postwar Eastern Europe. Five decades of Soviet domination had a profound impact on the countries of the region. Their economic and political structures as well as civil societies were completely recast through coercive processes of attempted political, economic, and ideological homogenization. The imposition of the Leninist project on the diverse countries of the region created new and lasting institutional and cultural realities. In many ways, however, Leninism also reinforced some of the more traditional features of Eastern European societies (see Jowitt, 1992: 287). Moreover, traditional subregional boundaries persisted in a remarkable way (Berend, 1986).

The regime transformation and the disintegration of the Soviet empire that took place between 1989 and 1992 was first and foremost a reconstitution of the geopolitical space in this part of the European continent, with dramatic consequences not only for the region but also for the entire framework of world politics. Despite the uncertainties and political fuzziness of the post–Cold War world, geopolitical influences, boundaries, and pressures are as relevant today as they are different. Laurence Whitehead has recently argued that "geopolitical constraints and crosscurrents can powerfully affect: (1) the interstate distribution of democratization; (2) the scope of democracy within the states affected; and (3) the viability of the resulting democratic regimes" (1999: 75). The new geopolitical space within which the East European transformations have been taking place is complex, characterized by a significant degree of fluidity and uncertainty, as well as the ever present potential for a major crisis. As a result, various postcommunist countries have to adjust continuously their foreign and domestic policies to respond to opportunities and constraints emerging within these changing geopolitical boundaries. Accordingly, as Whitehead emphasized, "Each of the new and potential democracies of postcommunist Central and Eastern Europe is fixed in a territorial matrix that exposes it to powerful international crosscurrents.... in the region bounded on the west by the European Union, on the east by the residues of the Soviet experiment, and to the south by the resurgent forces of Islam, external cross pressures hold considerable explanatory power" (1999: 76).

Clearly, geopolitical pressures within the vast postcommunist space differ in terms of their nature, effectiveness, and constraining power. Some locations are more responsive to Western influences and are more propitious to democracy and market reforms than others. It may well be that the success of Central East European countries was "overdetermined" by virtue of their geographical location. We need more-systematic research in order to understand better the impact and nature of geopolitical pressures on domestic politics in more-successful countries and in other parts of the region. One possible way to explore this issue is to look at the "neighbor effect" (investigated by Kopstein and Reilly, Chapter 4 in this volume) and systematically assess constraints and crosscurrents affecting transformation politics in various countries. Another approach is to view these dynamics through the prism of international security. Scholars have investigated, for example, debates about Russian identity and their effects on Russian foreign policy in the post-Soviet global context (Hopf, 1999).

The influence of geopolitics works through the creation of institutional regimes, economic and political cooperation, and security alliances as well as through military threats and interventions. We have seen all of these mechanisms in action during the past decade. Their impacts, however, have been uneven across the region as different countries experienced significantly different levels of international pressure and different kinds of security incentives. The conditionality attached to membership in the Council of Europe or the Organization for Security and Cooperation in Europe had a relatively similar impact on the majority of postcommunist countries, but other actions and initiatives have not. The admission of three Central European countries (the Czech Republic, Hungary, and Poland) into NATO, and the invitation of several additional new members in the years to come, has changed the security equation in the region in the most fundamental way. Similarly, the selection of eight postcommunist countries (the Czech Republic, Estonia, Hungary, Latvia, Lithuania, Poland, Slovakia, and Slovenia) for the "first wave" of European Union expansion has redrawn intraregional boundaries and dramatically altered the context of postcommunist transformations. These decisions have created powerful geopolitical boundaries and distinctive subregions within the new Eastern Europe, with far-reaching economic and political consequences. The relegation of other countries such as Bulgaria, Romania, and Croatia to the much less certain "second wave" creates a less immediate set of incentives for these countries, while leaving other parts of the region in a sort of geopolitical limbo. In short, during the first decade of postcommunism a three-tier geopolitical hierarchy emerged in the region that threatened to magnify already existing divisions in Europe. The western-located leaders of reforms are likely to become the winners who take all.

The unequal extent and density of relations between the West and Eastern Europe reflect a complex interaction between domestic developments in particular countries and Western interests, expectations, and sympathies. Western sympathies toward Central Europe and the assumption that this part of the postcommunist world was the most likely candidate for joining a developed and liberal European space had as much to do with the political construction of subregional boundaries as with geographic location per se. The notion of Central Europe by itself became a geopolitical reality, in part, as a result of a political and intellectual project that Rupnik (1989: 4) described as "more a state of mind than a scientific concept." The constructed category of Central Europe, significantly different from the prewar concept of Mitteleuropa, simultaneously engaged the state of mind of Western policy makers and that of East European intellectuals opposing Soviet domination and advocating a return to Europe. Reviewing Timothy Garton Ash's work, which profoundly shaped Western public opinion, Perry Anderson argued that

> if there was a single leitmotif of his writing until the mid-Nineties, it was the special character of the countries of central Europe in the spectrum of captive nations, and their quite particular call on the sympathies and resources of Western Europe. The notion of "Central Europe" – as expounded by spokesmen like Milan Kundera or Czeslaw Miłosz – designated Czechoslovakia, Hungary and Poland.... Its function was, on the one side, to draw a cultural line demarcating this zone from such truly East European (viz. backward) countries as Romania or Yugoslavia – and even more from perpetually barbarian, totalitarian Russia; on the other, to link it, as a cradle of political tolerance and high culture, to the homelands of liberty and prosperity in Western Europe, from which, on Kundera's showing, only malign fate had wrenched it away. (1999: 6)

The cultural construction of the notion of Central Europe embraced by opposition movements in these countries proved to have a real impact on Western policies vis-à-vis the region.[6] As Susan Woodward (1993: x) has

[6] This point should not be exaggerated, however. Western and especially American policies toward the region always pursued a strategy of differentiation, selecting countries for special

argued, "As early as 1989 Western governments began to declare that the central European countries were better prepared to make the economic and political transition from socialism to capitalism than those in south-eastern Europe." Thus, power politics and cultural politics came together to redefine new geopolitical boundaries dividing the eastern part of the continent.

The recent restructuring and redefinition of East European geopolitical space will have profound consequences for the long-term economic development of particular countries and for the consolidation of their democratic regimes. In short, new geopolitical divides have been emerging in postcommunist Eastern Europe, and the boundaries between newly defined subregions have become more rigid and permanent. These new divisions have already had a significant impact on patterns of foreign assistance and investment, trade and political cooperation, and the scope and limits of Western political involvement. As Whitehead rightly points out, "geography may not entirely dictate any nation's democratic destiny, but Central and Eastern Europe is a region where its effects are likely to remain pivotal" (1999: 79). The new geopolitical patterns emerging in Eastern Europe have interacted in a powerful way with domestic transformations by shaping the preferences and expectations of political actors as well as by creating turning points, critical junctures, and discontinuities in unfolding processes of change in particular locations.

This brings us to the third, most contextualized approach to studying postcommunist political space – the interactional level of analysis. In contrast to conceptualizing geographical spaces as natural environments or as a hierarchy of qualitatively different regional spaces, the third perspective implies the understanding of space as the combination of networks that often ignore natural and constructed regional boundaries. The spatial distribution, density, and robustness of such networks may have a critical impact on political and economic outcomes. Consequently, the progress of political and economic transformations may indeed depend on characteristics of social space as mediated by these networks. The concept of diffusion is at the center of this way of thinking about spatial patterns. From this point of view, the relevance of the diffusion literature to the study of postcommunist transformations seems obvious. In recent years, there has been significant growth in research on diffusion across organizations and social movements (see, e.g., Strang and Soule, 1998; Rucht, 1995). Although most of the recent work in this tradition was concerned with microlevel processes, especially in the field of technological innovations, democratization processes provide fruitful settings for investigation of why institutional and behavioral practices

treatment on the basis of their potential for creating divisions within the Soviet bloc. For example, Yugoslavia received American aid and loans since 1949. Poland was granted most favored nation status in 1960, and Romania was rewarded in a similar way in 1964 (see Baylis, 1994).

embedded in markets and liberal democracy are diffused at different rates in different settings. In fact, many current applications of the concept involve macrolevel issues. As Strang and Soule (1998: 268) show, "contemporary work on organizations and social movements typically examines the spread of behavioral strategies and structures rather than technical innovations, emphasizes adoption by social collectivities more than individuals within those collectivities, works with a much larger historical and spatial canvas, and incorporates diffusion as one sort of explanation rather than as the overarching framework."

Contemporary transition processes involve the extension of democratic and market institutions, mechanisms, and norms from geographically located centers of global capitalism and democracy to other more or less distant locations. They generate a great deal of "contagion" – transfer of ideas, behavioral patterns, and cultural practices, as well as mimicry and imitation in institution building and policy innovations. As a result of these transnational transfers, outcomes can emerge that are relatively independent from underlying structural conditions (for an application of these ideas in the field of social movements, see McAdam, 1995). This regularity may account for the obvious discrepancy between internal conditions and the timing of transitions in Eastern Europe. The temporal decline in the effects of internal factors on the pace and rate of adoption of specific institutions and policies or the spread of contention has been documented in many studies (Strang and Soule, 1998). Diffusion is mediated by network structures that differ across space and is predicated on the existence of an extensive system of weak bridging ties to other spatial or geographic units (Granovetter, 1973). Accordingly, the investigation of contextual spatial patterns requires closer inspection of different pathways through which diffusion takes place, the types of actors and networks that facilitate the diffusion processes, and the role of proximity.

Spatial proximity is commonly considered as a precondition for effective diffusion processes. As Strang and Soule (1998: 275) point out, "perhaps the most common finding in diffusion research is that spatially proximate actors influence each other. No distinctive logic can be proposed – rather, spatial proximity facilitates all kinds of interaction and influence. Where network relations are not mapped directly, proximity often provides the best summary of the likelihood of mutual awareness and interdependence." Whereas the transformation and recasting of geopolitical space and its impact on the transformation process in specific parts of postcommunist Eastern Europe can be easily described, the impacts of other spatial patterns based on cultural and organizational diffusion are more difficult to untangle. The strong correlation between geographical location and the progress of transition may be fleshed out by an examination of the nature of networks and diffusion patterns that existed before 1989 and those that developed after the collapse of communism. The increased travel opportunities, significant migrations and formations of political diasporas, more-extensive trade links and industrial cooperation with the West, and wider participation in international organizations (see Ekiert, Chapter 3 in this volume) that characterized the countries of Central Europe before 1989 exposed both elites and ordinary people to practices of democracy and the market economy, as well as establishing links between intellectual and political elites in these countries and influential global "epistemic communities." Such links involved "discovering that something is possible, witnessing it in action, or hearing secondhand about its objectives, rationale, and operation" (Strang and Soule, 1998: 269). Thus diffusion patterns based on network proximity can provide a significant element in explaining both the patterns of dissolution of communist rule and the successes of postcommunist Central Europe during the past decade.

The impact of spatial proximity, however, should not be construed in mechanistic terms. Strang and Soule (1998: 276) also emphasize that "structural opportunity for meaningful contact cannot tell us what sort of practices are likely to diffuse and such opportunities may lead to conflicts or boundary formation as well as diffusion." Accordingly, the analysis of the cultural and social bases of diffusion becomes critical. Cultural similarities and common reference points will facilitate diffusion processes.[7] Such similarities can be conceptualized in terms of "civilizations" (see, e.g., Huntington, 1996) but also in a more specific way, through mapping out religious, ethnic, ideological, or cultural boundaries within and between countries that create opportunities and impediments for the diffusion of norms, beliefs, institutions, and social behavior. From this perspective, it is not only for deep structural reasons that Central Europe and the Baltic republics are the most successful adopters of democracy and the market economy. It is true that their links to Western Europe have long historical roots, and the western part of the continent has long been a cultural, political, and economic reference point for these countries. In addition, however, they also maintained closer ties with the West in many formal and informal ways during the communist period. Some countries experienced crisis-generated emigration waves (during the post–World War II communist takeover and in 1956, 1968, and 1981) that produced large political diasporas living in Western Europe and the United States. In addition, countries like Poland, Hungary, or Slovenia had more-open political regimes that imposed fewer travel restrictions. The presence of large emigrant communities opened many informal channels facilitating diffusion processes. Finally, such transnational networks were not restricted to official elites. The congruence between elite and popular actors in adoption of ideas, attitudes, and institutions has had a profound impact on patterns

[7] According to Strang and Meyer (1992), diffusion is facilitated by the process of social construction through which the adopters emulate the innovators in defining themselves and the situation they face. In turn, as McAdam (1995: 233) argues, "this fundamental 'attribution of similarity' makes actions and ideas of the innovator relevant to the adopter."

and effectiveness of diffusion. Rowan (1982) has advanced the argument that innovations diffuse more rapidly when core actors are in agreement and tend to fail when they are not. In fact, it could be argued that in successful postcommunist countries the divisions between state and society and among various segments of the postcommunist elites were less pronounced, and the political as well as ideological boundaries more porous. This situation, which facilitated the emergence of a strong proliberal consensus, had its sources in part in pre-1989 politics. It seems that less exclusionary politics under the old regime facilitated both diffusion processes and the post-1989 liberal consensus about the direction of reforms.

This short overview was intended to make a simple point: location matters. If this is the case, it is necessary to investigate possible effects various spatial patterns may have on transformation processes. The available evidence indicates that, indeed, there are "right" or "better" places for democracy to take hold and for a market economy to emerge. The East European cases we compare have specific spatial locations that intersect with old and new patterns and boundaries that divide the postcommunist world. We suggest – as the research presented in this volume by Kopstein and Reilly convincingly shows – that attention to and inclusion of spatial factors in our explanatory models may provide a better understanding of the initial outcomes of postcommunist transformations. At the same time, we are acutely aware that most spatial patterns have historical origins; therefore, geographic space may ultimately need to be considered in a more geological fashion – that is, as a component of social "time-space."[8]

Conclusion: Toward a Disciplined Contextual Approach

Clearly, this chapter has provided only a preliminary sketch of how scholars might distinguish among the three levels of analysis and identify distinct causal mechanisms operating on these levels, in order to clarify their understandings of the impact of historical and spatial contexts on social outcomes. Efforts to theorize this "dual contextuality" more fully require further conceptual work and research. The biggest intellectual challenge is to resolve such problems as how to combine the temporal and spatial dimensions in investigation of particular social outcomes, and how to relate and reconcile the results of research done at different levels of analysis. In principle, of course, all three levels of analysis are connected to a single social reality, and causal mechanisms at work at these levels interact; thus there must be principles of "transformation" that explain how outcomes of particular event sequences diffused through particular social networks at the interactional level sometimes develop into standardized "regime types" patterning

[8] For an interesting effort to construct a set of categories combining temporal and spatial dimensions, see Wallerstein (1991a: 135–48). See also Kiser and Wesler (1999).

institutional outcomes in a wider range of times and spaces – and how, at an even more encompassing temporal and spatial level, the rise and fall of various regime types occur in patterned ways observable only in the *longue durée* and over vast geographical territory. Ultimately, such problems must be addressed through the development of a more comprehensive evolutionary theory of institutional change in the social sciences that is able to synthesize research at different temporal and spatial levels into a new, empirically verifiable explanatory framework.

At a minimum, though, we hope the present essay has helped to clarify somewhat the advantages and disadvantages of research at each of the three levels of analysis. In particular, it seems clear from this review of the literature that specialists on the communist and postcommunist region have already made enormous strides in understanding many of the most important historical and geographical influences on social change there. In this respect, research on postcommunist societies is no longer peripheral to mainstream social scientific inquiry but instead finds itself located at the cutting edge of the field.

References

Abbott, Andrew. 1988. Transcending General Linear Reality. *Sociological Theory* 6: 169–86.

1997a. Of Time and Space: The Contemporary Relevance of the Chicago School. *Social Forces* 75(4): 1149–82.

1997b. On the Concept of Turning Point. *Comparative Social Research* 16: 85–105.

2001. *Chaos of Disciplines*. Chicago: University of Chicago Press.

Aminzade, Roy. 1992. Historical Sociology and Time. *Sociological Methods and Research* 20(4): 456–80.

Anderson, Perry. 1999. A Ripple of the Polonaise. *London Review of Books*, November 25, 3–10.

Armijo, Leslie, Thomas Biersteker, and Abraham Lowenthal. 1995. The Problem of Simultaneous Transitions. In Larry Diamond and Marc E. Plattner, eds., *Economic Reform and Democracy*, pp. 226–40. Baltimore: Johns Hopkins University Press.

Bates, Robert. 1997. Area Studies and the Discipline: A Useful Controversy. *PS: Political Science and Politics* 30(2): 166–69.

Baylis, Thomas. 1994. *The West and Eastern Europe*. Westport, Conn.: Praeger.

Berend, Iván T. 1986. The Historical Evolution of Eastern Europe as a Region. *International Organization* 40(2): 329–46.

1996. *Central and Eastern Europe, 1944–1993: Detour from the Periphery to the Periphery*. Cambridge: Cambridge University Press.

Berend, Iván T., and György Ránki. 1982. *The European Periphery and Industrialization, 1780–1914*. Cambridge: Cambridge University Press.

Bernhard, Michael. 2000. Institutional Choices after Communism: A Critique of Theory-Building in an Empirical Wasteland. *East European Politics and Societies* 14(2): 316–47.

Böröcz, József. 2000. Informality Rules. *East European Politics and Societies* 14(2): 348–80.
Bourdieu, Pierre. 1977. *Outline of a Theory of Practice*. Cambridge: Cambridge University Press.
1998. *Practical Reason*. Stanford: Stanford University Press.
Braudel, Fernand. 1980. *On History*. Chicago: University of Chicago Press.
1981–84. *Civilization and Capitalism, 15th–18th Century*. 3 vols. London: Collins.
Breslauer, George. 1992. In Defense of Sovietology. *Post-Soviet Affairs* 8(3): 197–238.
Brzezinski, Zbigniew. 1969. The Soviet Political System: Transformation or Degeneration? In Zbigniew Brzezinski, ed., *Dilemmas of Change in Soviet Politics*, pp. 1–44. New York: Columbia University Press.
Bunce, Valerie. 1995a. Should Transitologists Be Grounded? *Slavic Review* 54(1): 111–27.
1995b. Comparing East and South. *Journal of Democracy* 6(3): 87–100.
1999. *Subversive Institutions: The Design and the Destruction of Socialism and the State*. Cambridge: Cambridge University Press.
Calhoun, Craig. 1998. Explanation in Historical Sociology: Narrative, General Theory, and Historically Specific Theory. *American Journal of Sociology* 104: 846–71.
Chirot, Daniel, ed. 1989. *The Origins of Backwardness in Eastern Europe: Economics and Politics from the Middle Ages until the Early 20th Century*. Berkeley: University of California Press.
Collier, David, and Ruth Berins Collier. 1991. *Shaping the Political Arena: Critical Junctures, the Labor Movement, and Regime Dynamics in Latin* America. Princeton: Princeton University Press.
Collier, David, and Steven Levitsky. 1997. Democracy with Adjectives: Conceptual Innovations in Comparative Research. *World Politics* 49: 430–51.
Collier, David, and James E. Mahon Jr. 1993. Conceptual Stretching Revisited: Adapting Categories in Comparative Analysis. *American Political Science Review* 87(4): 845–55.
Comisso, Ellen. 1991. Where Have We Been and Where Are We Going. In W. Crotty, ed., *Political Science: Looking to the Future*, pp. 77–122. Evanston, Ill.: Northwestern University Press.
Crawford, Beverly, and Arend Lijphart, eds. 1997. *Liberalization and Leninist Legacies: Comparative Perspectives on Democratic Transitions*. Berkeley: International and Area Studies Press.
David, Paul A. 1985. Clio and the Economics of QWERTY. *American Economic Review* 75: 332–37.
Diamond, Jared. 1997. *Guns, Germs, and Steel: The Fates of Human Societies*. New York: W. W. Norton.
EBRD. 2000. *Transition Report, 1999*. London.
Ekiert, Grzegorz. 1991. Democratization Processes in East Central Europe: A Theoretical Reconsideration. *British Journal of Political Science* 21(3): 285–313.
1996. *The State against Society*. Princeton: Princeton University Press.
Esping-Andersen, Gøsta. 1990. *The Three Worlds of Welfare Capitalism*. Cambridge: Polity Press.

Eyal, Gil, Iván Szelényi, and Eleanor Townsley. 1998. *Making Capitalism without Capitalists: Class Formation and Elite Struggles in Post-Communist Central Europe.* London: Verso.

Feshbach, Murray. 2001. Russia's Population Meltdown. *Wilson Quarterly* 25(1): 12–21.

Feshbach, Murray, and Alfred Friendly Jr. 1992. *Ecocide in the USSR: Health and Nature under Siege.* New York: Basic Books.

Fish, M. Steven. 1998a. The Determinants of Economic Reform in the Post-Communist World. *East European Politics and Societies* 12(1): 31–77.

1998b. Democratization's Requisites: The Postcommunist Experience. *Post-Soviet Affairs* 14(3): 212–47.

Friedrich, Carl J., and Zbigniew K. Brzezinski. 1956. *Totalitarian Dictatorship and Autocracy.* Cambridge, Mass.: Harvard University Press.

Fukuyama, Francis. 1992. *The End of History and the Last Man.* New York: Free Press.

Gallup, John, Jeffrey Sachs, and Andrew Mellinger. 1999. Geography and Economic Development. CID Working Paper No. 1, Harvard University, March.

Gellner, Ernest. 1983. *Nations and Nationalism.* Oxford: Blackwell.

Gerschenkron, Alexander. 1965. *Economic Backwardness in Historical Perspective.* Cambridge, Mass.: Belknap Press of Harvard University Press.

Goldstone, Jack A. 1998. Initial Conditions, General Laws, Path Dependence, and Explanation in Historical Sociology. *American Journal of Sociology* 104(3): 829–45.

Gould, Stephen Jay. 1989. *Wonderful Life: The Burgess Shale and the Nature of History.* New York: W. W. Norton.

Grabher, Gernot, and David Stark, eds. 1997. *Restructuring Networks in Post-Socialism: Legacies, Linkages, and Localities.* Oxford: Oxford University Press.

Granovetter, Mark. 1973. The Strength of Weak Ties. *American Journal of Sociology* 78: 1360–80.

Greenfeld, Liah. 1992. *Nationalism: Five Roads to Modernity.* Cambridge, Mass.: Harvard University Press.

Greskovits, Bela. 2000. Rival Views of Postcommunist Market Society: The Path-Dependence of Transitology. In Michel Dobry, ed., *Democratic and Capitalist Transition in Eastern Europe: Lessons for the Social Sciences*, pp. 19–49. Dordrecht: Kluwer Academic Publishers.

Griffin, Larry. 1993. Narrative, Event-Structure, and Causal Interpretation in Historical Sociology. *American Journal of Sociology* 98: 1094–1133.

Grossman, Gregory. 1990. Sub-Rosa Marketization and Privatization in the USSR. *Annals of the American Academy of Political and Social Science* 507: 44–52.

Grzymała-Busse, Anna. 2002. *Redeeming the Communist Past: The Regeneration of Communist Parties in East Central Europe.* Cambridge: Cambridge University Press.

Hall, Peter. 2003. Aligning Ontology and Methodology in Comparative Research. In James Mahoney and Dietrich Rueschemeyer, eds., *Comparative Historical Analysis in the Social Sciences.* Cambridge: Cambridge University Press.

Hall, Peter, and Sidney Tarrow. 1998. Globalization and Area Studies: When Is Too Broad, Too Narrow? *Chronicle of Higher Education*, January 23, B4.

Hall, Peter, and Rosemary Taylor. 1995. Political Science and the Three New Institutionalisms. *Political Studies* 44(5): 936–57.

Handelman, Stephen. 1995. *Comrade Criminal: Russia's New Mafiya*. New Haven: Yale University Press.

Hanson, Stephen E. 1995a. Social Theory and the Post-Soviet Crisis: Sovietology and the Problem of Regime Identity. *Communist and Post-Communist Studies* 28(1): 119–30.

1995b. The Leninist Legacy and Institutional Change. *Comparative Political Studies* 28(2): 306–14.

1997. *Time and Revolution: Marxism and the Design of Soviet Institutions*. Chapel Hill: University of North Carolina Press.

Hedström, Peter, and Richard Swedberg, eds. 1998. *Social Mechanisms: An Analytical Approach to Social Theory*. Cambridge: Cambridge University Press.

Higley, John, Jan Pakulski, and Włodzimierz Wesołowski, eds. 1998. *Postcommunist Elites and Democracy in Eastern Europe*. London: Macmillan.

Holmes, Stephen. 2001. Simulations of Power in Putin's Russia. *Current History* 100(648): 307–12

Hopf, Ted, ed. 1999. *Understandings of Russian Foreign Policy*. University Park: Pennsylvania State University Press.

Huntington, Samuel. 1996. *The Clash of Civilizations and the Remaking of World Order*. New York: Simon & Schuster.

Hupchick, Dennis. 1994. *Culture and History in Eastern Europe*. New York: St. Martin's Press.

Janos, Andrew. 1982. *The Politics of Backwardness in Hungary, 1825–1945*. Princeton: Princeton University Press.

1995. Continuity and Change in Eastern Europe: Strategies of Post-Communist Politics. In Beverly Crawford, ed., *Markets, States, and Democracy*, pp. 150–74. Boulder, Colo.: Westview Press.

2000. *East Central Europe in the Modern World: The Politics of the Borderlands from Pre- to Postcommunism*. Stanford: Stanford University Press.

Johnson, Chalmers. 1997. Perception vs. Observation, or the Contribution of Rational Choice Theory and Area Studies to Contemporary Political Science. *PS: Political Science and Politics* 30(2): 170–74.

Jones, E. L. 1981. *The European Miracle: Environments, Economies, and Geopolitics in the History of Europe and Asia*. Cambridge: Cambridge University Press.

Jowitt, Ken. 1992. *New World Disorder: The Leninist Extinction*. Berkeley: University of California Press.

Kassof, Allen. 1964. The Administered Society: Totalitarianism without Terror. *World Politics* 16(4): 558–75.

King, Gary, Robert Keohane, and Sidney Verba. 1994. *Designing Social Inquiry: Scientific Inference in Qualitative Research*. Princeton: Princeton University Press.

Kiser, Edgar, and Michael Hechter. 1998. The Debate on Historical Sociology: Rational Choice Theory and Its Critics. *American Journal of Sociology* 104(3): 785–86.

Kiser, Edgar, and Ted Welser. 1999. The Relationship between Theory and History in Evolutionary Biology: A Model for Historical Sociology? Paper presented at the Social Science History Meetings, Fort Worth, November.

Kitschelt, Herbert. 1999. Accounting for Outcomes of Post-Communist Regime Change: Causal Depth or Shallowness in Rival Explanations? Paper presented at the annual meeting of the American Political Science Association, Atlanta.

Kitschelt, Herbert, Zdenka Mansfeldova, Radosław Markowski, and Gábor Tóka. 1999. *Post-Communist Party Systems: Competition, Representation, and Inter-Party Cooperation*. Cambridge: Cambridge University Press.

Kopstein, Jeffrey, and David Reilly. 1999. Explaining the Why of the Why: A Comment on Fish's Determinants of Economic Reforms in the Post-Communist World. *East European Politics and Societies* 13(3): 613–26.

Kornai, János. 1992. *The Socialist System*. Princeton: Princeton University Press.

Krugman, Paul. 1991. *Geography and Trade*. Cambridge, Mass.: MIT Press.

1995. *Development Geography and Economic Theory*. Cambridge, Mass.: MIT Press.

Kundera, Milan. 1984. The Tragedy of Central Europe. *New York Review of Books* 31(7): 33–38.

Laitin, David. 1995. Disciplining Political Science. *American Political Science Review* 89(2): 454–56.

Ledeneva, Anna. 1998. *Russia's Economy of Favours: Blat, Networking, and Informal Exchange*. Cambridge: Cambridge University Press.

Linz, Juan, and Alfred Stepan. 1996. *Problems of Democratic Transition and Consolidation: Southern Europe, South America, and Post-Communist Europe*. Baltimore: Johns Hopkins University Press.

Lustick, Ian. 1997. The Disciplines of Political Science: Studying the Culture of Rational Choice as a Case in Point. *PS: Political Science and Politics* 30(2): 175–79.

Lynch, Allen. 2002. Roots of Russia's Economic Dilemmas: Liberal Economics and Illiberal Geography. *Europe-Asia Studies* 54(1): 31–49.

Lynn, Nicholas J. 1999. Geography and Transition: Reconceptualizing Systemic Change in the Former Soviet Union. *Slavic Review* 58(4): 824–40.

Mahoney, James. 2000. Path Dependence in Comparative-Historical Research. *Theory and Society* 29: 507–48.

Mahoney, James, and Dietrich Rueschemeyer, eds. 2003. *Comparative Historical Analysis in the Social Sciences*. Cambridge: Cambridge University Press.

Mann, Michael. 1986. *The Sources of Social Power*. 2 vols. Cambridge: Cambridge University Press.

McAdam, Doug. 1995. Initiator and Spin-off Movements: Diffusion Processes in Protest Cycles. In Mark Traugott, ed., *Repertoires and Cycles of Collective Action*, pp. 217–39. Durham, N.C.: Duke University Press.

McAdam, Doug, and Dieter Rucht. 1993. The Cross National Diffusion of Movement Ideas. *Annals of the AAPSS* 528: 56–74.

McAuley, Mary. 1997. *Russia's Politics of Uncertainty*. Cambridge: Cambridge University Press.

McDonald, Terrance, ed. 1996. *The Historic Turn in the Human Sciences*. Ann Arbor: University of Michigan Press.

McNeill, William. 1974. *The Shape of European History*. Oxford: Oxford University Press.

North, Douglass Cecil. 1990. *Institutions, Institutional Change, and Economic Performance*. Cambridge: Cambridge University Press.

O'Donnell, Guillermo. 1979. *Modernization and Bureaucratic-Authoritarianism*. Berkeley: Institute of International Studies.

Offe, Claus. 1991. Capitalism by Democratic Design? Democratic Theory Facing the Triple Transition in East Central Europe. *Social Research* 58(4): 865–92.

Olson, Mancur. 1981. *The Rise and Decline of Nations*. New Haven: Yale University Press.

Pierson, Paul. 2000a. Increasing Returns, Path Dependence, and the Study of Politics. *American Political Science Review* 94(2): 251–67.

2000b. Not Just What, but When: Timing and Sequence in Political Processes. *Studies in American Political Development* 14: 1–21.

Poznański, Kazimierz, ed. 1995. *The Evolutionary Transition to Capitalism*. Boulder, Colo.: Westview Press.

Putnam, Robert, with Robert Leonardi and Raffaella Y. Nanetti. 1993. *Making Democracy Work: Civic Traditions in Modern* Italy. Princeton: Princeton University Press.

Ragin, Charles. 1987. *The Comparative Method*. Berkeley: University of California Press.

2000. *Fuzzy-Set Social Science*. Chicago: University of Chicago Press.

Ramet, Sabrina, ed. 1999. *The Radical Right in Central and Eastern Europe since* 1989. University Park: Pennsylvania State University Press.

Rigby, T. H. 1990. *The Changing Soviet System: Mono-Organisational Socialism from Its Origins to Gorbachev's Restructuring*. Aldershot, Hants: Edward Elgar.

Róna-Tas, Ákos. 1997. *The Great Surprise of the Small Transformation: The Demise of Communism and the Rise of the Private Sector in Hungary*. Ann Arbor: University of Michigan Press.

Rothschild, Joseph. 1993. *Return to Diversity: A Political History of East Central Europe since World War II*. New York: Oxford University Press.

Rowan, B. 1982. Organizational Structure and the Institutional Environment. *Administrative Sciences Quarterly* 27: 259–79.

Rucht, Dieter. 1996. The Impact of National Contexts on Social Movement Structures: A Cross-Movement and Cross-National Comparison. In John McCarthy, Doug McAdam, and Mayer N. Zald, eds., *Comparative Perspectives on Social Movements: Opportunities, Mobilizing Structures and Framing*, pp. 185–226. Cambridge: Cambridge University Press.

Rueschemeyer, Dietrich, Evelyn Huber Stephens, and John D. Stephens. 1992. *Capitalist Development and Democracy*. Chicago: University of Chicago Press.

Rueschemeyer, Dietrich, and John Stephens. 1997. Comparing Historical Sequences – A Powerful Tool for Causal Analysis. *Comparative Social Research* 17: 55–72.

Rupnik, Jacques. 1989. *The Other Europe*. New York: Pantheon Books.

Sachs, Jeffrey, and Andrew Warner. 1996. Achieving Rapid Growth in the Transition Economies of Central Europe. Development Discussion Papers, Harvard Institute for International Development, Harvard University, July.

Sartori, Giovanni. 1970. Concept Misformation in Comparative Politics. *American Political Science Review* 64: 1033–53.

Schmitter, Philippe C., and Terry Lynn Karl. 1994. The Conceptual Travels of Transitologists and Consolidologists: How Far to the East Should They Attempt to Go? *Slavic Review* 53(1): 173–82.

Schöpflin, George. 1989. Central Europe: Definitions Old and New. In George Schöpflin and Nancy Wood, eds., *In Search of Central* Europe, pp. 7–29. Cambridge: Polity Press.

1993. *Politics in Eastern* Europe. Oxford: Blackwell.

Sewell, William H., Jr. 1996. Three Temporalities: Toward an Eventful Sociology. In Terrence J. McDonald, ed., *The Historic Turn in the Human Sciences*, pp. 245–80. Ann Arbor: University of Michigan Press.

Shama, Avraham. 1996. Inside Russia's True Economy. *Foreign Affairs* 103: 110–27.

Skocpol, Theda, ed. 1984. *Vision and Method in Historical Sociology*. Cambridge: Cambridge University Press.

Słomczyński, Kazimierz, and Goldie Shabad. 1997. Systemic Transformation and the Salience of Class Structure in East Central Europe. *East European Politics and Societies* 11(1): 155–89.

Solnick, Steven. 1998. *Stealing the State: Control and Collapse in Soviet Institutions*. Cambridge, Mass.: Harvard University Press.

Somers, Margaret. 1998. "We're No Angels": Realism, Rational Choice and Relationality in Social Science. *American Journal of Sociology* 104(3): 722–84.

Staniszkis, Jadwiga. 1989. *Ontologia Socjalizmu*. Warsaw: In Plus.

1991. *The Dynamics of the Breakthrough in Eastern Europe: The Polish Experience*. Berkeley: University of California Press.

1995. Polityka postkomunistycznej instytucjonalizacji w perspektywie historycznej. *Studia Polityczne* 4: 39–60.

Stark, David, and László Bruszt. 1998. *Postsocialist Pathways: Transforming Politics and Property in East Central Europe*. Cambridge: Cambridge University Press.

Stark, David, and Victor Nee. 1989. Toward an Institutional Analysis of State Socialism. In V. Nee and D. Stark, eds., *Remaking the Economic Institutions of Socialism: China and Eastern Europe*, pp. 1–31. Stanford: Stanford University Press.

Stinchcombe, Arthur. 1978. *Theoretical Methods in Social History*. New York: Academic Press.

1998. Monopolistic Competition as a Mechanism: Corporations, Universities and Nation-States in Competitive Fields. In Peter Hedstrom and Richard Swedberg, eds., *Social Mechanisms*, pp. 267–305. Cambridge: Cambridge University Press.

Stokes, Gale. 1997. *Three Eras of Political Change in Eastern Europe, Part I: The Origins of East European Politics*, pp. 7–66. New York: Oxford University Press.

Strang, David, and J. W. Meyer. 1993. Institutional Conditions for Diffusion. *Theory and Society* 22: 487–512.

Strang, David, and Sarah A. Soule. 1998. Diffusion in Organizations and Social Movements: From Hybrid Corn to Poison Pills. *Annual Review of Sociology* 24: 265–90.

Strohmayer, Ulf. 1997. The Displaced, Deferred or Was It Abandoned Middle: Another Look at the Idiographic-Nomothetic Distinction. *German Social Science Review* 20(3–4): 279–344.

Sztompka, Piotr. 1992. Dilemmas of the Great Transformation. *Sisyphus* 2: 9–27.

Szücs, Jenö. 1988. Three Historical Regions of Europe. In John Keane, ed., *Civil Society and the State: New European Perspectives*, pp. 291–332. London: Verso.

Thelen, Kathleen. 1999. Historical Institutionalism in Comparative Politics. *Annual Review of Political Science* 2: 369–404.

2000. Time and Temporality in the Analysis of Institutional Evolution and Change. *Studies in American Political Development* 14(1): 101–8.

Tilly, Charles. 1990. *Coercion, Capital, and European States, A.D. 990–1990*. Cambridge, Mass.: Basil Blackwell.

Tismaneanu, Vladimir. 1998. *Fantasies of Salvation: Democracy, Nationalism, and Myth in Post-Communist Europe*. Princeton: Princeton University Press.

Tucker, Robert C. 1971. *The Soviet Political Mind: Stalinism and Post-Stalin Change*. New York: W. W. Norton.

Venables, Anthony, and Nuno Limao. 1999. Geographical Disadvantage: A Heckscher-Ohlin–von Thunen Model of International Specification. World Bank, Policy Research Working Papers, no. 2256.

Verdery, Katherine. 1996. *What Was Socialism, and What Comes Next?* Princeton: Princeton University Press.

Walder, Andrew. 1986. *Communist Neo-Traditionalism: Work and Authority in Chinese Industry*. Berkeley: University of California Press.

Wallerstein, Immanuel. 1974. *The Modern World-System: Capitalist Agriculture and the Origins of the European World-Economy in the Sixteenth Century*. New York: Academic Press.

1991a. *Unthinking Social Science: The Limits of Nineteenth-Century Paradigms*. Cambridge, Mass.: Polity Press in association with Basil Blackwell.

1991b. *Geopolitics and Geoculture: Essays on the Changing World-System*. Cambridge: Cambridge University Press; Paris: Editions de la Maison des Sciences de l'Homme.

Weber, Max. 1968. *Economy and Society*. 3 vols. Berkeley: University of California Press.

Whitehead, Laurence. 1999. Geography and Democratic Destiny. *Journal of Democracy* 10(1): 74–79.

Woodward, Susan. 1993. *Balkan Tragedy: Chaos and Dissolution after the Cold War*. Washington, D.C.: Brookings Institution.

2

Accounting for Postcommunist Regime Diversity

What Counts as a Good Cause?

Herbert Kitschelt

A single hegemonic power ruled the East European and Central Asian regions until the late 1980s and stamped its ideological doctrine and basic institutions on every single polity, with the partial exception of Yugoslavia and Albania. Its demise, however, has resulted in a highly diverse set of more than twenty-five sovereign polities with features that range from those of full-fledged competitive democracies with well-protected civic and political rights all the way to authoritarian, personalist, if not despotic, rule. Measured in terms of the civic and political rights indexes developed by Freedom House, there is no region or set of countries on earth with a currently larger diversity of political regimes.[1] The fact that before 1989 all of today's East Central European and Central Asian polities had communist single-party rule and socialist economic planning systems cannot possibly account for the tremendous diversity of political regimes that emerged in this region in the early 1990s. This postcommunist diversity came about in the short window of about three years (1990–93). Since that time, new regime structures have been more or less "locked in" in almost all polities. Countries that by 1994 were more democratic have stayed that way. Countries that were authoritarian have not reversed course and become democratic. There may even be a tendency toward a *polarization of regime types* such that polities with initially intermediate levels of civic and/or political rights eventually became entirely democratic or fully authoritarian.[2] In a similar vein, postcommunist

[1] The standard deviation of countries' civic and political rights scores for the set of postcommunist polities serves as the mathematical indicator of regional regime diversity. The comparatively high standard deviation of civic and political rights is so high because, in contrast to other regions, the postcommunist area polities display no central tendency. In Latin America and East Asia, by contrast, that central tendency has gravitated toward democracy or mixed regimes since the 1980s. In the Middle East and Africa, regimes are overwhelmingly authoritarian.

[2] Several countries in the intermediate range of the Freedom House indexes (3.5–5.0) in the mid-1990s appear to be moving toward more-democratic civic and political rights

countries that were leaders in economic market reform in 1992–93 are still in that position by the end of the millennium, if we accept European Bank of Reconstruction and Development (EBRD) indexes of economic reform effort as our critical measure.

The impressive diversity of political regimes and economic reform efforts evidenced by the postcommunist polities poses a provocative puzzle for the social sciences. Why is there no uniform and persistent "communist legacy" detectable among the numerous communist successor regimes? What led to the appearance of great variance in the modes of dismantling communist rule as well as the resulting new political power relations and institutional codifications almost overnight in the early 1990s? The great physical, economic, social, and cultural diversity of postcommunist countries allows us to eliminate some explanations with great ease. Conversely, some essential similarities shared by all polities also rule out important explanations for lasting regime diversity. For example, the best confirmed generalization about democratization is that rich countries are more likely to become and then stay democratic than poor countries (Bollen, 1979; Burkhart and Lewis-Beck, 1994; Geddes, 1999). But differentials in economic wealth and development cannot account for the observed pattern in postcommunist Europe and Central Asia. On that account, Belarus should display more civic and political democratic rights and economic reform effort than Lithuania, Armenia more than Poland, and Russia more than Hungary. Broadly speaking, all formerly communist polities are "middle income" economies whose political regime patterns are underdetermined by socioeconomic levels of wealth and development. The only generalization from theories of economic modernization that applies to all of them is that members of this group are likely to display diverse and volatile regime properties (Huntington, 1991; Przeworski and Limongi, 1997).

Although similar levels of economic development and shared experiences with a "Leninist legacy" cannot serve as explanations of postcommunist regime diversity, scholars have proposed a bounty of competing hypotheses to account for that outcome. Students of postcommunist regimes have nominated religion, geographical location, precommunist regimes and state formation, post-Stalinist reforms in communist regimes, modes of transition to postcommunism, and winners or losers in the "founding elections" of the new regimes as explanations of current regime diversity, to name only some of the most important arguments. Most of these variables tend to be plausible candidates for explanation because they display striking patterns of

(Croatia, Macedonia, and Moldova). Others initially in a semiauthoritarian halfway house have lately gravitated toward authoritarianism (Belarus and Kyrgyzstan, as well as possibly Albania or Armenia). Some countries have stayed in this intermediate category (Georgia, Russia, Ukraine). But no country has joined the intermediate category since 1995 through a degradation of preexisting democratic accomplishments or an improvement over authoritarianism.

covariance with the dependent variables, political regime properties, or economic reform effort. Nevertheless, scholars disagree on which of them qualify as reasonable *causal* explanations. Because the rival explanatory variables are highly collinear both in cross-national as well as intertemporal perspective after the initial outburst of diversification in 1989–91, it is impossible to settle on a single superior causal account based on inductive statistical computation alone, regardless of which multivariate statistical model one might accept as most adequate for the explanatory task. In order to discriminate among explanations, one has to draw on more-subtle methodological, metatheoretical, and ontological considerations about the conceptualization of causality when faced with the theoretical problem of explaining postcommunist regime diversity.

The nature of this chapter is therefore primarily epistemological. I do not develop any single substantive explanation of postcommunist regime diversity in detail, but I draw upon them in order to illustrate different conceptions of causality. Empirical evidence does constrain what we can reasonably consider or dismiss as a good cause of postcommunist regime diversity. But this empirical evidence, by itself, leaves sufficient ambiguities to necessitate a reflection on further criteria and qualifications in order to discriminate among more or less satisfactory causal explanations.

What We Can(not) Ask Causal Analysis to Achieve in the Social Sciences

Let me begin by rebutting a common misunderstanding of what causal analysis should accomplish in the social sciences. We will make headway in the causal analysis of social processes only if we abandon misplaced aspirations and expectations. To put it in one proposition: sciences of complexity in general, and the social sciences in particular, cannot explain singular events and, conversely, therefore cannot advance point predictions of what is likely to happen in a particular instance.

In the mid-1990s Japan was the last technologically advanced country to close down its earthquake prediction program. All other countries with significant earthquake risks, including the United States, had done so earlier. Policy makers and scientists concluded that earthquake prediction is unable to reduce the margin of error sufficiently to sound operational warnings, for example, to evacuate certain areas. Does the fact that earthquake prediction programs have globally failed lead us to conclude that geology in general and geotectonics more specifically have failed? Scientists would respond to that question with a resounding no. Our understanding of continental plate tectonics has substantially improved over time, and scientists can identify the areas that are vulnerable to major earthquakes quite precisely. What cannot be achieved, however, is to predict the specific occurrence of earthquakes. Scientific knowledge about earthquakes is probabilistic because it is practically impossible to assemble a full account of all forces that impinge on a time-space event. Such singular events are the result of multiple causal chains that interact. Even if all causal mechanisms were known, an extraordinary amount of data would have to be gathered from countless sites, some of them deep underground, to be fed into an encompassing theoretical model of plate tectonics. As a consequence, it is not feasible to predict a particular earthquake event with sufficient certainty to allow policy makers to take expensive decisions based on such information – for example, the evacuation of a city. The weather is a case in point. In most regions of the world, meteorologists have so far failed to predict seasonal weather features with sufficient precision to enable growers to adjust the crops they plant.

The case of earthquake prediction can be generalized to all sciences that deal with moderate or high complexity. It is all but impossible to predict singular events with a sufficient measure of precision and certainty to improve the ability of policy makers and citizens to act in a more rational, strategic, future-oriented fashion in addressing particular situations. For ontological reasons, the prediction of events is even more difficult in the social sciences than in the study of natural phenomena with high complexity. Merton (1957) drew our attention here to the problem of *reflexivity*, precipitating self-fulfilling or self-destroying prophecies. Many of the people who make public event predictions are not just disinterested social scientists (even if we grant that there are such people), but actors in whose interest it is to bring about or avert the predicted events. They will attempt to change the boundary conditions assumed in the event prediction. Thus, social predictions often generate their own social dynamic of hypothesis falsification or verification. In light of recent experiences with stock markets around the world, any reader can spell out the logic of such individual and collective conduct for stock market bubbles.

In addition to complexity and reflexivity, also *uncertainty* from the perspective of the actors sets limits on the causal account of individual social events. With the benefit of hindsight and with time and resources to collect data, scholars may have a much better grasp of the objective constraints and the diverse actors' perceptions and calculations at the time of political decision making than any of the actors had themselves ex ante. Particularly in times of regime crisis, political actors often may not have the time and the access to gather the information that would allow them to choose their best course of action. Faced with ambiguities about the past and the present, they have to *interpret* the prospective yield of alternative courses of action. These interpretations may have a systematic and a random component. The systematic component is amenable to causal analysis within a cognitive "political culture" framework. What are the theoretical concepts and idioms that allow actors to interpret their choice situation? What were the causal propositions within their zone of attention that enabled them to construct payoff matrices resulting from alternative strategies of action chosen by themselves, their (potential) allies, and their adversaries? In social science accounts of regime change, the cultural semantics of breakdown becomes one causal chain that, on average, may show a statistically significant probabilistic relationship to the occurrence of regime breakdowns.

The other component of uncertainty and interpretation is random. How individual and collective actors define a particular historical situation may depend a great deal on contingent social networks (who gets to know what) and idiosyncratic psychological processes (the personality of actors in high-impact positions). Whether "persuasive," "charismatic," and thus "entrepreneurial" and "innovative" leaders are situated at critical nodes of social networks in times of accelerating regime decay and thus may organize collective action that brings about regime collapse can never be predicted by a systematic causally oriented social science. Similarly, social science can never determine the conditions under which entrepreneurial leaders have a "correct" or "foresighted" interpretation of the situation in which they choose a course of action. Such leaders and their entourage, just like other citizens, are subject to cognitive errors. Revolutionary situations may thus slip by simply because leadership failed at critical moments, either because it was insufficiently bold and persuasive and/or because it cognitively misconstrued the situation. Conversely, political leadership may define situations as revolutionary and attempt insurrections when the objective circumstances are not conducive. Scholars here face a random component of collective action with the intent of regime change that will always make it impossible to predict singular events with certainty.

The challenge to theorize political regime change thus exemplifies the general limits of explanation and prediction in the social sciences. *Complexity, reflexivity*, and *actor uncertainty* about the parameters of the situation make it impossible for social scientists to predict singular events. The postdiction of past events ("explanation") always leaves residual unexplained variance. We may know that, on average, a higher level of affluence, the onset of a sharp economic recession, and discord within the ruling authoritarian elites, particularly if they are military juntas or single-party regimes, make a transition of authoritarian rule to durable democracy more likely. This general knowledge, however, will help us little to predict the occurrence and precise timing of democratization in individual cases, such as Indonesia or Malaysia, Singapore or South Korea. Nevertheless, as scholars we work on making our general knowledge about cause-effect relations more precise and calibrate the average contributing effect of each variable to the phenomenon of regime breakdown. This will, however, still never permit us to predict individual events with certainty.

In the retrospective account of regime change, we may distinguish between conditions that made regimes more conducive to change in the long run, as well as conditions that acted upon regimes over short periods of time and precipitated their ultimate collapse. Nevertheless, this does not allow us to draw a simple divide between "necessary" and "sufficient" causes of regime change. Each cause may have functional equivalents. No single long-term or short-term condition may be necessary or sufficient in its own right, but only the concatenation and configuration of forces that yield particular historical constellations (cf. Gerring, 1999: 26). These considerations only repeat a thesis advanced by Max Weber (1988: esp. 286–89) almost one hundred years ago. The social sciences deal with general correlations and causations that permit only probabilistic explanations and predictions. It is up to historians and historical-comparative sociology to show how multiple causal chains interact in unique contexts and produce often irreproducible results.

If events result from multiple causal chains, the construction of "analytic narratives" (Bates et al., 1998) may be instructive, but of limited use for causal analysis. Analytic narratives "are motivated by a desire to account for particular events and outcomes" (1). They reconstruct the logic of reasoning and interaction that is presumed to motivate actors in a particular case. As long as we examine individual cases, however, it is difficult to draw causal inferences about any logic of action attributed to social actors in a theoretically conceptualized structure of constraints, even though we can ascertain which theoretical accounts fit the facts of the case (15–17). In that sense, the study of particular cases only provides "data points," each of which is open to multiple causal inferences. Taken together, in a comparative analysis of multiple cases, they may narrow down the range of plausible causes of an outcome and identify distinct causal chains that contribute to that outcome.

Because multiple causal chains interact in many contexts, it is misleading to blame the social sciences for not predicting the "event" of communism's sudden demise in 1989–91 in most countries governed by that system of governance.[3] Beginning with the debate between Max Weber and his anarchist students in 1919, and documented in Weber's ruminations about socialist economics in *Economy and Society*, soon followed by von Mises's and the Austrian school's work on planned economies, a great deal has been known for a long time about the principal weaknesses of economic institutions with a hierarchical allocation of scarce resources. Of course, these basic economic liabilities of socialism, taken by themselves, were neither necessary nor sufficient conditions for the breakdown of communism. Any satisfactory historical account of the communist breakdown must incorporate the many facets of decay and cumulative comparative inferiority on multiple economic, political, social, and cultural dimensions of performance that characterized these regimes as they entered the 1980s.

[3] Following a chorus of scholars since 1989, Kalyvas (1999) subscribes to this charge and provides an impressive review of the voices that have tried to explain communism's fall after the fact.

From a purely social scientific point of view, interested in the causal analysis of human social action, institutions, and processes, the prediction of singular historical events is thus neither interesting nor feasible. The focus of attention is on the general mechanisms and causal linkages that make the occurrence of certain events more likely. For this reason, the knowledge of financial economists does not necessarily render them to be better stock market speculators, business economists will not necessarily help a particular company to beat its profit targets, and political scientists can never claim to tell politicians with certainty how to improve the margin of their electoral support. The hiatus between analytical, cause-seeking social science and public policy remains large. Students of political regime change have to appreciate that as much as practitioners, whether they are average citizens or political professionals, including professional revolutionary cadres.

A further example may clarify the limits and possibilities of causal analysis in the social sciences. According to most accounts, both the Czech Republic and Poland are examples of postcommunist polities that have advanced market-liberal economic reform most, when compared to the entire cohort of polities that resulted from the breakdown of communism (cf. Hellman, 1996; 1998; EBRD, 1998; Fish, 1998b; Kitschelt and Malesky, 2000). Yet the Czech Republic experienced an economic recession and then a weak recovery in the final years of the twentieth century, whereas Poland's economy sustained very high rates of growth in that period. Theories that predict why both the Czech Republic and Poland are better off in terms of reform effort and reform outcome than most postcommunist economies cannot account for the particular details of differential performance since 1996.

Other, more short-term causal chains may influence these particularities, including the role of leadership and of subjective interpretations of economic uncertainty by influential politicians, something that social science is less equipped to explain than psychology. For example, we may argue that for electoral reasons the governing politicians in the Czech Republic engaged in a hasty privatization program in 1992 that overlooked problems of moral hazard in the governance structures of banks, investment funds, and corporations outside the financial sector. We may also surmise that idiosyncrasies of the political leadership, such as Vaclav Klaus's exposure to Chicago-style economics and his admiration of Margaret Thatcher, translated into a fanaticism of market-liberal reforms that ignored the importance of market-complementing political-regulatory institutions that avert market failures generated by unrestrained contracting and lower transaction costs in the privatization of economic assets. From the vantage point of social science theory, the leaders' psychological dispositions or the details of the electoral calendar are entirely coincidental external "shocks" intertwined with a particular historical situation, which will always guarantee a measure of randomness in explanations and predictions of postcommunist economic reform effort and success. What is consoling for a social science account of postcommunist economic reform, however, is that the particularities of Czech politics did not let the country's performance drop to levels encountered among countries to which scholars attest much less promising social and political capabilities for economic reform.

Having now approximately clarified what causal analysis cannot do in the study of postcommunist political regime change and economic reform, let us inspect more closely what social science may be able to contribute, or at least what social scientists aspire for it to accomplish. When social scientists talk about causes, they usually have in mind what Aristotle referred to as the "efficient" cause(s) of some outcome under study – that is, the forces that brought it about, produced it, or created it (Gerring, 2001: chap. 7). It is no simple question, however, to determine what exactly is meant by creation and what qualifies a good causal analysis. Before we turn to concrete examples of rival causal accounts of postcommunist political and economic trajectories, we need to generate some epistemological criteria to evaluate the status of causal claims.

What Counts as a Good Cause?

Assessing the quality of inferences in general and of causal inferences in particular involves multiple dimensions and calls for judgments that go beyond the arbitration among claims purely grounded in formal logic.[4] Ultimately, what "counts" as an acceptable cause in a community of scholars involves trade-offs among a variety of criteria. Debates among scholars of postcommunism are thus often as much about the quality of causal attribution as the correct specification of empirical tests or the nature and validity of the data brought to bear on the theoretical question. Let me first sketch an unsatisfactory conceptualization of causal analysis, then move on to criteria of causal analysis in the social sciences, and finally address the problem of trade-offs between such criteria.

The "Covering Law" Schema as Explication of Causal Analysis

The debate about Hempel-Oppenheim's standard "covering law" explanation illustrates the ontological rather than the logical nature of the epistemological debate about causal analysis. For these authors, a complete explanation involves a time-space invariant proposition about the relationship between two variables and a statement of empirical conditions that assert the presence of one of the two terms. We can then draw the inference that the facts corresponding to the other term must be present too. Explanation, then, is the inference of an observable fact from knowledge of a general relationship among antecedent and consequent variables together with

[4] In this section, I heavily draw on Gerring's (2001: 128–51) extremely useful discussion of formal criteria and empirical confirmation of causal inferences.

empirical knowledge about the antecedent conditions. The problem is, however, that this standard "covering law" explanation cannot separate lawful (causal) and accidental ("correlational") generalizations (Salmon, 1989: 15).[5] The same problem is patent in Stinchcombe's (1987: 29) conception of a causal law as a "statement that certain values of two or more variables are connected in a certain way," even though the author later reminds us that correlation is not the same as causation (32). A similarly deficient statistical-epistemological definition of causation appears in King, Keohane, and Verba (1994: 81–82): "The causal effect is the difference between the systematic component of observations made when the explanatory variable takes one value and the systematic component of comparable observations when the explanatory variable takes on another value." The ontological intuition behind causation is that some x helps to create some y in the sense of "bringing it into existence." Substantive scientific theories, not reconstructive epistemology, must elaborate conceptual primitives and entities that constitute an acceptable ontology of causation in a particular domain. To demonstrate that questions of causation involve ontological and pragmatic considerations unique to each science is the purpose of Richard Miller's *Fact and Method*:

> [A]n explanation is an adequate description of the underlying causes bringing about a phenomenon. *Adequacy, here, is determined by rules that are specific to particular fields at particular times.* The specificity of the rules is not just a feature of adequacy for given special purposes, but characterizes all adequacy that is relevant to scientific explanation. *The rules are judged by their efficacy for the respective fields at the respective times* – which makes adequacy far more contingent, pragmatic and field-specific than positivists allowed, but no less rationally determinable. (1987: 6, emphasis added)

Ontological Criteria of Causal Analysis

In order to specify the meaning of what Miller calls "adequacy" of explanation for a particular scholarly field, such as the study of postcommunist regime change, let us draw on Gerring's (1999: 20–29; 2001: 130–46) three criteria pertaining to causal inference and four criteria involved in the confirmation of causal relationships. They demonstrate how difficult it is for social

[5] This critique is different from the following advanced by Somers (1998: 737), which is inappropriate: "Because it [the Hempel-Oppenheimer scheme] subsumes explanation under the rubric of predictive universal laws, the covering law model cannot disclose the underlying causal mechanisms underwriting chains of events; it cannot allow for the contingency of outcomes or explain how temporal sequences, conjunctures, and spatial patterns matter to theory construction." There is nothing in the H-O scheme that would not allow us to explain events by the conjuncture of multiple general laws and their corresponding initial conditions. Goldstone (1998: 834) is correct that also Somers's insistence on historical specificity does not get around general lawlike propositions.

scientists to agree on an account of a phenomenon's causes. The criteria are temporal priority of the cause vis-à-vis the consequence, the independence of the cause from the effect, and the (ab)normality condition. The first two need no explication. The last criterion follows from comparative logic: all sorts of processes are necessary to bring about a certain outcome, but only few of them covary with the specific outcome consistently. They are "abnormal" against the background processes that go on all the time without bringing about the phenomenon to be explained. The four empirical criteria to identify causality are covariation between cause and effect, comparison with alternative explanations across settings, process tracing to establish the temporal order of things, and plausibility arguments about cause-effect relations.

The third criterion of causal inference ([ab-]normality) and the first two of the criteria of empirical verification are manifestly insufficient to allow identification of causality for familiar reasons: covariation does not establish causality. The first and second criterion of causal inference and the second criterion of causal empirical analysis go to the heart of our subject matter: temporal sequence, independence of cause from effect, and process tracing. Gerring's fourth empirical criterion, plausibility, is too vague to be of much use for our discussion. What is striking is that the key analytical and empirical criteria of causal analysis – temporal sequence, independence, and process tracing – are inherently ambiguous and leave a great deal of room for interpretation by social scientists and the scholarly communities within which they operate.

With regard to sequence, how much temporal priority do we require a variable to exhibit in order to count as a cause? Gerring notes that proximate causes temporally close to the outcome "are often referred to as 'occasions' for specific outcomes, rather than causes" (Gerring, 1999: 22). In a similar vein, how independent must an "independent variable" be from its purported effect to count as a cause? The problem that looms large over explanatory hypotheses is that they border on tautologies. Gerring (2001: 138–40, 142–43) quite rightly claims that there are hardly any tautologies in the strict sense, but that the informational value of a proposition with causal intent is a matter of degree. How informative is it to say that party identification, measured as a citizen's electoral registration as supporter of a particular party, is the best predictor of voting for that particular party in an actual election, controlling for citizens' political attitudes and social position? This proposition is clearly not a tautology in the logical sense but may construct a sufficiently short causal nexus to count as an "occasion" more than as a "cause" in what many social science scholars would aspire to in the causal account of a phenomenon. They would try to "endogenize" party identification by uncovering the elements of a citizen's social, cultural, and political experience that contribute to party identification.

No abstract logical proof or quantifiable decision rule but substantive debates about alternative accounts in a scholarly community draw the line between insightful explanation and uninformative tautology. Let us refer to the problem of temporal priority as that of *causal depth*.

Those who are seeking considerable causal depth may run into a conflict with another empirical criterion of verification in causal analysis, that of *process tracing*. A causal account needs to demonstrate a temporal sequence of events and processes. The "deeper" the causes are, the more distant they are from the ultimate explanandum and the more tenuous may be the causal sequence that leads to the ultimate outcome. The criteria of causal depth and process tracing thus involve trade-offs. Before we examine the trade-offs, let us illuminate the activity of process tracing in the social sciences by drawing on a closely related concept, that of a *causal mechanism*.

To accept something as a cause of a social phenomenon, it must involve mechanism(s) that brought about the effect. Mechanisms are processes that convert certain inputs into outputs (Hedström and Swedberg, 1998: 7). In addition to temporal precedence over outputs, there must be some intelligible linkage between antecedent and consequence. In the spirit of Max Weber (1978), we may say that a causal mechanism is intelligible when it involves the rational deliberation of human beings in the production of some outcome. This proposal has several implications.

First, the concept of causal mechanism in the social sciences implies *methodological individualism* in the weak sense that causal mechanisms rely on human action, even though each action may be constrained by collective and aggregate phenomena external to the individual actors (resource distributions, the temporal structure of events, the physical distribution of actors, and the collectively understood rules and anticipated consequences of action that are often codified in formal institutions). Employing causal mechanisms in explanation, we move from a highly aggregate level of social entities (sets of human beings, structures, and institutions) to the individual-level conduct of particular actors in order to account for higher-level outcomes. This weak methodological individualism is not inimical to the consideration of structural and collective phenomena. It only requires that we treat individuals' actions as critical ingredients in any account of structural transformation, such as that of political regimes.

Second, a mechanism working through human action is intelligible only if it is based on the actors' more or less explicit, deliberate preference schedules. As Boudon (1998) argues, the finality of a social science explanation is grounded in the understandability of human action. This requires that actors can invoke some higher objectives that inform their conduct (Weber's *Wertrationalität*). Pushed to its ultimate consequence, intelligible action is rational when actors choose among different objectives, explicitly ranked in their preference schedules, in light of scarce means at their disposal in such ways as to maximize their overall value satisfaction (Weber's *Zweckrationalität*). Purely affective or "traditional," habitual conduct is unintelligible and does not count as a *social* mechanism in explanatory accounts. The same applies to physical causes of behavior.[6]

Third, mechanisms require that we specify the *social knowledge* actors bring to bear on intelligible action. Given that actors often encounter risk or uncertainty, they must make empirically unproved assumptions about the consequences of alternative strategies in the pursuit of their objectives, usually without being able to assign objective probabilities to them. Identifying these interpretations of the situation is often as important in understanding human action as determining the actors' preferences and the "objective" constraints of the situation, observed by the social scientist with the benefit of hindsight.

This ontological conception of mechanism (weak methodological individualism with intelligibility or rationality and social knowledge) differs from a purely epistemological conception of mechanism recently invoked by Elster (1998). Elster wishes to reserve the conception of mechanism for causal linkages that operate sometimes but not always. They explain, but do not predict, according to the logic "If A, then sometimes B" (Elster, 1998: 49). There may always be intervening causes that suppress the causal link between A and B or functionally equivalent causes that create B without A. Moreover, the relationship between A and B may be of an inherently probabilistic rather than a deterministic kind. There are no laws in the social sciences in the strict sense of deterministic processes without intervening variables, functional equivalents, or stochastic fuzziness.

I propose to separate the problem of nondeterministic relations between causes and consequences, broadly conceived (stochastic laws, intervening causes, etc.), from the ontological conception of causal mechanism in the social sciences. The latter calls for social explanations that shift the level of causal process analysis from that of aggregates and structures to individual action under constraints. It is entirely open whether these causal mechanisms are stochastic or deterministic or whether intervening causes (mechanisms?) suppress their effects.

Trade-offs between Causal Depth and Causal Mechanisms

According to Hedström and Swedberg (1998: 24–25), the virtue of causal mechanisms is their reliance on action, their precision, their abstraction from concrete contexts, and their reductionist strategy of opening black boxes. This, they claim, is in line with the striving of all science "for narrowing the

[6] Of course, physically induced conduct, such as the lethargy of a starving population, has social consequences. Moreover, the physical processes (famine, etc.) may themselves be brought about by social mechanisms based on deliberate action, such as the destruction of food crops in warfare.

gap or lag between input and output, cause and effect" (25). This statement signals a potential conflict with at least one formulation of the criterion of temporal causal depth elaborated earlier. Advocates of the need for causal mechanisms could embrace the call for temporal causal depth of an explanation, as long as linkages across time can be partitioned into infinitesimally small steps. Each step is linked to the next by a causal mechanism. Causal depth results from assembling very long chains of proximate causes expressing causal mechanisms. No single step, however, must be too large.

What is a small or a large step, of course, is a question of ontology and not logic or methodology. If we take the imperative literally, however, that causal mechanisms should be very close to the explanandum in spatiotemporal terms, the proximity criterion has, in my view, little merit in many explanatory contexts of the social sciences, most certainly in the case of postcommunist political and economic regime change.

Precommunist political regimes across Eastern Europe displayed striking diversity.[7] In some regards, postcommunist polities reproduce this pattern. Countries that were democratic or semiauthoritarian in the interwar period, such as the Baltic countries, particularly if they also had older semiauthoritarian roots in the Habsburg Empire with its mechanisms of political representation, such as Czechoslovakia, Hungary, Poland, Slovenia, and Croatia, tend to become full-fledged democracies with civic and political rights immediately after 1989, with the Slovak and Croatian laggards fully converging toward the rest of the group by the late 1990s. Countries with authoritarian patrimonial regimes tend to yield greater postcommunist regime diversity and instability. Some of them gravitate toward formal electoral democracy with tenuous levels of civic and political rights (Russia, Ukraine); some start out in this category but appear to make headway toward full democracy (Bulgaria, Macedonia, Romania, and, to a lesser extent within the former Soviet Union, Armenia, Georgia, and Moldova); others relapse into authoritarianism after a fleeting moment of liberalization (Belarus, Serbia until 2000). The colonial periphery of the former Soviet Union, finally, almost uniformly drifts toward authoritarian solutions. Here, there are no precommunist precedents of civic mobilization.

At first sight, this account of postcommunist diversity lacks actor-related causal mechanisms. There are two not necessarily conflicting ways to remedy that problem, but they remain inherently controversial. *One of these ways* operates through cognitive processes within and across generations of actors. Those who were alive in the interwar period, survived communism, and lived to welcome postcommunist politics draw on skills and experiences they never quite lost during communism. Such a cognitive capital stock helps them formulate expectations about the dynamics of the new polities and

[7] In this and the following paragraphs, I am drawing on Kitschelt et al. (1999), chaps. 1 and 2.

contributes to political rejuvenation – for example, in the formation of political parties with distinctive programmatic appeals. Moreover, even where postcommunist actors are too young to have experienced precommunist rule or even much of communism, their elders may have handed them down crucial skills, interpretations, and experiences. In addition to politics, this may apply also to the business sphere. Róna-Tas and Böröcz (2000: 221), for example, found that family history matters for the new postcommunist political entrepreneurs, and here the experience of grandparents who lived most of their lives before communism is of substantially greater influence than that of their parents. Moreover, postcommunist entrepreneurialism is negatively correlated with precommunist family landownership in some countries, such as Bulgaria and Poland, where it involved essentially subsistence farming divorced from market involvement.

Those who accept cognitive causal mechanisms over the span of more than fifty years and two generations would argue that the human mind is a robust deposit of ideas and information. In periods of societal crisis, people are capable of activating their long-term memory and scan its content in order to interpret their strategic options under conditions of uncertainty. Moreover, technical and institutional memory enhancers (scripture, literacy, media of communication, education, professionals in charge of preserving memories) and Kubik's "cultural entrepreneurs" (Chapter 10 in this volume) extend the capacity of human actors to retrieve and process information over lengthy periods of time.[8]

The other way to make plausible the efficacy of intermediate distance explanations focuses on political practices and institutional arrangements rather than beliefs and cultural orientations. In this vein, the efficacy of causal mechanisms in the choice of political regimes and economic activities operating across periods of more than fifty years can also be made plausible by decomposing their operation into smaller steps, each linking more proximate phenomena. Thus, precommunist politics and economics had an impact on the way communist states were formed under Soviet tutelage with differential bargaining power of the new communist rulers vis-à-vis what was left of civil society after the Nazi war. These nationally and even subnationally different bargaining constellations reasserted themselves in the period of de-Stalinization from 1953 to 1956, when Stalinist rulers had to confront domestic societal forces that were acting on precommunist experiences then only five to fifteen years old. The increasing post-Stalinist diversification of communist rule inside and beyond the Warsaw Pact, including that between republics of the Soviet Union itself, constitutes a mechanism that then explains why communist countries and regions responded differently to the challenges of technology, political elite turnover, and changing societal

[8] For a critique of an overly narrow construction of the criterion of spatiotemporal proximity, see also Goldstone (1998: 838).

demands (induced by education, different family structures, etc.) from the 1960s through the 1980s. The diversification of communist rule, in turn, causes distinct patterns of oppositional mobilization and incumbent elite response in the ultimate crisis of communism. These configurations, finally, influence the initial and ultimate political and economic outcomes of the communist breakdown. Grzymała-Busse's chapter on communist successor parties (Chapter 5 in this volume) highlights the linkage among the last two causal steps in the chain.

Even this cascade of probabilistic causal linkages between precommunist politics and society, the establishment of communist rule, its post-Stalinist transformation, and its ultimate collapse, however, may not satisfy those who insist on very close spatiotemporal proximity in causal mechanisms (Kiser and Hechter, 1991; 1998). Drawing on the epistemological principle of Ockham's razor, they tend to discard "deeper" explanations as inefficient and causally irrelevant for an outcome. This epistemological move in the evaluation of alternative causal accounts constitutes the main bone of contention between different camps in the study of postcommunist regime transition.

As a rule of thumb, causal mechanisms that are temporally proximate ("close") to the effect they claim to explain account for more statistical variance in the effect than deeper and less proximate causes most of the time, even though not always. Intervening external shocks reduce the path dependence of ultimate outcomes and dilute the measurable effects of temporally more distant causes. But is a shallower causal explanation really "better" just because the statistically explained variance is greater than that of a deeper alternative? Advocates of causal proximity engage in a statistical modeling strategy to which their adversaries object. The former rely on single-equation statistical models to account for an ultimate outcome and enter rival candidates for causal explanation on the right-hand side of the equation, regardless of their temporal position within a chain of causation. Temporally deeper causes with less direct impact on the ultimate outcome then tend to wash out in the hunt to find the statistically most efficient explanation. Single-equation models constitute the technical implementation of Ockham's razor. By emphasizing multivariate statistical efficiency over ontological criteria of temporality and human action in causal mechanisms, Ockham's razor promotes explanatory shallowness, with the ultimate danger of explanations approaching tautological reasoning.

Alternatively, one might conceive of the statistical explanation of an ultimate outcome (regime change) as a multiequation model that links temporally prior to subsequent causes of an outcome in a stepwise estimation procedure. This analysis reveals the temporal interconnections between causes that are directly pitted against each other in the single-equation multivariate statistical tournament inspired by Ockham's razor. A multiequation model of causal chains may reveal that some proximate cause is, to a considerable extent, *endogenous* to a deeper cause. Moreover, it may reveal interaction effects between deeper causes ("structural conditions") affecting shallower causes ("triggers"). Finally, the same variable may appear in different cases at different stages in the temporal causal chain that must be reconstructed to arrive at a satisfactory causal account. These are just examples for a general epistemological rule adversaries of Ockham's razor advance: respect the temporal complexity of causal relations.

The search for causal mechanisms and causal depth are mutually supportive but also mutually constraining criteria in the construction of satisfactory explanations. The requirement that causal mechanisms run through intentional action limits the spatiotemporal depth of explanations, while causal depth criteria militate against minimizing lags between cause and effect, accompanied by the dangers of tautological reasoning. How far we wish to push back the envelope of causal analysis in terms of spatiotemporal depth and history is a pragmatic and ontological question, not a matter of epistemology, logic, or statistics. Reasonable minds may disagree on what counts as a good explanation of a particular phenomenon. I employ the next two sections of this chapter to persuade readers that many explanations currently offered to account for postcommunist regime variance are either too shallow (temporally proximate, bordering on tautology by blurring the line between explanans and explanandum) or too deep (without a chain of causal mechanisms) to be fully satisfactory in an account of postcommunist pathways.

Excessively Deep Explanations of Postcommunist Regime Diversity

The current paradigmatic case of an excessively deep comparative-historical explanation in political science is Robert Putnam's (1993) account of democratic processes and performance in northern and southern Italy, claiming that twelfth- and thirteenth-century polity formation in the two parts of Italy shaped both the institutional practices as well as the economic outcomes in the different Italian regions in the second half of the twentieth century. What Putnam lacks is a convincing account of the transmission from thirteenth-century Italian conditions to those of the twentieth century. No mechanisms translate the "long-distance" causality across eight hundred years into a more proximate chain of closer causal forces acting upon each other. Margaret Levi (1996: 46) therefore identifies in Putnam's work a "metaphorical use of path dependence without the rigorous analytics a compelling application of the concept requires." When one tries to supply such causal mechanisms across historical time, one soon discovers that civicness and governance wildly fluctuated in Italy and that, if anything, the eighteenth-century governmental institutions should serve as the reference point for twentieth-century development, not the thirteenth- and fourteenth-century city-states in northern Italy and the Kingdom of Sicily (Sabetti, 1996: esp. 27–37).

In a similar vein, in the analysis of postcommunist political change, observers often invoke different *religious doctrines* and *zones of administrative-political control* under tutelage of either Prussia, Habsburg Austria, Russia, or the Ottoman Empire as determinants of late twentieth-century politics but generally do not specify the mechanisms that lead from these antecedents to the political consequence. This explanatory gap occurs even in the better historical comparative analyses, such as Schöpflin's (1993) broad comparative sweep, even though his study provides, in principle, the facts and tools to work out the causal mechanisms that link the institutional transformations of diverse polities across different historical "stages" and "rounds of struggle" in Eastern Europe.[9] Schöpflin (1993: 19–22) discusses the different levels of professionalization in the state bureaucracies of post–World War I East and Central European polities, yet his later description of communist regime differentiation in the 1960s and 1970s does not systematically draw on such earlier regime variations and their influence on actors' strategic capabilities and constraints. For example, in contrast to Hungary and Poland with a bureaucracy penetrated by the gentry, Schöpflin attributes to interwar Czechoslovakia "a relatively well-functioning administration and considerable autonomy of the law" (20). Yet he does not explore a linkage of those earlier administrative practices with the later prominence of "illiberal technocrats" (214) in communist Czechoslovakia at a time when the state party apparatus of Hungarian and Polish communism was already crumbling and a generation of reformist apparatchiks took control of the ruling parties.

In terms of correlational statistics, religion provides a surprisingly strong association with regime outcomes.[10] But it is unclear what mechanisms causal analyses are really picking up with religion. Is it religious doctrines about the relationship between economic activity, politics, and religious organization that matter for the founding of new political regimes? Or is religion simply a tracer of institutional historical correlates – for example, the timing of state formation and the construction of rational bureaucratic administrations that facilitated the rise of market capitalism and the development of civic societies? In this latter case, there is nothing intrinsically crucial about religious beliefs that affect postcommunist regimes. Instead of starting from religion, we would need to construct a causal chain starting from state formation to account for postcommunist regime diversity.

9 Incomplete "deep" accounts of postcommunist regime variation also tend to characterize Ágh (1998: chap. 1), Crawford (1996: chap. 1), and the typological approach in Offe (1994: 241–49).

10 The precise statistical strength of that association depends on intricacies of operationalization. It is slightly weaker, if dummy variables signal the cultural dominance of a religion (cf. Fish, 1998b). It is somewhat stronger if we create a single ordinal-scale variable with the highest value for compatibility with democracy and market liberalism going to Western Christianity, followed by Eastern Orthodoxy and then Islam (cf. Kitschelt, 1999).

Religion could also be a variable that simply measures proximity to the West (cf. Fish, 1998a: 241). Long-distance causality accounting for post-communist regimes sometimes takes the form of geostrategic considerations within the international system. According to this view, proximity to the West and a resentment of Russian domination under the shadow of the Brezhnev doctrine translate into adoption of a market-liberal representative democracy. It is not easy, however, to spell out the causal linkage between geographical location and postcommunist regime change. There are at least four analytical modes to bring geography to bear on the problem of causally explaining postcommunist regime diversity. First, the causal chain is historical in nature and would run from state formation through interwar politics and post-Stalinism to the regime transitions of the 1989–91 period. In that sense, geographical location does not add anything that could not be gleaned from variables more informative in the social scientific sense of permitting the construction of causal mechanisms that account for the ultimate outcome.

The second view of geography treats it as a proximate cause of regime forms. The implied causal mechanism here is focused on the economic incentives Western countries have offered to their postcommunist neighbors, for now more than a decade, to adopt political and economic rules of the game that are similar to their own. If this account is correct, trade flows between the OECD West and postcommunist countries, as well as patterns of foreign direct investment (FDI) should signal a close link to postcommunist political regime form. As a matter of fact, the statistical association between these variables is quite modest, however, and certainly much weaker than that between regime form and "deep" variables, such as religion, precommunist regime, or mode of communist rule.[11] Some countries, such as Poland, engaged in vigorous economic reform, but did not benefit from FDI flows until some time later. FDI here certainly did not work as a proximate stimulus to economic reform. Moreover, it appears that the causal direction goes in opposite ways, namely that FDI and trade are endogenous to previously enacted economic reform.

A third way to think about geography is in the fashion proposed by Kopstein and Reilly (Chapter 4 in this volume), namely as physical contiguity and communication with neighbors whose economic and political reform strategies mutually influence each other. Kopstein and Reilly have made an interesting opening move on this worthy avenue of research, but in order to convince me they would have to address at least the following issues. First, their index of neighborly communication is a murky amalgam of numerous elements that I would like to see analyzed separately in order to determine (1) the unidimensionality of the concept that is postulated to inform the index and (2) the relative influence of index components on the dependent variable. My suspicion is that the index is not unidimensional and that the

[11] I have reported evidence in Kitschelt (1999: 37).

components most influential in establishing neighbor effects are of a simple modernization theoretical logic. Moreover, as I already suggested, some elements of the index (FDI, trade) are in fact endogenous to the explanatory variable. Second, Kopstein and Reilly do not submit their neighborhood effects index to what I have called the multivariate tournament of variables. How collinear is their index with other variables, and how can they establish causal primacy for the neighborhood effect?

Finally, none of the case studies explains how neighborhood effects trump other variables. All structural theories would predict that Slovakia and also Croatia would have returned to the cohort of postcommunist economic and political reform vanguard polities. In a similar vein, structural theories would predict backsliding in Kyrgyzstan and an intermediate, volatile trajectory in Moldova, Georgia, and Macedonia, as well as in Armenia, all countries where new titular majorities find it imperative to protect the autonomy of their new polities by catering to Western institutional principles in order to receive support and resources from new allies. Kyrgyzstan, a country distant from the West but initially pushing for economic and political reform after the collapse of the Soviet Union, may have experienced a relapse into authoritarianism not so much because of its distance from the West and the political practices of its neighbors, but simply because from the very beginning its reform politicians were unable to build political parties and professional bureaucratic administrations in a domestic environment inhospitable to the institutional correlates of a Western capitalist and democratic polity. Structural but maybe not geographical theory can explain the backsliding into semiauthoritarianism among a final group of countries, those in relative physical proximity to the West but emerging from institutional legacies and practices of collective action that should make the establishment of liberal democracies relatively difficult (Albania, Belarus, Serbia).

The strongest, most convincing version of geographic influence trumping structural factors would have to be established through a fourth mechanism and micrologic, the *future-oriented expectations of postcommunist politicians*. Political and economic elites in countries close to the European Union (EU) anticipate benefits through trade and FDI in the *near or medium-term future*, if they embrace economic reform and democratic civic and political rights. As Przeworski (1991: 190) suggested early on, "geography is indeed the single reason to hope that Eastern European countries will follow the path to democracy and prosperity." The best way to show the independent influence of geography through expectations would be to detect extraordinary economic reform efforts among countries with weak structural predictors to establish democracy and economic reform, yet plausible expectations to join the European Union in the foreseeable future (Bulgaria and Romania). So far, the evidence on these cases is mixed. Both countries clearly stand out within the cohort of formerly patrimonial communist countries in terms of instituting liberal democracies with firmly protected civil and political rights. Yet their economic reform efforts, in terms of short-term stabilization, medium-term market liberalization, and long-term construction of market-supporting political institutions certainly lends little support to the proposition that expectations of EU accession enabled them to move ahead of the pack of other formerly patrimonial communist polities and to close the gap to the lead countries of the postcommunist region in Central Europe (cf. Kitschelt, 2001). Geography as a "deep" explanation may therefore still lack an empirically corroborated mechanism to count as a plausible reason for patterns of regime diversity and economic reform strategy among postcommunist countries.

Excessively Shallow Explanations of Postcommunist Regime Diversity

Shallow explanations provide mechanisms and high statistical explanatory yields but little insight into the causal genealogy of a phenomenon. This danger is evidenced by Philip Roeder's (1994; 1997; 2001) analysis of diversity in the regime types of Soviet successor states. Let me focus on his most refined recent statement of that perspective and particularly on the analysis of regime outcomes from 1994 to 2000. Roeder recounts in admirable detail how bargaining configurations between different interests propelled different fission products of the Soviet Union toward democracies with full contestation, exclusionary democracies with disenfranchised Russian minorities, oligarchies, or autocracies. The more incumbent power elites were fragmented before the initial republic-level elections of 1990, then before the initial postindependence elections, and finally in subsequent years to the turn of the millennium the more the dynamics of bargaining promoted a democratic outcome. The two key variables are the dominance of agrarian or urban-industrial agencies before 1990 and the presence of indigenized or Russian party and managerial elites. The prevalence of urban-industrial agencies and nonindigenized Russian elites threatened the viability of hegemonic autocratic solutions, presumed to be the first preference of incumbent Union Republic party elites belonging to the titular majority. Where urban-industrial agencies prevailed, the result was either full democracy (in Armenia, Lithuania, Russia, and the Ukraine) or exclusionary democracy (in Estonia and Latvia). Four cases with mixed control structures oscillate between autocracy (predominant in Azerbaijan, Kazakhstan, and Belarus) and oligarchy (Georgia). Starting from rural-agricultural dominance and nonindigenized party elites, Kyrgyzstan ends up with a halfway house between democracy and authoritarianism, whereas Moldova inches toward democracy. Three cases of rural-agricultural agency dominance yield authoritarianism (Tajikistan, Turkmenistan, and Uzbekistan).

Roeder's meticulous process tracing (Roeder, 2001: 52) remains unsatisfactory in two ways that mutually reinforce each other. First, the model says nothing about the origins of the power configurations on the eve of the Soviet

Union's disintegration. Second, the model fits the data only because of the rather odd characterization of some of the regime outcomes in the late 1990s, and even then it is sometimes difficult to see the linkage between stipulated mechanisms and regime consequences over time.

Let me work backward from the unsatisfactory characterization of regime outcomes and show that "deeper" explanations actually account for properly described postcommunist regimes in more satisfactory ways, even though such explanations treat some of the short-term event history, coalitional struggles, and victories of individuals and their followers as not worthy of detailed theoretical explanation.[12] In contrast to Roeder, I consider the long-term practice of state building and the mobilization of secondary associations (interest groups, parties) before incorporation into Russia or the Soviet Union as well as the mode of incorporation in the Soviet Union as critical variables that shape the capacity of counterelites to threaten autocratic self-transformations of the elites. Roeder's approach focuses on intraelite bargaining in order to explain short-term regime outcomes, ignoring the potential for mass action as a critical element in elite calculations. I do not deny the importance of elite fragmentation, but I emphasize the collective action potentials of citizens and incipient counterelites that result from the history of state building, precommunist patterns of political mobilization, and resulting modes of organizing civic compliance under communism.[13]

Roeder's class of democracies is incoherent. Serious infringements on civil and political rights in Armenia, Russia, and the Ukraine (even including electoral manipulation) make it impossible to place them in the same category as full democracies. Conversely, not only Lithuania but also Estonia and Latvia qualify as full democracies after their revision of citizenship laws. The Freedom House rankings reflect this, but not Roeder's unusual and contrived measure of accountability.[14] What we need to explain is a division

[12] Actually, it is hard to see how some of Roeder's own process tracing – for example, of the oscillations of regime patterns in Azerbaijan, Belarus, or Tajikistan – follow a tight analytical logic (2001: 40–42). Had the outcomes been otherwise, Roeder could have told a slightly different story about victory or defeat of factions at war.

[13] Roeder attempts to disqualify my approach as building on the distinction between "rational-legal and patrimonial cultures" (2001: 51). He makes the rhetorical move to associate any analysis of temporally deeper causes with the pursuit of "bad" cultural explanation against "good" (and shallower) rational-instrumental and institutional explanation. The final section of my chapter discusses the inadequacy of this dichotomy. Needless to say, I have always placed the emphasis of my approach on political practices and institutions, but I would not want to exclude the importance of cultural elements in a very specific sense: even good game theorists would not want to discount elements of culture (corporate and otherwise), such as memories of past (inter)actions and beliefs about the expectations those episodes generated among current players in order to model how current actors calculate the payoffs resulting from alternative strategic choices.

[14] For good reason, the Freedom House annual rankings attribute to Russia and the Ukraine barely "semi-free" status, scoring them below the median value on their democracy scales

of four groups: (1) full democracies (Baltic countries); (2) semidemocracies with a pattern of improvement throughout the 1990s (Armenia, Georgia, Moldova); (3) initial semidemocracies with a pattern of slower or faster deterioration in the 1990s (Belarus, Russia, Ukraine); and (4) full autocracies.

Group 1 countries were precommunist interwar semidemocracies with considerable associational mobilization based on class, nation, and economic sector in an environment of beginning industrialization and bureaucratic state building with a formal-legal rule of law. Soviet rule built on this organizational infrastructure and responded to the collective action threat with a mixture of repressive *and* accommodative practices to co-opt and depoliticize a potentially formidable civic mobilization. When hegemony crumbled, this mobilizational potential came to the fore and made indigenous and nonindigenous elites seek a regime transition through negotiation. Eventually, even the nonindigenous population finds it advantageous to assimilate into the new independent, Western-oriented democracies (Laitin, 1998).

By contrast, in group 2, the core of long-standing patrimonial Russian state building without broad precommunist interest group and party mobilization and only very limited ethnic differentiation and autonomy movements in different historical episodes (in Belarus and Ukraine in 1905, 1917–21, after 1989), the realm of communist elite action in the late 1980s was much less constrained by bottom-up challenges and involved factional efforts to engineer preemptive reform while converting public assets into the private property of managerial and party elites. It resulted in an unstable oscillation between semidemocratic and oligarchical regime forms in an environment of volatile parties and interest associations. The high level of education of at least the urban population, however, makes a suppression of autonomous secondary associations inauspicious in the longer run. Even elite fragments bent on authoritarianism, such as those that asserted themselves in Belarus in the late 1990s, are likely to encounter increasingly stiff resistance to the realization of their preferences.[15]

Group 3 are countries incorporated late into the Russian empire in the late eighteenth and first half of the nineteenth century (Armenia, Georgia,

on civil rights and political liberties ranging from 1 (highest) to 7 (lowest). By 2001, Russia receives a mere 5 + 5 and the Ukraine 4 + 4, whereas all Baltic countries are rated as 1 + 2.

[15] In line with Przeworski et al. (2000), I assert that economic development in the longer run matters for political mobilization and durable democracy, though constrained by the legacies of past regime formation and associated experiences. Roeder (2001: 20) initially appears to deny the explanatory power of economic development to predict regime outcomes but later brings this variable in through the back door by attributing to regions with a prevalence of urban-industrial elites a greater threat potential vis-à-vis the autocratic designs of party elites. His early assessment is faulty because he does not correct per capita GDP in the Soviet republics by purchasing-power parity. Doing so places them exactly in that second-highest quintile of economic development to which Huntington (1991) and Przeworski et al. (2000) attribute the highest probability of making a durable move toward democracy.

and Bessarabia/Moldova). Here the new masters engaged in inconclusive efforts to assimilate indigenous ruling classes, such as the Armenian diaspora pariah entrepreneurs and the Georgian nobility and Orthodox Church. In repeated episodes of struggle, indigenous ethnic movements pressed for greater autonomy, even under the Soviet administration. The presence of a patrimonial state apparatus and the lack of twentieth-century experiences with democratic or semidemocratic associational self-organization, however, constrain the transition of postcommunist regimes in these countries toward full democracy. The anti-Russian dispositions of the new titular majority elites make them receptive to Western incentives to adopt democratic practices in exchange for economic resources and political assurances that prop up their independence against an overbearing Russian neighbor. As noted by Kopstein and Reilly, geography and power distribution in the international system may, at the margin, tip the balance of regime dynamics in these countries toward democratization.

The six countries of group 4, finally, have all evolved into unambiguously authoritarian regimes (Azerbaijan, Kazakhstan, Kyrgyzstan, Tajikistan, Turkmenistan, and Uzbekistan). Setting aside many differences among them, they have in common a legacy of (1) virtual stateless societies before (2) very late incorporation into the Russian empire in a (3) more colonial rather than assimilative mode (Kappeler, 1993: 174). Earmarking these regions for strategic resource exploitation, Russian rulers sought to subordinate indigenous elites, organized along primary relations of kinship and tribe, under a light colonial administration that did not fully assert even patrimonial techniques. Later, under Soviet rule, those indigenous clientelist and kinship-based practices of governance were not entirely displaced, but transformed into regional-spatial clientelist patrimonial networks co-opting the existing networks of elders and tribal headmen (Jones Luong, 2001). The assimilation of indigenous ethnic elites into the communist apparatus of domination perpetuated the incapacity of clients and constituencies for collective action. Both the earlier breakdown of tsarist rule (1917–21) and the recent fall of the Soviet Union thus did not spawn powerful ethnopolitical autonomy movements in any of these incipient countries, with the partial exception of the Baku region of Azerbaijan in 1917. When the Soviet Union imploded, either the indigenous elites simply endowed their existing system of rule with a new ethnonational ideology and perpetuated well-worn practices (Kazakhstan, Uzbekistan), or brief interludes of uncertainty, internal competition, and civil war enabled new (or returning) rulers to reestablish these old patterns of autocracy within the short span of a handful of years (Azerbaijan, Kyrgyzstan, Tajikistan).

I have gone beyond a mere critique of Roeder's analysis in order to show that shallow explanations may not only be shortsighted but, in their zeal to explain processes in all their details, also distort the characterization of outcomes. Instead, by homing in on state formation (including ethnic incorporation), economic development, and political experience with autonomous secondary associations and collective action before the advent of and under communist rule, a more satisfactory explanation emerges that involves longer but, from the perspective of an actor framework relying on beliefs and experiences, not excessively long causal chains. The specific techniques of communist rule to create civic compliance serve as the transmission belts that link precommunist to postcommunist experiences. My explanatory strategy is quite similar to that proposed by Laitin (1998) to account for different patterns of language assimilation by Russian minorities faced with non-Russian-speaking titular majorities since 1991.

Shallow explanations of regime and policy change are quite common in the comparative literature on postcommunist polities. After having covered Roeder in some detail, because in my view his work represents the most rigorous and interesting effort to date to spell out the logic of postcommunist transformation inspired by the imperative of short cause-effect chains and "mechanisms" operating in small time-space intervals, I can now only mention a few more examples of "shallow" explanations without detailed discussion. Higley, Pakulski, and Wesołowksi's (1998) work, building on Higley and Gunther (1992), argues that stable democracies result from elites that agree on basic regime parameters, while simultaneously displaying pluralist differentiation into parties, interest groups, and movements with their unique objectives. Whereas the authors conceive of these attributes of intraelite relations as an explanation for the rise and persistence of democracy, I see it as a simple redescription of democratic practices. In a similar vein, Fish's (2001) intentional explanation of authoritarian backsliding in postcommunist regimes borders on tautology. If chief executives promote the degradation of democracy, and if that process is particularly pronounced where superpresidential constitutions have been adopted, in order to provide a causal account we had better ask why superpresidentialism could entrench itself and subjugate the fate of political regimes under the whims of individual rulers. The self-serving intentions of rulers faced with this opportunity structure certainly do not supply a satisfactory causal account of the regime outcomes. In a similar vein, the fact that the replacement of old communist successor parties by noncommunist parties and alliances in initial postcommunist elections is the statistically most efficient predictor of economic reform effort in subsequent years (Fish, 1998b) is not much of an insight. And that this variable "beats" deeper explanatory variables of economic reform in a single-equation statistical model is not surprising, given the proximity between favored cause and effect.[16] I would voice similar concerns about explanatory shallowness with regard to propositions that treat

[16] Similar problems apply to Fish's (1998a) explanation of democratization. In both cases, single-equation models, often with high to very high collinearity among the independent variables, do not help to shed light on temporal patterns of causality.

greater or lesser executive and legislative powers of a presidential office in new postcommunist democracies as the ultimate independent variable accounting for economic reform trajectories.[17]

Deep and Shallow Explanations: Rivalry or Complementarity?

The recent prominence of causally shallow explanations is due not exclusively to fashionable multivariate reasoning, driven by the criterion to maximize explained variance in statistical terms. The historical experience of the "Third Wave" of democratization (Huntington, 1991) powerfully influences the penchant for such approaches. What appeared as the sudden sweep of democracy across Latin America, Southeast Asia, the communist hemisphere, and even parts of Africa in the 1980s and early 1990s made deep structuralist and comparative-historical theories appear to be of little use (O'Donnell and Schmitter, 1986; Przeworski, 1991: 3). The problem here is that the explanatory focus is on the "event" of authoritarian regime breakdown, but, as I argued before, all sciences of complexity, and not just the social sciences, are bad at making point predictions to account for individual events. This event-oriented framing of the object of explanation is furthered by studies that follow the now fashionable pooled cross-sectional time-series analyses in which the dependent variable is really short-term historical fluctuation, rather than lasting regime parameters that have entrenched themselves.[18]

In order to avoid misunderstanding, let me nevertheless reiterate two points. On the one hand, I do not doubt that strong *correlations* between what Roeder, Fish, and others offer as explanations for postcommunist regime types and regime performance in terms of economic reform actually do exist, but I question their status in explanatory accounts of regime diversity, *even if* they turn out to prevail over rival causal candidates by purely statistical criteria of significance in single-equation tournaments. On the other hand, I do not deny that short-term accounts sometimes, but not often, do provide the ultimate explanation and that further backward-oriented process tracing is futile. Before we conclude that explanatory chains cannot be temporally deepened, however, we must have carefully specified a model of explanatory layers that takes into account the temporal ordering of forces that may impinge on the final outcome. With these qualifications in mind, let

[17] This critique applies to Hellman's (1996) attribution of causal efficacy to executive-legislative relations in the comparative analysis of economic reform. For a different perspective, see Kitschelt and Malesky (2000) and Kitschelt (2001).

[18] This focus is technically entrenched by employing the lagged dependent variable (regime change) as a control on the right-hand side of the equation and/or by including a full set of country dummies that suck out a great deal of cross-sectional variance. Structural variables are superior to country dummies but require more theoretical work.

me outline four different ways to frame the relationship between short-term and long-term factors in explanatory accounts.

First, one can argue that *long-term factors actually trump short-term factors as causal explanations.* Although ideally it is neat to specify micromechanisms that establish an unbroken chain of causal linkages between deep, distant causes and ultimate outcomes, sometimes an external shock may yield a crisis in a system such that actors engage in a randomized trajectory of trial-and-error in search of new solutions. This trial-and-error process may be unpredictable experimentation with fluctuating short-term political coalitions that do not lend themselves to any systematic explanations. In the longer run, however, those experiments will prevail that are consistent with long-term structural parameters of resource distributions and actors' capabilities, beliefs, and aspirations. In that spirit, Ekiert (Chapter 3 in this volume) asserts that broadly perceived legacies of the past offer the most consistent explanations of successful postcommunist trajectories. The short-term problem solving of actors may generate a great deal of noise that cannot be explained or patterns of action that are not worth explaining if the explanatory objective is more durable long-run steady states of postcommunist political rule and economic governance.

Second, one can argue that *short-term factors serve as proximate links in the chain of causation.* In this view, deeper structural and shallower, agency-related explanations are mutually complementary in some kind of funnel of explanation. Shallow explanations rely on proximate causal mechanisms that become useful only if complemented by causally deeper analyses of regime diversity. Conversely, the search for depth must not ignore the provision of causal mechanisms that make plausible how structural, institutional, and cultural parameters translate into strategic, calculated action, which, in turn, creates new macrolevel outcomes. Intermediary "links" in the chain between deeper and shallower causes of current outcomes must be specified. In this sense, Grzymała-Busse's (2002 and Chapter 5 in this volume) discussion of the transformative capacities of communist parties in the 1970s and 1980s provides an intermediate causal mechanism to link precommunist and postcommunist political rule.

To adapt and modify a statement from the German philosopher Kant, shallow explanations without depth are empty, deep explanations without mechanisms are blind. The complementarity of "deep" and "shallow" explanations echoes the call for "layered" structural, institutional, and interactional levels of analysis proposed by Ekiert and Hanson in the introduction to this volume. Let me nevertheless throw some cold water on this happy "peace formula" in the battle between structuralist and process-oriented analysts of regime change. Where deeper structural causes (such as diversity of communist regimes, predicated on variance among precommunist interwar regimes) are highly collinear with proximate causes (such as the outcome of founding elections, or the power of presidencies in postcommunist constitutions) of the ultimate outcomes (regime form, economic reform effort), then at least two different conceptualizations of the relationship between deeper and shallower causes are empirically equally plausible. Either the deeper causes x "work through" the shallower cause y to bring about the final outcome z ($x \rightarrow y \rightarrow z$); or the causes x bring about both what appears as the shallower cause y as well as the outcome z ($x \rightarrow y; x \rightarrow z$). Because of collinearity, we cannot statistically distinguish between these alternatives.

Our only way to conduct at least a plausibility check of which alternative is more reasonable is to conduct case-oriented process tracing of outliers that conform either to the structural or to the process-oriented explanation or to neither of them. We are interested in two temporal perspectives when dealing with outliers. Retrospectively, what causes outliers not to conform to the expected patterns on the deeper structural or the shallower process-oriented variables? Prospectively, do we detect changes that make outliers gravitate toward the expected patterns on one or both of them? In other words, is outlier status a transitional nonequilibrium state or permanently "locked into" a new institutional and political-economic compact?

Third, one can argue that *short-term factors serve as the ultimate causes of outcomes*. Consider outlier outcomes that conform to shallower, process-oriented explanations but not to deeper structural explanations. Particularly if this configuration persists over time and there is no "equilibrium" process that makes outcomes gravitate toward the result expected based on structural predictions, then short-term causal arguments are key to bringing about the ultimate result of what appear to be outliers in the structural perspective. In the face of otherwise high collinearity between deeper and shallower causes of some ultimate outcome, such outlier constellations generate at least some plausibility for the proposition that deeper causes affect outcomes only by "working through" shallower causes.

Now consider other constellations and processes. An outcome initially conforms to predictions based on shallow causation, but over time changes such that it is in line with predictions based on structural causation as well. Or initially an outcome is at variance with both structural and process-based forces, but over time gravitates to what underlying structure would predict. In those instances, such outliers suggest that the collinearity between x and y vis-à-vis z really involves a long-run equilibrium with a structural determination of both y and z through x.

Fourth, one can argue that *some cases are pure outliers; neither short-run nor long-run factors have explanatory power*. Some outliers may always be outliers, regardless of whatever systematic shallow or deep causal analysis we may explore. There may, however, be structural reasons for randomness. As Przeworski and Limongi (1997) point out, in middle-income countries political regimes can be quite volatile, tipped by minor disturbances. Structural background conditions tend to lock them in less firmly than those that characterize very poor or very affluent polities.

To move beyond this rather abstract discussion, let us examine a few outliers and their dynamics in studies by Fish (1998b) and papers I recently (co)authored (Kitschelt and Malesky, 2000; Kitschelt, 2001). Fish (1998a: 242) argues that economic reform has a "possible causal effect" on democracy, while in another piece he advances the proposition that the victory of democratic forces in initial elections furthers economic reform (Fish, 1998b). In that piece there are no substantial outliers, so it is impossible to conduct an analysis of divergent cases.[19] Taking the two pieces together shows how ambiguous causal attributions are when the temporal priority of the forces to which causality is attributed is so tenuous. This critique, however, underlines only what I have already said about shallow explanations and is not my main point here. I rather focus on outliers in the analysis of economic reform as predictor of democratization.

When Fish employs economic reform as predictor of the democratic quality of postcommunist regimes, major outliers are Albania, Croatia, Kyrgyzstan, and Slovakia, all of which should have exhibited more political democracy in 1996, if economic reform was the critical driving force. Conversely, Slovenia displayed too little reform, given its level of democracy (Fish, 1998a: tables and figures on pp. 217, 225, and 227). Because structural theories usually also predict a high correlation of political democratization and market liberalization, they cannot account for these anomalies. We can, however, examine the adjustment process outlier countries have undertaken over time.

In Kyrgyzstan and Albania, since 1996 the outlier status has become more pronounced. These developments are consistent with a structural theory that identifies citizens' skills and resources as unconducive to democratic stabilization. Here, democratic civil and political rights have eroded, while economic reform has made only small advances.[20] In a third country, Slovenia, increased economic reform caught up with the level of democratization already reached by the mid-1990s. In all three processes, either the causal relationship is the inverse of what Fish claims (democracy influences economic reform), or there are underlying structural factors that, over time, generate a compelling equilibrium between politics and economics. While these cases tend to be inconsistent with Fish's theoretical logic, two others

[19] The only countries marginally approaching outlier status are Albania (too little initial democratization for its level of economic reform) and Armenia (a great deal of democracy, but little reform). In both cases, there may be measurement problems that create the anomalies. Compared with other measures of economic reform effort in Albania (cf. Kitschelt and Malesky, 2000: table A-1), Fish's measure is on the high side. In Armenia, there may have been less initial decoupling from communist elites in the first election than Fish's score implies.

[20] For change rates of economic reform between 1994 and 1999, see Kitschelt and Malesky (2000: table 3).

confirm his argument through process analysis. The outliers Croatia and Slovakia have recently become more democratic, in line with high levels of economic reform achieved earlier.[21] Nevertheless, only a minority of outliers show dynamic processes consistent with Fish's causal-temporal argument.

Now let us see how dynamic processes of economic reform reflect on proximate and structural causes (Kitschelt and Malesky, 2000). Regardless of whether one selects geography (proximity to the West), religion, mode of communist rule, and interwar regimes, or even closely related proximate correlates (pervasiveness of corruption, displacement of communists in the first election), measures of structural divergence among postcommunist countries are quite strongly related to institutional arrangements (powers of the presidency) in these countries in 1994 and very closely related to the same measure in 1999.[22] Both, in turn, are excellent predictors of postcommunist economic reform effort, regardless of the point in time one chooses, at least for the entire universe of postcommunist countries (Kitschelt and Malesky, 2000: table 2). Can we infer from these correlations among structural and institutional predictors of reform that structural conditions "work through" proximate executive-legislative arrangements to achieve the economic policy outputs? In other words, is high presidential power the proximate cause of weak economic reform effort?

If structural and proximate explanations of economic reform were complementary, we should observe that outliers with structural features conducive to economic reform (closeness to the West, Western Christianity, bureaucratic-authoritarian or national-accommodationist communist regime, low levels of corruption), but comparatively strong presidential powers, should display *weak* economic reform effort. Conversely, we should observe polities with inauspicious structural background conditions and parliamentary government, but *strong* economic reform effort.

Only one of the six postcommunist outlier countries that do not contribute to the strong correlation between structural conduciveness and institutional arrangements, however, has economic reform efforts that correspond to a pattern suggesting that institutions are the proximate cause of economic reform efforts. Three countries with good structural conditions had comparatively strong presidential powers from 1990 on, but they nevertheless engaged in vigorous economic reform efforts from the very start. Here, clearly, structure trumps institutions (Croatia, Lithuania, Poland). Not by chance, politicians in at least two of these reform-oriented countries have

[21] Of course, Kopstein and Reilly's argument (Chapter 4 in this volume) that leaders and citizens adjust both political structures and economic reform strategies to the expectation of (West) European integration provides a possible alternative mechanism for the equilibration between political and economic reform. Furthermore, the change in Croatia's and Slovakia's levels of democratization is broadly consistent with a structuralist argument as well.

[22] Based on the operational measures of these concepts in Kitschelt and Malesky (2000), these correlations are +.66 in 1994 and +.79 in 1999 (cf. p. 23 and tables 1B and A-1).

attempted to weaken presidential powers based on the legislative experience of the first decade.

Two further countries had weak presidencies up to 1994 and underlying structures not conducive to economic reform (Belarus, Ukraine). Contrary to the institutional hypothesis, but in conformity with the structural hypothesis, these configurations yielded weak economic reform efforts. In both countries, the introduction of stronger presidencies since 1994 has not changed that outcome. Only in the sixth case, Russia, do changing rates of economic reform between 1994 and 1999 appear to reflect institutional efficacy. Until 1993, with a formally weak presidency that was enhanced by presidential emergency powers granted after the failed 1991 coup, Russia engaged in rather intensive economic reform efforts, given its comparatively unfavorable structural circumstances. Once Russia empowered the presidency through the 1993 constitution, however, its economic reform effort languished throughout the subsequent seven years. Empirical support by only one of six cases is not reassuring for the institutional thesis that weak presidencies further economic reform. Reviewing eighteen cases with collinearity between structural conditions and institutional arrangements and six outliers with separable effects of these variables on economic reform provides preciously little evidence that economic reforms have to "work through" institutional arrangements as the proximate cause.

The examples taken from Fish's and my own work are meant to cast doubt on epistemological prescriptions that demand very tight spatiotemporal proximity of causes and consequences. Of course, my defense of "structuralism" in these instances does not suggest that political actors and strategic action play no role. However, what affects deliberate, calculated political action works often through longer chains of causal determination than short-term mechanisms. Nevertheless, my analysis does not suggest a historical determinism that puts everything into structural conditions. There are several limitations to structural arguments, even when accompanied by a micrologic of action that makes strategic choices intelligible. First of all, there is the element of uncertainty in the crisis of a political regime. Depending on the personalities who are at the right place at the right time, whole polities may take a "leap into the dark" for which no systematic theory, whether building on structural or proximate causes, can account. For example, at least one country in the postcommunist universe is recalcitrant to whatever structural and institutional theories predict about economic reform efforts – Kyrgyzstan. Despite inauspicious conditions and a strong presidentialist constitution, Kyrgyzstan has engaged in quite vigorous reform efforts.

Second, actors in new political regimes undergo rapid learning processes, triggered by the success or failure of initially chosen strategies. Policy feedbacks become the cause of new initiatives (Pierson, 1993). Learning may yield results not predicted based on structural background conditions or proximate factors. An important mechanism in postcommunist democracies here is retrospective economic voting in the face of manifest failure of economic policy strategies. Thus, the failed social protectionist economic policies of the Bulgarian, Moldovan, and Romanian communist successor parties in the mid-1990s eventually led to the electoral victory of market-liberalizing parties promoting more-vigorous reform. In other instances, where voters interpreted unsuccessful efforts to bring about economic reform as the cause of their socioeconomic misery, victorious challengers, elected on social protectionist tickets, then changed their tune and actually promoted reform (e.g., in the Ukraine). Even without electoral politics, under authoritarianism rulers may learn from economic policy failure and try new strategies (cf. Ames, 1987). In this vein, authoritarian leaders in Kazakhstan and Kyrgyzstan have engaged in rather vigorous reform efforts in the 1990s that cannot be covered by other explanations.

Finally, external "shocks" that no systematic domestic theory of economic reform effort incorporates affect the trajectory of postcommunist countries. Thus, the general trend toward market liberalism in the global system has subjected all postcommunist countries to pressures to accommodate, though at different speeds. Moreover, economic reform efforts receive a boost from the end of civil and international wars. The sharp leaps in economic reform effort in Armenia, Georgia, Moldova, and Tajikistan since 1994 certainly suggest a linkage between pacification of a country and economic reform.

The relevance of innovative learning and policy feedback, conjunctural uncertainty, and exogenous shocks shows the limits of systematic, causally oriented social science more generally. It underlines the impossibility of crisp point predictions for individual cases, regardless of whether structural conditions or precipitating factors are the analytical focus. With regard to the cohort of postcommunist countries, this indeterminacy is structurally enhanced by the very fact that they are middle-income countries that, as a cohort, display very high levels of regime volatility (Przeworski and Limongi, 1997).

Modes of Causal Explanation and Social Science Paradigms

In this final section, let me reject a stereotypical rendering of principles of theory construction and explanation often encountered in epistemological and metatheoretical debates in comparative politics. According to this stereotype, the particular model of social actor and choice, the explanatory depth of the theory, and the reliance on causal mechanisms are necessarily linked to each other. Those who rely on an instrumental rational choice conception of human action, centering on actors' pursuit of "interests" in fungible private goods (wealth and power), also emphasize proximate causal mechanisms and rely on "shallow" explanations according to the strictures of Ockham's razor. Conversely, supporters of "deep" explanations allegedly emphasize culture and discourse and therefore rely on a less instrumental conception of human action concerned with collective identities and idealistic preferences (solidarity, salvation, beauty). They are said to shun the elaboration of causal mechanisms.

A closer examination of the substantive comparative politics literature, however, reveals no a priori association between conceptions of human action, causal depth, and the reliance on causal mechanisms. The elective affinities constructed between rational-interest-driven, shallow, but mechanism-endowed explanations, on the one hand, and cultural, normative, and deep explanations without mechanisms, on the other, are misleading. Some of the shallowest accounts of social and political action are cultural, particularly in the currently popular stream of studies about discourse formation and framing. They offer mechanisms without causal depth.[23] I see a similar danger in much of what is now advertised as a "historical institutionalist" explanation of political processes. Such undertakings often do not move beyond the thick description of historical processes.[24] Conversely, as Thelen (1999) correctly points out, many explanatory accounts that rely on rational actor calculations are averse neither to spatiotemporally extended chains without or with "long distance" causal mechanisms nor to cultural analysis. Long causal chains, for example, play a role in Douglass North's (1981) rational choice analysis of why England dominated the early stages of the Industrial Revolution, while other European powers, such as Spain or France, fell behind. Rogowski's (1989) influential study of trade-related political cleavage patterns lacks microfoundations (cf. Alt et al., 1996). More recently, a whole host of rational choice theorists has realized the importance of actors' cognitive frameworks and cultural orientations in accounting for their strategic choices in light of instrumental self-interest (cf. Denzau and North, 1994; Greif, 1994; Bates, Figueiredo, and Weingast, 1998).

In this sense, the benchmark that good explanations should involve causal mechanisms, but also causal depth, rules out neither rational choice nor cultural (cognitive, normative) mechanisms. These ontological requisites of causal analysis do not prejudice the nature of the substantive theories that

[23] An example is discursive frame analysis in studies of social movements. See Snow et al. (1986) and the subsequent sizable literature derived from this paradigm.

[24] Metatheoretical works on the new historical institutionalism reveal and often even recognize this danger. See Immergut (1998), Somers (1998), and Thelen (1999). Inasmuch as historical institutionalism focuses on configurative, conjunctural interactions of causal chains and their unique temporal sequencing, it postulates an unpredictability of collective outcomes. It thus concentrates on what cannot be causally explained either in terms of actors' preexisting cognitive and cultural frames or strategies resulting from instrumental interests constrained by scarce resources, institutions, and rival players. The danger is that this institutionalism simply gives up on explanation. For good reason, Immergut (1998: 27) worries that historical institutionalist accounts lack falsifiability and therefore cannot promote alternative theories to those inspired by principles of structuralist or rational choice institutionalism. Immergut notices that, as a consequence, "in eschewing systematization, the historical institutionalists undercut the cumulative impact of their work."

account for empirical social outcomes. The ontological criteria I support also do not necessarily imply an affinity to what is now called "historical" (neo)-institutionalism (cf. Thelen and Steinmo, 1992). The latter's distinctive claim is that institutions shape actors' preferences (March and Olsen, 1989; but see Thelen, 1999) and that historical processes have contingent outcomes (Immergut, 1998). With regard to preference formation, I have not found a single avowedly historical institutionalist account that would explain actors' preferences rather than merely their strategies, constrained by institutions and cognitive frameworks. Concerning the historical contingency of social phenomena, every comparativist recognizes the stochastic nature and complexity of social processes. But focusing on the random component of such processes gives up the quest for causal explanations that imply some reliance on causal mechanisms pertaining to a multitude of cases. Only general causal propositions, applying to an indefinite number of cases, are empirically testable. A historical institutionalism that focuses on idiosyncratic individual events and unrepeatable processes is empirically irrefutable.

Finally, the recognition that structuralist and actor-oriented, voluntarist approaches, those with long and short causal chains, are often mutually complementary should not lead to the search for some grand "synthesis." What is advertised as such is usually not much more than a taxonomic addition of the different frameworks (e.g., Snyder and Mahoney, 1999). For substantive theory building and empirical analysis, it is in fact more fruitful not to emphasize synergisms but to take each mode of explanation and theory building in its purity and push it as far as possible. Hence I agree with Lichbach's (1998: 401) conclusion, derived from an analytical reconstruction of rival collective action theories, that "we need creative confrontations, which should include well-defined combinations rather than grand syntheses, of rationalist and structuralist approaches to contentious politics."

Conclusion

So what "counts" as a good cause in explanations of postcommunist political regime diversity? I have suggested that to answer this question is to embark on an ontological and transscientific enterprise more so than a narrowly methodological and empirical one. Different scientific communities may reasonably disagree on the appropriate answer to the challenge of causality. A treatise that tries to separate good from bad causal analysis involves as much persuasion about what should be important in social scientific analysis as straightforward logical inference from patterns of empirical evidence.

This chapter has argued for a deep version of causal analysis, yet one that does not lose sight of social mechanisms. The latter show how human beings with deliberative faculties and capacities to choose objectives can act on constraints and opportunities. It is human action that brings about collective outcomes, even though broader socioeconomic, institutional, and cognitive parameters influence the choice set from which individuals and groups select their courses of action. This chapter tries to steer a middle course between an uncompromising structuralism that has a penchant toward excessively deep analysis without human action, on the one hand, and purely conjunctural theories that favor only the shallowest, most proximate of intertemporal social mechanisms, on the other.

In addition to the qualified preference for deep causal analysis, I have repeatedly warned that not everything in social processes is causally explicable and therefore predictable through good social science. This limitation applies certainly to individual events, even if they are macropolitical in nature and consequence, such as the collapse of communism in 1989–90. Complexity, reflexivity, and inherent uncertainty in social life render it impossible to ever construct exhaustive explanations of macropolitical processes (cf. Lichbach, 1997: 278, 288–89). An explanatory account usually provides neither necessary nor sufficient causes for what we intend to explain. This indeterminacy of social science models makes it practically impossible ever to achieve the equivalence of explanation and prediction. Knowing what explains one set of events does not necessarily help to predict another set of events with a high level of confidence. Even though path dependence is an important feature of political regime change, it never exhausts the empirical richness of history. To tell the story of how communism collapsed in 1989–90 and of the trial-and-error processes that led to the emergence of new political and economic systems to replace them therefore remains a task of historical event analysis no social scientist could ever exhaustively replace with causal models of regime decay, breakdown, and replacement.

References

Ágh, Attila. 1998. *The Politics of Central Europe*. London: Sage.

Alt, James E., Jeffrey Frieden, Michael J. Gilligan, Dani Rodrik, and Ronald Rogowski. 1996. The Political Economy of International Trade: Enduring Puzzles and an Agenda for Inquiry. *Comparative Political Studies* 29(6): 689–717.

Ames, Barry. 1987. *Political Survival*. Berkeley: University of California Press.

Bates, Robert H., Rui J. P. de Figueiredo Jr., and Barry R. Weingast. 1998. The Politics of Interpretation: Rationality, Culture, and Transition. *Politics and Society* 26(4): 603–42.

Bates, Robert H., Avner Greif, Margaret Levi, Jean-Laurent Rosenthal, and Barry R. Weingast. 1998. *Analytical Narratives*. Princeton: Princeton University Press.

Bollen, Kenneth. 1979. Political Democracy and the Timing of Development. *American Sociological Review* 44(5): 572–87.

Boudon, Raymond. 1998. Social Mechanisms without Black Boxes. In Peter Hedström and Richard Swedberg, eds., *Social Mechanisms: An Analytical Approach to Social Theory*, pp. 172–203. Cambridge: Cambridge University Press.

Burkhart, Ross E., and Michael Lewis-Beck. 1994. Comparative Democracy: The Economic Development Thesis. *American Political Science Review* 88(4): 903–10.

Crawford, Keith. 1996. *East Central European Politics Today*. Manchester: Manchester University Press.
Denzau, Arthur, and Douglass C. North. 1994. Shared Mental Models: Ideologies and Institutions. *Kyklos* 47(1): 3–31.
Elster, Jon. 1998. A Plea for Mechanisms. In Peter Hedström and Richard Swedberg, eds., *Social Mechanisms: An Analytical Approach to Social Theory*, pp. 45–73. Cambridge: Cambridge University Press.
European Bank of Recovery and Development (EBRD). 1998. *Transition Report, 1997*. London: EBRD.
Fish, M. Steven. 1998a. Democratization's Requisites: The Postcommunist Experience. *Post-Soviet Affairs* 14(3): 212–47.
1998b. The Determinants of Economic Reform in the Post-Communist World. *East European Politics and Societies* 12(1): 31–78.
2001. The Dynamics of Democratic Erosion. In Richard D. Anderson Jr., M. Steven Fish, Stephen E. Hanson, and Philip G. Roeder, *Postcommunism and the Theory of Democracy*, pp. 54–95. Princeton: Princeton University Press.
Geddes, Barbara. 1999. What Do We Know about Democratization after Twenty Years? *Annual Review of Political Science* 2: 115–44.
Gerring, John. 1999. What Is a Good Cause? Causation in Social Science Reconsidered. Paper presented at the annual meeting of the American Political Science Association, Atlanta.
2001. *Social Science Methodology: A Criterial Framework*. Cambridge: Cambridge University Press.
Goldstone, Jack A. 1998. Initial Conditions, General Laws, Path Dependence and Explanation in Historical Sociology. *American Journal of Sociology* 104(3): 829–45.
Greif, Avner. 1994. Cultural Beliefs and the Organization of Society: A Historical and Theoretical Reflection on Collectivist and Individualist Societies. *Journal of Political Economy* 102(3): 912–50.
Grzymała-Busse, Anna M. 2002. *Redeeming the Communist Past: The Regeneration of Communist Parties in East Central Europe*. Cambridge: Cambridge University Press.
Hedström, Peter, and Richard Swedberg. 1998. Social Mechanisms: An Introductory Essay. In Peter Hedström and Richard Swedberg, eds., *Social Mechanisms: An Analytical Approach to Social Theory*, pp. 1–31. Cambridge: Cambridge University Press.
Hellman, Joel. 1996. Constitutional and Economic Reform in Postcommunist Transition. *East European Constitutional Review* 5(1): 46–57.
1998. Winners Take All: The Politics of Partial Reform in Postcommunist Transitions. *World Politics* 50(2): 203–34.
Higley, John, and Richard Gunther, eds. 1992. *Elites and Democratic Consolidation in Latin America and Southern Europe*. Cambridge: Cambridge University Press.
Higley, John, Jan Pakulski, and Włodzimierz Wesołowski. 1998. Introduction: Elite Change and Democratic Regimes in Eastern Europe. In John Higley, Jan Pakulski, and Włodzimierz Wesołowski, eds., *Postcommunist Elites and Democracy in Eastern Europe*, pp. 1–3. London: Macmillan.
Huntington, Samuel P. 1991. *The Third Wave*. Norman: University of Oklahoma Press.

Immergut, Ellen M. 1998. The Theoretical Core of the New Institutionalism. *Politics and Society* 26(1): 5–24.

Jones Luong, Pauline. 2001. (Re-)Forging Clientelistic Links after the Fall: The Persistence of Regionalism and Prospects for Democracy in Former Soviet Central Asia. Paper presented at the Workshop on Citizen-Politician Linkages in Democratic Politics, Duke University, March 30–April 1.

Kalyvas, Stathis N. 1999. The Decay and Breakdown of Communist One-Party Systems. *Annual Review of Political Science* 2: 323–43.

Kappeler, Andreas. 1993. *Russland als Vielvölkerreich: Enststehung, Geschichte, Zerfall.* Munich: Beck.

King, Gary, Robert O. Keohane, and Sidney Verba. 1994. *Designing Social Inquiry: Scientific Inference in Qualitative Research.* Princeton: Princeton University Press.

Kiser, Edgar, and Michael Hechter. 1991. The Role of General Theory in Comparative-Historical Sociology. *American Journal of Sociology* 97(1): 1–30.

1998. The Debate on Historical Sociology: Rational Choice Theory and Its Critics. *American Journal of Sociology* 104(3): 786–816.

Kitschelt, Herbert. 1999. Accounting for Outcomes of Post-Communist Regime Change: Causal Depth or Shallowness in Rival Explanations? Paper presented at the annual meeting of the American Political Science Association, Atlanta.

2001. Post-Communist Economic Reform: Causal Mechanisms and Concomitant Properties. Paper presented at the annual meeting of the American Political Science Association, San Francisco, August 29–September 2.

Kitschelt, Herbert, and Edmund Malesky. 2000. Constitutional Design and Postcommunist Economic Reform. Paper presented at the Midwest Political Science Conference, Chicago.

Kitschelt, Herbert, Zdenka Mansfeldova, Radosław Markowski, and Gábor Tóka. 1999. *Post-Communist Party Systems: Competition, Representation, and Inter-Party Cooperation.* Cambridge: Cambridge University Press.

Kitschelt, Herbert, and Regina Smyth. 2002. Programmatic Party Cohesion in Emerging Post-Communist Democracies: Russia in Comparative Context. *Comparative Political Studies* 35(10): 1228–56.

Laitin, David. 1998. *Identity in Formation: The Russian-Speaking Populations in the Near Abroad.* Ithaca: Cornell University Press.

Levi, Margaret. 1996. Social and Unsocial Capital: A Review Essay of Robert Putnam's *Making Democracy Work. Politics and Society* 24(1): 45–55.

Lichbach, Mark. 1997. Reformulating Explanatory Standards and Advancing Theory in Comparative Politics. In Mark Irving Lichbach and Alan S. Zuckerman, eds., *Comparative Politics: Rationality, Culture, and Structure*, pp. 277–310. Cambridge: Cambridge University Press.

1998. Contending Theories of Contentious Politics and the Structure-Action Problem of Social Order. *Annual Review of Political Science* 1: 401–28.

March, James Gardner, and Johan P. Olsen. 1989. *Rediscovering Institutions.* New York: Free Press.

Merton, Robert K. 1957. *Social Theory and Social Structure.* Glencoe, Ill.: Free Press.

Miller, Richard. 1987. *Fact and Method.* Princeton: Princeton University Press.

North, Douglass C. 1981. *Structure and Change in Economic History.* New York: Norton.

O'Donnell, Guillermo, and Philippe C. Schmitter, eds. 1986. *Transitions from Authoritarian Rule: Tentative Conclusions about Uncertain Democracies*. Baltimore: Johns Hopkins University Press.

Offe, Claus. 1994. *Der Tunnel am Ende des Lichts*. Frankfurt am Main: Campus Verlag.

Pierson, Paul. 1993. When Effect Becomes Cause: Policy Feedback and Political Change. *World Politics* 45(4): 595–628.

Przeworski, Adam. 1991. *Democracy and the Market*. Cambridge: Cambridge University Press.

Przeworski, Adam, Michael Alvarez, Jose A. Cheibub, and Fernando Limongi. 1996. What Makes Democracies Endure? *Journal of Democracy* 7(1): 39–55.

2000. *Democracy and Development: Political Institutions and Well-Being in the World, 1950–2000*. Cambridge: Cambridge University Press.

Przeworski, Adam, and Fernando Limongi. 1997. Modernization: Theory and Facts. *World Politics* 49(2): 155–83.

Putnam, Robert, with Robert Leonardi and Raffaella Y. Nanetti. 1993. *Making Democracy Work: Civic Traditions in Modern Italy*. Princeton: Princeton University Press.

Roeder, Philip G. 1994. Varieties of Post-Soviet Authoritarian Regimes. *Post-Soviet Affairs* 10(1): 61–101.

1997. Why Is Russia More Democratic Than Most of Its Neighbors? Paper presented at the annual meeting of the American Political Science Association, Washington, D.C., August 28–31.

2001. The Rejection of Authoritarianism. In Richard D. Anderson Jr., M. Steven Fish, Stephen E. Hanson, and Philip G. Roeder, *Postcommunism and the Theory of Democracy*, pp. 11–53. Princeton: Princeton University Press.

Rogowski, Ronald. 1989. *Commerce and Coalitions*. Princeton: Princeton University Press.

Róna-Tas, Ákos, and József Böröcz. 2000. Bulgaria, the Czech Republic, Hungary, and Poland: Presocialist and Socialist Legacies among Business Elites. In John Higley and György Lengyel, eds., *Elites after State Socialism*, pp. 209–28. Latham, Md.: Rowman and Littlefield.

Sabetti, Filippo. 1996. Path Dependency and Civic Culture: Some Lessons from Italy about Interpreting Social Experiments. *Politics and Society* 24(1): 19–44.

Salmon, Wesley C. 1989. Four Decades of Scientific Explanation. In Philip Kitcher and Wesley C. Salmon, eds., *Scientific Explanation: Minnesota Studies in the Philosophy of Science*, pp. 3–219. Minneapolis: University of Minnesota Press.

Schöpflin, George. 1993. *Politics in Eastern Europe*. Oxford: Blackwell.

Snow, David A., E. Burke Rochford, Steven K. Warden, and Robert D. Benford. 1986. Frame Alignment Processes, Micromobilization, and Movement Participation. *American Sociological Review* 51: 464–81.

Snyder, Richard, and James Mahoney. 1999. The Missing Variable: Institutions and the Study of Regime Change. *Comparative Politics* 32(1): 103–20.

Somers, Margaret. 1998. "We're No Angels": Realism, Rational Choice and Relationality in Social Science. *American Journal of Sociology* 104(3): 722–84.

Stinchcombe, Arthur. 1987. *Constructing Social Theory*. 1968. Reprint, Chicago: University of Chicago Press.

Thelen, Kathleen. 1999. Historical Institutionalism in Comparative Politics. *Annual Review of Political Science* 2: 369–404.

Thelen, Kathleen, and Sven Steinmo. 1992. Historical Institutionalism in Comparative Politics. In Sven Steinmo, Kathleen Thelen, and Frank Longstreth, eds., *Structuring Politics: Historical Institutionalism in Comparative Analysis*, pp. 1–32. Cambridge: Cambridge University Press.

Weber, Max. 1978. *Economy and Society*. 1968. Reprint, Berkeley: University of California Press.

1988. *Gesammelte Aufsätze zur Wissenschaftslehre*. 7th ed. Tübingen: Mohr.

PART II

POSTCOMMUNIST EUROPE

Continuity and Change in Regional Patterns

3

Patterns of Postcommunist Transformation in Central and Eastern Europe

Grzegorz Ekiert

Understanding Postcommunist Transformations

Conceptualizing and explaining the rapid and unexpected collapse of state-socialist regimes in Central and Eastern Europe between 1989 and 1991 as well as the ensuing patterns of democratization and transition to a market economy pose a challenge for students of comparative politics. These momentous events not only provide unprecedented research opportunities but also force us to reexamine the nature of social science inquiry, our theoretical assumptions, and our methodologies. The contention of this chapter is that legacies of the communist period had the most important impact on specific paths of reform and types of transformations unfolding across the region during the first decade of postcommunism. Consequently, I argue that a historical institutionalist approach provides a uniquely useful set of analytical and methodological tools for understanding this "great transformation" and that macrolevel modes of analysis are more effective in accounting for the initial trajectories and outcomes of postcommunist transformations than other competing approaches employed by students of political and economic developments in the region.

The simultaneity of the communist regimes' breakdown, despite varied political and economic conditions in each country, reinforced a notion that these regimes were basically identical one-party states kept in power by the Soviet military presence. This view is obviously incorrect. East European state socialist regimes underwent complex processes of transformation during their four decades in power and developed distinct institutional forms and modes of relations between the state and society. Domestic political developments differed from country to country. Specifically, patterns

I would like to thank István Majoros and Peter Ciganik for research assistance as well as Cecilia Chessa, Anna Grzymała-Busse, Peter Hall, Stephen Hanson, Yoshiko Herrera, Robert Kaufman, Jan Kubik, Andy Markovits, Paul Pierson, Anne Sa'adah, Jacek Wasilewski, and Jan Zielonka for their helpful comments and friendly criticism of the earlier drafts of this chapter.

of political conflict, institutional reforms and breakdowns, and strategies of regime reequilibration left long-lasting legacies. As a result of political crises and economic challenges, fundamental changes and adjustments were introduced not only into policies of these regimes but also into political and economic institutions, altering relations between institutional orders of the party-state and between the state and society. Such developments produced significant institutional and policy dissimilarities (see Ekiert, 1996). Whereas transformations in some countries were crisis-driven, in others they were more evolutionary in nature and highly sensitive to cross-regional diffusion processes. Thus each state socialist regime left behind distinct legacies that should be carefully examined if we are to explain the present rapidly diverging trajectories of political, social, and economic change taking place in the region.[1]

These diverse initial conditions were magnified even further through interaction with the modes of regime dissolution and types of power transfer that occurred at the outset of transitions. Despite the clustering of regime breakdowns in 1989, there were important differences in the way particular countries exited state socialism and entered the transition process. For example, the "pacted" transitions that took place in Poland and Hungary, the displacement of the communist regime through "popular upsurge" that occurred in Czechoslovakia and East Germany, or the transformation from above that took place in Bulgaria produced different transitional institutions and patterns of political conflicts. These distinctive modes of power transfer were in part engendered by specific conditions in each country and interacted with both domestic communist legacies and broader regional developments. The specific legacies of the communist period and modes of power transfer shaped subsequent political developments and the capacity of various political actors in each country (see, e.g., Ekiert, 1990; Kamiński, 1991; Stark and Bruszt, 1998: esp. chap. 1). In addition, the introduction of political competition and results of initial democratic elections varied across the region. In many countries former communists were able to retain political power; in others newly organized noncommunist oppositions emerged victorious. In sum, the period of regime breakdown was a complex and highly contingent process forged together by a multitude of causes, events, and interaction effects. It is possible, nevertheless, to identify several distinctive features of this process that varied across the region and generated specific sets of opportunities and constraints for political actors in particular countries.

A decade after the collapse of communist rule, distinctive regions or groups of countries with contrasting policies and transformation outcomes have emerged within the former Soviet bloc. In Valerie Bunce's words (1999: 759), "the dominant pattern of postsocialism has been one of variation, not

[1] For an exemplary effort to correlate developments under state socialism and their constraining impact on the current transformation process, see, for example, Kornai (1996) and chapters in this volume.

uniformity." In fact, postcommunist transformations have produced striking differences among the countries in all major dimensions: the extent of structural reform, economic performance, levels of inequality, the nature of party systems and civil societies, and quality of democracy. This should not come as a big surprise. Postcommunist regimes have been confronted with specific challenges engendered by their dissimilar initial conditions and have pursued different strategies of political and economic reforms. Thus, David Stark (1992: 18) is correct when he argues that we should regard Eastern Europe "as undergoing a plurality of transitions in a dual sense: across the region, we are seeing a multiplicity of distinctive strategies; within any given country, we find not one transition but many occurring in different domains – political, economic, and social – and the temporality of these processes are often asynchronous and their articulation seldom harmonious."

Although it may be tempting to argue that each country represents a unique case and distinct type of transformation, striking subregional similarities have emerged across the postcommunist world.[2] While some subregions have progressed with political and economic reforms in a consistent way, others have stagnated or even slid back. Moreover, these subregional trajectories of transformation present an increasingly constant and stable picture. The gap between the countries that emerged as front-runners of reforms and the laggards has become more apparent with every passing year. In this chapter, I examine the initial outcomes of post-1989 transformations in postcommunist countries outside the former Soviet Union. My goal is to identify the patterns of transformation emerging in the region and to propose some tentative ideas that may help to account for the existing disparities in initial outcomes of these transformations.

In comprehensive, macrolevel systemic change, numerous factors have the potential to shape the course and outcomes of transformations. Different theories can suggest specific sets of such factors and describe particular causal mechanisms that link them to observable outcomes. This multiparadigmatic nature of social science inquiry provides us with alternative and often incompatible sets of explanatory factors and competing causal accounts. As a result, the attributed importance of and causal relations among these factors are highly uncertain, and specific explanatory accounts are highly sensitive to one's initial assumptions and theoretical predilections. More generally, efforts to explain complex macrolevel processes are not well suited for constructing parsimonious models and a larger number of factors and mechanisms can be plausibly employed in comparative explanatory accounts. Finally, as David Cameron (2001: 3) noted, "given the relatively small n of

2 As the EBRD (2001: 3) acknowledged in its report, "There is a wide variation in the level of reforms and performance in the 26 countries.... The EBRD's transition indicators ... and the evidence of macroeconomic performance and structural change do not tell a single, common story but 26 distinct stories." But EBRD research also shows distinct and consistent subregional trends (2000: 26–27).

countries involved, the relatively short period of time that has elapsed in the post-Communist era, and the quite exceptional degree of multicollinearity that exists in the data, we are necessarily limited to the most elementary of statistical methods and the analysis can be no more than suggestive." Consequently, it is often more appropriate to think about the initial outcomes of postcommunist transformations in terms of "lessons" or "elective affinities" than in terms of causes and effects.

In the existing literature on democratization authors usually point to at least four groups of factors that need to be included in any effort to explain patterns of the ongoing transformation: legacies of the past and initial conditions, institutional choices, policies of new governments, and the extent of external support. Although the stark dichotomy of "Leninist legacies" and institutional choices as well as some reductionist approaches focused exclusively on reconstructing a microlevel logic underlying political choices are not very helpful in unraveling the nature of the multifaceted process of postcommunist transitions,[3] we can show with a reasonable degree of certainty that specific sets of factors are more important in particular stages of transformations and can be persuasively linked to specific outcomes. This is best done by employing a version of the "systematic process analysis" advocated by Peter Hall and others (see Hall, 2003; Bennett and George, 2001). I adopt a similar analytical strategy in the analysis that follows.

I intend to argue that broadly perceived legacies of the past offer the most consistent set of explanatory factors that distinguish successful transitions, especially in their initial phase. This statement, however, needs some clarification. Although the concept of legacies is intuitively evident and, in the most general sense, refers to material, institutional, and cultural factors inherited from the past (see Kubik, Chapter 10 in this volume), it is not analytically precise in contemporary social science discourse. In the introductory chapter to this book the claim was made that legacies can be understood in three contrasting ways based on their spatiotemporal context and ontological status. In the present analysis, I am not concerned with the impact of distant legacies operating in long historical periods (structural time). Instead, I focus on the category of legacies that we described as institutional and interactional time. These are the institutional, social, and political legacies of the communist period. My claim is that they account in the most persuasive way for the initial outcomes of postcommunist transformations.

It should be emphasized that these legacies not only consist of the institutional and attitudinal features inherited from communism that are inimical to markets and democracy (Leninist legacies or inhibiting legacies) but also include many transition-facilitating factors produced by specific developments under communist rule (facilitating legacies or legacies of state

[3] See, for example, Crawford and Lijphart (1995). In the same volume, Stephen Hanson (1995) argued that the dichotomy between Leninist legacies and institutional choices was a false one and argued for a more complex and contextual understanding of legacies.

socialism).[4] Broad modernization policies pursued by communist regimes (industrialization, urbanization, mass communication, education, etc.), relatively low levels of social inequality, and efforts to introduce various economic reforms and market mechanisms into centrally planned economies produced conditions that facilitated democratic breakthroughs and subsequent economic and political reforms and made economic structures more amenable to market conditions. Similarly, even inconsistent or interrupted political liberalization efforts under the old regime produced specific social and political cleavages, resources, and networks that made the introduction of democracy easier. For example, legacies of conflict and liberalization efforts account for the presence of pragmatic and divided communist elites and well-defined opposition groups and movements that, in turn, shaped the modes of power transfer, institutional choices, and the outcomes of initial elections.

The presence and strength of facilitating and inhibiting legacies differed across the region. Countries with easily identifiable and stronger facilitating legacies have made more-consistent progress in building democracy and a market economy. It seems, therefore, that the paramount lesson from the initial stages of postcommunist transition is that history matters. Despite the emerging consensus on the critical role of institutional choices, even the best institutions may fail to induce the behavior their designers had in mind (see Stark and Bruszt, 1998: 80–84). Moreover, historical legacies determine the available alternatives and make some institutional choices more likely. Robert Putnam (Putnam et al., 1993: 179) makes a similar claim when he argues that "where you can get to depends on where you're coming from, and some destinations you simply cannot get to from here. Path dependence can produce durable differences in performance between two societies, even when the formal institutions, resources, relative prices, and individual preferences in two are similar."

The varied legacies of the communist period were decisively influenced by modes of power transfer and the outcome of the first competitive elections.[5] In fact, legacies can only be actualized through events; indeed, the interaction

[4] Philip Roeder (1999: 751) has made a similar point about the double nature of communist legacies: "[W]e tend to treat communism as simply the source of a series of problems that must be overcome on the way to a better life. Yet with time we must come to grips with the ways in which communism also transformed these societies for the better." See also Greskovits (1998).

[5] For an argument linking the outcome of initial elections with the extent of economic reforms, see M. Steven Fish (1998). The outcomes of initial elections, however, can and should be explained by the specific legacies of communist rule in particular countries and should be considered only as an important element in the interactive sequence of events (see Kopstein and Reilly [1999] for a critique of Fish). Similarly, Easter (1997) shows that the institutional choice between the presidential and parliamentary system was shaped by the nature of cleavages among communist elites. Such cleavages, of course, had their source in the communist past, and the specific institutional choice is an element of the interactive sequence of events.

of legacies and events should be at the center of macrohistorical analysis. In short, the interaction of legacies of the communist period with modes of power transfers and initial outcomes of democratic competition offers the most convincing account of why some countries have accomplished more and been more successful than others. Consequently, I place less emphasis on the role of new institutional constraints and institutional engineering as prime factors that structure incentives for collective actors and shape mass behavior as well as policy choices of the elites. I agree with Valerie Bunce (1995: 97) that "in postcommunism, political institutions seem to be more a consequence than a cause of political developments."

Assessing the Evidence

Since 1989 the progress of political and economic transformations in post-communist countries has been uneven. In order to illustrate the diverging outcomes of transition across the region, it is useful to compare a number of indicators and rankings produced by various organizations (see Table 3.1). It is obvious that each ranking has its own problems and inconsistencies, and regional experts could argue about specific scores or places assigned to specific countries. Yet the simple exercise of comparing several rankings reveals a relatively consistent picture of disparities among countries of the former Soviet bloc. This first set of indicators shows that four Central European countries – the Czech Republic, Hungary, Poland, and Slovenia – scored significantly higher on all indexes. Economic transformations in these countries are more advanced, as the European Bank for Reconstruction and Development (EBRD) index of transition progress indicates. Their economies are more open and liberalized in comparison with those of other countries. Economic policies are more stable and transparent, the level of corruption is moderate, privatization has had a more consistent record, and a large private sector has emerged. In these countries poverty rates remain relatively low and income inequality is still below the OECD average. Their progress is acknowledged by the international financial community, as illustrated by *Euromoney*'s country risk index. More importantly, the quality of democracy in these four countries (as approximated by the Freedom House index) is high and comparable with established Western democracies. Democratic institutions are not contested, procedures are followed, and political rights and liberties are more extensive and secure than in the rest of the region. Moreover, civil societies are more developed, and the media are free. These countries are also better integrated politically and economically with the West and actively participate in regional and international multilateral organizations. Three of them have been members of the NATO since 1999, and all four have been named in the first group of countries to join the European Union (EU).

The second group comprises the Balkan countries (Bulgaria, Romania, Croatia, and Albania) and Slovakia. In these countries the progress of

TABLE 3.1. *Comparative Measures for Selected Postcommunist Countries*

	Index of Transition Progress[a]	Economic Freedom Index[b]	Country Risk Index[c]	Press Freedom Index[d]	Political Freedom Index[e]	Corruption Perception Index[f]
Czech Republic	36.0	2.20 (27)	60.19 (44)	20 (F)	3 (F)	4.3 (42)
Hungary	38.0	2.55 (42)	61.83 (42)	30 (F)	3 (F)	5.2 (32)
Poland	36.5	2.75 (54)	61.67 (43)	19 (F)	3 (F)	4.1 (43)
Slovenia	34.0	2.90 (63)	71.28 (32)	27 (F)	3 (F)	5.5 (28)
Albania	25.0	3.50 (110)	28.18 (146)	56 (PF)	9 (PF)	2.3 (84)*
Bulgaria	30.5	3.30 (95)	39.75 (84)	30 (F)	5 (F)	3.5 (52)
Croatia	32.5	3.45 (106)	47.8 (70)	63 (NF)	8 (PF)	3.7 (51)
Romania	29.5	3.65 (124)	33.80 (107)	44 (PF)	4 (F)	2.9 (68)
Slovakia	33.5	2.85 (59)	48.44 (66)	30 (F)	3 (F)	3.5 (52)
Belarus	16.0	4.25 (146)	29.11 (140)	80 (NF)	12 (NF)	4.1 (43)
Ukraine	26.0	3.85 (133)	29.96 (134)	39 (PF)	7 (PF)	2.6 (75)

[a] *Source:* European Bank for Reconstruction and Development, *Transition Report, 2000* (London, 2001), 14, 34, and 36 (economic transition indicators are combined with legal transition indicators).

[b] *Source:* Gerald O'Driscoll Jr., Kim R. Holmes and Melanie Kirkpatrick, *2001 Index of Economic Freedom* (Washington, D.C.: Heritage Foundation, 2001). Lowest score 5.0, highest score 1.25. The index is composed of nine factors, including political risk, trade policy, taxation, government intervention in the economy, monetary policy, wage and price control, property rights, capital flows and foreign investment, banking, regulation and black market.

[c] *Source: Euromoney* (March 2000). Highest possible score 100.

[d] *Source:* Leonard R. Sussman, ed., *Press Freedom Survey, 2000* (New York: Freedom House, 2000). Countries scoring 0–30 on 100-point scale are regarded as having a free press; countries scoring 31–60 are partly free.

[e] *Source: Freedom in the World: The Annual Survey of Political Rights and Liberties, 1999–2000* (New York: Freedom House, 2000). Highest possible score 2, lowest possible score 14.

[f] *Source:* Transparency International, 2000 Corruption Perception Index, available: <http://www.transparency.de>. This index is constructed as compilation of a number of surveys conducted in each country and ranges between 10 (highly clean) and 0 (highly corrupt). The score for Albania is from the 1999 index.

political and economic transformations has been slower and less consistent, and the policies of postcommunist governments displayed greater shifts. For example, Bulgaria, Albania, and Romania had recurring recessions and more than one economic stabilization attempt. Market reforms have been less advanced, privatization lagged behind, and their legal and institutional infrastructure has been less developed and transparent. Moreover, corruption has become a widespread phenomenon. The recurrent setbacks in economic transformation, illustrated by macroeconomic indicators, are reflected in higher poverty rates, lower income, greater inequalities, and meager foreign capital inflows. Similarly, politics in these countries has been less predictable, reformist forces weaker, and the potential for a sudden crisis – as developments in Albania in 1998 illustrate – much greater. Political rights and liberties have been less secure, and the media are not fully free. These countries have been characterized by more dramatic and frequent policy shifts, and ruling elites have been less willing or able to maintain consistent reform strategies. Slovakia, which was initially a part of the group of leading reformers, fell behind in the mid-1990s. Economic transformations slowed down, political liberties were seriously curtailed, and the rule of law was frequently subverted by the Mečiar government. The result of the 1999 elections helped Slovakia to regain a reform momentum, although it already missed the opportunities afforded by earlier accession to NATO.

The countries of the former Soviet Union present an extremely complex picture. They range from the Baltic countries, which have emerged as very successful reformers, to new countries in Central Asia plagued by civil wars, ethnic and border conflicts, the revival of authoritarianism, and disastrous economic performance. Russia itself, in its sheer size, turbulent politics, and regional disparities, embodies all the problems and dilemmas of postcommunist transformation. For these reasons I exclude these countries from systematic analysis. The selected data on the former Soviet republics that I present only serve as a contrasting illustration of difficulties experienced by some postcommunist countries and of the possible range of variation in the initial outcomes of transition. For similar reasons, Serbia, Bosnia-Herzegovina, and Macedonia are excluded from systematic analysis.

The second set of indicators comes from public opinion research. The popular evaluation of the new political and economic order differs significantly across the region. Although public opinion data are notoriously difficult to interpret because of their short-term fluctuations and sensitivity to specific events, they, by and large, show that the more advanced economic transformations and more solid establishment of democracy and protection of rights confer more legitimacy for the new political and economic order. This situation is reflected, for example, in public opinion surveys conducted in many postcommunist countries since 1989 by Richard Rose and his associates (see Rose and Haerpfer, 1996; 1998). The data show that in more successful countries the level of approval of the new economic and political system is higher than in less successful countries (see Figures 3.1–4). This is particularly evident for the Czech Republic, Poland, and Slovenia. In these countries there is also less nostalgia for the old regime. Moreover, the popular acceptance of the new political and economic order has a tendency to increase, despite costs and uncertainties of the transition. In less successful countries, on the other hand, a positive view of the communist past has been gaining strength. Interestingly, in Hungary the level of support for the new order is lower than in other leading countries, which in part reflects better living standards at the outset of transition, the less rapid progress of economic reforms, austerity measures introduced in response to severe problems with internal and external imbalances in 1994–95, and the more pragmatic nature of the old regime. In fact, these evaluations reflect among other things the impact of legacies that vary with the nature of communist rule before 1989.

Although the initial political transition is largely completed and at this stage the consolidation of these new democracies is the major task, the transition to a market-based internationally competitive economy is still far from being achieved. The progress of economic transformations and differences among the three groups of countries is well reflected by macroeconomic indicators such as GDP growth, inflation, and unemployment. Patterns of economic performance have diverged significantly from country to country. Such disparities have resulted not so much from differences in transition strategies, which were basically similar across the region, but to a considerable extent from the initial economic conditions and timing of reforms. Nicholas Stern (Hirschler, 2000: 3), the chief economist of the World Bank, acknowledged this: "Indeed, we now realize that initial conditions were very different in the individual transition economies – something I don't think we attached enough significance to initially.... No doubt geography, cultural background, and historical familiarity with the market economy helped Central Europe quickly restore its traditional ties to Western Europe." The role of these initial factors, however, is gradually decreasing in favor of policy choices and strategies. Already in the 1997 report, EBRD analysts (1998: 2) argue that economic transformations in the region entered another phase, the challenges of which "will be determined not only by the conditions in the countries at the start of the transition but also by the events and actions of the first phase. This new phase of transition will be shaped therefore by both the broader history of each country and, more particularly, the very recent history of the first phase."

The data show that countries of East Central Europe resumed economic growth faster, their recovery has been more consistent, and their price stability has been greater (see Table 3.2). A number of factors have contributed to the initial success of economic reforms. Economists have attempted to quantify the impact of contextual factors (natural endowment, proximity to Western Europe), initial conditions (economic situation and structures,

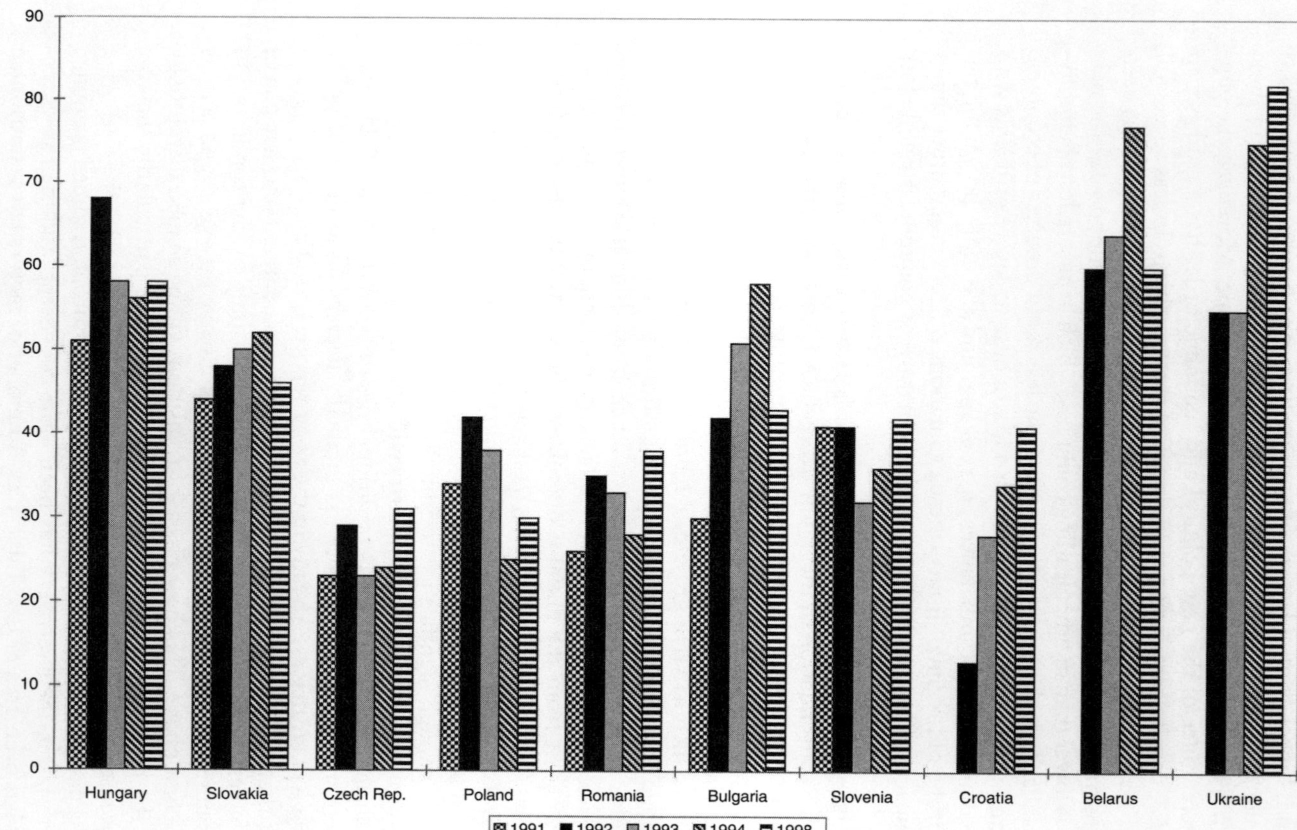

FIGURE 3.1. Approval of the communist regime. Data for Croatia, Belarus, and Ukraine are for 1992, 1993, 1994, and 1998 only.

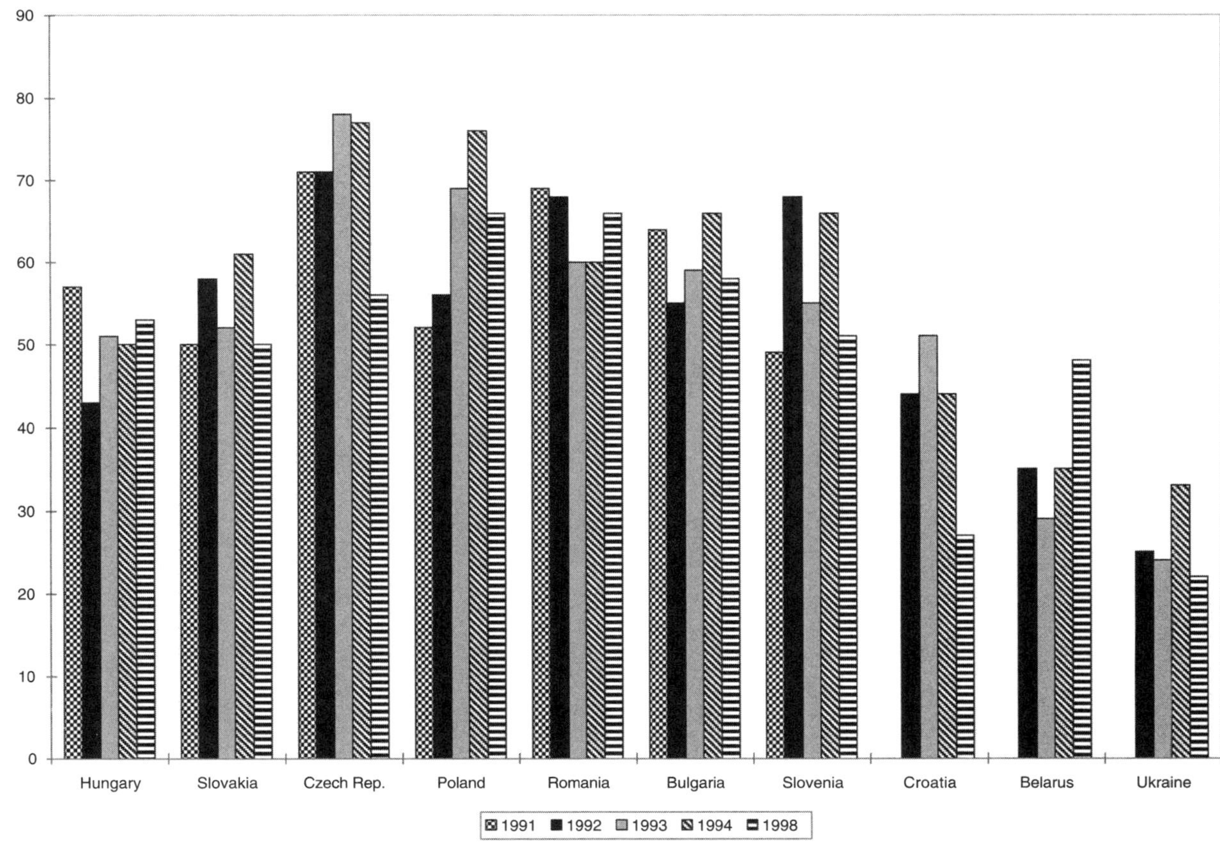

FIGURE 3.2. Approval of the current regime. Data for Croatia, Belarus, and Ukraine, are for 1992, 1993, 1994, and 1998 only.

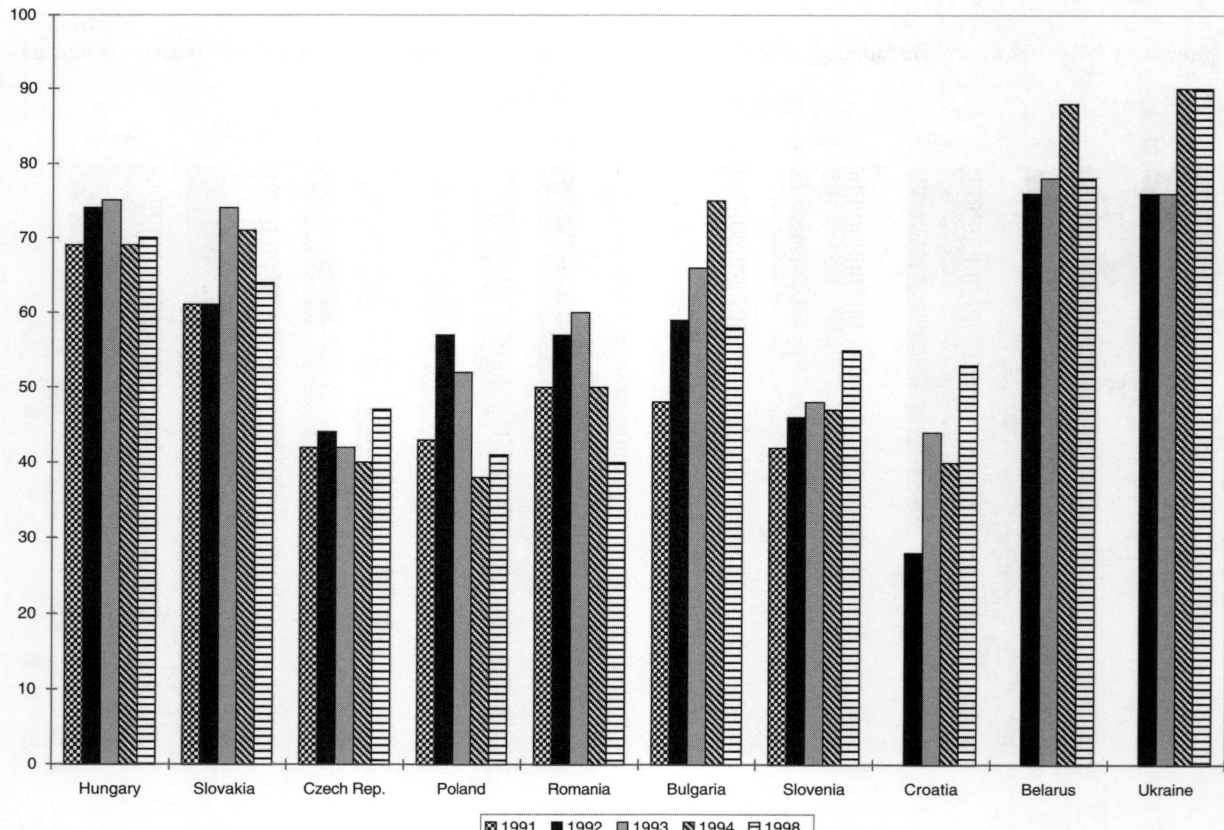

FIGURE 3.3. Approval of the communist economic system. Data for Croatia, Belarus, and Ukraine are for 1992, 1993, 1994, and 1998 only.

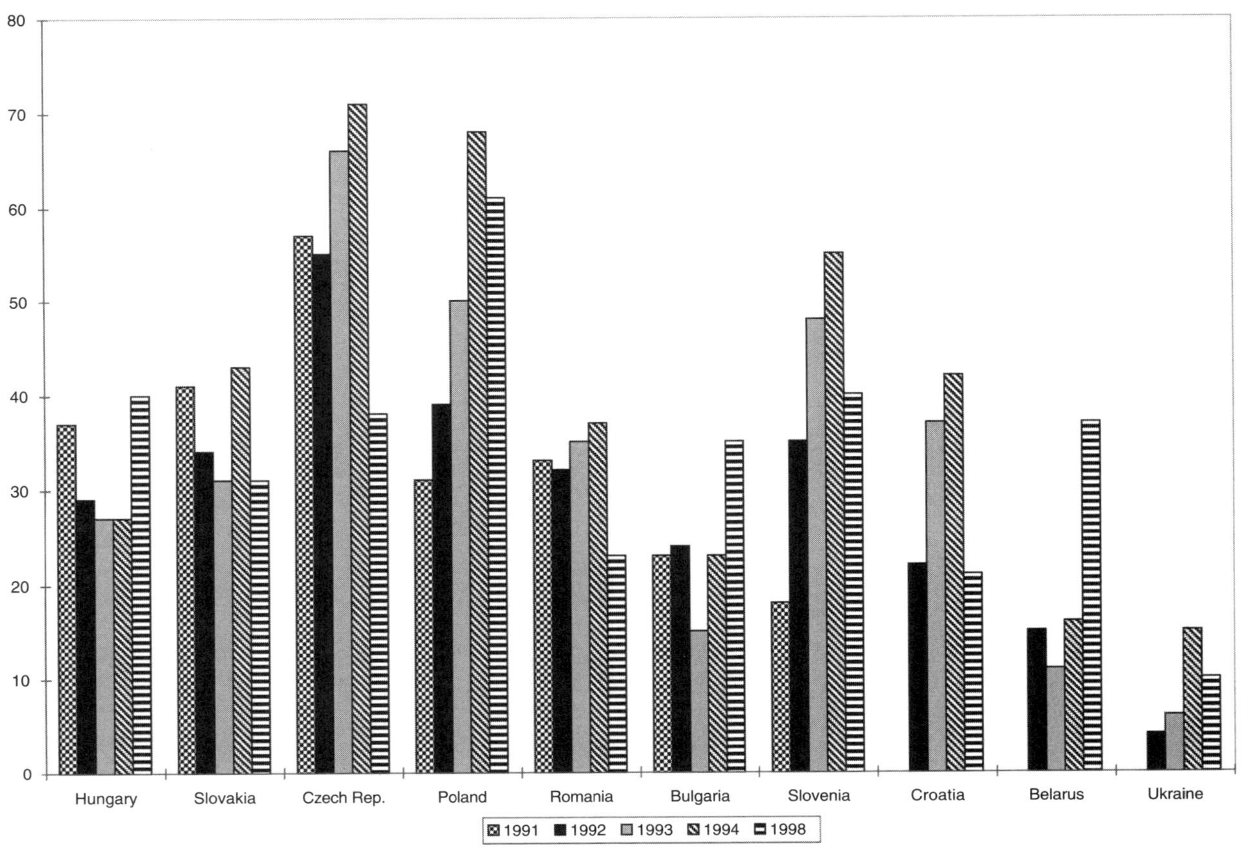

FIGURE 3.4. Approval of the current economic system. Data for Croatia, Belarus, and Ukraine are for 1992, 1993, 1994, and 1998 only.

TABLE 3.2. *Selected Economic Indicators, 1989–1999*

	Years of GDP Decline	GDP Fall after Recovery	GDP Growth 1989–94	GDP Growth 1995–99	GDP Growth 1989–99	1999 GDP (1989 = 100)	GDP per Capita 1999($)	Unemployment 1999
Czech Republic	6	Yes	−2.0	1.5	−0.4	95	5,189	9.4
Hungary	4	No	−2.6	3.4	0.1	99	4,853	9.1
Poland	2	No	−1.1	5.8	2.0	122	3,987	13.0
Slovenia	4	No	−2.1	4.0	0.7	109	10,020	7.5
Albania	4	Yes	−2.9	6.3	1.3	96	1,102	18.0
Bulgaria	6	Yes	−4.6	−1.6	−3.2	67	1,513	16.0
Croatia	6	Yes	−7.3	4.3	−2.0	78	4,467	12.6
Romania	7	Yes	−4.6	−0.8	−2.9	76	1,517	11.5
Slovakia	4	No	−3.5	4.0	0.6	100	3,650	19.2
Belarus	6	No	−4.3	3.1	−1.0	80	777	2.1
Ukraine	10	No	−10.3	−5.5	−8.1	36	619	4.3

Source: GDP data from EBRD, *Transition Report, 2000* (London, 2001).

patterns of trade), and transition factors (timing and scope of reforms, economic policies, foreign assistance), but the results are inconsistent. The causal relations among these factors are not clear, and their contribution to successful reforms are hard to measure and interpret (see De Melo et al., 1997: esp. 13–16). It is evident that initial conditions differed significantly among Soviet bloc countries. Some had more decentralized and institutionally diverse centrally planned economies. Moreover, their economic performance and the level of macroeconomic imbalances were greatly dissimilar. According to Salvatore Zecchini (1997: xix), this may explain "why policy outcomes differ widely across countries even though their strategies were broadly similar, as they included essentially the same components, namely price and trade liberalization, macroeconomic stabilization, creation of market institutions and privatization."

The timing, sequencing, and scope of reforms are commonly considered as the best explanation of more-successful economic transitions. The World Bank (1996) analysis supports the view that countries that liberalized rapidly and extensively recover faster and experience a decline in inflation rates.[6] Similarly, Zecchini (1997: xix) argues that "some countries have shown more determination than others in introducing radical changes and in maintaining the reform momentum, mostly by taking maximum advantage of the window of opportunity that the political upheaval offered them initially." Although the data show that countries that introduced economic reforms differ systematically from the late reformers, it is not easy to establish an unambiguous causal explanation. Johannes Linn (1996) is right when he cautions that "we will never be able to disentangle what part of today's better growth performance of Central Europe and the Baltics is due to better and early reform policies and what can be attributed to [the] initial conditions: but what we do know is that the quality of policies matter – and these are under the control of governments."

Finally, the most successful countries were able to attract considerable foreign aid and private capital (see Table 3.3). The patterns of foreign capital flows indicate that external help was not so much a cause but a result of successful reforms and political stability. Initially, large sums were invested in Hungary, which had the most liberalized economy under the communist regime. Then, the Czech Republic became a leading recipient of foreign capital due to the bold and comprehensive nature of its mass privatization scheme. Subsequently, Poland has been attracting a growing share of foreign investment, capitalizing on its successful stabilization program and fast recovery from the recession. As a World Bank report (1996: 138) concluded, "official support from the international financial institutions and individual

[6] This finding, however, is still a subject of debates among economists – see, for example, Aage (1997).

TABLE 3.3. *Direct Foreign Investment, 1989–1999*

	Cumulative 1989–99	Per Capita 1989–99
Czech Republic	14,924	1,447
Hungary	17,770	1,764
Poland	20,047	518
Slovenia	1,400	701
Bulgaria	2,332	284
Croatia	3,234	716
Romania	5,647	252
Slovakia	2,111	391
Albania	454	137
Belarus	681	67
Ukraine	2,751	55

Note: Cumulative in US$ millions, per capita in US$.

Source: European Bank for Reconstruction and Development, *Transition Report, 2000* (London, 2001).

country donors has typically been much larger, relative to population or GDP, for those countries that have advanced further with reforms."

This brief overview of political and economic developments in postcommunist Eastern Europe indicates wide disparities among the countries emerging from four decades of communist rule. Since at least 1995 the gap between East Central European front-runners and other postcommunist countries has become apparent, and it seems to be "locked in" across the region. How can we account for such differences and their persistence? What factors make some countries more successful than others? How should we conceptualize relations among various dimensions of East European transformations? In the next section I explore several explanatory leads offered in the literature on postcommunist transformation and on transitions to democracy in general.

Explanatory Leads

As I have already suggested, the diverging trajectories and initial outcomes of postcommunist transformation may be explained by several factors. Initial conditions, timing and sequencing of reforms, quality of policies, institutional choices, and the extent of external support provide important clues for the range of outcomes emerging in the region. The causal impact of these factors and interaction effects among them, however, are not obvious or easy to determine. Moreover, timing and sequencing matter (see Pierson, 2000b); therefore, their influence may decrease or increase in different stages of transition and differ depending on temporal ordering. In this section I briefly comment on the role of some of these factors, and in the conclusion I outline the sequence of factors that accounts for the pattern of successful transformations.

International Factors

In contrast to earlier transitions to democracy, the role of international factors in East European cases is much more profound. International factors decisively shaped all phases of transition: the deconstruction of the old regime, the transfer of power, and the consolidation phase (see, e.g., Linz and Stepan, 1996: 235–44). The international context of postcommunist transitions has many different dimensions, including the expansion of the global economy, the end of the Cold War and changing East-West relations, the collapse of the Soviet bloc's political and economic structures, new relations emerging among East European countries, and the deepening of European integration and prospects for EU enlargement. Accordingly, various international actors – states, international organizations, transnational movements, multinational corporations, and multilateral financial institutions – have all played specific roles and influence developments in postcommunist countries. As a result, the international environment within which postcommunist transitions take place is exceedingly complex. As Valerie Bunce (1995: 94) has emphasized, "transitions to democracy in Eastern Europe, with all their fluidity and uncertainty, are taking place in the context of a fluid and uncertain international environment."[7]

I focus here only on two issues. First, in both political and economic dimensions international factors should be perceived as facilitating conditions, not as causes determining specific outcomes. As I have already argued, the inflow of foreign direct investment should be viewed as a result, not as a cause, of successful economic reforms. Similarly, membership in international organizations almost always requires the fulfillment of certain initial conditions. Consequently, countries striving for international recognition and acceptance must first sufficiently marketize their economies and democratize their political systems in order to benefit from international economic and political support. Such integration, in turn, fuels faster growth of productivity, trade volumes, national incomes, and foreign capital investment. Thus expanded international participation propels countries onto the path toward more-open and -liberal economies and imposes powerful constraints on their domestic policies. According to the EBRD, "the discipline imposed

[7] At the same time, however, Bunce (1999: 757) argues that "the larger world into which successor regimes entered was remarkably consensual in its ideological messages." Of course, fluidity, uncertainty, and ideological consistency can easily go together.

by EU Association Agreements, WTO accession negotiations, and other regional trade agreements (CEFTA, EFTA) has generally provided an effective counterweight to protectionist pressures." As a result, "the trade regimes [of leading reformers] do not look very different from those in mature market economies" (EBRD, 1998: 28). Similarly, membership or a promise of membership in international institutions facilitated domestic institution building and adherence to international laws and standards.

Second, foreign support is extended to those countries that are willing and able to attract and cultivate potential foreign partners. In short, the ruling elites must be familiar with modes of operation and institutional rules that govern transnational communities, develop necessary skills, and prove willing to conform to such rules. The existing evidence shows that more-successful postcommunist countries have been more closely integrated with global economic and political structures and that such integration was established earlier rather than later in the sequence of transformations. Moreover, these are the countries that have been more willing to cooperate politically and economically with their neighbors and that have a longer history of participation in international institutions. Their elites had more opportunities and time to learn necessary skills allowing effective participation in the global economy and politics. Table 3.4 presents the membership of East European countries in selected international organizations and dates when particular countries were admitted.

The data on international integration show that countries that have been more integrated in international institutions and have joined various multilateral and new regional political and economic organizations earlier are more advanced in the economic and political transitions. Such countries also had a longer history of international relationships because they joined these organizations either under communist rule or at the outset of the transition period. In sum, international integration with its economic and political benefits and constraints on domestic policies clearly facilitates political and economic transformation. Countries included in the first round of the NATO and EU enlargement already have benefited and will certainly continue to benefit economically and attract an ever growing share of foreign investment as well as transfers from the EU.[8] However, such integration is only possible when the progress of political and economic reforms is already secured. Consequently, one should look at other factors in order to explain the initial outcomes of East European transitions.

[8] It is expected that the EU candidate countries will get a total of 2.9 billion euro in transfers from the Phare, Ispa, and Sapard programs between 2000 and 2006 (*Business Central Europe*, June 2001: 59). For efforts to quantify the cost and benefits of the EU enlargement, see, for example, Baldwin, Francois, and Portes (1997).

TABLE 3.4. *Participation in Selected International Organizations*

	UN	World Bank	IMF	WTO (GATT)	Council of Europe	EU Associate Agreement	CEFTA	OECD	NATO	EU Accession Negotiations
Czech Republic[a]	1945	1990	1990	1947	1991	1993	1993	1995	1999	1998
Hungary	1955	1982	1982	1975	1990	1992	1993	1996	1999	1998
Poland	1945	1986	1986	1967	1991	1992	1993	1996	1999	1998
Slovenia	1992	1993	1992	1995	1993	1995	1996			1998
Albania	1955	1991	1991	2000	1995					
Bulgaria	1955	1990	1990	1996	1992	1995	1999			2000
Croatia	1992	1993	1992	2000	1996					
Romania	1955	1972	1972	1972	1993	1993	1997			2000
Slovakia	1993	1993	1993	1995	1993	1993	1993	2000		2000
Belarus	(1945)[b]	1992	1992		1995 (SP)[c]					
Ukraine	(1945)	1992	1992		1995					

[a] For Czech and Slovak Republics a date before 1993 means the membership of Czechoslovakia.
[b] Until 1991 both Belarus and Ukraine were integral parts of the USSR but had separate UN membership.
[c] SP means a special guest status. Belarus's special guest status was suspended on January 13, 1997.

Source: Compiled from the websites of the individual organizations, the OMRI Daily Digest reports, and various editions of *The Europa World Year Book* (London) and *Transition Report, 2000* (London, 2001).

TABLE 3.5. *Institutional Choices and Elections, 1989–2000*

	Constitutional Type	Electoral System	Executive Power P/PM[a]	Elections PA/PR	Effective Parties[c]
Czech Republic	Parliamentary	PR (4%)	3/5	5/0	3.6/5.2
Hungary	Parliamentary	Hybrid (5%)	6/7	3/0	2.9/3.7
Poland	Semipresidential	PR (5%)	7/11	4/3	2.9/10.8
Slovenia	Parliamentary	PR (4%)	4/6	4/2	2.5/6.6
Albania	Semipresidential	Hybrid (4%)	7/5	4/0	1.3/2.2
Bulgaria	Parliamentary	PR (4%)	1/6	4/2	2.4/2.5
Croatia	Presidential	Hybrid (3%)	9	4/2	2.4/2.6
Romania	Semipresidential	PR (3%)	6/9	4/4	2.2/4.8
Slovakia	Parliamentary	PR (5%)	4/6	4/1	3.3/4.4
Belarus	Presidential	Majoritarian	18	3/1	
Ukraine	Presidential	Majoritarian[d]	8	2/3	

[a] Joel Hellman's index of executive power ranks powers of presidents (P) in all countries and prime ministers (PM) in parliamentary and mixed systems in ten categories. Countries with highest scores have the most extensive executive powers. These are Belarus (18), Uzbekistan (18), Turkmenistan (18), and Russia (15). See Joel Hellman and Joshua Tucker, Post-Communist Elections Project <www.wws.princeton.edu/jtucker/pcelections.html>.

[b] Until the end of 2000 for parliamentary (PA) and presidential (PR) elections.

[c] Laakso/Taagepera index calculated for the elections with the lowest number of effective parties and with the highest number of effective parties.

[d] In 1998, Ukraine adopted a mixed (hybrid) electoral system.

Institutional Choices

The issue of institutional choices has received much attention in the literature on democratic transitions (see, e.g., Lijphart and Waisman, 1996; Diamond and Plattner, 1996; Merkel, 1996; Crawford and Lijphart, 1995). Scholars have concluded that new institutions can be crafted in such a way as to provide constraints and incentives that facilitate consolidation of democracy. Beverly Crawford and Arend Lijphart (1995: 176–77) reconstructed such a view in the following way: "[I]f new democratic institutions are constructed, then vested interests in those institutions will develop rapidly and will have long-term consequences that overshadow past legacies. If those institutions provide incentives to economic and political liberalizers and constrain those actors who oppose the liberalization process, then the odds that the outcome will be a successful transition to liberal capitalist democracy will increase." The design of electoral systems and executive-legislative relations are considered to be the most critical institutional choices. Table 3.5 presents some major institutional choices of postcommunist democracies.

This overview of institutional choices in postcommunist democracies yields several preliminary conclusions. First, the process of institution building is still very much underway, especially when economic institutions are concerned. One may expect that these new democracies will endure more institutional changes resulting from conflicting interests before a relatively stable institutional framework is in place. In fact, Robert Putnam (Putnam et al., 1993: 184) reminds us that "most institutional history moves slowly. Where institution building (and not mere constitution writing) is concerned, time is measured in decades." If this is the case, the impact of institutions can only be adequately assessed and measured in the long term.

Second, there is great variation in institutional design in Eastern Europe. Postcommunist systems of government range from pure presidentialism to pure parliamentarism, with most countries opting for a mixed system. Similarly, postcommunist electoral systems range from relatively pure proportional representation to majoritarian systems, whereas the majority of countries adopted mixed proportional representation (PR)–majoritarian electoral institutions. The impact of mixed systems is more difficult to discern, especially in a situation in which such systems constantly change and evolve in many fundamental ways. Nevertheless, there is an interesting regularity emerging in the region that is supported by various empirical data.

The progress of economic reforms tends to be more advanced and democracy more secure and fair in countries that adopted systems of government closer to a pure parliamentary type and in countries with various PR systems. This observation confirms Juan Linz's (1996: 125) contention that "parliamentarism provides a more flexible and adaptable institutional context for the establishment and consolidation of democracy" (see also Linz and Valenzuela, 1994; Horowitz, 1996; Bunce, 1997; Easter, 1997). Parliamentary systems promote power sharing among various political actors, facilitate moderation, and provide for a more efficient processing of conflicts. Although they are, in principle, less stable than presidential systems, as reflected in the number of elections and cabinet changes, it seems that democratization is better served when there are more frequent government turnovers and changes of ruling coalitions. The EBRD report (1998: 23) points out that "the advanced countries have, on average, held a larger number of democratic elections, have had more frequent government turnovers, and have had shorter government tenures than the less advanced reformers."[9] Such changes allow policy acceleration and adjustments and prevent policy stagnation and the stabilization of clientelistic relations. Thus, despite views that the democratization process and electoral politics might disrupt the implementation of necessary economic reforms, "the [experience] of transition in

[9] It should be noted that this contrast is more apparent when the Soviet successor states that on average had fewer elections are included in the comparison. Also, following the recent series of interim elections in the Balkan countries, they do not differ from the more successful reformers of East Central Europe in number of elections and governmental turnover. The recent governmental instability in these countries had effects similar to earlier instability in Central Europe. It generated serious reforms as new governments scrambled to make up for years of neglect by their predecessors.

post-communist countries . . . suggests that the institution of democratic elections can play an integral role in strengthening the robustness of economic reforms and generating the necessary resolve to implement comprehensive reform programmes" (EBRD, 1998: 23).

It should be noted, however, that governmental instability seems to have a more advantageous effect when frequent government turnover is concentrated at the beginning of the transition rather than in its latter phases. The experience of Poland, which endured much political volatility in the early years of the transition and later emerged as a successful reformer, illustrates this regularity well. In contrast, Bulgaria and Romania only recently experienced a period of accelerated government turnover and interim elections, in part as a result of political and economic failures. Similarly, successful reformers are characterized by more-fragmented party systems as illustrated by the index of effective political parties in Table 3.5.

It is not only politics, however, that benefits from the more flexible institutional system offered by parliamentary democracy. Economic transitions are far more advanced in countries with more-dispersed political power as well. Joel Hellman (1996: 3–4) concluded his analysis of the implementation of macroeconomic stabilization programs in postcommunist countries in the following way: "Postcommunist countries with a greater dispersion of political power and a larger number of veto points in the policymaking process have stabilized faster and more effectively than countries in which political power is more concentrated. Coalition/divided governments and constrained executives . . . appear to hasten stabilization in the postcommunist cases. . . . Postcommunist countries with more competitive political systems appear to have a 'competitive advantage' in the process of macroeconomic adjustment."

While the evidence about the relationship between institutional choices and initial outcomes of transitions seems to be persuasive, the great institutional variation and continuing fluidity of new East European institutions suggests some caution. As with other factors discussed so far, it is relatively safe to assume that institutional systems with a greater dispersion of political power tend to promote more-effective economic policies and secure better democracy. This statement has to be qualified by pointing out that general institutional constraints provide only a framework for policy-making processes. There are indeed notable policy differences across the region in terms of substance, style, and effectiveness. One can observe among postcommunist governments different degrees of determination and capacity to pursue consistent reform strategies. According to Salvatore Zecchini (1997: 12), in the realm of economic policies these differences "lie in the relative priority assigned to different goals, in the speed, depth and timing of the various reforms, in the extent to which market-based incentives were offset or blunted by other government interventions and in the determination shown in redressing macroeconomic imbalances."

Legacies

The final explanatory lead to be discussed in this chapter draws attention to the impact of historical legacies and initial conditions in shaping diverging trajectories of East European transitions. On a formal institutional level, state socialism can be analyzed as a highly uniform political and economic system. Yet, at a more contextual level of analysis, state socialism assumed a variety of political, economic, and cultural forms, with differences among countries as striking as similarities. Consequently, the collapse of communist regimes took place in the context of highly dissimilar domestic conditions and institutions across the region. Some countries such as Poland and Hungary had already experienced significant political liberalization, had opened to the West, and had developed organized opposition movements. Similarly, their economies departed from the orthodox command economy model in many fundamental ways (see, e.g., Nee and Stark, 1989; Walder, 1995; Poznański, 1996). Other countries experienced little political liberalization and their economies remained highly centralized. There were not only differences in institutional designs and policies, but also in the level of economic problems and imbalances. Paradoxically, countries with the least reformed economies, such as East Germany or Czechoslovakia, were in better economic shape than the reformers.

The initial experience of transitions shows that the most successful East Central European countries share common historical legacies. First, all these countries had a history of major political conflicts and political reforms. As a result they were more liberal in the declining years of communism than their neighbors. Czechoslovakia is here an exception. However, it too experienced a significant liberalization drive in the 1960s that left important resources and residues, especially in the Czech lands. Second, the extent of marketization and economic liberalization prior to the end of communist rule was larger. These countries had a relatively large private sector and many state-owned firms had cooperated with Western firms or produced goods for Western markets. Third, these countries had pragmatic communist elites and/or substantial political and cultural opposition. Finally, these countries had stronger ties to the West. It seems that such histories of political struggle and reform engendered a learning process on the level of elites and society alike that facilitated a faster transition to democracy, a better quality of democratic institutions, and more extensive liberties and freedoms. The kinds of knowledge and skills that were acquired by relevant collective actors (ruling elites, oppositional movements and civil society organizations, private entrepreneurs) under decentralized and pragmatic state socialism were an important asset after its demise. As a result, these countries and their new elites were more consistent and effective in implementing political and economic reforms.

The institutional legacies of reforms and the pool of available skills and experiences made political cleavages more transparent and the break with the communist past more radical. The initial stages of transition in these countries were dominated by noncommunist opposition forces. In fact, in all four leading countries former communist parties lost power in the first round of democratic elections. New democratic governments were formed by the members of opposition movements who set up to dismantle economic and political vestiges of state socialism as quickly as possible. Thus, Steven Fish (1998: 57) is correct when he argues that "the outcome of initial elections is the best predictor of the extent of economic reform." But the fact that in several countries communist parties lost initial elections begs for explanation. The presence of facilitating legacies accounts for the ability of noncommunist political forces to win the first elections. It would be imprudent, however, to assume that liberalized and marketized state socialism mechanically produced better democracies and better-performing economies. Czechoslovakia neither was liberal nor did it have a reformed economy. It seems, however, that in successful countries legacies of dissent, opposition, and reform facilitated the process of political and economic transformation, even despite the fact that such reforms were reversed under the old regime. The difference between the Czech Republic and Slovakia illustrates this point. The bulk of reform movement in 1968 concentrated in the Czech lands. Consequently, the Czech Republic inherited better-developed and larger opposition movements and other legacies that facilitated the democratic breakthrough. It should also be emphasized, however, that the explanatory power of legacies declines over time. As the analysts of the EBRD (1998: vi) rightly note, "the difference in the depth of reforms are increasingly the result of policy choices rather than the initial conditions in each country."

Conclusion: Lessons of the Postcommunist Transition

This chapter is intended as a preliminary assessment of patterns of political and economic transitions in postcommunist Eastern Europe. I have focused specifically on the former Soviet-bloc countries. This analysis excluded the Soviet-successor states and some post-Yugoslav countries in order to reduce the level of complexity added by the independence drive and struggle for self-determination, the nationality question, military conflicts, the greater variation of initial conditions, and the dissimilar timing of transition. I imagine that a similar analysis focused exclusively on post-Soviet states would yield similar conclusions.

Experiences of postcommunist transformation vary significantly across the region. The group of leading countries (the Czech Republic, Hungary, Poland, and Slovenia) has made quite extraordinary progress. These countries are followed by the Balkan states and Slovakia, which have had an inconsistent and much less impressive record. They have lagged behind in both political and economic transformations, and their new democracies have been more uncertain and crisis-prone. Finally, among Soviet-successor states the progress of transformations has been highly uneven, and in many countries reforms have stalled. One thing should be strongly emphasized: the transition processes are still unfolding, and it would be highly imprudent to overgeneralize the lessons of the early experiences. It is still possible and even likely, as Katherine Verdery (1996: 16) has argued, that "these transformations will produce a variety of forms, some of them perhaps approximating Western capitalist market economies and many of them not..... Polities more closely resembling corporatist authoritarian regimes than liberal democracies are a distinct possibility in several countries... whereas military dictatorship should not be ruled out for others." In fact, as Herbert Kitschelt has noted (in Chapter 2 in this volume), the postcommunist countries represent more varied scores on the Freedom House indexes than any other region of the world. On the other hand, in most of the postcommunist world, transformations so far have progressed in the direction of liberal democracy and an open-market economy. The emerging patterns of these transformations suggest several preliminary conclusions.

First, the countries with the most advanced and successful economic transformations have at the same time the most secure and effective democratic systems, as well as a greater extent of freedom and liberties. Thus, what transpires from postcommunist experiences in Eastern Europe is that the simultaneous transitions characteristic of the recent wave of democratization can only be successful when democracy is inclusive, stronger, and more competitive; all rights and liberties are protected; civil society is more robust; and the media are free from censorship and government control.

Second, all successful countries had earlier histories of political conflict, attempts at liberalization, economic reforms and experiments, and oppositional activities. Such developments under state socialism produced more pragmatic communist elites, more viable private domains within state-run economies, and stronger cultural and political counterelites. All these developments facilitated the democratic breakthrough and subsequent political and economic reforms.

Third, these countries also maintained more extensive relationships with Western democracies, international organizations, and the global economy during the communist period. They benefited from broader cultural, scientific, and technical cooperation; maintained better trade relations; and received extensive aid in the form of expertise and capital inflows. All these factors clearly contributed to speedier and more successful transformations. The kinds of knowledge and skills acquired by all relevant economic and political actors in the past played a major role in the designing and implementing of transition strategies and the shaping of institutional change. Moreover, as the EBRD (1998: 22) report suggests, these countries "have achieved a high level of integration into world markets and into existing multilateral institutions which generates powerful incentives to maintain and deepen market-oriented reforms." However, the leading countries have shared additional similarities that have made certain outcomes more likely.

Fourth, these were the countries where former communist parties lost power in the first round of democratic elections and opposition forces formed the first democratic governments. New political elites were more committed to change and used the initial window of opportunity to accelerate the exit from state socialism. In short, initial electoral victory by the opposition allowed for the consolidation of the advantages of the democratic breakthrough and the "locking in" of the "increasing return" dynamics of the transformation process.

Fifth, the more successful countries were characterized by more-dispersed political and economic power and relatively fragmented party systems and had more-competitive political systems. As a result, they experienced more frequent government turnovers and shorter electoral cycles. All these factors contributed to better accountability of decision makers, facilitated coalition building and policy innovation, and prevented political stagnation.

Finally, these countries introduced more-comprehensive macroeconomic stabilization reforms, extensively liberalized their economies, and privatized a large percentage of state-owned assets. Moreover, these reform measures were introduced earlier rather than later in the transition process and were maintained with an often surprising level of consistency, despite government turnover and even in the face of significant opposition. In addition, both the costs and benefits of reforms were more equally distributed. In short, the leading countries succeeded in "creating sufficiently large domestic constituencies with a stake in sustaining the reform process" (EBRD, 1998: 22; see also Balcerowicz, 1995).

The role of the main factors discussed in this chapter and the temporal sequence of developments that account for more-advanced levels of economic and political transformation are summarized in Figure 3.5. This overview of East European experiences allows us to draw some more general points as well. The collapse of state socialism and the unfolding transformation processes provide a unique opportunity to reexamine and to test theoretical and methodological tools of contemporary comparative politics. The evidence presented in this chapter suggests that we are well advised not to create artificial and simplistic analytical distinctions and causal accounts. Even the most appropriate and efficiently implemented institutional engineering cannot create successful democracies and market economies, although institutional choices are critically important in facilitating successful transformations and locking in virtuous paths of development. Similarly, foreign aid and support can only expedite but not create working democracies and market economies. I have suggested that in order to understand East European experiences we should pay more attention to legacies of the old regime and path-dependent dynamics, even despite the fact that these cases are characterized by a sharp break in institutional continuity. Douglass North

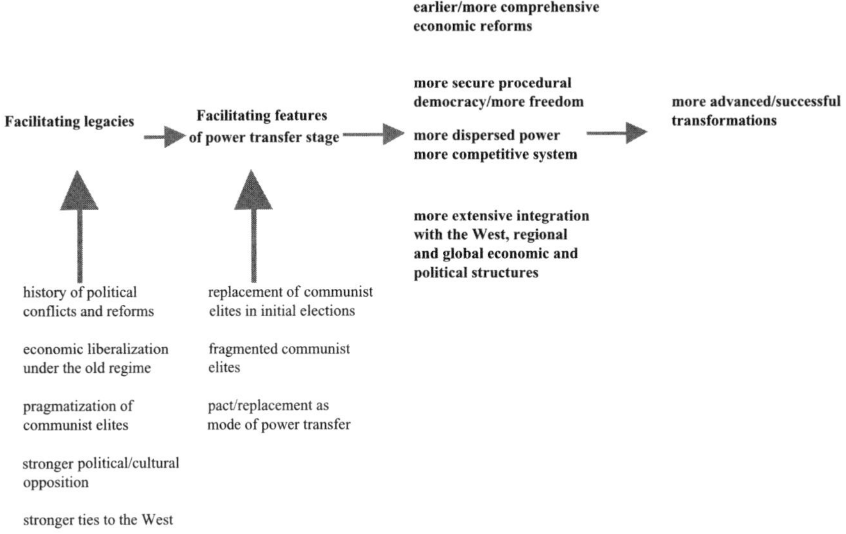

FIGURE 3.5. Pattern of successful transformations.

(1990: 6) reminds us that "even discontinuous changes (such as revolutions and conquest) are never completely discontinuous." Similarly, Robert Putnam's (Putnam et al., 1993: 161) study of Italian regional reforms illustrates in an insightful way "the power of historical continuities to affect the odds of institutional success."

I have also proposed that we conceptualize these legacies in a more complex and precise fashion. Experiences of East European countries have not only been shaped by the "Leninist legacies" identified by Ken Jowitt (1992) that are inimical to markets and liberal democracy. The contours of broad modernization processes; critical events such as past political crises, reform attempts, and institutional tinkering with the architecture of the party-state and centrally planned economy; and learning processes among elites are critical factors in explaining divergent trajectories of transition in the postcommunist context. They help to explain why some countries have been able to respond to the challenges and opportunities of the collapse of the Soviet empire much more effectively than other countries. In short, a path-dependent approach that combines the investigation of timing and sequencing and a serious reflection on the historical experiences of countries in transition with attention to contingent events such as initial elections, as well as institutions and institutional choices, should replace thinking in terms of the simplistic dichotomy between "Leninist legacies" and "institutional engineering."

The second theoretical conclusion concerns our capacity to develop parsimonious models in order to understand and explain large-scale processes of political and economic transformation. Contemporary political science strives to generate analytical models that try to specify precisely causes and effects. As I have suggested, a number of factors of a highly uncertain and interdependent nature are at work behind specific patterns of transition that we can discern in the postcommunist world. The temporal status of these factors is also complex. Some of them reflect distant historical processes and events, others the more recent legacy of communist rule. Still others are the product of transition politics. Multicollinearity among these factors is evident, and interaction effects are intricate. Thus, any single-factor interpretation is problematic. Moreover, although many factors clearly facilitate the transformation process, their causal power is not certain. As Robert Putnam (Putnam et al., 1993: 162) reminds us, in explaining complex political processes, "we must think not merely in terms of cause and effect."[10] Thus, most of the attempts to determine a limited set of specific causes and to establish simple linear relationships to outcomes are likely to be questionable. The metaphor of vicious and virtuous circles captures much better the relationship among these factors. They interact together in a complex fashion, producing the "increasing returns" that characterize path-dependent development.[11]

Such self-reinforcing, interactive processes are clearly detectable in many postcommunist countries. Poland, Czechoslovakia, and Hungary, for example, received more attention from the international community at the start of the transition not only for being among the first to reject communism, but also for their past experiences of political struggle and economic reforms and their openness and historical links to the West. In contrast to other countries of the region, they had vocal and well-known cultural and political counter-elites, and in two of these three countries communist elites were pragmatic, reform-minded, and liberal. The advantage of being first and familiar as well as these past experiences not only provided intellectual capital and skills but also led to a faster and more extensive cooperation with the West and greater inflows of foreign expertise and capital. This in turn had a growing impact on the policies of newly democratized regimes, the normative orientations of political actors, and their economic preferences, expectations, and behaviors. Better-developed market institutions, improved economic performance, and stronger democracy in turn invited more cooperation, assistance, and investment.

[10] On the ontological complexities of political and social reality and their relation to methodological concerns, see, for example, Hall, 2003; Jervis, 1997; Ragin, 2000.

[11] For an excellent review of the concept of path dependence and its application to political analysis, see Paul Pierson (2000a: 251), who argues that "the notion of path dependence is generally used to support a few key claims: that specific patterns of timing and sequence matter; that a wide range of social outcomes are often possible, and large consequences may result from relatively small and contingent events." See also the debate in *Studies in American Political Development* 14(1): 72–119.

If this self-propelling virtuous dynamic of the transition process among leading East European reformers with its increasing returns and positive feedbacks explains a great deal of their success, other countries have experienced vicious cycles of political and economic setbacks, stalled reforms, and a wait-and-see attitude of potential foreign partners. Investigation of such self-destructive paths is very important because, as Kathleen Thelen (2000: 106) has noted, "increasing returns arguments focus mostly on winners." The interesting question is how and when the vicious cycles that characterize developments in these countries can be reversed in order to change these countries' logic of development. What kind of events have the capacity to recalibrate entrenched path-dependent developments? Similarly, what configuration of events may lead to the destruction of self-reinforcing virtuous cycles? Even the most successful East European countries still have a long way to go before their new democracies are fully consolidated, economies are sufficiently depoliticized and integrated with global markets, and resources for coping with the inherent volatility of economic and political processes are sufficiently developed.

References

Aage, Hans. 1997. Transitions in Central and Eastern Europe. TKI Working Papers on European Integration and Regime Formation, South Jutland University, 12.

Balcerowicz, Leszek. 1995. *Socialism, Capitalism, Democracy*. Oxford: Oxford University Press.

Baldwin, Richard E., Joseph F. Francois, and Richard Portes. 1997. EU Enlargement: Small Cost for the West, Big Gains for the East. *Economic Policy* 24: 127–76.

Bennett, Andrew, and Alexander George. 2001. *Case Studies and Theory Development*. Cambridge, Mass.: MIT Press.

Bunce, Valerie. 1995. Comparing East and South. *Journal of Democracy* 6(3): 87–100.

1997. Presidents and the Transition in Eastern Europe. In Kurt von Mettenheim, ed., *Presidential Institutions and Democratic Politics*, pp. 161–76. Baltimore: Johns Hopkins University Press.

1999. The Political Economy of Postsocialism. *Slavic Review* 58(4): 756–93.

Cameron, David. 2001. The Return to Europe: The Impact of the EU on Political and Economic Reform in the Post-Communist Countries. Paper presented at the annual meeting of the American Political Science Association, San Francisco, August 29–September 2.

Crawford, Beverly, and Arend Lijphart. 1995. Explaining Political and Economic Change in Post-Communist Eastern Europe: Old Legacies, New Institutions, Hegemonic Norms and International Pressures. *Comparative Political Studies* 28(2): 171–99.

De Melo, Martha, Cevdet Denizer, Alan Gelb, and Stoyan Tenev. 1997. Circumstances and Choices: The Role of Initial Conditions and Policies in Transition Economies. World Bank, Policy Research Working Paper 1866, December.

Diamond, Larry, and Marc Plattner, eds. 1996. *The Global Resurgence of Democracy*. Baltimore: Johns Hopkins University Press.

Easter, Gerald. 1997. Preference for Presidentialism: Postcommunist Regime Change in Russia and the NIS. *World Politics* 49(2): 184–211.

Ekiert, Grzegorz. 1990. Transitions from State-Socialism in East Central Europe. *States and Social Structures Newsletter* 12: 1–7.

1996. *The State against Society: Political Crises and Their Aftermath in East Central Europe*. Princeton: Princeton University Press.

European Bank of Recovery and Development (EBRD). 1998. *Transition Report, 1997*. London: EBRD.

2000. *Transition Report, 1999*. London: EBRD.

2001. *Transition Report, 2000*. London: EBRD.

Fish, M. Steven. 1998. The Determinants of Economic Reform in the Post-Communist World. *East European Politics and Societies* 12(1): 31–78.

Greskovits, Bela. 1998. *The Political Economy of Protest and Patience: East European and Latin American Transformations Compared*. Budapest: Central European University Press.

Hall, Peter. 2003. Aligning Ontology and Methodology in Comparative Research. In James Mahoney and Dietrich Rueschemeyer, eds., *Comparative Historical Analysis in the Social Sciences*. Cambridge: Cambridge University Press.

Hanson, Stephen E. 1995. The Leninist Legacy and Institutional Change. *Comparative Political Studies* 28(2): 306–14.

Hellman, Joel S. 1996. Competitive Advantage: Political Competition and Economic Reform in Postcommunist Transitions. Paper presented at the annual meeting of the American Political Science Association, San Francisco.

Hirschler, Richard. 2000. Ten Years Transition: Recalling the Events of a Historic Decade with World Bank Chief Economist Nicholas Stern. *Transition Newsletter* 11(5): 1–4.

Horowitz, Donald. 1996. Comparing Democratic Systems. In Larry Diamond and Marc Plattner, eds., *Global Resurgence of Democracy*, pp. 143–49. Baltimore: Johns Hopkins University Press.

Jervis, Robert. 1997. *System Effects: Complexity in Political and Social Life*. Princeton: Princeton University Press.

Jowitt, Ken. 1992. *New World Disorder: The Leninist Extinction*. Berkeley: University of California Press.

Kamiński, Bartłomiej. 1991. Systemic Underpinnings of the Transition in Poland: The Shadow of the Roundtable Agreement. *Studies in Comparative Communism* 24(2): 173–90.

Kopstein, Jeffrey, and David Reilly. 1999. Explaining the Why of the Why: A Comment on Fish's "Determinants of Economic Reforms in the Post-Communist World." *East European Politics and Societies* 13(3): 613–26.

Kornai, János. 1996. Paying the Bill for Goulash-Communism. Discussion Paper Series no. 1749, Harvard Institute for Economic Research, Cambridge, Mass.

Lijphart, Arend, and Carlos H. Waisman, eds. 1996. *Institutional Design in New Democracies: Eastern Europe and Latin America*. Boulder, Colo.: Westview Press.

Linn, Johannes F. 1996. The Transition in Europe and Central Asia: Progress and World Bank Assistance. Tokyo, November 25.
Linz, Juan. 1996. The Perils of Presidentialism. In Larry Diamond and Marc Plattner, eds., *The Global Resurgence of Democracy*, pp. 124–42. Baltimore: Johns Hopkins University Press.
Linz, Juan, and Alfred Stepan. 1996. *Problems of Democratic Transition and Consolidation.* Baltimore: Johns Hopkins University Press.
Linz, Juan, and Arturo Valenzuela, eds. 1994. *The Failure of Presidential Democracy.* Baltimore: Johns Hopkins University Press.
Merkel, Wolfgang. 1996. Institutions and Democratic Consolidation in East Central Europe. Juan March Institute Working Papers, Madrid, no. 1996/86, December.
Nee, Victor, and David Stark, eds. 1989. *Remaking the Economic Institutions of Socialism.* Stanford: Stanford University Press.
North, Douglass C. 1990. *Institutions, Institutional Change and Economic Performance.* Cambridge: Cambridge University Press.
Pierson, Paul. 2000a. Increasing Returns, Path Dependence and the Study of Politics. *American Political Science Review* 94(2): 251–67.
2000b. Not Just What, but When: Timing and Sequence in Political Processes. *Studies in American Political Development* 14(1): 72–92.
Poznański, Kazimierz. 1996. *Poland's Protracted Transition: Institutional Change and Economic Growth, 1970–1994.* Cambridge: Cambridge University Press.
Putnam, Robert, with Robert Leonardi and Raffaella Y. Nanetri. 1993. *Making Democracy Work.* Princeton: Princeton University Press.
Ragin, Charles. 2000. *Fuzzy-Set Social Science.* Chicago: University of Chicago Press.
Roeder, Philip G. 1999. The Revolutions of 1989: Postcommunism and the Social Science. *Slavic Review* 58(4): 743–55.
Rose, Richard, and Christian Haerpfer. 1996. Change and Stability in the New Democracies Barometer: A Trend Analysis. Centre for Study of Public Policy, Glasgow, University of Strathclyde, no. 270.
1998. New European Barometer V. Centre for Study of Public Policy, Glasgow, University of Strathclyde, no. 306.
Stark, David. 1992. Path Dependence and Privatization Strategies in East Central Europe. *East European Politics and Societies* 6(1): 17–54.
Stark, David, and László Bruszt. 1998. *Postsocialist Pathways: Transforming Politics and Property in East Central Europe.* Cambridge: Cambridge University Press.
Thelen, Kathleen. 2000. Timing and Temporality in the Analysis of Institutional Evolution and Change. *Studies in American Political Development* 14(1): 101–8.
Verdery, Katherine. 1996. *What Was Socialism and What Comes Next.* Princeton: Princeton University Press.
Walder, Andrew, ed. 1995. *The Waning of the Communist State.* Berkeley: University of California Press.
World Bank. 1996. *From Plan to Market: World Development Report, 1996.* New York: Oxford University Press.
Zecchini, Salvatore. 1997. Introduction. In Salvatore Zecchini, ed., *Lessons from the Economic Transition*, pp. 1–34. Dordrecht: Kluwer.

4

Postcommunist Spaces

A Political Geography Approach to Explaining Postcommunist Outcomes

Jeffrey S. Kopstein and David A. Reilly

Questions

What explains the wide variation in postcommunist political and economic outcomes? Why should all of the big winners of postcommunism be located in close proximity to the West? What explains the persistence of the centuries-old continental gradient of political and economic performance running roughly from the north and west to the south and east in Europe into the postcommunist era? Why does the interregional variation in postcommunist outcomes grow as one moves eastward and southward along the continental gradient? This chapter uses the methods and insights of political geography to answer these questions and explain the variation in postcommunist outcomes. Our argument is that both aggregate data and the experience of individual cases demonstrate powerful and independent spatial and neighborhood effects that cannot be reduced to other factors and that therefore need to be explained. Although we do not offer a conclusive account of the observed spatial and neighborhood effects, we do suggest two fruitful lines for research that are supported by both quantitative and qualitative evidence: the diffusion of norms, institutions, and resources across borders; and the impact of external actors, especially the European Union (EU) but also China and the crisis zone of Islamic fundamentalism, and other regional actors, on political and economic behavior.

In what follows, we test this "geographic" or spatial dependence explanation against competing hypotheses using the entire universe of postcommunist cases. We then explore the spatial dependence hypothesis and its implications more deeply and offer a preliminary attempt to identify the causal channels through which the approach offered might be working. What we maintain is that most alternative explanations have ignored, to their detriment, the role of geographic position on the Eurasian landmass and the spatial diffusion of influence, norms, and expectations across borders in accounting for variations in political and economic outcomes. Although we do not argue that ours is the only possible explanation, we do insist that such a perspective provides a powerful lens through which to understand postcommunist developments. We conclude the essay with a meditation on whether new regions are emerging out of the postcommunist world and whether these new regions have both objective characteristics and subjective meaning for scholars and the broader public.

Competing Explanations

The literature on the diverging trajectories of postcommunist states and economies is dominated by variations on a single theme: temporal path dependence.[1] One finds, however, various kinds of path-dependent types of explanations. Institutional path dependence stresses the consequences of initial institutional choices. In particular, Linz and Stepan maintain that while parliamentary systems tend to produce stable and consensus-driven democracies, presidential systems produce unstable, conflict-driven, and semiauthoritarian democracies (Linz and Stepan, 1996; Stepan and Skach, 1993; Linz and Valenzuela, 1994). In the creation of market economies, a related proposition has been put forward by a number of scholars. The logic here runs as follows: countries that quickly adopted secure property rights and independent central banks, liberalized their prices and tariffs, privatized their state-owned property, and balanced their budgets succeeded in laying the path to rapid market-oriented growth (Lipton and Sachs, 1990; Hellman, 1997). By contrast, countries that delayed this process, for whatever reason, allowed rent seekers and "oligarchs" to entrench themselves in power and resist further reform. The result was a stable, if bad, equilibrium of a semireformed, semicommunist economy.

The utility of the path dependency literature lies in its account of why successful democratic reformers and successful marketizers seem to be the same countries. Genuine democracy permits the distributional beneficiaries of the old system (the rent seekers) to be removed from power. Semiauthoritarian democracy, on the other hand, as in Russia, worked to the benefit of the rent seekers, who could use existing institutions to ensure the continuity of their power.

The problem with this literature is that, on the whole, it does not include within its theoretical ambit an explanation for why some countries could choose the right policies and institutions and why others could not. As useful as this literature is, it calls out for a deeper causal analysis. Two scholars, in particular, Steven Fish and Herbert Kitschelt, have put forward well thought out temporal path-dependent explanations for variation in political and economic change, and it is worth considering their studies briefly.

[1] In the literature, path dependence implies two things: multiple possible equilibria and critical junctures forestalling certain paths of development due to increasing returns or sunk costs.

In a multivariate statistical study of economic reforms using the universe of postcommunist cases, Fish has convincingly argued that the crucial variable in explaining good versus bad equilibria is the result of the first postcommunist elections (Fish, 1999a). This critical juncture theory maintains that the quick displacement of communists or their successor parties permitted rapid reform and staved off a return to power of rent-seeking coalitions. When pitted against competing explanation, such as religious traditions, institutional choice, and preexisting levels of economic development in a multivariate equation, the inaugural elections come up as the only statistically significant explanation. Again, the logic here is one of temporal path dependence, and one is inevitably left asking the question of why the noncommunists won in some countries more decisively than in others.

Kitschelt asks a different but related question: why have some countries managed to lock in high levels of political and civic freedoms while others lag behind (Kitschelt, 1999, and Chapter 2 in this volume)? In accounting for the variation in postcommunist political regimes, Kitschelt begins by criticizing what he calls the "tournament of variables" of the sort undertaken by Fish on a number of statistical and methodological grounds, the most important of which is that the different variables at work in Fish's argument reside at different conceptual distances from what they are trying to explain. Such a research design accords the variables most "proximate" to the outcome a better chance of being the winner in the "tournament" and therefore biases the test from the outset. This objection suggests the need, Kitschelt argues, for "deeper" explanations that cannot necessarily be set off against more proximate or "shallow" ones in a statistical tournament. Kitschelt's alternative is a series of causal chains (backed up with a series of bivariate correlations) that link one set of more general or deeper explanations to more proximate ones. Ultimately, however, Kitschelt's explanation too is temporally path dependent (he argues specifically against spatial dependence) – the key variable is the precommunist and communist legacies of bureaucratic rectitude. States with traditions of the rule of law in the precommunist period (Czechoslovakia and East Germany) carried on this tradition into the communist period and were thus left with a better chance of setting up liberal states that could respect and defend all kinds of rights in the postcommunist era. The critical juncture in Kitschelt's scheme is thus much more distant from the outcomes he is trying to explain. Although he never provides us with a causal mechanism by which these continuities are sustained through a century of turmoil and two, three, or even four different political regimes, Kitschelt has taken the causal chain one step backward (at least) in time.[2] In his case the critical juncture is the timing of precommunist bureaucratic and civic development.

[2] Not all path-dependent explanations are the same, nor do they all go back as far in the past. Whereas Kitschelt's legacies reflect state traditions of bureaucratic rectitude that go back

As in the case of Fish's work, in general we find Kitschelt's argument convincing. It may be worth considering, however, whether paths of continuity may be established not only over time but also over space. That is, in searching for the ligatures of continuity, we argue that it is also worthwhile to explore the connections not only between generations within the same state but also in the contact among people and institutional actors between states. It is here that explanations that stress the spatial diffusion of norms, lines of communication, resources, and institutions have something to offer in a causal explanation of postcommunist outcomes. Whereas Kitschelt is quick to disregard the merit of spatial explanations, we believe that cross-border interactions, the flow of ideas and resources, and the openness of states are important explanations for postcommunist reform. We also contend that the empirical evidence is available for evaluating these effects.

The main theoretical implication of our chapter is that the spatial location of a country can and should be considered an important contextual dimension that profoundly changes the nature of postcommunist dilemmas across the region and provides powerful constraints that shape available and actual choices of transforming elites. This is an important alternative position to the temporally based sociopolitical causality that dominates the literature on postcommunism. As we shall see, temporal and spatial patterns interact in complex ways, producing contextual constraints that are unequally distributed across the postcommunist world. Time and space cannot therefore be theoretically truncated and separated or altogether ignored.

Research Design

In what follows, we first engage briefly in a small "tournament of variables" of the type criticized by Kitschelt, testing statistically the types of factors put forward by Fish and Kitschelt against spatial measures. We do so not in order to refute alternative, temporally based, approaches (indeed, as we shall see, all come up as statistically significant), but rather to demonstrate the validity of the proposition that spatial context has an independent effect on political and economic outcomes that deserves further investigation. We therefore set up a geographical distance variable against an initial elections variable (as in Fish's study) and a bureaucratic rectitude variable (as a proxy for precommunist and communist legacies of the type of independent variable advanced by Kitschelt) as competing explanations for both economic reform and political democracy. What we find, however, is that even though

into the nineteenth century, the discussion by Grzegorz Ekiert (Chapter 3 in this volume) reflects a consideration of more recent developments, especially the development of civil society and reform communism in the 1970s and 1980s. The problem with this latter legacies explanation, as Ekiert repeatedly acknowledges, is that a major "winner" of postcommunism, the Czech Republic, had little civic development in the 1980s and no experience with reform communism.

it "works" statistically, conceiving of spatial context simply in terms of distance from the West does not do justice to the concept of spatial dependence. Distance is not the only way, or even the best way, of getting at geographic effects. All that distance can tell us is that factors moving over space matter. In the following two sections, therefore, we develop and deploy a much more complex measure of the spatial effects of neighbors. There we attempt to show where the most likely channels of spatial diffusion have developed, which states are exercising the greatest impact on their neighbors, and which states are resisting the effects of their external environment. The penultimate section illustrates the relationships at work through case studies of Hungary, Slovakia, and Kyrgyzstan.

The Crude Model: Distance from the West

As a starting point to the empirical examination of postcommunist reform, we consider the relative importance of initial elections, bureaucratic rectitude, and spatial factors to economic and political outcomes.[3] There are two objectives to this first model. First, we intend to demonstrate that geographic factors have a viable influence on political and economic reform above and beyond what is accounted for by path-dependent explanations. In other words, our objective is to determine whether spatial issues deserve further investigation as determinants of state behavior. Including all three variables in the model not only reveals the relative importance of each, it also indicates the independent effect. So, although the result is a "tournament of variables," this model is useful for gauging the effect of distance when controlling for path-dependent factors.

A second concern of these initial tests is the temporal realm. We use a pooled cross-sectional time-series model in order to examine how these factors relate to discrete changes over time. In Fish's and Kitschelt's work on this topic, as well as an earlier review of Fish's study, single-year results were examined (Kopstein and Reilly, 1999). Although their studies provide a snapshot view of postcommunist reforms, they do not address the process of change. The results of these studies are also unreliable because of the small number of cases analyzed. Our model addresses a five-year period of economic (1995–99) and six-year period of political (1993–98) data as a means of capturing the ongoing reform process.

[3] Although Fish does not maintain that his initial elections are crucial in determining *political* (as opposed to economic) outcomes, following Kitschelt, we believe that there is a strong enough logic here to warrant including them in the model. Similarly, although Kitschelt's legacies are meant primarily in his article to explain political outcomes, the logic of their influencing economic reforms is strong enough to warrant their inclusion in the economics model too. In fact, they remain the primary determinants in explaining outcomes in his work on political party formation (Kitschelt et al., 1999: 19–41).

Political reform is evaluated using the Polity IV data.[4] We chose the democracy measure from this data set for two reasons. First, it is conceptually relevant for our study. The democracy and autocracy scores are aggregated from a variety of authority measures that address participation, liberties, and competition. These scores also address institutional constraints and regulations that are pertinent to the determination of political reform. In contrast, Freedom House's surveys of political rights and civil liberties relate to a more narrow conception of political reform.[5] Second, Polity IV offers a more discrete indication of change than other indicators of democracy. With the calculated "Democracy minus Autocracy" score, a 21-point scale of political level is produced. When Freedom House's scores are combined, a 14-point scale results. This is important because the identification of slight changes in the institutions, practices, and policies of postcommunist governments is crucial for understanding the process of reform.

For the measure of economic reform we chose the *Index of Economic Freedom* (Johnson, Holmes, and Kirkpatrick, 1999). Not only are the economic freedom data available from 1995 to the present, but the study scores countries on ten economic factors: trade policy, taxation, government intervention in the economy, monetary policy, capital flows and foreign investment, banking, wage and price controls, property rights, regulation, and black market.[6] Political and economic scores for all postcommunist states are listed in Table 4.1, sorted by distance from the West.

In terms of independent variables, we chose three basic indicators of the aforementioned causal explanations. To evaluate the "first election" hypothesis, we employ Fish's 1990 election scores (Fish, 1999a). This variable scores countries on a scale of 1 through 5 as a result of their initial elections, with scores aggregated on the basis of who won, whether the results persisted, and whether the elections were competitive and complete. As a means of investigating bureaucratic rectitude, we create a composite score of government corruption based on the economic freedom measures of property rights, government intervention, and black market.[7] We chose this indicator over

4 See Jaggers and Gurr (1995) for a detailed explanation of the scoring criteria. From the democracy and autocracy measures, we calculate a "democracy minus autocracy" score from the data. This practice follows earlier research on democratization.

5 In fact, the Freedom House scores have been frequently used to evaluate the human rights behavior of states (Stohl et al., 1986).

6 Missing data for all variables were addressed using one of two methods. If country data revealed a pattern of consistent change (uniform increases or decreases), the prior year's numbers were used for missing years. If country data revealed no clear, uniform pattern, the mean score of all available country data was used. Missing data pose a particular problem for spatial analysis where geographic factors are investigated using a proximity matrix. In these instances, analysis cannot be performed if any data are missing.

7 The measure of property rights is based on the following criteria: freedom from government influence over the judicial system; commercial-code-defining contracts; sanctioning of foreign arbitration of contract disputes; government expropriation of property; corruption

Kitschelt's own score because our corruption indicators vary over time, and because we believe this measure provides a more robust tally of the issues Kitschelt describes in his account of bureaucratic legacies. The final variable measures the distance, in miles, between postcommunist country capitals and Vienna or Berlin, whichever is closer. These cities are chosen as important economic and cultural referents for the countries of the former communist world.[8]

Table 4.2 lists the results of regressing political level on the three independent variables in a pooled cross-sectional time series running from 1993 to 1998, yielding 145 cases.[9] The statistics indicate that the further away from the West a country is, the less likely it is to be democratic. Although not as significant, the relationship between bureaucratic rectitude and democracy also is empirically validated. Lower levels of corruption within the government are correlated with higher levels of democracy. The relationship between the initial elections and political level is not supported, however.

The substantive effect of this relationship can be described as follows. For a country that made a clean break from communism in the 1990 elections and that has an average bureaucratic rectitude score, we can predict that if it borders the West it should have a political score of 7.1. That score for a country with the same election results and bureaucratic rectitude score, but located 500 miles from the West, should decrease to 6.1. The same circumstances for a country 1,000 miles from the West should result in a score of 5.1, and so forth. We can see from these results that distance matters – especially in the context of a region where capital cities are located anywhere between 35 miles (Slovak Republic) and 3,965 miles (Mongolia) from the nearest Western capital city.

within the judiciary; delays in receiving judicial decisions; and legally granted and protected private property. Regulation and intervention is a function of licensing requirements to operate a business; ease of obtaining a business license; corruption within the bureaucracy; labor regulations; environmental, consumer safety, and worker health regulations; and regulations that impose a burden on business. The black market score is defined in terms of smuggling; piracy of intellectual property in the black market; and agricultural production, manufacturing, services, transportation, and labor supplied on the black market (Johnson, Holmes, and Kirkpatrick, 1999: 64–67).

8 One alternative to this coding would simply be to have substituted "distance from Brussels" as the independent variable. This choice is justifiable on conceptual grounds, because joining the EU and NATO remain important goals for most postcommunist states. Substituting Brussels does not alter the statistical results substantively at all. Jeffrey Sachs (1997; 1999) has recently turned to a distance variable in his explanation of postcommunist outcomes.

9 Analysis producing the results in Tables 4.2–4 performed on Intercooled Stata ver. 6.0 using the *xtreg* function. This command estimates cross-sectional time-series regression models. We employed a population-averaged model to produce a generalized estimating equation that weights the countries by their available data. Standard errors are semirobust and adjusted for clustering around countries. OLS assumptions are relaxed for pooled data – in other words, so that multiple observations for each country are not assumed to be independent of one another.

TABLE 4.1. *Political and Economic Reform Scores*

Country by Distance from the West	Political Reform Score, 1998	Economic Freedom Score, 1999
35–500 miles		
Slovak Republic	8	3.05
Hungary	10	2.90
Czech Republic	10	2.05
Croatia	−1	3.65
Slovenia	10	3.10
Bosnia-Herzegovina	1	4.80
Poland	9	2.95
Macedonia	9	
501–1,000 miles		
Albania	6	3.85
Bulgaria	8	3.45
Lithuania	10	3.00
Latvia	8	2.85
Romania	8	3.30
Moldova	7	3.35
Belarus	−7	4.15
Estonia	8	2.15
Ukraine	7	3.80
1,001–1,500 miles		
Russia	4	3.45
Georgia	5	3.65
Armenia	6	3.45
1,501–4,080 miles		
Azerbaijan	−6	4.30
Turkmenistan	−9	4.45
Uzbekistan	−9	4.40
Tajikistan	−2	4.40
Kyrgyzstan	2	4.00
Kazakhstan	−3	4.05
Mongolia	9	3.20

TABLE 4.2. *Effect of Independent Variables on Political Level, 1993–1998 ($n = 145$)*

Variable	Coefficient	Standard Error	z	$P > \|z\|$
1990 elections	.965	.597	1.616	0.11
Bureau, rectitude	−.799	.486	−1.645*	0.10
Distance from West	−.002	.001	−1.933**	0.05
Constant	11.469	6.327	1.813*	0.07

*p ≤ 1; ** p ≤ .05.

TABLE 4.3. *Effect of Independent Variables on Levels of Economic Freedom, 1999 (n = 24)*

Variable	Coefficient	Standard Error	z	$P > \|z\|$
1990 elections	−.203	.047	−4.302**	0.000
Corruption	.056	.036	1.533	0.125
Distance from West	.0002	.00007	2.616**	0.009
Constant	3.674	.249	14.735**	0.000

** $p \leq .05$.

On the issue of levels of economic reform (Table 4.3), we find that once again distance from the West is statistically significant even when controlling for corruption and initial elections. In contrast with the political results, however, distance from the West is not a substantively significant influence on economic reform. This model predicts, in other words, that moving away from the western border of postcommunist states results in a trivial change in the overall economic reform score. Note that our results in Table 4.3 are based on a small number of cases (n = 24); we have replaced bureaucratic rectitude with Kitschelt's "corruption" variable in order to reduce multicollinearity[10] as well as to address the issue of economic reform more directly. This adjustment requires that we examine a single year (1999) rather than a pooled time series.[11] In this model, an additional significant variable is the results of the initial elections – the more definitive the break from communist rule, in other words, the more likely a state is to have an economy free from government control.

So how do we interpret these findings? Our intent is not to prove that path dependence is irrelevant to political and economic reform. It is obvious from an examination of the raw scores of economic and political reforms in the former Soviet Union (see Table 4.1) that there are countries that do not conform to the distance explanation. Belarus, Croatia, and Mongolia stand out in particular as outliers in the Western proximity model; from these cases alone we can see that a more elaborate account is required for explaining postcommunist reforms. Rather, we seek to demonstrate at this stage, and the findings appear to support the contention, that geography has been underspecified in research on postcommunist states. Our goal is to demonstrate that cultural models of "Leninist legacies" and bureaucratic rectitude,

[10] Because the factors from which the bureaucratic rectitude score is composed are also components of the overall economic freedom score, we could not include the bureaucratic rectitude measure as an explanation for economic freedom. Kitschelt's corruption score correlates with our bureaucratic rectitude score at .8669, so it is an adequate substitute.

[11] Kitschelt's bureaucratic rectitude scores are measured for a single year, rendering a time-series model irrelevant.

and the broader historical context are themselves spatially bound. If we think of their effects in terms of how they condition behavior across the landscape of the postcommunist states, we can imagine them as generating the channels of communication that facilitate diffusion. It may be the case that spatial factors not only affect the reform process but also were instrumental in the choices that leaders made historically. In other words, we may find that geography, in addition to influencing the process of reform, can also help to account for the developmental paths and critical junctures themselves.

Before we take this leap, however, we believe it is important to disaggregate the concept of space. Diffusion, after all, is a complex process that involves information flows, networks of communication, hierarchies of influence, and receptivity to change. To attribute all of this to a simple indicator of distance from the West is unnecessarily vague. In order to begin to disentangle these plausible causes, the way we understand spatial influence itself needs to be disaggregated and reformulated.

Diffusion: Stocks and Flows

One way of establishing which factors may be moving over space and thus separating specific spatial effects from those of mere distance is to hypothesize, on the one hand, a relationship between a country's external environment and openness to outside influences and, on the other hand, its political and economic performance. In spatial analysis, the objective is to identify and make sense of the patterns that emerge from interactions.

The geographic pattern of success and failure in the postcommunist world, a pattern that is surprisingly strong even when controlling for cultural legacies and institutional choice, suggests a spatial diffusion of the resources, values, and institutions that are necessary for successful transformation. What exactly do we mean by diffusion, and how do we propose to get at this? The core of any diffusion explanation of politics and economics involves a relationship between stocks and flows, on the one hand, and discrete political and economic outcomes, on the other. Stocks represent the assets, liabilities, or general qualities of a given unit, in this case a given postcommunist country. These qualities may be physical, political, economic, or cultural and may either be helpful or harmful to democracy and economic development. Among these qualities are the environmental and structural conditions that shape the alternatives available to decision makers. In a diffusion model, the stock of a country can be represented by its external environment. Flows, on the other hand, represent the movement of information and resources between countries. Even if a country has a certain spatial stock, it may be more or less open to flows of goods and information from the outside world, whether by choice or by circumstance.

Diffusion is difficult to disaggregate from other processes of change because it encompasses a variety of qualifying factors. As Strang and Soule note, "Diffusion arguments ... verge on the one hand toward models of individual choice, since diffusion models often treat the adopter as a reflective decision-maker. They verge on the other hand toward a broader class of contextual and environmental processes, where conditions outside the actor shape behavior" (Strang and Soule, 1998). For the purposes of this study we posit a given country's spatial stock to be who its neighbors are. This is best indicated by the Polity IV democracy scores and the economic reform scores of the countries geographically contiguous with it. Such a definition has its obvious limits, especially when one considers the different sizes and geographical contours of the units under investigation, but it does provide a convenient and comparable way of summing up the stock of a country's external political and economic environment.

Flows, on the other hand, are best represented by examining both the actual movement of resources and people between countries and the potential for this movement. These tend to reflect the choices made by the relevant actors – in our case the willingness and capacity of states to interact within their larger environment. The diffusion process, in other words, is in large part a function of how open and interactive states are. Accordingly, states that interact extensively are likely to exhibit similar political and economic behavior.[12] Although the most likely units to interact are those closest together,[13] social patterns do not always follow this logic. States may choose to ignore the behavior of their neighbors, erecting barriers to resist surrounding change.[14] In addition, states may attempt to promote their agendas to specific countries beyond their neighbors. By examining flows of resources and information, we can capture these interactions that occur beyond (the stocks of) neighboring states.

In order to evaluate these flows, an openness criterion must be employed. Research by Brams employs such a measure, but his operationalization of "relative acceptance" is based exclusively on elite transactions.[15] Our objective is to devise a measure that reflects both public and elite receptivity, because the process of change in the postcommunist states was a hybrid of

[12] This should come as no surprise to students of Eastern Europe who are familiar with the contagion effect during the revolutions of 1989. See Ash (1990).

[13] As Strang and Soule (1998: 275) state, "Perhaps the most common finding in diffusion research is that spatially proximate actors influence each other.... Where network relations are not mapped directly, proximity often provides the best summary of the likelihood of mutual awareness and interdependence." An operationalization of this dynamic is Boulding's (1963) loss-of-strength gradient.

[14] One of Stalin's strategies for establishing absolute power was the systematic monopolization of communication channels within the Soviet Union and, after World War II, in Eastern Europe. His control over all facets of the media not only facilitated the spread of communist ideology but also limited the possibility of undesirable interactions.

[15] Brams (1967) uses diplomatic exchanges, trade, and shared memberships in intergovernmental organizations as indicators of transaction flows.

elite reform and mass mobilization. This measure is also intended to reflect the choices state actors make. Whereas stocks are representative of structural conditions within which states operate, flows indicate the willingness and capacity of states to behave in particular ways.[16]

Our measure of openness is a composite score based on indicators that are conceptually linked to the exchange of ideas and associated in prior research studies to processes of diffusion.[17] The set of six indicators gathered from the *World Development Indicators* (World Bank, 1998) includes the number of televisions per 1,000 households; newspaper circulation per 1,000 people; outgoing international telecommunications, measured in minutes per subscriber; international inbound tourists; total foreign direct investment as a percentage of GDP; and international trade (sum of exports and imports) as a share of GDP, using purchasing power parity conversion factors. Each individual indicator is assigned a score ranging from 1 to 5, based on its raw number.[18] These scores are then aggregated into an overall openness measure, which ranges from a low of 6 to a high of 27, and is intended to reflect the awareness of external ideas within the population and the willingness and capacity of elites to permit their exchange. The period of coverage (1991–96) begins with the early years of democratization efforts and includes a sufficient period of time for postcommunist countries to develop exchanges and establish patterns of interaction.

The results of regressing the openness measure on political and economic reforms are displayed in Table 4.4. These results reveal a significant and

[16] Most and Starr's (1989) research presents the opportunity/willingness framework, which corresponds with our stocks and flows to some extent. However, flows in our model involve more than just willingness. The capacity of states is important for determining the extent of interaction and exchange of resources and ideas. Although we admit that this leads to a blurring of the line between stocks and flows, we expect that any operationalization of flows is likely to overlap with stocks.

[17] It could be argued that some of these measures, such as the number of televisions or newspaper circulation, reflect modernization rather than the diffusion of information. This is precisely why we developed a composite index; our intent is to capture a variety of sources that could contribute to diffusionary processes of reform. Furthermore, most of our indicators have been frequently cited as tools of interaction in diffusion studies. Newspapers, television, and the mass media in general have been studied extensively as mechanisms of diffusion. See, for example, Spilerman (1984), Koopmans (1993), and Oberschall (1994). Foreign direct investment (FDI) has been identified as an important channel for the diffusion of ideas and information. See, for example, Barrell and Pain (1997). Trade is also recognized as a source of diffusing ideas. See, for example, Eaton and Kortum (1999). The telephone is a mechanism of within-group information exchange and seems an obvious indicator for our purposes. Tourism is not only a means of communication, but it also provides a means by which individuals can compare their own political and economic circumstances to those of others.

[18] Scores are assigned in such a manner as to provide for the greatest distribution of cases across the 1–5 categories.

TABLE 4.4. *Effect of Openness on Political and Economic Reforms*

Variable	Coefficient	Standard Error	*z*	*P* > |*z*|
Political level (n = 162)				
Openness	.268	.111	2.410**	0.016
Constant	−.324	1.950	−0.166	0.868
Economic freedom (n = 98)				
Openness	−.096	.015	−6.365**	0.000
Constant	4.940	.208	23.764**	0.000

** $p \leq .05$.

substantive effect to both political and economic reforms resulting from openness.[19] The results show that a country with the highest level of openness would be likely to have an economic reform score of 2.35 (a medium-high level of reform), whereas a country with the lowest should have a score of 4.36 (a very low level of reform). For political level, the lowest level of openness corresponds with a democracy score of 1.3 (an autocracy), and the highest with a democracy score of 6.9 (full-fledged democracy). In short, it appears that the independent effect of a state's receptivity and openness to external ideas and resources is an important factor in both political change and economic reforms.

Neighbor Effects: Spatial Dependence

We have established a relationship between a country's openness to outside influences and its political and economic performance. How much does a country's locational stock determine its performance? Do neighboring states affect a country's democratic and economic freedoms? Do domestic conditions of openness and awareness affect the process of diffusion? What is the independent influence of these two factors? Are there particularly influential states or blocs of states that encourage or discourage liberalization and marketization? In this section of the chapter, we attempt to answer these questions as a means of integrating domestic factors and international influences.

Our methods stem from research in political geography, where the central expectation of research is that the conventional explanations of domestic political change are often inadequate. In order to uncover the dynamics of political and economic change, geographers argue that place-specific factors

[19] The lag between openness measures (1991–96) and the dependent variables of political level (1993–98) and economic reform (1995–99) is intentional. Our expectation is that interaction will influence political and economic behavior over time. Although there may be some immediate effects, we expect that a period of 3–4 years is most likely to capture the learning and implementation processes that would result from new information.

must be included in these models.[20] In our case, this would suggest that where a state is located can influence the extent to which that state is dependent upon its path of prior circumstances.

The concept of spatial dependence is central to geographic research. It is often termed the "friends and neighbors effect" because the contention is that "behavior in a place is related, in part, to conditions in neighboring places" (O'Loughlin, Flint, and Anselin, 1994). Because of this association, patterns of diffusion can be identified where spatial dependence, or clustering, exists. A first step in disaggregating the concept of space is to create a more sophisticated measure – one that would operationalize spatial context differently. To this end we have created new variables that measure the economic and political levels of a state's physically contiguous neighbors. The logic behind the relevance of a neighbor's performance to a given state's economic and political performance is straightforward. If we believe that geographical proximity to the West may help a country or that geographical isolation in the East (or proximity to other, nondemocratic, weakly marketized or authoritarian states) may hurt a country, then it makes sense to say that a state will be influenced by its neighbors wherever it is located. These measures are intended to establish similarities and differences between economic and political choices and developments of states. We expect that the extent of similarity between states partially represents the contextual factors that are associated with geography.

In order to analyze the postcommunist states in the context of their surroundings, we look at the scores for these states as well as their neighbors. Accordingly, our population of cases includes the postcommunist states as well and the countries immediately bordering them. We include these because our interest is in identifying which neighbors influence each other – it is certainly the case that some countries outside of the formerly communist world are promoting democracy and open markets, but whether these countries are actually affecting the reform processes is an empirical question. Accordingly, the following tests pertain to forty-one countries, twenty-seven of which are postcommunist states.

The results of Tables 4.5 and 4.6 reveal the extent to which neighbors influence democratization and marketization. In the same manner that a temporal lag measures the extent to which a state's characteristics are a function of its past, we use a spatial lag to determine how dependent states are upon their neighbors. We regress democracy and political levels on a state's neighbor scores in order to evaluate the proposition that ideas are most likely to be shared among states in close contact. Given that geographical proximity is one determinant of interaction, the extent to which states are influenced by their neighbors can be addressed through the use of spatial

[20] See, for example, O'Loughlin, Flint, and Anselin (1994); Johnston (1991); Agnew (1987).

TABLE 4.5. *Neighbor Effects and Political Level ($n = 41$)*

	Coefficient	Standard Deviation	*t*-value	Probability
Democracy, 1998				
Spatial lag	.680	.205	3.313**	0.002
Openness	.469	.208	2.258**	0.030
Constant	−5.149	2.817	−1.828*	0.075
$r^2 = .501$				
Democracy, 1996				
Spatial lag	.546	.216	2.531**	0.016
Openness	.754	.256	2.945**	0.005
Constant	−8.555	3.239	−2.641**	0.012
$r^2 = .555$				
Democracy, 1994				
Spatial lag	.794	.194	4.091**	0.000
Openness	.486	.214	2.273**	0.029
Constant	−4.839	2.467	−1.961*	0.057
$r^2 = .595$				

Note: Analysis performed using SpaceStat. *$p \leq .1$; **$p \leq .05$.

TABLE 4.6. *Neighbor Effects and Economic Freedom ($n = 41$)*

	Coefficient	Standard Deviation	*t*-value	Probability
Economic Reform, 1999				
Spatial lag	.707	.190	3.714**	0.000
Openness	−0.100	.025	−3.954**	0.000
Constant	2.278	.899	2.533**	0.016
$r^2 = .685$				
Economic Reform, 1997				
Spatial lag	.180	.226	.797	0.430
Openness	−.155	.030	−5.171**	0.000
Constant	4.901	1.111	4.409**	0.000
$r^2 = .580$				
Economic Reform, 1995				
Spatial lag	.835	.205	4.066**	0.000
Openness	−.078	.022	−3.462**	0.001
Constant	1.650	.922	1.791*	0.081
$r^2 = .649$				

Note: Analysis performed using SpaceStat. *$p \leq .1$; **$p \leq .05$.

lags. In addition, we include the openness score for each state to assess its importance, independent of neighbor effects.

The results suggest that both neighbors and openness are strong determinants of political and economic behavior. These variables are consistently and robustly related to political levels in 1994, 1996, and 1998, as well as economic freedom scores in 1995, 1997, and 1999. Equally important to our argument is the fact that both variables – openness and neighbors – are statistically significant when controlling for the other. This suggests that internal conditions as well as the external environment have played an important role in the reform process of the postcommunist states. It also suggests that spatial proximity permits a more extensive level of diffusion that, in turn, exercises a strong and independent effect on political and economic outcomes. Alternatively, we can think of this result as revealing the importance of *both* stocks (neighbors) and flows (openness) to the process of diffusion in the postcommunist world.

Spatial dependence involves more than neighbor effects, however. As stated already, the types of patterns that we expect to reveal include the extent to which openness, receptivity, and influence matter for processes of reform. In order to assess the extent of spatial dependence, we rely on two additional spatial statistics. The first is the Moran's I, a measure of the spatial pattern for the entire population of cases under investigation.[21] This statistic indicates the clustering of similar values of political and economic reform, as well as their significance level. Whether the reforms of postcommunist states are randomly distributed across space or subject to identifiable patterns is revealed by this statistic. Second, we employ a localized measure of spatial association. The G_{i*} statistic, like the Moran's I, offers an indication of clustering.[22] The difference between the two is that the Gi* measure addresses the extent of clustering around each particular state, rather than the overall level of clustering within the system. Its usefulness is for assessing the extent to which each state influences those around it, as well as the extent to which states resist external influences.

The Moran's I scores are reported in Table 4.7.[23] Again, this score indicates whether bordering states are the most similar in terms of the variables tested. The strength and uniformity of positive spatial autocorrelation reveals that this is in fact the case – there is significant clustering for all three years tested and for all three measures of political level, economic freedom score, and openness. This indicates that there is a substantial spatial component to these variables that warrants investigation.

[21] For technical notes on the logic and use of Moran's I, see Getis and Ord (1992); Anselin (1995).

[22] G_{i*} statistics and other local indicators of spatial association are explained in Anselin (1995).

[23] Spatial weights matrix is in row-standardized form.

TABLE 4.7. *Moran's I Test for Spatial Autocorrelation: Scores for Political Level, Economic Level, Openness, and Bureaucratic Rectitude*

Variable	Moran's I-Score	Z-Value	Probability
1994 political level	.504	5.096**	0.000
1996 political level	.462	4.688**	0.000
1998 political level	.455	4.626**	0.000
1995 economic reform	.466	4.729**	0.000
1997 economic reform	.315	3.283**	0.001
1999 economic reform	.428	4.361**	0.000
1992 openness	.299	3.122**	0.002
1994 openness	.400	4.100**	0.000
1996 openness	.285	2.989**	0.003
1992 bureaucratic rectitude	.441	4.494**	0.000
1994 bureaucratic rectitude	.416	4.247**	0.000
1996 bureaucratic rectitude	.349	3.601**	0.000

Note: Analysis performed using SpaceStat. **$p \leq .05$.

Finally, we address the importance of receptivity and influence to reform. Using the G_{i*} statistic (Table 4.8), we seek to identify those states that promote change and those that resist it. In Table 4.8 and Map 4.1 we see that thirteen of the forty-one countries are significantly associated with their neighbors (denoted by asterisks). Nine are negatively associated, or grouped at the low end of the spectrum of political scores, and four are positively correlated around high levels of democracy. Clustering among high similar scores is apparent along the border between Western and Eastern Europe, where Austria, Germany, Slovakia, and the Czech Republic display the highest scores. Low-score groupings can be seen to the east of the Caspian Sea, where Uzbekistan, Turkmenistan, and Afghanistan display particularly significant scores. One can think of these scores as suggesting the substantial influence of these states on their neighbors. To the west we can conceptualize this in terms of democratic promotion, whereas in the post-Soviet "Near Abroad" we see a regional trend of autocratization.

The middle category, denoted by medium gray in Map 4.1, represents those states that resist the influences of their neighbors. We see subregions of resistance within the Caucasus – the territory between the Black, Azov, and Caspian Seas, bordering on Turkey and Iran in the south – as well as in the former Yugoslavia. Interestingly, these are two areas of violent conflict. It stands to reason that states in the midst of violent turmoil are less likely to be receptive to the diffusion of ideas and more concerned with the outcome of their disputes. Accordingly, these states reject the influences of surrounding countries and focus on their domestic issues.

A second set of middle-level countries are not clustered – Russia, Turkey, and Mongolia. Instead, these states appear as the remnant cores of formerly

TABLE 4.8. G_{i*} *Results for Democracy and Economic Reforms*

Country	Z-Score: Democracy 1998	Probability: Democracy 1998	Z-Score: Economic Reform 1999	Probability: Economic Reform 1999
Afghanistan	−4.051**	0.000	−2.877**	0.004
Albania	0.250	0.803	−0.390	0.697
Armenia	−0.870	0.385	−1.381	0.167
Austria	2.425**	0.015	2.800**	0.005
Azerbaijan	−0.801	0.423	−1.137	0.255
Belarus	0.474	0.635	−0.143	0.886
Bosnia	−1.538	0.124	−1.784*	0.075
Bulgaria	0.856	0.391	0.453	0.650
China	−2.525**	0.012	−2.313**	0.021
Croatia	−0.388	0.698	−1.113	0.266
Czech Republic	1.884*	0.060	2.377**	0.018
Estonia	0.711	0.477	1.252	0.211
Finland	1.057	0.291	1.657*	0.010
Georgia	−0.181	0.856	−0.308	0.758
Germany	1.768*	0.077	2.452**	0.014
Greece	1.471	0.141	0.068	0.946
Hungary	0.829	0.407	0.347	0.729
Iran	−2.394**	0.017	−1.883*	0.060
Italy	1.576	0.115	1.927*	0.054
Japan	0.643	0.520	1.281	0.200
Kazakhstan	−2.904**	0.008	−1.634	0.102
Korea, North	−2.057**	0.040	−1.446	0.148
Kyrgyzstan	−2.660**	0.008	−1.918*	0.055
Latvia	0.232	0.817	0.766	0.444
Lithuania	0.301	0.764	0.229	0.819
Macedonia	0.507	0.612	−0.200	0.841
Moldova	0.884	0.377	−0.091	0.923
Mongolia	−0.500	0.617	−0.097	0.923
Norway	1.057	0.291	1.657*	0.098
Poland	1.113	0.266	1.012	0.312
Romania	0.665	0.506	0.106	0.916
Russia	0.057	0.955	0.518	0.605
Serbia	0.204	0.839	−1.116	0.265
Slovakia	1.940*	0.052	1.348	0.178
Slovenia	1.333	0.182	1.303	0.193
Tajikistan	−2.935**	0.003	−2.187**	0.029
Turkey	−0.149	0.882	−0.935	0.350
Turkmenistan	−3.692**	0.000	−2.724**	0.007
Ukraine	0.829	0.407	0.125	0.900
United States	0.643	0.520	1.281	0.200
Uzbekistan	−3.286**	0.001	−2.380**	0.017

Note: Analysis performed using SpaceStat. $^{**}p \leq .1$; $^{*}p \leq .05$.

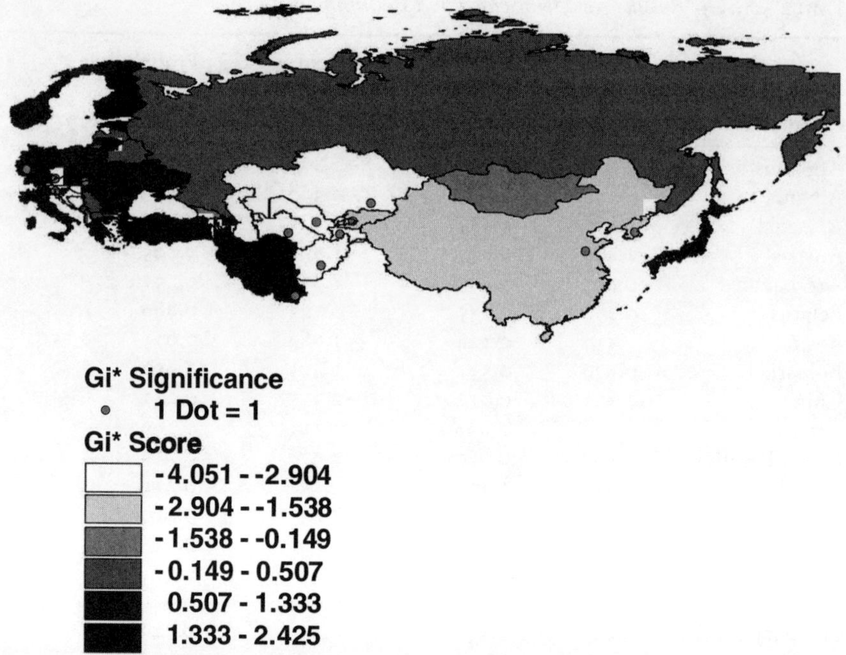

MAP 4.1. G_{i*} for democracy, 1998.

imperial powers that are especially impervious to outside influences. They are insignificant now, statistically speaking, but hold the potential to be key power centers once again if the circumstances were right (Hanson and Kopstein, 1997). A second way of thinking about these states is by way of the shatterbelt literature, which describes these as countries caught between competing ideologies, histories, and cultures (Cohen, 1991; Diehl, 1999). The case of Mongolia is, to date, the true outlier in the postcommunist world, not conforming to the expectations of any extant theory (Fish, 1998).

Table 4.8 and Map 4.2 show the G_{i*} statistics for economic freedoms. In this instance we see a uniform shift from high positive association in the West to high negative association in the southwestern portion of the map. Note that the fourteen statistically significant scores (six positive, eight negative) are located in these two areas, with a large buffer zone of states displaying intermediate scores in between. Economic reforms are promoted from the bordering states of Western Europe – Austria, Germany, and Italy – while economic corruption and government control of the economy is the norm in Iran, Afghanistan, Turkmenistan, Uzbekistan, and China. The diffusion of these competing economic orientations is evident in Map 4.2, where the middling scores fall geographically between these polar opposite – evidenced by the medium gray shading of Eastern and Central Europe. Poland, Slovakia, Latvia, and Estonia appear inclined toward the West, whereas Azerbaijan and Armenia are leaning toward Central Asia.

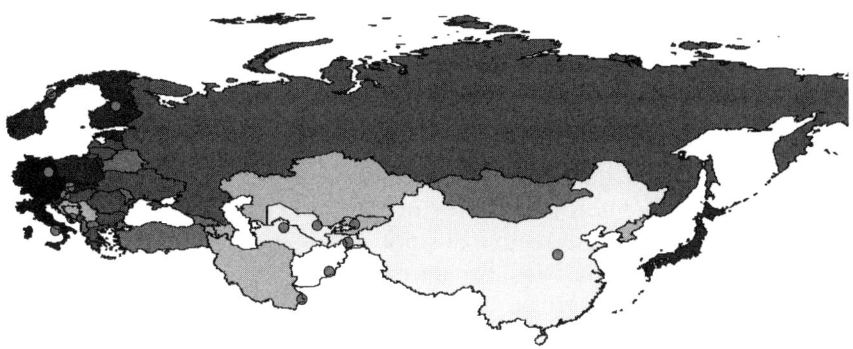

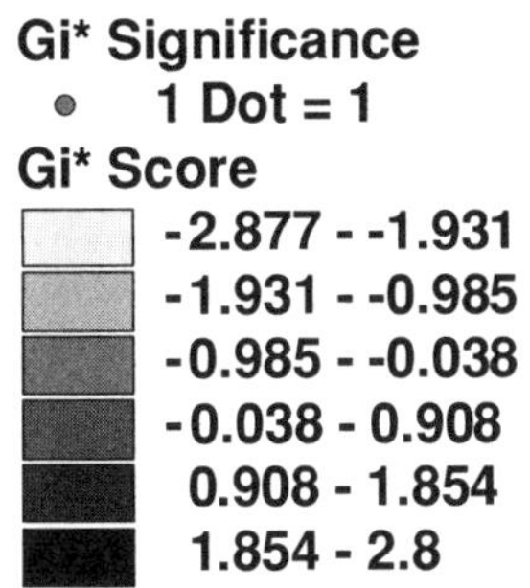

MAP 4.2. G_{i*} for economic reform, 1999.

This map may provide the clearest visual representation of the sort of effect we seek to demonstrate. It is certainly the case that path dependence and the historical evolution of political and economic choices and values are important explanations for postcommunist reforms. The evidence presented in Maps 4.1 and 4.2, however, suggests that this path dependence is in large part a function of the geopolitical landscape. Cultures certainly shift, and ideas spread across space, but the shortest route between two points is the most likely one for information to travel. The path dependence of political and economic reforms may explain the process of change, but these maps indicate that location determines the path.

How Does Geography Matter? External Promoters and the Constitution of Interests

Put most boldly, our statistical treatment suggests that location matters more than domestic policy itself in determining outcomes or at least appears to influence which policies are chosen.[24] A country that chooses all the right policies but is poorly located, if our explanation is correct, should ultimately

[24] In a similar vein Vladimir Popov (1999) has recently argued that policy choices cannot account for variation in the recessions in the postcommunist world between 1990 and 1993.

not perform well. Conversely, bad policies should be mitigated by good location. Why would this be the case?

In this section we deepen the explanation for how geography might matter. Our data analysis of spatial dependence has suggested a purely structuralist tale, one in which stocks and flows determine outcomes. Such an explanation stands up to statistical scrutiny and constitutes an important part of the diffusion story. But it is only part of the story. A country's external environment not only is the product of its spatial stock and its openness to outside influence but is also strongly affected by the decisions of other states or groups of states. The G_{i*} statistics, for example, indicate that the countries bordering Western Europe are being strongly influenced, in a positive direction, by their western neighbors. Similarly, states in close proximity to Afghanistan and Iran are being influenced in a direction that hinders democratic and capitalist development.

One explanation for the effects of spatial context is the impact of external actors on the structure of domestic interests and the policies chosen by elites. We expect, for example, the possibility of EU and NATO membership for the countries of Central Europe bordering on the eastern and northern frontier of "Western Europe" to alter the expected utilities of elites and masses in ways that would not be the case in Eastern Europe and Central Asia.[25] The potential for integration into "just in time delivery systems" in regional production chains or the stabilizing effects of probable membership in a larger military alliance, we hypothesize, has altered the relative expectations of future economic success and political stability. Elites and masses in Central Europe have calculated that economic and political institutions similar to those of the EU will improve the chances that such benefits will actually be realized. We expect the real changes to come about in the region not so much as a result of actual EU or NATO membership but as a result of *anticipated* membership. These divergent, externally induced incentives are part of what accounts for differences in institutional reform, state behavior, and popular discourse in the countries of postcommunist Europe.

Presumably, one could tell a similar tale in reverse, about the baneful effects of poor location on the structure of interests, institutional reform, state behavior, and political discourse. From our Maps 4.1 and 4.2, for example, it would appear that proximity to the general crisis zone of Islamic

[25] The EU logic of enlargement, one based mostly on a logic of geographical contiguity, is a topic that remains mostly unexplored, due principally to the sub rosa nature of most real discussions of the matter among policy makers. Such an explanation, of course, represents a departure from a purely structuralist logic of diffusion, in that the decisions of the EU and NATO to admit particular countries are themselves an element of the spatial context, and these decisions were influenced by a whole range of not only strategic but also *cultural* considerations of where EU members consider Europe's boundaries properly to lie and who should be a member of "Europe." If culture is to reenter the picture in our spatial diffusion analysis, we suspect that this is the proper place for it.

TABLE 4.9. *Postcommunist Policies and Spatial Advantage/Disadvantage, 1999*

	Location	
	Good	**Bad**
Policies		
Good	Hungary, Poland, Czech Republic, Estonia, Slovenia, Lithuania, Latvia	Kyrgyzstan, Moldova, Georgia, Mongolia, Macedonia
Bad	Slovakia, Croatia	Ukraine, Russia, Belarus, Turkmenistan, Kazakhstan, Tajikistan, Azerbaijan, Bulgaria, Armenia, Albania, Romania

fundamentalism that has engulfed Afghanistan and Tajikistan or the war in the Balkans should subvert even the hardiest of domestic political reformers and ardent marketizers.

In order to get at this logic and begin to disentangle the causal connections between spatial context, domestic processes, and political and economic outcomes, a brief examination of the cases is in order. If we sample on the independent variable of location, while at the same time controlling for the rival independent variable of policy and institutional choice, the universe of postcommunist countries can be illustrated in a simple two-by-two table (see Table 4.9). From the four possible groups, we have chosen three cases for more-detailed examination based on their theoretical interest. Hungary is selected in order to illustrate the effects of close institutional ties to the EU based on its good location. Slovakia is chosen as a country that is well located and was initially considered for rapid EU and NATO accession but, in the years after its independence in 1993, made a series of exceedingly poor political and economic choices, a combination that yields better-than-expected outcomes. Kyrgyzstan, on the other hand, is chosen because it is very poorly located, in close proximity to semiauthoritarian states of Central and South Asia, but adopted in the first years of independence most, if not all, of the policies and institutions that Western experts and advisers maintained were important for success in the political and economic transition. Because the outcomes of the cases of "bad location, bad policy" are so overdetermined, it makes little sense to discuss them here in any detail.

Hungary

The first quadrant in Table 4.9 depicts the countries that are both well located and have chosen "good policies."[26] Hungary provides a good example of the

[26] Of course, some countries in this group have restructured their polities and economies more than others. Hungary and Poland, for example, have clearly restructured their economies more than the Czech Republic and Slovenia.

trends in this quadrant. As in the cases of Poland and the Czech Republic, after 1989 Hungary became the recipient of a significant amount of foreign investment as a result of the publicity of being among the "first" to exit from communism and its close proximity to Western markets.[27] Quickly following on these early public relations coups came the possibility of relatively rapid accession to the EU, a possibility formalized when the European Commission drew up a list of the postcommunist countries that would be considered for admission in a "first round" (Jacoby, 1999).[28] During the second half of the 1990s, the flow of domestic political legislation and the shape of domestic discourse revolved around the issue of accession to the EU. Even accounting for differences over such contentious domestic issues as privatization and social policy, political competition in Hungary, as in Poland and the Czech Republic, were heavily influenced by the question of which party was more competent to guide the country to accession. In the 1990s it was all but impossible to understand politics in these countries without considering the effects of prospective EU enlargement (Tőkés, 1997; Kovrig, 1999; Ágh, 1994).

The effects were not only political but also, perhaps more importantly, legislative and institutional. As a "tutor and monitor," the European Commission helped to usher in a flood of new institutional legislation and organizational reforms, as Hungarian ministries and successive governments rushed, in a competition with other prospective states, to alter their own legislation and institutions to conform with the 88,000-page *acquis communautaire* with its more than 10,000 directives (Jacoby, 1999).[29] EU monitors regularly evaluated Hungary's progress in institutional change and issued reports about lacunae in legislation and offered checklists and blueprints to follow (Franzmeyer, 1999).[30]

[27] Between 1989 and 1998 Hungary received, by far, the largest share of FDI in the formerly communist world. In second and third place came Poland and the Czech Republic (Coolidge, 1999).

[28] In March 1998 the EU formalized two tiers of accession candidates. The Czech Republic, Poland, Hungary, Estonia, and Slovenia were in the first group for accession, and Bulgaria, Slovakia, Latvia, Lithuania, and Romania were in the second group. However, by 2002, Slovakia, Latvia, and Lithuania, plus Cyprus and Malta, had also been invited to join the first five candidates in the first wave of EU expansion.

[29] In Hungary's June 1999 parliamentary session, for example, 180 laws were passed, 152 of which were not subject to any debate because they were part of the *acquis communautaire*. *Magyar Nemzet*, June 19, 1999. We thank Andrew Janos for providing us with this information.

[30] According to one Brussels-based Bulgarian diplomat involved in negotiations on EU admission, "These are not classic negotiations, you are not sitting there bargaining in the true sense of the word. You are an applicant, and the rules of the club are as follows, so basically if you are aspiring to become a member of this particular club, you will have to accept the rules that are being laid out for you." And on the *acquis*, "on the bulk of the rules, or the so-called acquis communautaire, there won't be any bargaining, simply we must find ways to incorporate them in our legislation and to also effectively implement them in our daily work in Bulgaria, and not argue whether we accept them or not." Quoted in O'Rourke (2000).

The point is not that domestic politics did not matter. Indeed, privatization of state assets and stabilization of the national budget, the establishment of a free press, legislation on national minorities, and social policy reform were strategies common to all postcommunist states. But what the EU did, especially since the mid-1990s, was to provide the crucial external push that has altered domestic interests in favor of accomplishing some of the key tasks of postcommunism. Even where legislative changes have not occurred, EU influence has put the question on the agenda. A good example in Hungary is in the area of foreign ownership of land. In Hungary, as of 2001, foreigners were still forbidden to own land, and economists had identified a number of drawbacks to this policy for domestic capital formation and the modernization of the agricultural sector (a key feature of Hungary's economy). In order to gain acceptance into the EU, however, Hungary will have to permit foreigners to own land. Although no government since 1989 has attempted to push through the kind of legislation that will be required, there is a general consensus that such legislation will eventually pass, a consensus that would not have come about as easily if the prospect of EU membership were not on the horizon (Marer, 1999).

Taken together, this tutoring and monitoring helped to embed political and economic reform practices and legislation more deeply than if the countries of Central Europe had been left on their own. The rapid marginalization of extreme populist and nationalist discourse from political life after an initial flirtation with it in several Central European countries after 1989 is a final example of how the prospect of EU accession has influenced domestic politics (Frank, 1995; Nelson, 1999). In Hungary, the extreme nationalist Istvan Csurka, after finding a home within the ruling conservative Hungarian Democratic Forum (MDF), was driven out of the party by moderate forces who feared the effects of his followers on prospects for EU admission.[31] The marginalization of the nationalists has also influenced Hungarian foreign policy. Given the large minority populations of Hungarians in Romania, Slovakia, and Yugoslavia, one could reasonably have expected Hungary's primary foreign policy aims after 1989 to have focused on the status of these groups. Yet, after an initial abortive orientation of this sort under the Antall government, Hungarian foreign policy was consistently guided by the larger policy goal of gaining entry to the EU, going so far as to risk retribution against ethnic Hungarians in Voivodina during Hungary's reluctant support for the Kosovo campaign in 1999.[32] In short, whatever

[31] In 2001, however, it appeared that Csurka was making a moderate comeback with a party of his own.

[32] At the same time, Hungary continues to monitor carefully the fate of Hungarians living abroad, especially in Romania, Slovakia, and Yugoslavia. In 2001 the conservative government of Viktor Orban passed a "status law" on the rights of Hungarians living abroad to work and live in Hungary. Although both the Romanian and Slovak governments protested the passage of what they saw as extraterritorial legislation, the Hungarian government, significantly, argued that the law did not contradict either EU legislation or practices.

democratic and capitalist forces were already strong and present in the post-communist countries of Central Europe in 1989, they received invaluable support based on their location on the European continent and the prospect for admission to West European institutions.

Slovakia

An interesting contrast to Hungary in this respect is Slovakia. Located in close proximity to West European markets, like the other countries of the Visegrad Group (Hungary, Poland, and the Czech Republic), Slovakia was considered to be a prime candidate for membership in the EU and NATO. Between 1990 and 1992, as part of the still existing Czechoslovakia, the Slovak Republic began to democratize its politics and made an impressive start in financial reform and small-scale privatization. After independence in 1993, however, and especially after Vladimir Mečiar's return to power as prime minister in 1994, Slovakia's course became increasingly undemocratic and corrupt. In a similar fashion to Croatia under Franjo Tudjman, Slovakia had fallen into a seemingly hopeless form of political and economic Peronism, a course that was not altered until the national elections in September 1998. Slovakia thus provides us with the crucial test case of a country that is well located but which, on the whole, pursued "bad" policies – a combination that yields much better than expected results.

After 1994 Mečiar ruled over an increasingly nondemocratic "thugocracy": competing parties to his misnamed Movement for a Democratic Slovakia (HZDS) worked under discriminatory procedures, critical intellectuals and journalists were intimidated, laws were simply ignored, opposition figures were detained or kidnapped, and political power was distributed to an incompetent group of Mečiar's political clients (Wolchik, 1997). After coming to power on an antireform program, Mečiar corrupted the privatization process by doling out the choicest parts of the economy to his cronies (Kotrba and Svejnar, 1994). This delayed the restructuring of the badly decaying, former military industries of central Slovakia.[33] Shunned by the EU, Mečiar shunned the EU in return (Walker, 1998). Instead of Western integration, Mečiar pursued an anti-Western alliance with Russia and spoke openly of his country's affinities with international pariahs of the day, such as Iraq, Yugoslavia, and Belarus (Fish, 1999b). In short, unlike Hungary, Slovakia after 1994 consistently pursued a course of political populism and economic cronyism.

[33] Having come to power on a platform that promised a less painful "Slovak path" to the economic transition, Mečiar's economic policies produced mixed results in the short run and very poor results in the long run. The Slovak economy's main weakness is its industrial core, which came into existence almost entirely during the communist era and was designed to support a much reduced (and now truncated) Czechoslovak military-industrial complex.

Despite having done so much to destroy its democracy and ruin its economy, by 1999 Slovakia appeared once again to be on track, even though the country faced formidable challenges in overcoming the ground lost in the previous half decade. A large part of the reason for Slovakia's remarkable turnaround, we wish to argue, is its favorable location in close proximity to the West and its good prospects for joining the EU and NATO. Again, as in Hungary, external influences have been channeled through domestic institutions and interests, and domestic political issues remain crucial in any consideration of Slovak politics. Civic groups and political parties that had come into existence during the Velvet Revolution did not disappear during the 1990s, even when they remained disorganized and at odds with each other. The Slovak presidency and the Supreme Court retained an important measure of autonomy, even at the height of Mečiarism, and acted as a brake on Mečiar's accumulation of power. The public broadcast media, although increasingly a pawn of the HZDS, was balanced by a vigorous free press and third sector (Butora, Meseznikov, and Butorova, 1999).

Yet, even these rudiments of democracy might have been undermined – the case of Kyrgyzstan, as we shall see, opens up such a possibility – were it not for Slovakia's position on the European continent and the influence of outside actors. Even with less than exemplary economic policies during Mečiar's rule, Slovakia's economic performance was buoyed by foreign direct investment levels that were surprisingly high and *rising*,[34] and the economy even enjoyed a mild level of prosperity.[35] The country's sustained cultural connections to Western and Czech political parties also ensured that Mečiar's moves were subject to constant critical scrutiny in the foreign press and Czech radio and television. Slovak nongovernmental organizations (NGOs) were sustained by their strong connections to their European counterparts.[36]

Under these circumstances Mečiar pulled back from outright dictatorship. As one student of the end of Mečiarism has noted, "[Slovakia's] location may have created counterpressures against the would-be dictator that were stronger than those endured by, say, the Belarusian or Kazakh rulers" (Fish, 1999b: 50). Despite some effort, Mečiar did not succeed in completely neutralizing his political opponents. Nor did he manage to subvert completely the formal rules and procedures of Slovakia's constitutional provisions.[37] Perhaps most important, his opponents could coalesce around the quite

[34] After an initial drop to $182 million of FDI in 1995 from $203 million the year before, in the subsequent three years FDI in Slovakia doubled its level by 1998 (Coolidge, 1999: 5).

[35] See especially the annual reports of the National Bank of Slovakia, an institution that retained a remarkable degree of autonomy under Mečiar: <http://www.nbs.sk/INDEXA.HTM>.

[36] "Slovak NGOs had their natural partners abroad, and they exchanged skills, technical advice, and moral encouragement with them" (Butora et al., 1999).

[37] In an attempt to take advantage of an opposition that was fragmented into a number of competing parties, he did effect a change in the electoral rules just before the 1998 election that would have made it impossible for the opposition to win had they not coalesced into a single party.

reasonable assertion that Slovakia was squandering its opportunity to join the West. Indeed, this is what transpired when Mečiar's HDZS lost to a broad coalition of parties in the parliamentary elections of 1998 (Naegele, 1998). Although it would be inaccurate to attribute Mečiar's defeat wholly to Slovakia's "location," the evidence is quite strong that Slovakia's continued close connections with other Central European states undermined Mečiar's populist project. It is also fair to say that the sustained criticism that the country received from the EU during the 1990s in regard to its "democratic deficit," combined with the implied prospect of EU membership if Mečiar could be ousted, helped the opposition solve its own internal collective action problems in a way that would not have otherwise occurred (Butora et al., 1999).

During and after 1998, Slovakia quickly began negotiations on accession to the EU, and the EU in turn has attempted to support the diverse coalition of parties that opposed dictatorial rule. Of course, Slovakia's future is not preordained by its position on the European continent. Any return to a new variation of Mečiarism or anti-Western populism, however, is likely to be confronted with the same kinds of capacities and resources that the Slovak opposition brought to bear on the would-be dictator of the 1990s – capacities and resources that are in large part a function of the country's location at the heart of Europe.

Kyrgyzstan

Our final case, Kyrgyzstan, illustrates the kinds of obstacles facing a geographically remote and disadvantaged country that is trying to integrate itself into Western political and economic structures. In the first few years after the breakup of the Soviet Union in 1991, Kyrgyzstan was the regional darling of Western governments and financial institutions. Under the leadership of a liberal physicist, Askar Akaev, who managed against long odds to win the presidency in 1991, Kyrgyzstan quickly privatized its main enterprises; it was the first Central Asian country to leave the ruble zone and introduce its own currency, the som; and it even managed to gain entry into the World Trade Organization (WTO) (Huskey, 1997). International financial institutions rewarded Kyrgyzstan with substantial loans (considering its small size), bolstering Akaev's popularity, and Western political organizations lauded its political record (Huskey, 1993). In the first few years of independence, civic organizations flourished, the print media became lively, a private television station began to broadcast from the capital, Bishkek, and opposition parties were formed (even though they lacked significant grass-roots support).

Even with this positive beginning, Kyrgyzstan did not have the capacity to attract the kind of Western attention that could have helped it overcome the pressures of its immediate international environment. Unlike other former Soviet republics, Kyrgyzstan did not possess nuclear weapons nor did it border on bodies of water adjacent to western states, removing any possibility of Western interest arising from nuclear or environmental fears. Typical of Central Asia as a whole, foreign direct investment focused primarily on resource extraction (gold mining), as opposed to the long-term manufacturing and services investment received by Hungary, Poland, the Czech Republic, and even Slovakia.[38] The effect of this pattern of economic engagement with the West, rather than training a new middle class, has been to restrict contact between business classes to the highest political levels, which in turn has fostered political favoritism and corruption.[39]

By 1995, despite the propaganda facade of Kyrgyzstan being portrayed as the "Switzerland of Central Asia" – a neutral, multiethnic, (relatively) prosperous, democratic mountain republic – the entire Kyrgyz political economy was slowly unraveling (Anderson, 1999). As in our previous two cases, any understanding of the Kyrgyz case must combine international and domestic forces. Confronting a stagnating economy and impatient foreign creditors, on the one hand, and the increasing power of provincial elites, on the other, President Akaev undermined his country's democratic institutions, rigging both parliamentary and presidential elections in the 1990s. During the parliamentary elections in the early spring of 2000, the irregularities were all but institutionalized, and by the late spring of that year Akaev's main opponent, Felix Kulov, was imprisoned on trumped-up charges.[40] The evidence is suggestive that Akaev learned this behavior from other postcommunist presidents, especially the experience of Leonid Kravchuk in Ukraine and Stanislau Shushkevich in Belarus, both of whom lost their positions in elections in 1994. In his December 1995 presidential race, according to one student of the region, Akaev manipulated "registration rules to keep strong opponents out of the race" but "left some small fish in the pond in order to create a plausible veneer of electoral competition" (Rutland, 1999). Even more compelling is the evidence that Akaev conformed to the expectations of the other Central Asian presidents who preside over more or less authoritarian dictatorships. Kazakhstan and Uzbekistan, larger and more powerful than Kyrgyzstan, have let their preferences be known for a noncompetitive political system in a country that has so much contact with their own (Huskey, 1999). Kyrgyzstan's powerful neighbors have also criticized its attempts to integrate more closely with the West.[41] Both the policy of leaving the ruble zone in 1993

[38] Although Slovakia and Kyrgyzstan both have about 5 million inhabitants, in 1998 Kyrgyzstan received $55 million of FDI while Slovakia received almost seven times that much, even though their rankings in the various economic freedom indexes were not so far apart (Coolidge, 1999).

[39] By 1999, for example, the son-in-law of President Akaev was reported to have managed to gain under his own control almost all of the energy, transport, communications, and alcohol industry, as well as air service. *Moskovskii Komsomolets*, December 9, 1999.

[40] The pattern has largely been one of serial temporary arrests.

[41] In 1998, for example, Uzbekistan's president Karimov criticized Kyrgyzstan's dreams of Westernizing its economy. "Kyrgyzstan," Karimov admonished the Kyrgyz leadership, "is

and the entry into the WTO in 1999, for example, were met by stoppages in natural gas deliveries and the imposition of tariffs and limitations on goods exported from Kyrgyzstan to Uzbekistan and Russia (Pannier, 1999). By the end of the decade, Kyrgyzstan's continued attempts to find a stable connection to the West that ran through other hostile Central Asian countries had largely run out of steam. Confronted by a steady increase in reports of human rights abuses, political and electoral corruption, and economic stagnation, Kyrgyzstan could no longer distinguish itself as distinctly from the other authoritarian countries of the region.[42] Despite its best efforts, during the 1990s Kyrgyzstan was unable to slip the bonds of its new regional politics.[43]

Conclusion: From Postcommunist Spaces to Postcommunist Places

In this chapter we have demonstrated, using various measures and methods, the plausibility of the thesis that geographical proximity to the West has exercised a positive influence on the transformation of communist states and that geographical isolation in the East has hindered this transformation. We have pursued the spatial logic further to examine the facilitating role that openness to outside influences has played in shaping the spatial diffusion of democracy and capitalism. Furthermore, we have conceived of geographical effects in a more complex manner than is traditionally done and attempted to operationalize this concept through a statistical test of "neighbor effects" on the postcommunist states' development. Finally, we have illustrated plausible mechanisms by which geography is influencing outcomes in three theoretically important cases.

We have attempted to unpack the phenomenon of the spread of democracy and capitalism by investigating what factors are at work in the diffusion process. Our research indicates that the political and economic behaviors of postcommunist states are related, in part, to the behaviors in neighboring states. There is, accordingly, some process of spatial diffusion operating. Underlying the idea of spatial diffusion, however, are two determinants of spatiality: spatial dependence and spatial heterogeneity. Spatial dependence represents the extent to which behavior in one state is a function of behavior in adjoining states. Spatial heterogeneity, by contrast, involves regional distinctions and is characterized by differentiation among states on similar

tied more closely to the IMF, which is your 'Daddy' and supervises everything." "O druzhbe, bez kotoroi ne prozhit,'" *Slovo Kyrgyzstana*, December 2, 1998, p. 2, cited in Huskey (1999).

42 "Human Rights Watch on Kyrgyzstan," *RFERL Daily Report on Kyrgyzstan*, December 10, 1999. Available: <http://www.rferl.org/bd/ky/reports/today.html>.

43 Most ominously, Kyrgyzstan's new regional politics have included a number of short-lived but intense skirmishes with Islamic fundamentalist insurgents in the country's mountainous border regions.

characteristics. O'Loughlin and Anselin present the concepts on a continuum of spatiality. "At one extreme, if high spatial heterogeneity exists, then every region is unique and no general statements or models are possible. At the opposite extreme, the same relationships hold for all scales and regions" (O'Loughlin and Anselin, 1992).

The postcommunist states fall between these extremes. The results of the Moran's I test reveal that there is strong spatial dependence across the full set of states. However, within the space of postcommunist states, there are different levels of political and economic reforms. At the high end are Poland, Hungary, and the Czech Republic, and at the low end are Uzbekistan, Turkmenistan, and Tajikistan. Table 4.8 and Maps 4.1 and 4.2 of the G_{i*} statistics indicate statistical significance for states within each of these subregions.

In order to explore the dynamics of diffusion, we have distinguished between two sets of factors: stocks and flows. These stocks and flows have been examined simultaneously in our model of neighbor effects. We have simplified the complexity of spatiality, geographic influence, and state choices into two variables that we believe capture the essence of stocks and flows in spatial diffusion: neighbor scores and openness. The neighbor scores reflect the stock of locale: where a state is positioned shapes the interactions that are likely to occur; the examples that elites and masses learn from; the resources that are readily accessible; and the cultural, religious, and ethnic affiliations that are often place-based. The openness score is indicative of the flow of ideas and the willingness and capacity of the ruling regime to allow interaction with surrounding states and to accept the influx of communication, transportation, and technology that has the potential to transform attitudes and behavior. The model provides support for the proposition that both of these factors are important. Even when controlling for the other, there is statistical significance to both stocks and flows.

In assuming that political and economic reforms in the postcommunist world involve a process of spatial interaction, we must also consider the dynamics of "origin" and "destination" or "target" states. The diffusion literature offers detailed discussion of the importance of promoter and receptor, and we believe that these concepts are applicable to the circumstances of postcommunist reform. The case studies included in our discussion illustrate this point. The strategy of EU enlargement based on geographical contiguity and proximity has altered the context of politics in the states of East Central Europe in important ways. The states of Central Asia, by contrast, even those that have tried to escape from their Leninist and pre-Leninist legacies, have been constrained by their isolation, their politically and economically unstable and undemocratic neighbors, and the absence of sustained outside sponsorship by economically powerful, democratic states.

Are we witnessing the creation of new regions out of the larger postcommunist world? Our analysis suggests that this is in fact happening. The question, however, may be more complicated. In getting at the question of when a region develops, it may be useful to return to the ideas of political geography. Political geographers like to distinguish between the concepts of space and place. Far from being mere wordplay, these two concepts denote important differences between the objective and subjective features of geography. A space becomes a place when it is invested with meaning by the people on the ground and by outside observers. Such a conceptual distinction can also help us think about the origins of regions. It is probably safe to say that an area becomes a region when it exhibits not only "objective" similarities but also when these similarities become hard, naturalized "facts" in the minds of people. We have demonstrated in this chapter the similarity of different spaces in different areas of the postcommunist world and argued that this fact can be plausibly traced to the effects of diffusion and outside promoters. However, we have not proved conclusively that these objective characteristics have in fact become naturalized at the popular or elite level. Even so, the differing behavior of Kyrgyz and Slovak elites suggests a profound understanding in both countries of the different realms of possibility in two very different places in the world. While hardly conclusive, such narratives open up the way for further research addressing the question of when postcommunist spaces become different kinds of postcommunist places.

At the same time we are keenly aware that the kind of research we have undertaken here itself contributes to the mental remapping of the postcommunist world. In social science the observer and the observed are never completely separable. If enough scholars characterize the Czech Republic as Western and Uzbekistan as Eastern, this may exercise a self-reinforcing dynamic of "orientalism." Still, the potential for orientalism is probably no worse in the study of spatial dependence than it is for temporal path dependence. Ultimately, however, as social scientists we believe that reality is not simply or merely the creation of outside observers and that therefore this reality can be meaningfully studied, described, and explained. In the case of postcommunism, the location of a country constitutes an important contextual dimension that exercises a profound impact on the nature of the postcommunist dilemma by altering the confining conditions and incentives to act of the relevant elites and masses throughout the region. This much appears difficult to deny. To be sure, these constraints act in tandem with those in the temporal and domestic political realm, but they cannot be reduced to either of them.

The integration of spatial and temporal factors is essential to a deeper understanding of the postcommunist world. It may be possible to separate and isolate these factors for methodological purposes. Indeed, this is what much of our paper has done. Any consideration of real cases, however, even the short discussions outlined here, suggests that variation in political and economic reform in the postcommunist states is best understood in the context of spatiotemporal analysis. Temporal or path-dependent arguments must be couched in a geographic context. Likewise, spatial factors cannot stand alone. Such considerations suggest that the task that stands before social science is the integration of history and geography into the analysis of political change.

References

Ágh, Attila. 1994. Die neuen politischen Eliten in Mittelosteuropa. In Hellmut Wollmann, Helmut Wiesenthal, and Frank Bönker, eds., *Transformation sozialistischer Gesellschaften: Am Ende des Anfangs*, pp. 442–36. Opladen: Westdeutscherverlag.

Agnew, John. 1987. *Place and Politics: The Geographical Mediation of State and Society*. Boston: Allen and Unwin.

Anderson, John. 1999. *Kyrgyzstan: Central Asia's Island of Democracy?* Amsterdam: Harwood Academic Publishers.

Anselin, Luc. 1995. Local Indicators of Spatial Association – LISA. *Geographical Analysis* 27(2): 93–114.

Ash, Timothy Garton. 1990. *The Magic Lantern: The Revolutions of '89 Witnessed in Warsaw, Budapest, and Prague*. New York: Random House.

Barrell, Ray, and Nigel Pain. 1997. Foreign Direct Investment, Technological Change, and Economic Growth within Europe. *Economic Journal* 107(445): 1770–86.

Boulding, Kenneth E. 1963. *Conflict and Defense: A General Theory*. New York: Harper.

Brams, Steven J. 1967. Transaction Flows in the International System. *American Political Science Review* 76(1): 880–98.

Butora, Martin, Grigorij Meseznikov, and Zora Butorova. 1999. Overcoming Illiberalism – Slovakia's 1998 Elections. In Martin Butora, Grigorij Meseznikov, Zora Butorova, and Sharon Fisher, eds., *The 1998 Parliamentary Elections and Democratic Rebirth of Slovakia*, pp. 9–23. Bratislava: Institute of Public Affairs.

Cohen, Saul B. 1991. Global Geopolitical Change in the Post–Cold War Era. *Annals of the Association of American Geographers* 81(2): 551–80.

Coolidge, Jacqueline. 1999. The Art of Attracting Foreign Direct Investment in Transition Economies. *Transition* 10(5): 5.

Diehl, Paul F. 1999. Territory and International Conflict: An Overview. In Paul F. Diehl, ed., *A Road Map to War: Territorial Dimensions of International Conflict*. Nashville: Vanderbilt University Press.

Eaton, Jonathan, and Samuel S. Kortum. 1999. International Technology Diffusion: Theory and Measurement. *International Economic Review* 40(3): 537–70.

Fish, M. Steven. 1998. Mongolia: Democracy without Prerequisites. *Journal of Democracy* 9(3): 127–40.

1999a. The Determinants of Economic Reform in the Post-Communist World. *East European Politics and Societies* 12(2): 31–78.

1999b. The End of Meciarism. *East European Constitutional Review* 8(1): 47–55.

Frank, Tibor. 1995. Nation, National Minorities, and Nationalism in Twentieth Century Hungary. In Peter F. Sugar, ed., *Eastern European Nationalism in the Twentieth Century*. Washington, D.C.: American University Press.

Franzmeyer, Fritz. 1999. Wirtschaftliche Voraussetzungen, Perspektiven und Folgen einer Osterweitung der Europäische Union. *Ost-Europa-Wirtschaft* 22(2): 146.

Getis, Arthur, and J. K. Ord. 1992. The Analysis of Spatial Association by Use of Distance Statistics. *Geographical Analysis* 24(1): 189–206.

Hanson, Stephen E., and Jeffrey S. Kopstein. 1997. The Weimar/Russia Comparison. *Post-Soviet Affairs* 13(3): 252–83.

Hellman, Joel. 1997. Winners Take All: The Politics of Partial Reform in Postcommunist Transitions. *World Politics* 50(2): 203–34.

Huskey, Eugene. 1993. Kyrgyzstan Leaves the Ruble Zone. *RFE/RL Research Report*, September 3.

1997. Kyrgyzstan: The Fate of Political Liberalization. In Karen Dawisha and Bruce Parrott, eds., *Conflict, Cleavage, and Change in Central Asia and the Caucasus*, pp. 242–76. Cambridge: Cambridge University Press.

1999. National Identity from Scratch: Defining Kyrgyzstan's Role in World Affairs. Department of Political Science, Stetson University. Unpublished manuscript.

Jacoby, Wade. 1999. Priest and Penitent: The European Union as a Force in the Domestic Politics of Eastern Europe. *East European Constitutional Review* 8(1): 62–67.

Jaggers, Keith, and Ted R. Gurr. 1995. Tracking Democracy's Third Wave with the Polity III Data. *Journal of Peace Research* 32(2): 469–82.

Johnson, Bryan T., Kim R. Holmes, and Melanie Kirkpatrick, eds. 1999. *1999 Index of Economic Freedom*. Washington, D.C.: Heritage Foundation and Dow Jones.

Johnston, R. J. 1991. *A Question of Place*. Oxford: Basil Blackwell.

Kitschelt, Herbert. 1999. Accounting for Outcomes of Post-Communist Regime Change: Causal Depth or Shallowness in Rival Explanations? Paper presented at the annual meeting of the American Political Science Association, Atlanta.

Kitschelt, Herbert, Zenka Mansfeldova, Radosław Markowski, and Gábor Tóka. 1999. *Post-Communist Party Systems: Competition, Representation, and Inter-Party Cooperation*. Cambridge: Cambridge University Press.

Koopmans, Ruvd. 1993. The Dynamics of Protest Waves: West Germany, 1965 to 1989. *American Sociological Review* 58(5): 637–58.

Kopstein, Jeffrey S., and David A. Reilly. 1999. Explaining the Why of the Why: A Comment on Fish's "Determinants of Economic Reform in the Post-Communist World." *East European Politics and Societies* 13(3): 613–26.

Kotrba, Josef, and Jan Švejnar. 1994. Rapid and Multifaceted Privatization: Experience of the Czech and Slovak Republics. *Moct-Most* 4(2): 147–85.

Kovrig, Bennett. 1999. European Integration. In Aurel Braun and Zoltan Barany, eds., *Dilemmas of Transition: The Hungarian Experience*, pp. 253–72. Lanham, Md.: Rowman and Littlefield.

Linz, Juan J., and Alfred Stepan. 1996. *Problems of Democratic Transition and Consolidation: Southern Europe, South America, and Post-Communist Europe*. Baltimore: Johns Hopkins University Press.

Linz, Juan J., and Arturo Valenzuela, eds. 1994. *The Failure of Presidential Democracy*. Baltimore: Johns Hopkins University Press.

Lipton, David, and Jeffrey Sachs. 1990. Privatization in Eastern Europe: The Case of Poland. *Brookings Papers on Economic Activity* 2: 351–80.

Marer, Paul. 1999. Economic Transformation, 1990–1998. In Aurel Braun and Zoltan Barany, eds., *Dilemmas of Transition: The Hungarian Experience*, pp. 157–202. Lanham, Md.: Rowman and Littlefield.

Most, Benjamin A., and Harvey Starr. 1989. *Inquiry, Logic, and International Politics*. Columbia: University of South Carolina Press.

Naegele, Joylon. 1998. Slovakia: Democratic Opposition Has Chance to Change Policies. *RFE/RL Weekly Report*, September 28. Available: <http://www.rferl.org/nca/features/1998/09/F.RU.980928134909.html>.

Nelson, Daniel. 1999. Regional Security and Ethnic Minorities. In Aurel Braun and Zoltan Barany, eds., *Dilemmas of Transition: The Hungarian Experience*, pp. 301–22. Lanham, Md.: Rowman and Littlefield.

Oberschall, A. 1994. The 1960s Sit-Ins: Protest Diffusion and Movement Takeoff. *Research in Social Movements, Conflict and Change* 11: 31–33.

O'Loughlin, John, and Luc Anselin. 1992. Geography of International Conflict and Cooperation: Theory and Methods. In Michael D. Ward, ed., *The New Geopolitics*. Philadelphia: Gordon and Breach Science Publishers.

O'Loughlin, John, Colin Flint, and Luc Anselin. 1994. The Geography of the Nazi Vote: Context, Confession, and Class in the Reichstag Election of 1930. *Annals of the Association of American Geographers* 84(2): 351–80.

O'Rourke, Breffni. 2000. EU Enlargement Negotiations: A Difficult Path to Tread. *RFE/RL Newsline* 4(56), part 2, March 20.

Pannier, Bruce. 1999. Central Asia: Concern Grows over Possibility of Trade War. *RFE/RL Weekly Report*, February 16.

Popov, Vladimir. 1999. Explaining the Magnitude of Transformational Recession. Department of Economics, Queens University, Canada.

Rutland, Peter. 1999. Count Them In or Count Them Out? Post-Socialist Transition and the Globalization Debate. Paper presented at the American Association for the Advancement of Slavic Studies, St. Louis.

Sachs, Jeffrey. 1997. Geography and Economic Transition. Harvard University, Center for International Development, Unpublished manuscript, November.

1999. Eastern Europe Reforms: Why the Outcomes Differed So Sharply. *Boston Globe*, September 19.

Spilerman, S. 1984. The Causes of Racial Disturbances: A Comparison of Alternative Explanations. *American Sociological Review* 354: 627–49.

Stepan, Alfred, and Cindy Skach. 1993. Constitutional Frameworks and Democratic Consolidation: Parliamentarism versus Presidentialism. *World Politics* 46(1): 1–22.

Stohl, Michael, David Carleton, George Lopez, and Stephen Samuels. 1986. State Violation of Human Rights: Issues and Problems of Measurement. *Human Rights Quarterly* 8(1): 592–606.

Strang, David, and Sarah A. Soule. 1998. Diffusion in Organizations and Social Movements: From Hybrid Corn to Poison Pills. *Annual Review of Sociology* 24: 265–90.

Tökés, Rudolf. 1997. Party Politics and Participation in Postcommunist Hungary. In Karen Dawisha and Bruce Parrott, eds., *The Consolidation of Democracy in East-Central Europe*, pp. 109–49. Cambridge: Cambridge University Press.

Walker, Christopher. 1998. Slovakia: Return to Europe Questionable. *RFE/RL, Weekly Report*, September 25. Available: <http://www.rferl.org/nca/features/1998/09/F.RU.980925133407.html>.

Wolchik, Sharon. 1997. Democratization and Political Participation in Slovakia. In Karen Dawisha and Bruce Parrott, eds., *The Consolidation of Democracy in East-Central Europe*, pp. 197–244. Cambridge: Cambridge University Press.

World Bank. 1998. *World Development Indicators*. Washington, D.C.

PART III

INSTITUTIONAL REDESIGN AND HISTORICAL LEGACIES

Case Studies

5

Redeeming the Past

Communist Successor Parties after 1989

Anna Grzymała-Busse

The persistence of communist successor parties is a peculiar paradox of democratic politics in East Central Europe. After all, the revolutions of 1989 fought to remove the communist parties from power and to end their discredited political and economic monopoly. Yet all these parties, even the most despised, survived. Several of their successors gained considerable popular support and a reputation for political professionalism. Some have even reentered government, this time through free elections.

The survival and regeneration of the successor parties is anomalous from two perspectives. First, many analysts assumed that the parties would disintegrate, along with other remainders of communist life, because "communist parties in Eastern Europe can only rule by force or disappear" (Zubek, 1990; Wałęsa, 1990; Kirsch, 1993; Sokorski, 1990). Second, scholars noted that political parties tend to resist wholesale transformation – party succession is extremely rare.[1] Because communist parties were not known for their flexibility or responsiveness, they were thus expected either to collapse or to retain their outdated ideology and structures (Przeworski, 1992).

Two related puzzles arise. First, how could the parties survive and adapt to democratic competition? Second, why is there variation in the subsequent patterns of party regeneration – why did some parties radically change their old organizations, symbols, and appeals (and find support for these changes), whereas others did not?

This chapter first examines the Czech, Slovak, Polish, and Hungarian communist successor parties in the decade after 1989. It then discusses the existing explanations and argues that specific legacies of the communist regime, corresponding to the "interactional" spatial level and "institutional" temporal level as set out in the introduction, determined the political resources

[1] Only 3 percent of parties manage to leave a successor, and only 13 percent persist when the regime collapses (Rose and Mackie, 1988: 551).

with which the parties would regenerate. It then examines how these political resources determined the strategies of regeneration and their outcomes.

Communist Successor Parties, 1989–1999

In all four cases, the communist successor parties are the formal descendants of the communist parties – that is, the political parties that arose from the ruling communist parties and which explicitly claim their successor status. Their "regeneration" consists of gaining long-term access to governmental power – the capacity to compete successfully for and enter democratic government. This capacity consists of *programmatic responsiveness* (the correlation between party programs and public concerns, and a focus on public issues rather than on internal party concerns), *popular support of the party* (both votes and public acceptance), and *parliamentary acceptance* (membership in coalitions, committees, and in the parliamentary leadership). These three dimensions[2] represent the hurdles a party has to clear to gain office in a parliamentary, proportional representation system.

The main cases under consideration illustrate the three types of party trajectories after 1989: from failed regeneration (the Czech KSČM) to regeneration on some dimensions but not on others (Slovak SDL' and Polish SdRP) to full regeneration (Hungarian MSzP). Because all four were forced to exit from power in 1989, they represent the "most difficult" cases for regeneration – unlike their counterparts in postcommunist countries, which could retain power and entrench themselves. At the same time, these parties all shared the same goal, of maximizing voter support and access to government.

The Czech successor party, the Communist Party of Bohemia and Moravia (Komunistická Strana Čech a Moravy, KSČM) has largely failed to regenerate. After 1989 it did not dissolve its organization or denounce its past symbols, name, or ideology. It is the largest successor party, with about 160,000 members and around 6,000 local organizations.[3] The party has consistently issued narrow appeals and spent a greater percentage of its programs on self-references than any other party. Its programs display little congruence with the public's chief concerns (the one shared emphasis was the provision of competent managers, but the wider public saw the KSČM as the party least likely to provide them). The party had no plans to change these emphases, since it had to retain the support of its orthodox members. As a result, its supporters are dominated by the elderly and the disaffected.[4] Its electoral

[2] I had initially included the *acceptance of democratic rules*. However, all the parties under consideration have declared themselves committed to democracy, and their subsequent behavior bears out these promises.

[3] The communist levels were 1,250,000 members and 25,000 organizations.

[4] Young, unemployed males tended to vote for the Republicans, an extremist right-wing party.

support has ranged from 10 to 14 percent, with occasional spikes in public support.[5] At the same time, the KSČM has a very polarized image – among the rest of the electorate, it is widely seen as the most controversial and least acceptable party in the Czech Republic.[6]

Despite its numerical gains, the party has not gained greater access to office. It continued to be excluded a priori from electoral or governmental coalitions. Its representatives have been marginalized in parliament, where the party was denied parliament leadership positions, and a parity of representation in the committees. Nor have its policy proposals been taken seriously.

Although ostensibly part of the same ossified federation,[7] the Slovak Party of the Democratic Left (Strana Demokratickej L'avici, SDL') took a different path after 1989, regenerating on some dimensions. In 1990 the party's new leaders forced the members to reregister in 1990, and so party membership dropped from 450,000 to 40,000, and the number of organizations, from 12,500 to 2,000.

In its programmatic development, the SDL' faced accusations of political inconsistency and programmatic ambiguity. Although the party consistently focused on important public issues, its stances on economic reform, administrative transformation, the Hungarian minority question, and Slovakia's NATO and European Union (EU) membership have shifted back and forth over the years, leading to charges of "fishtailing" and opportunism. While the public saw the economic burdens and competent managers as two of the most important programmatic issues, the party changed its views on the former and was unable to fully address the latter.

The SDL' has been widely accepted as committed to upholding democracy in Slovakia, even if it is not seen as the most administratively competent of parties. It received 13.8 percent of the vote in 1990 and 14 percent in 1992. However, its Common Choice Coalition (Spoločna Vol'ba) lost the 1994 election badly – instead of the expected 25 percent of the vote, the coalition

[5] *RFE/RL Newsline* 3(183), part 2, September 20, 1999. In a 1999 poll, KSCM support peaked at 20 percent. One explanation has been the implosion of the Republicans, the other extremist alternative. As one commentator noted, around 25 percent of the Czech electorate has voted for extremist parties after 1989, and with the collapse of Republicans in 1998, the communists may simply be taking over that protest electorate (Pavel Saradin, *Lidové Noviny*, July 31, 1999, p. 10).

[6] Throughout the post-1989 period, it was the party *least* likely to ensure democracy and competent governance, scoring even below the extremist right-wing Republicans; 55 percent of the Czech adult population did not want the party in parliament, the highest such percentage any party received (STEM Poll, May 26, 1992, *Mlada Fronta Dnes*).

[7] Officially, the Communist Party of Czechoslovakia (KSČ) was organized along federal lines after 1968. In practice, there was the Communist Party of Slovakia and the Communist Party of Czechoslovakia; a Communist Party for the Czech Republic was not deemed necessary, much as there was no Communist Party of Russia prior to 1991 in the USSR. The Slovak party was fully subordinate to the Prague center.

barely received 10 percent. In the September 1998 elections, SDL' rebounded with 14.7 percent of the vote, receiving third place.

The party was both widely accepted by the electorate and enjoyed a great deal of parliamentary acceptance. It achieved parity between its seats in parliament, and the percentage of committee representation and chairs.[8] It also had a relatively easy time forming coalitions. In March 1994 the SDL' led to the downfall of the government of Vladimir Mečiar and his ironically named Movement for a Democratic Slovakia (HZDS). The SDL' then entered a short-lived governing coalition with the Christian Democrats, presiding over renewed privatization efforts and political reforms. In government again after the 1998 elections with 15 percent of the vote, the party received nine out of twenty ministries.

The Polish successor party, the Social Democracy of Poland (Socjaldemokracja Rzeczpospolitej Polskiej, SdRP),[9] was largely successful in its regeneration efforts. The party dissolved in January 1990, dropping to 60,000 members and 2,500 organizations.[10] In its programs, the SdRP focused on public policy from the start, rarely mentioning internal party concerns. It corresponded to voters' concerns, calling for continuing economic and political reforms, but with greater administrative and managerial competence. Its addressed constituency was national and catchall, and its voters were increasingly better educated and better off than average.

Although the party lost every seat it could in the semifree elections in 1989, it steadily gained support. In the 1991 elections, the party formed the Democratic Left coalition (SLD), which also consisted of OPZZ, the communist-era official trade union, and other communist-era social organizations.[11] SLD received 12.0 percent of the vote, coming in second to the Democratic Union (UD), the main party emerging out of Solidarity after 1989. In 1993 the SLD won over 20 percent of the vote and formed a governing coalition. In 1997 the party actually *gained* voters in absolute numbers but lost to the Electoral Action Solidarity (AWS) coalition, a grouping of post-Solidarity political parties and movements.[12] Finally, it returned to power after the 2001 elections, having gained over 40 percent of the vote.

[8] The one exception was 1994–98, when the HZDS took over all committees.

[9] The party changed its name to the Alliance of the Democratic Left (Sojusz Lewicy Demokratycznej) in 2000, but this change did not reflect any organizational or programmatic transformations.

[10] Down from 2.1 million members and 75,000 organizations in 1988.

[11] Of the 171 seats held by the SLD in 1993–97, 61 represented the OPZZ. In April 1999, the party and the union coalition transformed itself into a party, also called the SLD. This move was in compliance with the new law on parties in 1997, which stipulates that only parties and their coalitions can run in the elections. The leadership of the new party is dominated by the SdRP elites.

[12] AWS leaders repeatedly commented that if the postcommunist forces succeeded with a disciplined coalition, forming a similar one was the only chance for post-Solidarity forces to regain power.

In addition to its broad support, the party is consistently seen as the most professional and competent of Polish parties.[13] In parliament, on the other hand, the party faced considerably more isolation. Initially, it was given no parliamentary leadership positions. The party parliamentary club was often marginalized, and its proposals ignored. However, the party has been slowly overcoming this isolation; by 1999 some leaders of the former communist opposition called for greater cooperation with the SdRP.[14]

While in power, the party formed the most stable governing coalition yet in Poland, which lasted its full term from 1993 to 1997, and continued the reforms of its predecessors.[15] However, because parties from the former opposition (including those closest to the SdRP ideologically) refused to ally with the communist successor, the SdRP could only form a coalition with the successor to the communist-era satellite Peasants' Party (PSL) in 1993.

Finally, the Hungarian Socialist Party (Magyar Szocialista Párt, MSzP) regenerated more fully than any other communist successor. The party also dissolved in October 1989, and its membership and local organizations dropped to 40,000 and 2,500, respectively.[16] In its programmatic appeals, the party's claims of managerial competence and administrative effectiveness appealed to broad constituencies, and a sizable portion of its electorate was made up of white-collar managers and well-educated professionals. The MSzP spent little time justifying its own internal policies in its programs and instead focused on public policy. Its focus was on maintaining social stability and a welfare safety net, two issues that especially resonated with the Hungarian electorate.

In the 1990 elections, the party came in fifth, with 8.5 percent of the vote and thirty-three seats. From the start, however, it was seen as an extremely competent party by a plurality of the electorate.[17] As various rifts appeared within the ruling Hungarian Democratic Forum (MDF),[18] such competence was seen as an antidote to the prevailing political turbulence. The April 1994 elections resulted in a first-place finish for the MSzP, with 33 percent of the

[13] The party's competence was the item most liked about the SdRP throughout the post-1989 period, and it was seen as the party most likely to provide competent managers and ensure democratic stability.

[14] Leszek Balcerowicz, most notably, has called for greater cooperation for the sake of economic and political development (*Donosy*, April 26, 1999). The Labour Union (Unia Pracy, UP) ran jointly with the SdRP in the 2001 elections.

[15] In contrast, there were five separate governments in the four years from 1989 to 1993.

[16] The communist levels, in 1988, stood at 870,000 members and 25,400 organizations.

[17] The party was seen after 1989 as consistently the most able to provide competent managers, ensure democracy, and maintain stability, even while in government.

[18] Most notably, the rise of an extreme nationalist faction led by István Csurka, government squabbling, minor scandals, and the death of József Antall, the popular prime minister in December 1993.

vote and 54 percent of the parliamentary seats.[19] The party continued to be seen as committed to democracy and effective in governance, even as it lost the 1998 election, with 32.3 percent of the vote, to the Young Democrats (Fidesz).

Unlike the Polish or the Czech party, the MSzP was less marginalized in the parliament, with effective representation in parliamentary committees from the start. After its 1994 electoral victory, the MSzP could form a coalition with the SzDSz, the Alliance of Free Democrats, a party that arose from the pre-1989 communist opposition.[20] Such coalitions were largely unthinkable for the former opposition in Poland and in the Czech Republic. Once in government, the MSzP continued to implement economic reform, most notably the 1995 Bokros austerity package, and maintained a relatively stable government coalition.

These outcomes are summarized in Table 5.1.

Explaining the Outcomes

Scholars of party politics and democratic transitions have accounted for these patterns using three main approaches. The first posits that electoral cleavages and changes in popular demands largely determine party strategies, and parties regenerate when they successfully address the electorate's concerns and cleavages (Lipset and Rokkan, 1967; Kitschelt, 1983; Robertson, 1976). Those parties that do not correspond to the shifts in the electorate are eliminated in electoral competition. Party regeneration should thus be the result of electoral selection.

In East Central Europe, one of the main cleavages to arise in the new polities is between those who have benefited from the economic transition and those whose well-being was tied to the old system (e.g., state enterprise workers). Communist successor parties could exploit this cleavage and represent the "losers" of the transition (Evans and Whitefield, 1995; Ágh, 1994; Cotta, 1994; Zubek, 1994). They would then achieve their greatest success where they were able to mobilize these voters. However, the electoral evidence is mixed: postcommunist parties gain votes and enter government where they attract a broad, cross-cutting electorate, not where they court either the losers or the winners of the transition (Szelényi, Fodor, and Hanley, 1997; Kovács, 1995; Körösényi, 1993; Tóka, 1996).

[19] While the MSzP initially had no contact with the trade unions, most of which were undergoing a massive crisis in 1989–90, an alliance developed from 1991 on with the MSzOSz, the main trade union organization. Six unionists stood as MSzP candidates, and union leader Sándor Nagy was given the second place on the party's electoral list in 1994.

[20] Of the twelve ministerial cabinet posts, the MSzP took nine, while the SzDSz took three: culture and public education; internal affairs; and the transport, telecommunications, and water management ministries.

TABLE 5.1. *Communist Successor Parties in East Central Europe*

	Popular Acceptance: Highest Vote % and Year	Parliamentary Relevance: Participation in Electoral and Governmental Coalitions, 1990–97	Programmatic Capacity	
			Average % of Programs Spent on Internal Party Issues	Congruence with Broader Electorate[a]
Czech Republic	14%, 1992	One electoral coalition, with civic groups; excluded a priori from all governmental coalitions, 1989–99	20–24% until 1993, 4% after	Very low congruence
Slovakia	14.7%, 1998	One electoral coalition, with four small groupings; two governmental coalitions, briefly in 1994, and since 1998 with the anti-HZDS opposition	18% in 1990, 0% in 1990–95, 8% after	High congruence
Poland	41%, 2001	Two electoral coalitions, mainly with postcommunist trade union; two government coalitions in 1993–97 and 2000–	12% in 1990, 2–6% after	High congruence, except secularism
Hungary	33%, 1994	Two electoral coalitions, with postcommunist trade union; one governmental coalition, with the SzDSz, 1994–98		High congruence

[a] As measured by party emphases on privatization, the free market, welfare state, redistribution, secularism, and competent managers.

A second explanation argues that the structure of the competition faced by the parties and the political rules constrain the appeals the parties can make (Przeworski and Sprague, 1986). The greater the competition, the fewer the unoccupied stances on policy and ideology and the greater the likelihood of challenges to the successor parties' claims and appeals. Therefore, we would expect communist successor parties to regenerate where they face weak competitors or where the party system revolves around a few large competitors, rather than many fragmented ones (Panebianco, 1988; Ishiyama, 1995; Arato, 1995; Millard, 1994). Successor parties should also do well where the electoral laws favor them (e.g., where electoral thresholds privilege large parties). Finally, a protracted transition also promotes party regeneration by giving the parties the time to adapt before other parties gain strength (Geddes, 1995; Cotta, 1994).

However, the structure of political competition does not seem to correlate with party regeneration. The Czech party faced no real competition on the left in 1989–93, yet failed to transform itself.[21] The Polish party, on the other hand, regenerated in the midst of the most fragmented and conflicted party system in the region, in 1991–93. Electoral laws also do not correlate fully with party regeneration, as neither electoral thresholds nor districting has affected the parties' ability to transform themselves or gain electoral success (Moraski and Loewenberg, 1997). Finally, the pace of the transition does not determine the outcome: the Slovak and Czech parties shared the same transition path but diverged rapidly within two months.

Finally, scholars posit that the parties' internal characteristics are responsible for the parties' successful transformation. First, most broadly, party institutionalization (the process by which a party becomes a self-perpetuating bureaucracy) makes initial party change more difficult, because it increases the organizational layers and departments that need to be changed (Panebianco, 1988; Waller, 1995; Kopecký, 1995; Lewis and Gortat, 1995). Second, if the leaders are accountable to members, and their ideological commitments are intense, it is increasingly difficult for a party to change its program or image (Sjöblom, 1983; Strom, 1990; Haraszti, 1995). Finally, elite change itself can be both a necessary and sufficient condition for party change – new elites change the organization or appeals to consolidate their power after an external shock (Harmel and Janda, 1994; Harmel et al., 1995; Wilson, 1980).

However, the mere presence of these factors does not seem to explain fully successor party regeneration. *All* the parties under consideration were both institutionalized and burdened with mass memberships in 1989. Their ideological commitment varied, from the orthodoxy of the Czechoslovak

[21] The Czech Social Democrats could not even clear the 5 percent threshold in the 1990 elections and received 6.5 percent of the vote in 1992, less than half the KSCM's vote.

party to the weary pragmatism of the Polish and Hungarian parties. Yet, an ostensible ideological stagnation did not prevent the Slovak party from regenerating. Despite the same external shock, and similar background conditions, party responses differed. New elites entered all leaderships, yet only some parties transformed, suggesting instead that elite change itself is not as important as the *kind* of party structures and elites that replace the old.

These variables and mechanisms clearly influence political parties. However, these accounts are less successful at accounting for the conditions under which parties can capitalize on the opportunities they present, the scope and direction of their transformation, or the subsequent success or failure of these efforts. Nor do they set out to account for the responses of parties to massive political destabilization, such as the regime collapse and subsequent democratic transition of 1989, where even the most entrenched political actors are temporarily unsettled.

Elites, Communist Legacies, and Adaptive Strategies

If we are to fill in the gaps in the explanations of communist party adaptation in East Central Europe, we need to link the agents of change, the resources and tools at their disposal, and the opportunities they had to transform the party.

To summarize, successful party regeneration demanded the centralization and streamlining of party organization, which then allowed the transformation of party ideology, appeals, and electoral or parliamentary strategies. For party regeneration to succeed, the new reformist elites had to move quickly and decisively in 1989–90. The old elites were then completely discredited and were either forced out or chose to leave. Their natural replacement was the midlevel party elites – the government ministers, regional party leaders, and party bureaucrats. The more rapidly and decisively these midlevel elites were able to advance and to consolidate power in the party, the greater the chance for their ideas to be implemented. In turn, the more extensive the initial changes, the greater the chance for the overall project to succeed.

If party elites were the agents behind the transformation of the parties, the differences in the political resources of the new successor party elites determined the strategies of regeneration. The elites' political resources consisted of their "portable skills" (the expertise and experiences gained in the previous regime) and their "usable pasts" (the historical record of state-society relations, and the subsequent references that could resonate with the public). As legacies, these two sets of resources can be categorized as interactional spatial legacies (the diffusion and transfer of elite skills and practices) and as institutional temporal legacies (the regularized patterns of party state response to the society, designed to maintain communist rule and constituting a public record of party behavior). The more experienced and skilled the new elites, the more rapidly and effectively they would move to break with the past and streamline party organizations; rely on broad programmatic appeals rather than on narrow, member-centered ones; and enforce moderation and discipline in the party's public behavior. The more usable the party's past, the more credible these efforts were to both the electorate and to other parties.

The communist past thus determined the composition of the midlevel communist party elites who took over power in the parties in 1989 and the political resources at their disposal. Three organizational practices of the communist regime determined elite political resources and, subsequently, the strategies of party regeneration after 1989. Each party had, to a different extent, fostered the advancement of a particular type of elites, reformed and implemented public policy, and negotiated with the representatives of societal opposition to the communist regimes. Although the link between elite background and its behavior is neither simple nor direct, these experiences generated a powerful set of elite skills and experiences with which the new party leaders in 1989 could envision and implement transformative strategies.

If this analysis is correct, we should see specific references to the past that justified or promulgated decisions regarding the party's new strategies in 1989. Personal and organizational capacities should be directly traceable to the communist party's policies of cadre training and societal engagement. We should also see that parties emphasize and rely on what they see as their historical strengths to survive beyond 1989, be it mass memberships, organizational entrenchment, elite experiences, or favorable references to the past. After discussing these legacies and demonstrating how they determined the political resources of the elites, I then show how the political resources translated into elite strategies of regeneration and party outcomes.

Elite Recruitment and Advancement

Elite recruitment and advancement policies not only selected the party's future leadership but also determined the extent to which ideological appeals trumped pragmatic solutions.

The conservative Czech party leaders reproduced a pattern of closed recruitment of party elites. The purges and recruitment policies of the Czech communist party rewarded neither education nor extramural experience but only ideological loyalty. The party's conservative attitude was exacerbated by the Prague Spring and the threat that this 1968 reform movement presented to party rule. Anxious to reassert control, and suspicious of any "reformist deviations," the party promoted only "safe" comrades. Elites could only rise within and through the party ranks, into increasingly ideologically stagnant elite layers, so that conformist and orthodox members were the primary ones to advance (Wolchik, 1987). The youth organization, completely under party control after 1968, provided no reformist elites. Moreover, an average of only 16 percent of the Czechoslovak Politburo turned over annually. As a result, the new party leaders in 1989–90 had a very limited grasp of reform and no experience in implementing it.

Ironically, however, in its desire to control the Czechoslovak party, the Czech leadership created the space for Slovak reform potential. The Slovak elites who led the party after 1989 arose only because, in their strict centralization of the Czechoslovak Communist Party, the Czech party leaders neglected the nominal center of the Slovak party. Pockets of reform thought, such as those in the Marxist Leninist Institute of the Central Committee of the Slovak party, survived.

Party reformists at the institute authored and circulated several reform documents throughout the 1980s (Žiak, 1996). These young scholars were unable to advance into the party's leadership prior to 1989 and thus gained far more theoretical than practical experience in policy making and implementation. They were ready, however, to assume power immediately after the regime collapse in November 1989. These new leaders, such as Pavol Kanis and Peter Weiss, assumed the leadership early in 1990 and rapidly changed the party's name, reregistered the membership, and reformed its image.

For their part, the Polish and Hungarian parties deliberately promoted different sets of elites. Polish and Hungarian elites were subject to a constant and deliberate shifting of personnel from one party position to another. Such personnel policies also meant that the cadres and midlevel elites received a variety of experiences in their advancement and gained considerable flexibility and diversity in their abilities.[22]

The Polish party, eager to rebuild its cadres and revitalize its image after repeated crises, pursued youth organization leaders, effectively educated in politicking and hungry for a chance to exercise their skills. Party youth auxiliaries served as both a candidate pool and training ground for future elites, via their democratic voting procedures, political bargaining, and coalition forming. Future elites learned how to win successive elections and manipulate coalitions, while learning legal and administrative norms.[23]

Many of the future party leaders advanced in these parallel organizations. By 1986, for example, 35 percent of the first secretaries had been youth organization leaders, and 80 percent of high-ranking party bureaucrats had

[22] Edward Gierek, the Polish party leader from 1968 to 1980, instituted the "cadre carousel" and constantly "parachuted" appointees from one region to another. In Hungary, János Kádár, the party leader after 1956, was notorious for constantly appointing and reappointing midlevel party leaders to different positions, following a policy of "lateral moves" designed to give the appointees experience in different areas (and to ensure that his power remained consolidated). Budapest Open Society Archives, Hungary File: Personnel Changes, December 4, 1980, MTI report.

[23] *Rzeczpospolita*, April 13–14, 1996: 3. The youth organization members, for example, learned trade laws long before anyone else had, giving them a considerable advantage when the market was liberalized in 1990.

belonged to the youth organization in Poland (Lewis, 1989; Wasilewski, 1990). Moreover, the 33 percent annual turnover rate in the leadership further created the demand for new elites. As a result, the new party leadership in 1990 consisted almost exclusively of youth organization alumni.

In Hungary, the party tried to co-opt the intelligentsia and administrative technocrats, especially in the 1970s and 1980s. It offered considerable incentives to join the party to these groups, whose expertise and experience made them valuable in formulating and implementing the party's reform policies. Moreover, the Kádárist policies of constantly shuffling elites meant that 25 percent of the party leadership turned over annually and midlevel cadres were recirculated, further creating demand for new elites (Tökés, 1996).

After 1956 the Hungarian Communist Party emphasized its recruitment of intelligentsia, as non–party members were offered grants and positions in higher administration (O'Neil, 1996). At the same time, party membership was a prerequisite for real career advancement. Party positions were lucrative, and so many nonparty technocrats, who spent the first decade or so of their career in local administration, moved horizontally to party structures. In short, the party promoted the rise of nonideological, experienced professional administrators, who would prove key to its post-1989 development.

Such policies of recruitment from the outside and higher rates of leadership turnover promote innovative and flexible policy making (Dogan, 1989; Putnam, 1973). They also keep elites from entrenching themselves in any position for too long and create competition for prized positions. Thus, the parties could foster different degrees of pragmatism, experience, and flexibility in their midlevel elites.

Reforms of Public Policy

Regime crises and public pressure provided an impetus to change the parties' political and economic policies. Although no party radically transformed the economy or the polity, the parties varied in the extent to which they tried to address the shortcomings of the system. Such policy innovation and reform implementation underlined the importance of cohesion and streamlined organizations, while providing the skills to overcome internal opposition, convince opponents, and build policy coalitions.

In Czechoslovakia, 1968 saw the only real economic or political reforms undertaken by the party-state. Stalinist political oppression and the extremes of communist economic centralization "lasted long after the death of Stalin and in many aspects was not basically modified until 1968" (Skilling, 1977). The "normalizing" leadership that assumed power in late 1968 was not interested in either further reform or societal negotiation. As the last party secretary, Miloš Jakeš, explained, "the anti-socialist opposition would rise up whenever the party changed its policies or self-criticized" (Jakeš, 1996: 103). Despite pressure from Gorbachev's Soviet Union, the party instituted no changes in either the economy or the polity until the announcement of minor reforms in 1987. At the same time, however, economic policies continued to promote the industrialization and urbanization of the rural Slovak republic, and political repression was not as severe in the Slovak republic as it was in the Czech. The party had also obliquely promoted Slovak national aspirations.

In Poland, waves of public protests brought in new leadership teams, each of which had an incentive to establish legitimacy by responding to public demands. Cycles of "reform" economic policies began in the 1960s, as "positive measures were enacted, usually immediately after leadership change or a particularly painful economic failure" (Brus, 1983). In the 1980s, a series of reforms and concessions followed, to reduce inflation and to provide a more rational pricing system.

In the political realm, even after martial law was instituted on December 13, 1981, to crush Solidarity, the party did not engage in the kind of long-term repression favored by the Czechoslovak party.[24] Once martial law was lifted in 1983, new local and national elections were held, in 1984 and 1985. These mandated multiple candidacies, in a modest liberalization. As a result of the earlier conflict, the Polish party engaged in what it termed "extensive consultation with society," including a 1987 referendum on further economic reform. Although these policies never fully opened up the political space in Poland, they attempted to justify party policies to a distrusting society.

For its part, the Hungarian party had done most to implement reform policies prior to 1989. The party sought to regain social peace after the 1956 Hungarian uprising and had the technocratic cadres to implement these reforms. In 1968 the New Economic Mechanism (NEM) freed up some prices, allowed enterprise managers greater nominal autonomy, and provided for a more flexible labor market. NEM was reversed in 1973, but new reforms were introduced in a piecemeal fashion. Personal taxes were eventually introduced, and between 1978 and 1982 the government officially recognized a second, private economy. These policies were both a response to the 1956 tragedy and to the country's worsening economic conditions in the late 1960s and early 1970s.

In the political sphere, the Hungarian party dabbled with liberalization. From 1966 on, the electoral law provided for multiple candidacies in the single-member parliamentary constituencies. A further liberalization of the election law in 1983 mandated multicandidate lists, while in 1985 the first parliamentary elections with two or more candidates in each district were held.[25]

The relevance of these reforms lies not in their admittedly meager results, but in the political and administrative elite education and the history of party

[24] Fifteen thousand were arrested in total, and several incidents of police brutality followed.

[25] Of the seventy-one unauthorized "spontaneously nominated" candidates who stood for election, thirty-five were actually elected.

responsiveness they provided. The more a party promoted policy innovation and negotiation prior to 1989, the more it emphasized the importance of cohesion, responsiveness to the public, and the streamlining of organizations. The more these innovations were implemented, the more party elites gained experience in convincing opponents, building coalitions, and overcoming administrative reluctance or entrenchment. The Polish and Hungarian successor party elites, several of whom had been in the government in the 1980s, thus had years of reform policy experience.[26] Their rule can best be described as continual tinkering with public policy in an attempt to keep social peace (as in Hungary) or in reply to social unrest and conflict (as in Poland).

Negotiation with Society and the Course of the Transitions

Finally, the extent to which the parties had engaged society also determined both the reformist credentials of the new elites and the credibility of their subsequent claims. In each of the countries under consideration, economic shortages and lack of basic freedoms led to popular pressures for change. The party response, however, had varied, from the massive crackdown that followed the Prague Spring in Czechoslovakia after 1968, to the official bargaining and negotiation, however conflictual, in Poland in 1980–81, to the gradual lifting of the many restrictions that followed the 1956 uprising in Hungary (Ekiert, 1996).

These communist party patterns of negotiation with representatives of the opposition showed a willingness to respond to society, to recognize imperfections in the political and economic systems, and to look beyond purely ideological solutions. The conflict between the party and society could thus create the expertise and the historical record that would benefit party elites as they moved to the democratic competitive system they tried so hard to avoid prior to 1989.

First, the Czechoslovak Communist Party refused to engage society or representatives of the opposition. Its refusal to recognize these demands led to the collapse of the party's regime in November 1989. The party's Extraordinary Congress was held barely a month after the Velvet Revolution, after the party was summarily removed from power but before the June 1990 elections could convince it of the necessity of change. Given the chaos surrounding its collapse, the presence of strong reform alternatives within the party was crucial – and, in the Czech party's case, scarce.

Under the Czechoslovak federation, the Slovak party also refused to negotiate with society and similarly capitulated in November 1989. However,

[26] For example, the first leader of the Polish successor party, Aleksander Kwaśniewski, was minister of youth in the 1980s, while the first leader of the Hungarian party, Gyula Horn, was the foreign minister in the late 1980s. Of the forty-three representatives of the MSzP in the first freely elected Hungarian parliament, five were former ministers, and three, former state secretaries.

it did have a ready pool of reformers, and the chaos of the rapid transition allowed them to enter the party's decision-making structures. Moreover, these reformists gained time to regenerate the party by consistently arguing that the federation with the Czech party was keeping the Slovak wing from developing its potential. The new party leaders argued that they had always been proponents of greater reform and societal negotiation, whose efforts were overcome by Czech intransigence and domination.

For their part, the Polish and the Hungarian parties had long engaged in negotiations – dominated by conflict between party and society in Poland and by a general consensus on the value of social stability in Hungary. As a result, these parties exited from political power not through a regime collapse, but through negotiations and elections. The parties took full advantage of the period before their Extraordinary Congresses of October 1989 and January 1990, respectively, to formulate strategies of organizational reform and to ensure that they would be implemented. Nor did these parties labor under delusions of popular support: after the June 1989 elections in Poland, for example, the party knew that it had very little popular support left and approached its upcoming January 1990 congress accordingly.

Although these policies of elite advancement, policy reform, and negotiation reflect patterns that began with the parties' takeover of power after World War II,[27] the recent past, the decades of the 1970s and 1980s, was the most significant source of the legacies that directly influenced post-1989 party trajectories. First, the cohort of elites currently leading the communist successor parties advanced through the communist organizations during those two decades, gaining the experiences and skills that proved crucial after 1989. Second, the more recent the historical memories, the more likely they were to influence popular perceptions of the party. For example, the Polish party elites, whose most recent crisis was in 1980–81, were held far more accountable for that crisis than the elites of the Hungarian party, whose major crisis occurred in 1956.

The Effects of Communist Legacies on Strategies and Outcomes of Regeneration

During 1989 these midlevel elites assumed power in the parties. The key moment at which the elites exercised their agency and chose the strategies of regeneration was during the Extraordinary Congresses of 1989–90. During this period, the legacies of the communist era – elite portable skills and usable

27 I refer specifically to the role played by the party organizations in this process – the greater the reliance on party organizations then, the more attention paid to its subsequent ideological orthodoxy. Pre–World War II influences are highly attenuated. First, the parties had changed their structure and ideology several times in the interwar period, so it is difficult to extrapolate what would be the template for postwar behavior. Second, many of the elites were decimated by the war, further diminishing any possible continuities.

pasts – exerted the most influence on the strategies of party transformation, as the new elites deliberately replicated earlier patterns of elite advancement, historical references, and stances toward reform in their efforts to transform the parties.

The differences in party trajectories quickly became apparent. First, the more skilled and experienced the elites, the more they perceived the need for immediate and radical change. Thus, the new Czech party elites were unable to articulate a vision of radical transformation. The one reference point was 1968, and the conclusion was that 1989 was another opportunity to *reform* communism. Czech party leaders therefore talked of a "programmatic return to 1968"[28] and regaining "socialism with a human face." However, these calls could not resonate within either the party or the society, given the party's consistent and deliberate rejection of reforms during 1968–89. The result was the emphasis on the party's history to the detriment of new party programs and reorganization.

Their Polish and Hungarian counterparts perceived instead a necessity to step back from the public eye and abandon any pretense of defending the Marxist ideal. The reformist factions within each party saw 1989 as the opportunity to remake the parties and promote a change not *within* the system but *of* it. Fully aware by now of how compromised the communist parties had become, these reformists had a much more radical reform agenda by 1989. Thus, by 1988, Hungarian party leaders already argued that "no progress is possible without a transformation of the entire structure of socialism,"[29] while Polish party reformers declared that "radical reform of the party is not a concession, but a political necessity."[30]

For the Polish, Slovak, and Hungarian parties, with few illusions regarding the relevance of old appeals and structures, democracy meant electoral competition. Having already been challenged by society, these parties' leaders understood that they were faced with considerable competition as political actors, and that under the new conditions after 1989, this competition was now given free rein. The disastrous elections of June 1989 dissipated any doubts the Polish party may have had about its monopoly on public support.[31] In short, although they gave up power reluctantly, the party elites knew they would have to compete and that appeals to continuing the past regime or policies would serve them badly.

Once the party elites realized the extent of change necessary, their first goal was to break with the past and centralize the party organizations. The more

[28] Jíri Machalik, the secretary of the Central Committee of the KSC, *Rude Právo*, January 31, 1990.

[29] *Radio Free Europe Situation Reports*, Imre Pozsgay, cited May 2, 1988.

[30] Jacek Zdrojewski, quoted in *Trybuna Ludu*, January 16, 1989.

[31] Further signals came in September 1989, when the opposition successfully called for further changes in the Round Table agreements (using the opposition activist Adam Michnik's famous formula: "your president, our prime minister").

skilled and pragmatic the new party elites, the more readily they broke with the party's past. Such a break consisted both of party dissolution or reregistration of the members and refounding of the local organizations and of the more symbolic changes in names, symbols, and stated ideologies. Speed was crucial – once the democratic transition had begun to consolidate and the tumult within the party organizations died down, the orthodox communist forces would otherwise begin to reemerge and act as a barrier to further transformation. Not only would they demand that the party programs and electoral appeals satisfy their interests, rather than the voters', but their continued presence and significance within the party would contradict any reformist signals sent out by the party. Therefore, early party streamlining was crucial to the subsequent success of the parties' transformation. Whether the elites could succeed, however, depended on the sort of political resources the elites had on hand.

The Czech party midlevel elites, having spent most of their professional lives in the highly orthodox party apparat, could neither envision nor implement a dramatic party transformation.[32] Dissolution was never even proposed, either at the Extraordinary Congress, or subsequently. The central party leadership argued that "KSČM is, was, and will be, the communist party of Czechoslovakia. We will not take on a different name, and 95 percent of members agree with us."[33]

With no reformist elites to put forth programmatic alternatives or experiences, and guided by the myth of the "socialist mass party," the Czech leaders saw the membership and its mobilization as the main chance at political survival, arguing that "the party has to be a mass party to be influential."[34] Party leaders immediately equated democratization with party decentralization and the end of fulfilling top-down directives.[35] To give the members an incentive to stay, the party proposed that the members vet policy, form opinion platforms, and decide the programmatic alternatives. However, the party members were largely conservative, elderly communist pensioners. An internal party referendum decided on the party name, and 78 percent of the conservative members voted to retain the communist name.

Moreover, the new Czech leaders proudly proclaimed that programmatic platforms would now be allowed in an attempt to "get back to the roots of real Marxist democracy." Old elites remained within the party, and the conservative regional offices continued to make crucial decisions. The old, pre-1989 leadership was *asked* to leave, rather than required to do so. As a

32 Interview with Jaroslav Ortman, November 7, 1996, and interview with Jaromir Sedlak, November 5, 1996, both in Prague.

33 Jírí Michalik, "Jsme komunisty" (We are communists), *Naše Pravda*, March 8, 1990, and KSČM, *Teze Zprávy ÚV KSČM o Cinnosti Ustavujicího sjezdu KSČM do 1. Sjezdu KSČM* ÚV KSČM (Prague, 1992), p. 14.

34 *Naše Pravda*, September 20, 1990.

35 *Rudé Pravo*, April 2, 1990.

result, 48 out of 109 Central Committee members elected in October 1990 were in the pre-1989 party leadership. The old party stalwarts thus continued to exert a considerable role in the party. At the same time, any voices for party reform were immediately denounced by the orthodox party members.

In contrast, the new Slovak leaders denounced communism immediately, changed the party name at the October 1990 congress, and adopted the symbols and language of social democracy, while calling for greater autonomy for the Slovak party.[36] However, the Slovak party did not dissolve, because the new leaders felt they did not have the experience or justification for this step.[37] Nonetheless, all members had to reregister, conditional on agreement with the radical reform of the party.[38] No attempt was made to encourage the party members to remain.[39]

The Polish and Hungarian party leaderships also immediately dissolved the parties in 1989–90 and forced all would-be members to reregister, pledging allegiance to the new reform orientation. Furthermore, not only did they change their names immediately, during the Extraordinary Congresses, but they also adopted the symbols of social democracy (such as the red rose), declared that their goal was to join the Socialist International, and denounced communism as an outdated ideology in which they never believed.[40]

The Polish, Hungarian, and Slovak party leaderships were also able to disregard the members and old party mainstays. Instead, they used their own expertise to set the congress agendas; change the party names, programs, and symbols; and neutralize the old organizational structures.[41] Orthodox members were actively encouraged to leave, and the rest told to either comply with the ideological and programmatic changes or leave. The Polish and Slovak parties further eliminated opinion platforms, although these were

[36] By December 1991, the SDL' unilaterally ended the federation (*Rude Pravo*, September 2, 1991).

[37] "Z uvodného vystupenia predsedu VV ÚV KSS Petra Weissa" (From the opening speech of the chair of the VV ÚV KSS Peter Weiss), KSS-SDL', *Dokumenty Zjazdu KSS-SDL' Presov, 20–21 Oktobra 1990* (Bratislava: ÚV KSS-SDL', 1990), p. 7.

[38] Interview with Peter Weiss, *Naše Pravda*, October 11, 1990.

[39] Pavol Kanis, *Pravda*, February 6, 1990.

[40] Paradoxically, the Hungarian congress also apologized more vigorously for a past that was by that point less objectionable than the Polish or Czechoslovak party history (for which those parties apologized halfheartedly). The MSzP condemned its past mistakes more than any other party, apologizing for its forcible merger with the Social Democrats after World War II, Stalinist repression, the 1956 suppression of the popular uprising (no longer called a counterrevolution), the party's inability in the mid-1970s to continue decentralizing reforms, the 1985 refusal by Kádár and his allies to liberalize further the decaying party system, and even the budget deficit. Documents of the Extraordinary Congress, quoted by Reuters, October 9, 1989.

[41] In both Slovakia and in Hungary, the party elites then had to backtrack in the face of rank-and-file apathy and passivity, and they attempted to garner members a greater role but did so not through member referenda or other direct involvement but by granting greater powers to the local organizations.

allowed to exist informally in the Hungarian party. Old elites were summarily removed or told to resign. Regional party leaders were also replaced. As a result, these party elites both consolidated their new positions and were able to implement further reforms with less opposition. Here again, however, the more experienced the leaders, the more effectively they implemented streamlining; thus, the new Slovak elites, with their minimal administrative experience, managed to alienate potential allies within the party, antagonizing loyal supporters and leading to severe internal clashes.

Elite skills also determined the degree to which the parties centralized or diffused their decision-making structures. In turn, the more the party elites were able to centralize the decision making within the parties, the more they were able to push through reform efforts. Given the lack of elite political resources either to take charge or to centralize the party leadership, the KSČM fell back on its myths of earlier party democracy. The Czech party remained decentralized until 1993.[42] The Central Committee declared it would only fulfill the directives of party members.[43] The party's organizational administration was diffuse: no central registry of members existed, and it was not until a change in the electoral law in 1991 that the party centralized its accounting practices.[44]

In contrast, in the other three parties that have regenerated, the organization and its leadership were centralized. The new leaders who assumed power in 1989–90 demanded that they could name the party leadership, as a condition of their assuming the executive positions. As a result, they all had immense leeway at the outset to implement reform, backed by loyal fellow reformists, and set the precedent for centralized leadership. In sharp contrast to the policies of the Czech party, the Slovak successor party completely ignored its members, disempowered regional leaders, and fused the parliamentary and central party leaderships to such an extent that its critics claimed the new party elites were adopting "Stalinist tactics." Polish party spokesmen admitted that "15–20 people decide about everything in our party."[45] The Hungarian party leadership was carefully chosen by the new reformist leaders: not one of its members was unpopular or discredited.[46] Although its regional leadership was not as integrated as that of the Polish or the Slovak parties, the central elites nonetheless maintained control.

42 During the June 1993 congress, new party leaders attempted to streamline the party: platforms were not allowed, local party leaders had less of a say, the members were not consulted as frequently, and the party executive got smaller and more powerful. However, by that point not only had the image of the party consolidated, but the only leaders left were conservative communists, who refused to consider more profound change in the party.

43 Vasil Mohorita speech at the first meeting of the ÚV KSČ, *Pravda*, January 9, 1990.

44 Interview with Miloslav Ransdorf, KSCM HQ, Prague, September 26, 1996.

45 *Polityka*, September 14, 1996.

46 MSzP, *The Hungarian Socialist Party* (Budapest: MSzP, 1996).

The more the party organization was streamlined early and unequivocally, the more the party elites could broaden the parties' programmatic appeals and formulate responsive programs (congruent with the policy priorities of the broad electorate). Moreover, a break with the past and organizational streamlining backed up the programmatic claims – otherwise, these appeals would be empty slogans. For example, the vociferous presence of orthodox activists would belie a party's claim that it had transformed itself completely and renounced the past. Thus, the Czech party's initial reformist stances were quickly subverted by the orthodox activists, and its programs rapidly reflected their concerns. In contrast, "early centralizers," such as the Polish and Slovak parties, cut themselves off from conservative members and organizations. They could pursue votes rather than members and responded to electoral concerns. These organizational preconditions for responsive programs mean that the trade-off between appealing to moderate supporters and to radical activists may not be exogenous, as many analyses have assumed, but of the parties' own making.

Centralized organizations also promoted effective campaigning to disseminate these claims (through both cohesive campaigns and attractive, new candidates) and the disciplined parliamentary behavior that would reinforce the parties' claims of professionalism and moderation. Parties that had not earlier centralized their organizations could neither make broad claims nor rely on the organizational backing to appeal to the voters effectively. This is not to say that organizational centralization was sufficient – the elites still had to have the experience and skill consistently to pursue broad electorates. Thus, the Slovak party's prior inexperience in societal negotiation and policy implementation made the party's appeals both inconsistent and often narrowly oriented. As a result of its organizational changes, the party could flexibly pursue different electorates, but its lack of cohesion and emphasis on broad appeals meant it could not retain these voters from election to election.

The Czech party fared even worse – it could not make broad claims or disseminate them effectively. In fact, where the party had its best organizations, it had the worst electoral results, as a consequence of its orthodox mobilization. In contrast, the Polish and Hungarian parties, with their broad appeal and skilled elites, won the 1993 and 1994 elections, respectively. Despite their "Social Democratic" and "Socialist" names, their extensive electoral support was based less on redistributive claims than on the parties' ability to commit credibly to continuing the market reforms, but with greater competence and sensitivity. The Polish party appeared especially competent next to its competitors – and, as a result, the party actually *gained* voters after it ruled for four years, in the 1997 elections.

Just as elite portable skills determined the extent of the transformation, the usable past made it credible. Specifically, the more opposed the party was to liberalization, and the less active a role it played in the democratic transition of 1989, the less credible its post-1989 commitments to democracy, its claims of managerial and administrative competence, or its acceptance of the free market. The democratic claims of the successor parties were thus either debunked or reinforced by their predecessors' records. After all, a commitment to democracy was that much more credible when declared by a Round Table participant than by a former communist apparatchik who denounced "bourgeois democracy" only a few years earlier.

Thus, the Czech party appeared completely out of touch with society, had no usable recent experience in pluralizing the polity or the economy, and its claims to a "better future with human socialism" verged on the absurd. This discreditation went so deeply as to convince the party leaders that the only rational strategy was to cling to its communist ideals since "no one will believe the change anyway."[47] Slovak party elites were in a slightly better situation, because they could claim that the Czech oppression under communism made a less repressive communist regime in Slovakia impossible. Because the new elites had little part in governing Slovakia prior to 1989, they were more credible than their Czech counterparts. At the same time, however, their lack of experience and previous visibility made their competence an unknown quantity.

In Poland, the communist elites were discredited to an extent, given the recent trauma of 1980–81, in which many of them played a role (unlike the distant events of 1956 in Hungary). They also faced a single opposition camp, Solidarity. Both factors led to the formation of a lasting cleavage in Polish politics between those who could forgive the party for its recent past and those who identified with the 1980s opposition instead. The Polish party thus faced a considerable credibility gap that made its past reform record an ambiguous asset. It also made bridging the divide between the successor party and its former opposition much more difficult, especially in the parliament.

The Hungarian elites were perhaps in the best situation of all. Their earlier liberalization, the creation of the social consensus, and considerable personal ties to the opposition made their claims of democratic commitment and administrative experience credible. Moreover, the defining crisis of their regime, and the oppression that followed, occurred over thirty years earlier, leaving fewer antagonisms. Thus, the MSzP was more widely accepted from the start and able both to form coalitions with the opposition and to present itself as a reform alternative.

The parties' usable pasts also exerted an influence over the credibility of the programmatic claims and electoral appeals – the more communist parties had engaged in reform policies and negotiation with society prior to the regime collapse, the more their successors could credibly claim they were experienced administrators and competent governors. Similarly, appeals to

[47] Radim Valenčik, KSČ spokesman, January 25, 1990, *Rudé Pravo*.

secularism, state-society consensus, and even nation building (in the case of the Slovak party) were also bolstered by the recent history of the communist regimes. The more usable their past, and the more skilled their elites, the more the parties credibly claim competence and managerial expertise. Such broad and catchall claims were key to obtaining broad support, because in all four cases the electorate's biggest concern was governmental competence and managerial expertise.[48]

The *nature* of the engagement also mattered: the more conflictual it was, the less subsequent cooperation after 1989 between parties from the opposition and from the former regime. The deeper the cleavages generated by the communist-era conflict, the less likely the communist successors were to find parliamentary partners, irrespective of their electoral achievements. The Czech party thus found no parliamentary acceptance, and its refusal to transform itself more radically made it even more of a pariah. Even otherwise regenerated parties, such as the Polish SdRP, had difficulty overcoming such cleavages, which continued to be a key source of identity for parties from the earlier anticommunist opposition. In countries where these cleavages were blurred either by the dispersion of communist politicians into other parties (Slovakia) or by a favorable past with relatively minimized conflict between state and society (Hungary), parliamentary cooperation was easier to achieve.

Conclusion

The regeneration of the communist successor parties is not only a lasting reminder of the authoritarian past and its influence after regime transitions. It also suggests conditions under which ancien regime institutions can adapt and the specific (and circumscribed) ways in which the past continues to matter.

For party regeneration to succeed, elites had to transform the parties quickly and radically, in a specific sequence that prioritized organizational transformation before changing the party programs or electoral appeals. Attempts to transform the parties' organizations or behavior after 1989–91 would make little difference. Once the new organizational, programmatic, and strategic choices were made, they influenced subsequent party development and the electoral and parliamentary performance of the parties. This self-reinforcing process made proper sequencing of reform necessary; without prior centralization of party organizations, subsequent programmatic, electoral, and parliamentary transformations could be easily subverted by the orthodox remainders within the parties.

48 Gábor Tóka, "Party Systems and Electoral Alignments in East Central Europe," machine readable data, Central European University, 1992–96.

These demands of timing and sequencing made elite political resources crucial. These resources, however, had their origin not in the transition, or in the months preceding it, but in the decades-long organizational practices of the communist parties. Authoritarian practices thus endowed some of the elite actors with political resources that were a considerable competitive advantage and allowed the parties to succeed in the new democratic regime.

References

Ágh, Attila. 1994. The Hungarian Party System and Party Theory in the Transition of Central Europe. *Journal of Theoretical Politics* 6(2): 217–38.

Arato, Andrew. 1995. Two Lectures on the Electoral Victory of the Hungarian Socialists. *Constellations* 1: 72–80.

Brus, Wlodzimierz. 1983. Economy and Politics: The Fatal Link. In Abraham Brumberg, ed., *Poland: Genesis of a Revolution*, pp. 6–41. New York: Random House.

Cotta, Maurizio. 1994. Building Party Systems after the Dictatorship: The East European Cases in a Comparative Perspective. In Geoffrey Pridham and Tatu Vanhanen, eds., *Democratization in Eastern Europe: Domestic and International Perspectives*. London: Routledge.

Dogan, Mattei, ed. 1989. *Pathways to Power*. Boulder, Colo.: Westview Press.

Ekiert, Grzegorz. 1996. *The State against Society: Political Crises and Their Aftermath in East Central Europe*. Princeton: Princeton University Press.

Evans, Geoffrey, and Stephen Whitefield. 1995. Economic Ideology and Political Success. *Party Politics* 1(4): 565–78.

Geddes, Barbara. 1995. A Comparative Perspective on the Leninist Legacy in Eastern Europe. *Comparative Political Studies* 28(2): 239–74.

Haraszti, Miklós. 1995. Animal Farm Scenarios: The Comeback of the Former Communists and Why It Is No Reason to Worry. *Constellations* 1 (January): 81–93.

Harmel, Robert, Uk Heo, Alexander Tan, and Kenneth Janda. 1995. Performance, Leadership, Factions, and Party Change: An Empirical Analysis. *West European Politics* 18(1): 1–33.

Harmel, Robert, and Kenneth Janda. 1994. An Integrated Theory of Party Goals and Party Change. *Journal of Theoretical Politics* 3: 259–87.

Ishiyama, John T. 1995. Communist Parties in Transition: Structures, Leaders, and Process of Democratization in Eastern Europe. *Comparative Politics* 27: 147–66.

Jakeš, Miloš. 1996. *Dva Roky Generalním Tajemnikem*. Prague: Dokumenty.

Kirsch, Henry. 1993. From SED to PDS: The Struggle to Revive a Left Party. In Russell L. Dalton, ed., *The New Germany Votes*, pp. 163–84. Providence: Berg.

Kitschelt, Herbert. 1983. *The Transformation of European Social Democracy*. Cambridge: Cambridge University Press, 1983.

Kopecký, Petr. 1995. Developing Party Organizations in East-Central Europe. *Party Politics* 1(4): 515–34.

Körösényi, András. 1993. Stable or Fragile Democracy? Political Cleavages and Party System in Hungary. *Government and Opposition* 1993: 87–104.

Kovács, András. 1995. Two Lectures on the Electoral Victory of the Hungarian Socialists. *Constellations* 1(January): 72–75.

Lewis, Paul. 1989. *Political Authority and Party Secretaries in Poland, 1975–1986.* Cambridge: Cambridge University Press.

Lewis, Paul, and Radzisława Gortat. 1995. Models of Party Development and Questions of State Dependence in Poland. *Party Politics* 4: 599–608.

Lipset, Seymour M., and Stein Rokkan. 1967. Cleavage Structures, Party Systems, and Voter Alignments: An Introduction. In Seymour M. Lipset and Stein Rokkan, eds., *Party Systems and Voter Alignments*, pp. 1–64. New York: Free Press.

Millard, Frances. 1994. The Shaping of the Polish Party System, 1989–93. *East European Politics and Societies* 8(3): 467–94.

Moraski, Bryon, and Gerhard Loewenberg. 1997. The Effect of Legal Thresholds on the Revival of Former Communist Parties in East-Central Europe. Paper presented at the annual meeting of the American Political Science Association, Washington, D.C., August 28–31.

O'Neil, Patrick. 1996. Revolution from Within: Institutional Analysis, Transitions from Authoritarianism, and the Case of Hungary. *World Politics* 48(4): 579–603.

Panebianco, Angelo. 1988. *Political Parties: Organization and Power.* Cambridge: Cambridge University Press.

Przeworski, Adam. 1992. *Democracy and the Market.* Cambridge: Cambridge University Press.

Przeworski, Adam, and John Sprague. 1986. *Paper Stones: A History of Electoral Socialism.* Chicago: University of Chicago Press.

Putnam, Robert. 1973. *The Beliefs of Politicians.* New Haven: Yale University Press.

Robertson, David. 1976. *A Theory of Party Competition.* London: Wiley.

Rose, Richard, and Thomas T. Mackie. 1988. Do Parties Persist or Fail? The Big Trade-Off Facing Organizations. In Kay Lawson and Peter Merkl, eds., *When Parties Fail: Emerging Alternative Organizations*, pp. 533–58. Princeton: Princeton University Press, 1988.

Sjöblom, Gunnar. 1983. Political Change and Political Accountability. In Hans Daalder and Peter Mair, eds., *Western European Party Systems*, pp. 370–403. London: Sage.

Skilling, Gordon H. 1977. Stalinism and Czechoslovak Political Culture. In Robert C. Tucker, ed., *Stalinism*, pp. 257–80. New York: W. W. Norton.

Sokorski, Wlodzimierz. 1990. *Udana Kleska.* Warsaw: Savimpress.

Strom, Kaare. 1990. A Behavioral Theory of Competitive Political Parties. *American Journal of Political Science* 34(2): 565–98.

Szelényi, Iván, Eva Fodor, and Eric Hanley. 1997. Left Turn in Post Communist Politics: Bringing Class Back In? *East European Politics and Societies* 11(1): 190–224.

Tóka, Gábor. 1996. Electoral Choices in East-Central Europe. In Geoffrey Pridham and Paul G. Lewis, eds., *Stabilising Fragile Democracies: Comparing New Party Systems in Southern and Eastern Europe*, pp. 100–25. London: Routledge.

Tökés, Rudolf. 1996. *Hungary's Negotiated Revolution.* Cambridge: Cambridge University Press.

Wałęsa, Lech. 1990. In *Życie Warszawy*, February 2.

Waller, Michael. 1995. Adaptation of the Former Communist Parties of East Central Europe. *Party Politics* 1(4): 473–90.

Wasilewski, Jacek. 1990. The Patterns of Bureaucratic Elite Recruitment in Poland in the 1970s and 1980s. *Soviet Studies* 42: 749–50.

Wilson, Frank. 1980. Sources of Party Transformation: The Case of France. In Peter H. Merkl, ed., *Western European Party Systems: Trends and Prospects*, pp. 526–51. New York: Free Press.

Wolchik, Sharon. 1987. Economic Performance and Political Change in Czechoslovakia. In Charles Bukowski and Mark Cichock, eds., *Prospects for Change in Socialist Systems*, pp. 35–60. New York: Praeger.

Žiak, Miloš. 1996. *Slovensko: Od komunizmu kam?* Bratislava: Archa.

Zubek, Voytek. 1990. Poland's Party Self-Destructs. *Orbis* 34: 179–94.

1994. The Reassertion of the Left in Post-Communist Poland. *Europe-Asia Studies* 5: 801–37.

6

Leninist Legacies and Legacies of State Socialism in Postcommunist Central Europe's Constitutional Development

Allison Stanger

With the Berlin Wall's fall now more than a decade behind us, it is an auspicious moment to assess the health of postcommunist Central Europe's new democracies. Has the time come to jettison the adjective "postcommunist" when referring to NATO's newest members, or does the weight of the Leninist past still lend distinctive features to the institutions and politics of these countries?

An extraordinary amount of scholarly attention has been focused on the efforts to institutionalize democracy's third wave.[1] These studies have tended to fall into one of two principal categories.[2] Structural explanations focusing on macrolevel variables have advanced our knowledge of the preconditions that facilitate successful democratic consolidation (Lipset, 1959; Stepan and Skach, 1993). Process-oriented analyses preoccupied with microlevel variables have increased our understanding of the interaction between government and opposition political strategies in shaping the trajectory of attempted transitions to democracy.[3] In Chapter 1 of this volume, Ekiert and Hanson reconceptualize this divide by breaking it down into structural, institutional, and interactional categories of explanation along both temporal and spatial lines. Although the transitions literature that has been generated to date is now voluminous, surprisingly little systematic attention has been devoted to the comparative study of the process by which new constitutions are made or what connections might exist between constitutional revision processes and subsequent political development. Social scientists by

[1] Samuel Huntington's (1991) book popularized the term "third wave."

[2] Dankwart Rustow was the first to suggest that one might study democratization as a phenomenon distinct from democracy itself; causes of and preconditions for democracy were not necessarily one and the same. See Lisa Anderson's (1997: 254) introduction to the special issue of *Comparative Politics* on Rustow's legacy.

[3] The literature here is voluminous, but the flagship of this approach is the four-volume series by O'Donnell, Schmitter, and Whitehead (1986). See, also, Di Palma (1990) and Linz and Shain (1995).

and large have "neglected" the comparative study of "the contexts in which constitutional formulas are adopted or retained" (Linz and Stepan, 1996: 81).[4]

The relative neglect of comparative constitutionalism in the study of postcommunist democratization is a significant oversight, for three principal reasons. First, the tenor and shape of constitutional dialogue in democratizing states has implications for both the likelihood of democratic consolidation and the form that democratic consolidation, if in the end attained, actually takes. Steering clear of this issue area because it is inevitably so methodologically messy may deprive us of valuable, policy-relevant insights. Second, one potential means of teasing out linkages between macro- and microlevel explanations of transition outcomes is through the comparative examination and evaluation of elite strategies for remaking the constitutional order. In this sense, an investigation of the character and conduct of constitutional politics can lay valuable groundwork for subsequent theoretical bridge building. Third, awareness of the processes by which institutions have been remade in postcommunist Central Europe can contribute to our assessment of the communist legacy and ultimately to our theoretical understanding of path-dependent institutional change.

Yale law professor Bruce Ackerman has argued that the immediate aftermath of revolution provides liberal democrats with a unique opportunity, what he calls "the constitutional moment," where circumstances are optimal for laying the legal foundations for a democratic order and mobilizing the requisite broad popular support for the constitutional initiative. Timing in tackling major constitutional controversies is critical, for the opposition to authoritarian rule will remain united only for a finite amount of time after it has become clear that a new order is in the making. If the constitutional moment passes in vain, therefore, it is very difficult to recreate it (Ackerman, 1992: 46–50). To what extent is Ackerman's constitutional moment a useful heuristic device for evaluating the potential for and limits on institutional transformation? Was the constitutional moment successfully exploited in Central Europe's transitions? Is the answer to this question of consequence for subsequent democratic development? Because Ackerman's constitutional moment is the path dependency theorist's critical juncture for the rule-creating issue area, assessing its salience in the postcommunist context promises to shed light on debates that are central to the literature on historical institutionalism.[5]

An investigation of the relationship between communism's institutional legacy and early constitutional decisions in Poland's, Hungary's, and the former Czechoslovakia's transitions to democracy frames some intriguing

[4] Jon Elster (1997: 123) has also noted this neglect. A noteworthy exception is Elster, Offe, and Preuss (1998). See also Zielonka (2001).

[5] On the defining features of this literature, see Hall and Taylor (1996: esp. 937–42).

empirical puzzles. In all three countries, aspiring democrats used the constitutions they inherited from the outgoing order as a point of departure for institutionalizing democracy. Although their approaches to constitutional renewal were surprisingly similar at the onset, despite differing modes of regime breakdown, the character of the constitutional conversation in each country quickly diverged. Thus, a decade after the official collapse of communism in Europe, democratic Hungary continued to be governed by a heavily amended version of its former communist constitution, despite repeated attempts to replace that text with a document specifically designed to govern democratic life. In contrast to the enduring constitutional gridlock in Hungary, Poland ratified a new constitution in May 1997, retiring what was first promulgated as an incomplete interim agreement, the so-called Little Constitution. Although the federal government of Czechoslovakia was unsuccessful in its quest for a new constitution, both successor states have since symbolically and legally renounced the constitutional framework bequeathed to them by the communist experiment, ratifying brand new constitutions in the latter half of 1992.

Through macrohistorical analysis, this chapter attempts to elucidate divergent constitutional outcomes in Poland, Hungary, and the former Czechoslovakia, those which were seemingly spawned by parallel points of departure.[6] It argues that modes of communist regime breakdown can explain neither the initial approach to constitutional reform that democratizers took in each of these countries nor the subsequent course of constitutional contestation.[7] In so doing, it becomes clear that the Leninist legacy in institutional forms was by no means uniform across the region, a fact in and of itself worthy of explanation. Although the trajectory of constitutional politics in the postcommunist context was certainly framed by both the form and timing of the old order's demise, choice on matters of constitutional import was ultimately bounded by more than institutional inheritance alone. Applying Ekiert and Hanson's distinction (Chapter 1 in this volume) between "Leninist legacies" (expressed through formal institutions) and "legacies of state socialism" (manifest in enduring norms and codes of conduct) serves to highlight the importance of evolving perceptions in shaping institutional choice. The political beliefs upon which former dissidents initially relied to make sense of revolutionary circumstances were themselves transformed by the practice of transition politics; individuals who first viewed the adoption of new constitutions as a secondary concern over time reassigned this task

[6] Stephen E. Hanson (1995: 310ff.) has broken down the Leninist legacy into four basic components – ideological, political, socioeconomic, and cultural – to which this chapter adds a fifth analytical lens: Marxism-Leninism's legal legacy.

[7] Along similar lines, in an illuminating essay, Grzegorz Ekiert and Jan Kubik (1998) have shown that modes of breakdown of communist regimes had no noticeable impact on the magnitude of protest activities in the former East Germany, Poland, Hungary, and Slovakia.

top priority. The perceptions of political elites were also affected in differing ways by the international context and Western pressures. These changing elite preferences are important for understanding the manner in which constitutional conflict was resolved, contained, or transcended in each country. Consequently, evaluating the impact of Leninist legacies and legacies of state socialism in the Czech and Slovak Republics, Poland, and Hungary demands consideration of the ways in which the dynamics of interaction with Western elites created opportunities for indigenous actors, as well as of the changing cognitive maps of those who govern.[8]

The discussion that follows is divided into three principal sections. In the first, I compare the circumstances that led to the method of radical continuity initially being chosen in Poland, Hungary, and the former Czechoslovakia. I argue that Czechoslovakia was headed down the same constitutional path as Poland's and Hungary's "pacted" transitions until the Czech-Slovak conflict intervened. In the second section, I explain how retaining the communist constitution as a stopgap measure in the Czecho-Slovak context posed serious problems for democratic consolidation, because it exacerbated rather than alleviated tensions between the federation's two members. The experience of constitutional deadlock at the federal level, however, actually facilitated constitution drafting at the republic level, making it possible for the successor states to learn from the mistakes of their parent. I conclude by applying Ackerman's framework to the Central European cases, exploring the implications of early legal choices in these four countries for their subsequent democratic development, and reflecting on the significance of my findings for theory building in the study of regime change.

Constitution-Drafting Patterns in Poland, Hungary, and the Former Czechoslovakia

The domestic opponents of communist regimes all faced a common and immediate problem once it became clear that the existing political order in their respective countries could no longer endure: what was to be done with the abundant legal inheritance from the totalitarian era, especially the fictional constitutions that allegedly laid out the foundational rules of political life in the people's paradise? Because the rulers of the one-party state had operated outside and above the law, it would seem to follow that their opponents should conduct themselves otherwise and simply demand that the existing laws be obeyed. Yet how could this be deemed democratic action, when those same laws were the embodiment of the very system that the proponents of democracy sought to transform?

[8] The key question here, as Herbert Kitschelt (1993: 417) has emphasized, is "when and why actors create particular cognitive maps."

While the actual choices faced in each state were all circumscribed by the realm of the politically possible, aspiring democratizers in the postcommunist context could follow three mutually exclusive paths to constitutional reconstruction. First, the custodians of the transition could restore precommunist constitutions, where they existed. Second, postcommunist elites had the option of pursuing a strategy of "radical continuity," whereby the communist constitution would be accepted as the law of the land only to be amended beyond recognition following its own amendment rules, in this way pursuing a "revolution by constitutional tinkering" (Arato, n.d.: 110; Holmes and Sunstein, 1995: 286). The path of radical continuity, in short, consists of grafting revolutionary amendments onto an undemocratic constitutional base. Third, proponents of change could renounce the constitution of the ancien régime and concentrate their efforts on drafting a brand new charter, either adopting an interim basic law to govern politics until that task was completed or promulgating a new constitution concurrently with the retirement of the old.

The third option is the one that citizens of the West, especially Americans, typically associate with liberal revolution. It is a course that democratizers in South Africa, for example, have pursued with success to date (a new constitution being ratified in 1996, replacing the 1994 interim document). Germany's, Italy's, Portugal's, Greece's, and Spain's contemporary democracies were also established in this general fashion.[9] Yet the transition to democracy in Poland, Hungary, and the former Czechoslovakia did not follow this course. Postcommunist elites in all three of these countries endorsed the constitutions of the outgoing order as a point of departure for democratization until new constitutions could be drafted and ratified. Each found the task of agreeing on a new constitutional framework to be more rather than less difficult as the initial revolutionary euphoria evaporated. In Poland, Hungary, and the former Czechoslovakia, the transition to democracy was negotiated through Round Table Talks between the outgoing communist order and the democratic opposition. In each country, the transfer of power transpired in complete legality – that is, through a negotiated settlement consistent with existing law, rather than radical renunciation of the ancien régime and its legal apparatus (Elster, 1993: 190). The precise reasons why this particular path was chosen, however, were different in each country.

Poland

Until May 1997 democratic Poland was governed by a patchwork collection of remnants of the heavily amended 1952 Stalinist constitution, with those unsystematic modifications supplemented by a constitutional law, the so-called Little Constitution, which was ratified by the Sejm in October 1992

[9] In the German case, of course, what was first promulgated as an interim constitution to govern only until a divided Germany could be reunited remains in force after reunification.

(Karpiński, 1995: 4–7). The Little Constitution attempted to clarify the legal relationship between executive and legislative power in postcommunist Poland but was mute on the organization of the judicial branch or the protection of civil rights.[10]

The Round Table Talks in the spring of 1989 between the leaders of Solidarity and the communist regime resulted in a compromise agreement on the future political structure of the country and the rules that would govern the first partially free elections. Convinced of the permanence of their power, the communists agreed to restore the upper chamber of the Polish Parliament, the Senate, which they had abolished after World War II. All 100 seats in that body would be contested, but 65 percent of the seats in the lower chamber, the Sejm, were to be reserved for representatives of the regime and its allies.[11] Both parties to these negotiations believed that the compromise gave the communists effective control of the political system. The June 4, 1989, elections, however, proved otherwise. Solidarity candidates swept 99 percent of the seats in the Senate and all of the contested seats in the Sejm, often by embarrassingly overwhelming majorities. Solidarity's resounding victory gave the opposition the upper hand in shaping the country's constitutional direction, as it had the only political actors who could claim to speak for the Polish people (Rapaczyński, 1991: 598–601; Elster, 1993: 203–4; Ash, 1990: 25–39).

After the semifree elections, the new Solidarity-led government proposed a series of constitutional amendments designed to modify the Stalinist constitution to facilitate democratic governance. From the start, however, these amendments were regarded as stopgap measures intended to smooth the transition to new constitutional forms. Restoring the so-called April Constitution of 1935 was not a viable option because of its unavoidable association with the Piłsudski dictatorship.

In early 1990 the Sejm appointed a special Constitutional Committee and assigned it the task of preparing a new constitution. The original plan was for the Constitutional Committee to submit its finished product to both houses of parliament for approval, followed by a national referendum to ratify the document as the law of the land. Although this plan was never formally renounced, the described sequence of events would never take place as envisioned (Rapaczyński, 1991: 601–2).

Andrzej Rapaczyński, a Columbia University Law School professor who served as an expert advisor to the Constitutional Committee of the Polish Parliament, cites four reasons why the plans for Polish constitutional renewal were initially derailed.

[10] On the content of the Little Constitution, see Vinton (1992).

[11] The representative of the communist regime responsible for suggesting this innovation at the Round Table Talks was Poland's current president, Aleksander Kwaśniewski. See Osiatyński (1996: 53–54).

First, the Round Table Sejm charged with drafting the new document was not the product of fully free elections; remember, 65 percent of the seats had been reserved for representatives of the outgoing order. Hence, the Sejm's Constitutional Committee did not have full democratic legitimacy; in contrast, the Senate did. Perhaps not surprisingly, the Senate quickly convened a rival Constitutional Committee and began work on a draft of its own, even though the 1952 constitution that was ostensibly governing Poland in the interim period delegated the matter of constitutional change to the Sejm (Rapaczyński, 1991: 602).

Second, the composition of the Sejm's Constitutional Committee caused some concern. Oddly enough, Solidarity members on the committee, who were the original force behind the new constitution project, had little interest in the substantive questions of institutional design. Consequently, despite Solidarity's domination of the Constitutional Committee as a whole, supporters of the undemocratic past controlled the Subcommittee on Institutions, which was charged with drafting the mechanics of government in the new document (Rapaczyński, 1991: 602–3).

Third, the rift in Solidarity that divided Lech Wałęsa's Gdansk group and that of the Warsaw intellectuals further undermined the prospects for a new constitution. That the rival Warsaw group dominated Solidarity's leadership in the Sejm led Wałęsa to denigrate the Sejm committee as an organization unfit to orchestrate the transition to a new order. From its perspective, the Warsaw group saw its work on constitution drafting as a vehicle for checking Wałęsa's power lust (Rapaczyński, 1991: 604–6).

Finally, Wałęsa's easy victory in the December 1990 presidential elections over the Warsaw intellectuals' candidate for president, Tadeusz Mazowiecki, only served to delegitimize irreparably the work of the Sejm's Constitutional Committee.[12] The Polish people had elected as their president one of the main critics of the Round Table Sejm's efforts to formalize the new rules of the game (Rapaczyński, 1991: 606–7). While no one could have been able to foresee that the national consensus forged in the revolutionary events of 1989 would so quickly unravel, a window of opportunity for drafting and ratifying a brand new constitution had for all practical purposes closed for Poland by the end of 1990, constitutional politics from that point on growing all the more politicized.[13]

Potentially complicating matters still further, postcommunist Poland's main supervisory and judicial review bodies were institutions that the

[12] A dispute over when to force General Jaruzelski out of office led to Solidarity fielding two candidates for president in 1990. Wałęsa favored pushing him out immediately, while many of his former associates, including Tadeusz Mazowiecki, thought that Polish interests were best served by temporarily keeping him in power to maintain unity. See Jasiewicz (1997: 132).

[13] "Bronisław Geremek on Constitution-Making in Poland," *East European Constitutional Review* 4(1) (1995): 42–43.

communist regime had founded in the 1980s as concessions to the Solidarity movement.[14] The Constitutional Tribunal, Poland's Constitutional Court, established in 1982, was first "elected" in 1985. The State Tribunal, a body that rules on potential legal violations by public officials, was created in March 1982. As these organs were designed to operate in a completely different context, it is not surprising that both their structure and their jurisdiction turned out to be less than fully adequate for democratic conditions. To make things worse, each of these institutions was and is staffed by the Sejm (Karpiński, 1995: 6–7). Yet because the Sejm was not a fully democratic body until the October 1991 parliamentary elections, these important structures continued to be dominated by representatives of the old order well after the revolutionary events of 1989.[15] In this sense, Poland's early democratic development was at first monitored and reviewed by less than ardent supporters of liberal democracy.

Efforts to complete the constitutional project were unsuccessful until reconstructed communist Aleksander Kwaśniewski's election as president in November 1995.[16] Since 1993, Kwaśniewski had served as chair of the Parliament's Constitutional Committee, the body charged with drafting a new constitution. Former president Wałęsa would surely have vetoed any constitution generated by the Kwaśniewski commission, prolonging the constitutional stalemate, but Kwaśniewski's election removed this impediment.

Arriving at a draft that might receive the approval of Parliament proved to be an arduous process. The proper relationship between church and state was the most contentious issue. Further, parties of the right wanted the new constitution to ban abortion. In this they were unsuccessful, but they did manage to secure constitutional guarantees that Poland would not legalize same-sex marriages.[17] The introduction to the draft that ultimately emerged reflects the conflicts that were part of its creation:

> With concern for the fate and future of our country, having in 1989 regained the opportunity for sovereign and democratic decisions upon its fate, we the Polish nation, all the citizens of the Republic, both those believing in God as the source of truth, justice, good, and beauty, as also those who do not share that faith and draw those universal values from other sources, equal in their rights and obligations in relation to the mutual good of Poland, grateful to our ancestors for their work, for their struggle for independence, bought with enormous sacrifices, for a culture rooted in the Christian legacy of the nation and in universal human values, drawing upon the best

[14] For a thorough investigation of the birth of judicial review in Poland, see Brzezinski (1993a).

[15] On the Polish Constitutional Tribunal, see Brzezinski (1993b).

[16] Kwaśniewski had campaigned as a member of the postcommunist Democratic Left Alliance (SLD), but after winning the election turned in his party card to become "President of All the Poles."

[17] "Hurry Up," *Economist*, January 18, 1997, p. 52.

traditions of the First and the Second Republic, with a sense of responsibility before God or else before our own, human conscience, bring into existence the constitution of the Polish Republic.[18]

Once both chambers of the Polish Parliament had endorsed a new constitution, it was then presented to the Polish people for final ratification via referendum.[19] Solidarity Electoral Action (AWS), an anticommunist coalition of no less than thirty-seven rightist parties, headed by the leader of the Solidarity Trade Union, Marian Krzaklewski, was the most vocal opponent of the document that was finally endorsed by the National Assembly. AWS urged Polish voters to reject the proposed constitution, arguing that it was a creation of former communists and consequently was inappropriate for a Catholic nation. In addition, it argued that adopting the new constitution would result in the surrender of hard-won Polish sovereignty to international organizations, such as the European Union.[20] In a variety of ways, the church itself weighed in against the Kwaśniewski draft (Eberts, 1998). In response, President Kwaśniewski sent a copy of the draft constitution to every Polish family, maintaining that it was precisely the prospect of EU and NATO membership that made ratification of the utmost importance. Poland, after all, did not want to enter negotiations with these international bodies with a provisional set of laws.[21]

On May 25, 1997, Polish voters went to the polls. Fifty-three percent of those voting endorsed the new constitution, but only 42 percent of the electorate participated in the referendum. In a strange twist of fate, democratic Poland had at last made a clean break with its communist past, yet the document that might have symbolized and embodied that action had been the creation of former communists, not of Solidarity. In the end, ironically, Polish democracy was sanctified by those who had once opposed its institution, rather than the courageous individuals who brought the old order crashing down.

Hungary

In contrast to the situation in Poland, where the communist regime was negotiating with Solidarity at a Round Table, the Hungarian communists were negotiating at a Round Table with a Round Table of opposition forces (hereafter designated by its Hungarian acronym EKA to minimize

[18] Text of report by Polish radio, March 22, 1997, BBC Summary of World Broadcasts (1997, March 24). Available: NEXIS Library: Europe File: All Europe.

[19] The vote was 461 deputies (and senators) in favor of the new draft constitution, 31 against, with 5 abstaining. Ibid.

[20] "An AWSome Future?" *Economist*, May 31, 1997, pp. 49–50.

[21] President interviewed on new constitution, Concordat, vetting law, Polish radio 1, April 24, 1997, BBC Summary of World Broadcasts (1997, April 26). Available: NEXIS Library: Europe File: All Europe.

confusion). EKA was an umbrella organization that brought together the most important groupings in the opposition (Ash, 1990: 56). The circumstances in which constitutional issues were addressed, moreover, were very different in Hungary than they were in Poland. In Hungary, the Communist Party (the Hungarian Socialist Worker's Party or MSzMP) first raised the issue of reforming the 1949 constitution well before its monopoly of power was seriously threatened. The ruling party began a process of legal reform in the 1980s that culminated in a draft constitution in 1988. As a result, EKA was in a difficult position vis-à-vis constitutional matters from the start of its negotiations with the communist regime. With a draft constitution in hand, the communist government had already devoted considerable time and energy to devising a legal strategy that would enable the regime to claim credit for democratic development, while preserving the party's privileged position in the reformed political order.

This unique history was reflected in the dynamics of the negotiations on matters of constitutional import at the Round Table Talks. Because the regime's representatives presented themselves to the opposition as resident experts on legal matters, every time a specific problem was not considered to be politically important by EKA, they would simply defer to the judgment of the Ministry of Justice. In instances where EKA was less than fully compliant, the party's negotiators would threaten the opposition with their power to rush new legislation through parliament, with or without their approval. In this way, the government drove the amending process, while simultaneously being able to claim that the legal products of their negotiations with the coalition of opposition forces had been endorsed by the opponents of communist legality (Sajo, 1996: 76–77).

The Round Table Talks produced a radically amended constitution – approximately 95 percent of the words were new – that sailed through the ancien régime–dominated parliament without any discussion. These changes were packaged, despite their radical nature, as an amendment to the existing Stalinist-era constitution, rather than as a brand new document, primarily because the 1989 law on referendum stipulated that a new constitution had to be put to the Hungarian people in the form of a referendum, and there was neither time for nor interest in traveling this road (Sajo, 1996: 88–89). The task of drafting a new constitution for postcommunist Hungary was instead delegated to the first democratically elected parliament. Meanwhile, in an attempt to distance themselves from the errors of the past, the members of MSZMP, all unavoidably associated with the old order, voted by a large majority on October 8, 1989, to create a new party, the Hungarian Socialist Party (MSzP) (O'Neil, 1996: 598). The amended constitution was then ceremoniously instituted on October 23, 1989, the thirty-third anniversary of the 1956 revolution (Paczoly, 1993: 24). The document itself explicitly states that it is meant to serve as the basic law of the land only until a new constitution can be enacted (Kukorelli, 1992: 41).

Despite the name change, the MSzP was soundly defeated in the March and April 1990 elections (Bruszt and Stark, 1992: 51). The main victors were two postcommunist political groupings, the Hungarian Democratic Forum (MDF) and the Alliance of Free Democrats (SzDSz). Together, they received 46 percent of the popular vote, but with the 4 percent threshold for entry into parliament stipulated by the 1989 electoral law, the two opposition parties wound up gaining more than two-thirds of the seats in parliament.[22] This had powerful implications for constitutional politics, since amending the constitution required but a two-thirds majority in Hungary's single-chamber parliament. Thus, the freely elected Hungarian parliament continued on the same road to democracy through constitutional reform as had their less than democratic predecessor, rather than changing course and pursuing a radical break with the legality of the communist system.

The idea that a wholly new constitution would one day be promulgated in a more traditional fashion persisted but was placed on the back burner, and the amendment process continued throughout 1990 until approximately 95 percent of the clauses had again been rewritten (Sajo, 1992). In this sense, the true framers of Hungary's present constitution span the political spectrum, with the principal framers including both the parties to the Round Table Talks of 1989, especially the ruling Communist Party as well as the two parties empowered by the 1990 elections, the MDF and the SzDSz (Arato, 1994: 27–28).

The newly elected parliament's fateful decision to work with the constitutional status quo rather than overturning it conferred a degree of "backward legitimacy" on those portions of the evolving document that had been forged by less than democratic means. In accepting the constitution bequeathed to them by the ancien régime, the new parliament legitimized that document, but at the same time missed the moment, difficult to recreate, when it might have been possible to make a radical break with the past by adopting an entirely new constitution (Paczoly, 1993: 31). Because the evolving text that emerged through perpetual amending was a creation of both old and new elites, the line between Hungary's outgoing order and its democracy in the making was inevitably blurred. In the process, since parliament was the province of constitutional change, the content of Hungary's ever changing constitution was rendered a potential tool in the hands of rival political parties, rather than providing a set of relatively permanent rules by which the democratic political game was to be played. Constitutional politics collapsed into ordinary politics.

The 1994 parliamentary elections, which marked the resurrection of reconstituted communists as the dominant political force, only rendered the story of constitutional renewal all the more Byzantine. The once dominant right-leaning MDF, which as of February 1996 had a mere 4 percent approval

[22] The threshold was raised from 4 to 5 percent in 1993 (Arato, 1994: 27).

rating among the Hungarian electorate, secured a mere 38 seats in parliament. The liberal SzDSz was also dealt a significant blow, winning only 69 seats in the 386-seat parliament. In contrast, the MSzP, led by a former communist who once served as Hungary's foreign minister, Gyula Horn, won a clear majority (209 seats). To allay international fears that the reform process had ground to a halt, the MSzP voluntarily governed in coalition with the SzDSz, which was given three of twelve ministerial posts.[23]

In the election campaign, a majority of the political parties had viewed the framing of a new constitution to be a top priority for Hungarian democracy (Arato, 1994: 28). The unlikely coalition that emerged recreated the two-thirds majority in parliament needed to pass a wholly new constitution, but the new coalition partners allayed the fears of those they had just defeated by agreeing to create a constitution-drafting committee in the new parliament with substantial opposition representation. To ensure that any new draft it produced was itself a product of consensus, that committee established further rules above and beyond the two-thirds parliamentary majority rule for ratification (Arato, 1996: 31–32).[24] Specifically, either a four-fifths majority or five of six parties had to sign off on any proposed amendment (Halmai, 1999; Mihalicz, 1999).

After a year and a half of work, the committee produced a set of detailed guidelines for a final draft of a new Hungarian constitution, as well as an accompanying set of ninety-three amendments expressing reservations about the content of that draft. Both were submitted to the unicameral parliament for approval in May 1996. The amendments were brought to a vote first and failed to pass by a mere five votes, largely due to unexpected foot-dragging on the part of members of the Hungarian Socialist Party. The guidelines themselves were never submitted to a vote, bringing the long-standing attempt to secure a new constitution to an at least temporary halt (Arato, 1996: 32–33).

In a final effort to enact a symbolic refounding, the Orban government proposed that a new constitution be symbolically created in January 2000 by simply renaming the XX. Law of 1949 the I. Law of 2000 and replacing the old preamble, which makes reference to the existing constitution's temporary status, with a new paragraph that refers to the Holy Crown, that is, the symbol of the Hungarian monarchy.[25] This renaming, however, never took

[23] Business Intelligence Report World of Information (on Hungary), Janet Matthews Information Services, Quest Economics Database (1996, October). Available: NEXIS Library: NEWS File: ALLNWS.

[24] For up-to-date information on Hungary's constitutional politics, consult the search engine of the OMRI web server. Bulashova, Natasha and Cole, Greg. Friends and Partners: Search RFE/RL Daily Digest. Online. Internet. Friends and Partners, 1996. Available: <http:// www.friends-partners.org/friends/news/rferl/search.htmlopt-tables-mac-english->.

[25] Endre Babus, "The Holy Crown," in *Heti Világgazdaság*, August 21, 1999, available: <http://folioweb.hvg.hu/cgi-bin/foliocgi.exe/hvg2.nfo/query=alkotm!E1ny++/doc/{t0,0,511,16504}/hit_headings/hits_only?>. Unlike Poland, or the Czech and Slovak republics,

place as proposed, although the Holy Crown itself was subsequently moved from the National Museum to a new home in the parliament.

Ten years after the collapse of communist authority, therefore, Hungary remained unique among its neighbors in being governed by a constitution forged in large part by what were then the opponents of liberal democracy. The constitutional synthesis of 1989–90, moreover, was never ratified by referendum, as the "Law on Referenda" stipulates that it must, if it is to be anything other than an interim constitution (Arato, 1996: 36). Yet while there have been repeated attempts to right this situation, both symbolic and substantive, calls for constitutional renewal seem to have faded as Hungarian democracy entered the twenty-first century. There are prominent voices on the Hungarian political stage – among them key members of the Hungarian Socialist Party as well as the president of the Constitutional Court, László Sólyom – who have stated publicly that the quest for a new basic law has become wholly unnecessary. In their view, the existing constitution "works" when it is informed by precedent, and precedent has accumulated over the course of Hungarian democracy's postcommunist existence.[26] As is well known, Hungary's present institutional arrangements bestow an enormous amount of responsibility on the Constitutional Court to rule on constitutionality where ambiguity prevails. By any measure, Hungary's Constitutional Court has been prepared to tackle this challenge.[27]

Czechoslovakia

The governing coalition that emerged from the Czecho-Slovak Round Table differed from its Polish and Hungarian counterparts in one critical respect: when the dust had cleared, the opposition had effective control of both domestic and foreign policy. While the interim Government of National Understanding formed by Marián Čalfa on December 10, 1989, looked like a power-sharing arrangement on paper, in practice it was not. Communist premier Ladislav Adamec had attempted to stack the first interim government but overplayed his hand and was forced to resign, which effectively handed de facto power to the dissidents (Kraus, 1995: 542–44). With

Hungary does not presently mention the historic past of the nation in its constitution. See "Visible Constitutions," in *Heti Világgazdaság*, August 21, 1999, available: <http://folioweb.hvg.hu/cgi-bin/foliocgi.exe/hvg2.nfo/query=alkotm!E1ny++/doc/{t0,0,511,16504}/hit_headings/hits_only?>. Both translations by Lorinc Redei.

[26] For example, see "Interview with László Sólyom," conducted by Andras Mink, *East European Constitutional Review* 6(1) (1997): 73. For a lucid presentation of the arguments for and against a new constitution, see József Debreczeni, "Do We Need a New Constitution?" *Magyar Szemle*, May 1997, available: <http://www.net.hu/magyarszemle/archivum/6_3–4/9.htm>. In the end, Debreczeni concludes that the time for a new constitution has passed. Translation by Lorinc Redei.

[27] Hungary's Constitutional Court has emerged as one of the most "authoritative" arbiters in the world (Holmes and Sunstein, 1995: 300).

respect to matters of constitutional import, therefore, the makers of the Velvet Revolution had unrivaled potential power to remake the institutions of the communist regime.

Even though the Czechoslovak communist regime was of the hard-line variety when compared with its reforming Warsaw Pact allies (the Czechoslovak Communist Party's initial reaction to glasnost in the Soviet Union, for example, was to stop selling *Pravda* in Prague), its minions had belatedly set out to work on a new constitution that might incorporate the Gorbachev agenda. The Communist Party member who was eventually to lead the Government of National Understanding, Marián Čalfa, had served the old regime since 1988 in the position of federal minister for legislation. In that capacity, he had been head of the committee in charge of drafting a new constitution, which had been scheduled to go into force in 1990 (Čalda, 1996: 148). By Čalfa 's own account, the party's new draft mentioned neither the leading role of the Communist Party nor Marxism-Leninism. Consequently, Civic Forum's request early on in the Round Table talks for the removal of the party's leading role from the constitution was immediately acceptable to the government in principle, so long as the changes were implemented according to existing legal procedures (Hanzel, 1991: 62ff.).

Although it was potentially part of its arsenal, the Czechoslovak government did not deploy constitutional reform as a strategic weapon for preserving the party's power in its negotiations with the opposition over the future of the country. Nor did it adopt the Hungarian strategy of attempting to outflank its opponents by posing as the real agent of democratization. The marked difference between the character of the Polish, Hungarian, and Czechoslovak Round Table Talks is the extent to which constitutional renewal was not a prominent topic for discussion in Prague. This decision merits explanation, given that the dissidents around Václav Havel had worked on constitution drafting prior to November 1989 and actually had a draft of a new federal constitution in hand as of December 5, 1989.[28]

Indeed, on several occasions the opposition seemed to treat the existing constitution with greater reverence than did its actual creators; for example, it was future finance minister Václav Klaus, not a member of the government negotiating team, who urged President Gustav Husák to appoint the members of the interim government before resigning, so as to adhere to the letter of the law (Hanzel, 1991: 323–24). Although in December 1989 the party's representatives proposed holding immediate direct elections to the presidency, which would have enabled the opposition to appeal over the heads of the Federal Assembly that had been "elected" in 1986 directly to the Czech and Slovak people, Civic Forum insisted that Czechoslovakia's

[28] See "Občanské Forum předkládá československé veřejnosti a ústavním orgánům republiky první návrh nové ústavy," December 5, 1989. Document in author's possession.

new caretaker president be appointed by the parliament, as specified in the old regime's constitution.[29]

The conciliatory approach of Civic Forum negotiators on constitutional issues in part explains why the outgoing order in Czechoslovakia never had to maneuver to co-opt the process of constitutional change; largely, it was not forced to do so. Both opposition and government were in surprising tacit agreement that the existing point of departure for the transfer of power would be the communist constitution, albeit for different reasons (Čalda, 1996: 48). Given that their demands for constitutional amendments were all accepted with little resistance, and that the balance of power was in their favor, why did the makers of the Velvet Revolution from the outset embrace a conservative approach to the necessary transformation of the country's basic law?

In framing an answer to this question, there are at least three factors that are of critical importance. First, the hard-line nature of the Czechoslovak communist regime certainly must be taken into account. It was difficult, at the time, to imagine that the apparatus would accept substantive change without a fight. Although the fear level at the Polish and Hungarian Round Table Talks was also palpable, given that both sets of negotiations, unlike their Czecho-Slovak equivalent, took place before the fall of the Berlin Wall, this must be weighed against the mitigating factor that the cost of a crackdown was higher for reform communists than it was for unreconstructed party members of the Czech and Slovak variety. In turn, since a crackdown could not be ruled out in the former Czechoslovakia, demanding too much all at once seemed to jeopardize the negotiations themselves, and the dialogue with the regime was something that Civic Forum sought to keep going at all costs.

Second, in many respects Civic Forum was understandably wholly unprepared for the breathtaking pace of possible change. As Timothy Garton Ash's oft-cited phrase aptly illustrates, it took ten years to make the revolution in Poland, ten months in Hungary, and ten days in Czechoslovakia (Ash, 1990: 78). Czechs and Slovaks did not have the luxury of self-consciously reflecting on the course that the revolution was taking while they were negotiating; there simply was not enough time in the day. Viewed in this context, it is perhaps unsurprising that when in round two of the negotiations communist premier Adamec unexpectedly asked the opposition to propose candidates for ministerial positions, Civic Forum first refused to do so, only presenting

[29] "The Position of the Coordinating Center of Civic Forum, 14 December 1989," and "Václav Havel's speech, 16 December 1989," both documents from the Archives of the Center for the Study of Constitutionalism in Eastern Europe, University of Chicago Law School. The reader should note that the center ceased operations in June 1997; because its archive is now maintained by the University of Chicago Libraries, the filing system may have changed since my visit.

the regime with a list of names a full week later. Small wonder, then, that Adamec complained that Havel and his compatriots wanted power without responsibility (Hanzel, 1991: 70–72, 158ff.).

Finally, and perhaps most important, Havel himself, Civic Forum's indisputable leader, does not seem to have believed that a new constitution belonged at the very top of the democracy movement's list of priorities. In his dissident writings and early presidential speeches, Havel repeatedly stressed that laws or systems, in and of themselves, can really guarantee nothing of value at all. Good laws alone can never create the quality of life on which human dignity relies because democracy is more than a collection of formal rules. For Havel, genuine political change could only be effected by the transformation of individuals and their interaction with political power and one another, not by systemic change (Havel, 1989: 95–100, 153–57). This supposition underlies Havel's argument in "The Power of the Powerless" that violent political revolution was unacceptable to the dissident, not "because the idea seems too radical, but on the contrary, because it does not seem radical enough" (Havel, 1989: 93). These long-held beliefs framed Havel's initial approach to politics in practice, particularly with respect to constitutional issues. As a result, the old dissident strategy of "demanding that the laws be upheld," "an act of living within the truth that threatens the whole mendacious structure at its point of maximum mendacity," as Havel once put it, carried the day (Havel, 1989: 98).

These ideas, of course, were not unique to Prague, though Havel perhaps expressed them most eloquently. Adam Michnik's "new evolutionism" and the subsequent Polish idea of a "self-limiting revolution" embraced the same basic assumptions. Rather than affirming complete allegiance to the Western political and economic model, many intellectuals in Prague and Warsaw instead envisioned a third way, a new order that was in its fundamental features both postcommunist and postcapitalist. In his exceptional book *Liberalism after Communism*, Jerzy Szacki deploys the term "protoliberalism" to describe this body of dissident thought, one characterized by its explicitly antipolitical approach to politics. Instead of seeking to topple the post-totalitarian order by confronting it directly, protoliberals challenged the system they sought to replace through the force of their own individual examples. Citizens of what Havel called the "parallel polis," therefore, renounced conventional revolutionary tactics, both because these were the weapons of their oppressors and because these methods stood absolutely no chance of successfully challenging the party's grip on all realms of daily life. Designed to sustain and nurture the democratic opposition under the threatening shadow of totalitarian power, protoliberalism never constituted an explicit political program. It provided a blueprint for interaction with the old regime, yet told one nothing about how to dismantle old institutions or build new ones. It provided a stance but not instructions on how to proceed after that stance had produced results (Szacki, 1995: 77–82).

This is why the question of whether Civic Forum might have chosen a standard liberal approach to founding new constitutional arrangements is ultimately more complicated than it initially appears. The actual balance of power on the ground suggests that Civic Forum had alternatives. Viewed in this light, the decision to postpone the quest for a new constitution might be attributed to a failure of leadership. Yet when the belief systems of the negotiating dissidents are factored into this equation, the range of alternatives narrows dramatically. Simply put, Civic Forum's leadership could have gone another way, but they would have had to become different people overnight for that alternative route to have been selected. They would have had to adopt immediately and without hesitation the outlook of ordinary politicians, after having spent years endeavoring to transcend politics as it was presently practiced. One of the reasons power went begging for a while in Prague was that those who were best equipped to seize control and shape the transition were initially the least interested in exercising conventional political power.

The Czech-Slovak Conflict and Constitutional Choice

Endorsing legal continuity had the most profound implications for political stability and constitutional choice in postcommunist Czechoslovakia. Because the Czecho-Slovak case highlights critical ways in which the institutional weight of the past can frame the perceived options of the present, it is worthy of close scrutiny. Although the Czecho-Slovak Federal Assembly was successful in passing a series of amendments to the federal constitution in 1990–91, its efforts to draft a new constitution, ironically, were undermined by voting rules that had been originally devised to generate the appearance of democratic procedure in the one-party state. The 1968 Law on the Federation, an amendment to the 1960 constitution that transformed Czechoslovakia from a unitary state to a federal one, provided for a Federal Assembly with two chambers. Representatives were elected to the upper chamber (the Chamber of the People) by the entire population on a proportional basis. In contrast, the lower chamber (the Chamber of the Nations) was comprised of seventy-five representatives elected in the Czech Lands and seventy-five representatives elected in Slovakia. In voting on any bill, both houses were governed by the antimajority principle (*zákaz majorizace*), which translates literally as the prohibition of majoritarian rule.[30] Ostensibly designed to protect the rights of the Slovak minority, it stipulated that the ratification of any extraordinary legislation – constitutional amendments, declarations of war, and the election of the president – required a three-fifths

[30] See "Ústavní zákon o československé federaci, z 27. října 1968, č. 143 Sb.," esp. articles 41 and 42. Act published in Jiří Grospič, *Československá federace*, pp. 139–263 (Prague: Orbis, 1972).

majority (supermajority) of both Czechs and Slovaks in the lower chamber (Mathernova, 1993: 64–65). What this meant, in practice, was that a mere thirty-one Slovak deputies in the Chamber of Nations could block any proposed constitutional amendment, even if the bill had the unanimous support of all the other deputies in both chambers (Cepl, 1993: 30). There was, in 1990–92, no democratic government anywhere else in the world "in which comparable minorities of legislative bodies [had] as much blocking power" (Cutler and Schwartz, 1991: 549).

To complicate matters still further, Czechoslovakia's communist constitution was a curiosity even among other federal systems of the Soviet variety. It proclaimed a federal state that presupposed the existence of republic-level constitutions, yet the charade had stopped short of actually promulgating these documents for the constituent states. Thus, Czechoslovakia's democratic forces inherited republican parliaments – the Czech and Slovak National Councils – whose precise mandate had never been formally codified. Upholding the communist constitution, consequently, required the immediate drafting of republican constitutions, yet this aim had to be pursued at the same time that the Federal Assembly was laboring to retire the old constitution. Put another way, demanding that the laws be upheld meant in practice that no less than three new constitutions had to be worked on simultaneously.

Who was to tackle the task of refounding the federation initially seemed relatively straightforward. The Federal Assembly would work on drafting a new federal constitution, yet it was to coordinate its endeavors closely with the efforts of deputies in the Czech and Slovak National Councils, who were charged with the simultaneous creation of the Czech and Slovak Republics' first constitutions.[31] That the Slovaks immediately after the revolution began work on their own constitution, having a first draft ready in April 1990, could be read as evidence of a budding Slovak quest for independence, but it might also be seen as their effort to uphold the basic law of the land.[32] National governments were also quite understandably "more afraid of preserving unsuitable structures" than the Government of National Understanding, since they were more intimately acquainted with the dysfunctionality of existing federal arrangements.[33]

The notion that the federation derived its legitimacy from the republics was already technically enshrined in law, as Article 1 of the 1968 law on the

31 As envisioned by President Václav Havel's speech to the first freely elected Federal Assembly, June 29, 1990 (Havel, 1990: 155–57).

32 "Návrh Ústavy Slovenskej Republiky (1. pracovná verzia)," Komisia Slovenskej národnej rady pre prípravu Ústavy Slovenskej republiky pod vedením Prof. JUDr. Karola Planka, predsedu Najvyššieho súdu Slovenskej republiky, Bratislava, April 1990. Archives of the Center for the Study of Constitutionalism in Eastern Europe.

33 President Havel's speech to the first freely elected Federal Assembly, June 29, 1990 (Havel, 1990: 162).

federation explicitly stated such.[34] That premise was further institutionalized, however, in a power-sharing agreement between federal and republican institutions, which after lengthy negotiations was passed in the form of a constitutional amendment by the Federal Assembly in December 1990. The power-sharing agreement devolved most economic powers to the republics, with the federation retaining control of foreign policy and financial strategy. It also tacitly implied that the ratification of a new federal constitution for Czechoslovakia would of necessity require the approval of both the Czech and Slovak National Councils.

Despite his initial disinterest in immediately replacing the communist constitution, with the June 1990 elections behind him President Havel placed the adoption of a new federal constitution at the top of his list of priorities. For the majority of Slovak politicians in early 1991, however, this now amounted to putting the cart before the horse. If the Czech-Slovak relationship was to be placed on a new footing, and the common goal was to build a federation "from the bottom up," as Czech and Slovak leaders had agreed in 1990, then a state treaty between the two republics, consistent with international law, must first be forged. Only after this treaty had been established and Czech-Slovak equality was therefore officially inscribed in law could the task of adopting a new federal constitution be tackled.[35]

Although Czechs expressed exasperation at the Slovak notion that citizens of the same country could forge something akin to an international agreement, at another level Slovak demands followed logically from the spirit of the earlier power-sharing constitutional amendment. That agreement stipulated that while the republics had the right to delegate authority to the federal government, the federation could not devolve powers to the republics without their consent. Whenever Slovak nationalist politicians felt that this basic principle had been compromised, they threatened to declare the supremacy of Slovak laws over federal ones, a move that their Czech counterparts almost uniformly interpreted as tantamount to treason. Discussions of constitutional matters, therefore, foundered on the question of the desired state treaty's meaning and significance, increasingly taking the form of a dialogue of the deaf. For most Czech politicians; in 1991, the locus of refounding was a new federal constitution; for Slovaks, it was a state treaty. The federation's president was forced to assume the role of mediator between two ethnically defined factions.[36]

[34] "Ústavní zákon o československé federaci, z 27. října 1968, č. 143 Sb.," čl. 1.

[35] David Franklin, interview with Pavel Rychetský, May 1991. Rychetský provided written answers to questions that Franklin had submitted. Archives of the Center for the Study of Constitutionalism in Eastern Europe, Chicago.

[36] Ibid. See, also, the interview with Václav Havel, October 17, 1991, BBC Summary of World Broadcasts (1991, October 19). Available: NEXIS Library: Europe File: All Europe, and the transcript of the November 1991 negotiations at Havel's summer home, published

With the prospects for attaining a new constitution before the June 1992 parliamentary election all but nil, President Havel attempted to break the constitutional deadlock in early 1992 by proposing several constitutional amendments for reform of both the antimajority principle and the Federal Assembly structure (Cutler and Schwartz, 1991: 549–51). All of them were blocked by the Slovak nationalist opposition. Although a good portion of these Slovak deputies seemed to vote against the proposals simply because they were President Havel's, their voting behavior can also be explained by simple self-interest: why should a minority with extraordinary power voluntarily vote it away, particularly when that power might be used as a bargaining chip in unrelated negotiations (Mathernova, 1993: 73–75)? This dynamic reached its logical point of culmination in June 1992, when the Slovak nationalist minority blocked the reelection of Havel as president, symbolizing the insurmountable impasse that had been reached. In a very real sense, then, the prospects for Czecho-Slovak democracy were undermined by the initial adoption of legal procedures that were never designed to govern a liberal democracy.

After the June 1992 elections, which brought to power in the Czech Republic and Slovakia two political parties – the Civic Democratic Party (ODS) and the Movement for a Democratic Slovakia (HZDS) – that shared very little common ground, the task of federal constitution drafting was formally abandoned, and efforts to recast the political order were reconcentrated at the republic level.[37] Czech and Slovak premiers Václav Klaus and Vladimír Mečiar were successful in forming a caretaker federal government that would eventually supervise its own retirement. The decision to create two independent states on January 1, 1993, was taken at the sixth meeting between HZDS and ODS on August 26, 1992.[38] Less than a week later, on September 1, the Slovak National Council made the split official when it approved Slovakia's first democratic constitution, to go into effect October 1. That document was written in such a way that it could theoretically function as both a charter for an entity that was part of a larger federal structure or as the basic law for a sovereign state, but its opening lines "We, the Slovak nation" and its definition of a citizen as a citizen of Slovakia signaled the official end of the Czechoslovak era.[39] The document was to be presented

as a series in *Slovenské Listy*, 1994, "Poločas rozpadu: Přepis stenografického záznamu ze setkání nejvyšších ústavních činitelů prezidenta Václava Havla na Hrádečku dne 3. listopadu 1991."

37 "Constitution Watch: Czechoslovakia," *East European Constitutional Review* 1(2) (1992): 3.

38 "Chronology of Discussions of Division of Czechoslovakia," CTK National News Wire (1992, November 27). Available: NEXIS Library: Europe File: All Europe.

39 *Ústava Slovenskej Republiky* (Bratislava: NVK International, 1992), preamble and article 52. Article 156 lists the sections that did not come into force on the day of the constitution's actual promulgation; the activation of these bracketed passages rendered the document a charter for a sovereign state.

to the Slovak people for ratification in the form of a referendum, although this never took place.[40]

With the formal date for the division of the country set, and the Slovak constitution already drafted and ratified, the Czech National Council faced an urgent task. It needed to draft and ratify a new constitution by the end of the year to avoid becoming the world's first democratic state without a body of basic laws to underpin its political order. With respect to constitutional concerns, the Czechs were far less prepared for independence than were the Slovaks. Political parties, which developed competing notions of what best served the republic's interest, drove the constitution-drafting process.[41] On the actual day the constitution was ratified, December 16, 1992, no fewer than ninety amendments to the evolving text were proposed, with twelve changes actually accepted.[42] Nevertheless, the Czech constitution was ultimately ratified by an overwhelming majority (172 of 200 deputies). Interestingly, the entire divorce process took place in ostensibly legal fashion, with the Federal Assembly narrowly passing a constitutional amendment in late November 1992 abolishing the Federal Republic as of January 1, 1993.[43]

The method of radical continuity, therefore, had the largest unintended consequences in the former Czechoslovakia. Abiding by the communist legal rules of the game, even against the backdrop of an ongoing series of significant amendments to the old constitution, underscored what divided rather than united citizens of the common state. Attempting to draft and agree on ratification procedures for the basic charter for three new political orders – Czech, Slovak, and Czechoslovak – with the *zákaz majorizace* in full force was an invitation to constitutional deadlock even had all three legislative bodies been composed of angels. The case of the former Czechoslovakia, however, when viewed in comparative perspective, provides a curious example of ethnic differences promoting the resuscitation of constitutionalism. Constitutional deadlock at the federal level served as a catalyst for constitutional revolution at the republic level. In this sense, both Czechs and Slovaks were granted a chance to learn from their past mistakes, an option that was unavailable to their Polish and Hungarian counterparts.

40 "Constitution Watch: Slovakia," *East European Constitutional Review* 1(3) (1992): 10.

41 See, for example, "Vládní návrh: Ústavy České Republiky," November 4, 1992, "Návrh ODA: Ústava České Republiky," 1992 (Daniel Kroupa draft), and "Návrh KDS," August 18, 1992. See also Václav Havel, "Několik poznámek na téma České ústavy," August 7, 1992. All party drafts and Havel's memorandum from the Archives of the Center for the Study of Constitutionalism in Eastern Europe.

42 "Czech Republic Adopts Constitution," United Press International (1992, December 16), available: NEXIS Library: Europe File: All Europe. One of the amendments accepted on the floor was no less than the inclusion of a bill of rights.

43 "Constitution Watch: Czech Republic," *East European Constitutional Review* 2(1) (1993): 4–5.

Conclusion

As a first cut, Ackerman's constitutional moment proves to be a useful heuristic device for illuminating the critical factors of timing and sequence in the challenge of institutional redesign. The cases considered in this chapter support Ackerman's theoretical claim at one level and reject it at another. In Poland, Hungary, and the former Czechoslovakia, the decision to follow the letter of communist constitutions never designed to function in conditions of genuine liberty facilitated the bracketing of the more difficult constitutional questions for resolution at a later date. While postponing these hard tasks allowed democratizing elites to focus on other pressing problems, it also meant that fundamental constitutional questions would have to be confronted after the salient cleavages dividing postcommunist societies had fully crystallized into rival political groupings. As a result, Hungary was slow to move into the realm of ordinary politics, where the constitution alone successfully provides the basic framework for political action, rather than being a tool in the hands of competing political parties and an uncommonly powerful constitutional court. Poland has successfully made this transition, but the politicized drafting and ratification process produced by the prolonged interim period stripped Poland's new constitution of the authority it might otherwise have had. Czechoslovakia's dissolution was in part a consequence of accepting an irrational legal apparatus that enshrined communist tactics of divide and rule, yet which the leaders of the Velvet Revolution volunteered to inherit. Ironically, the experience of interwar democracy notwithstanding, thanks in large part to communism's legal legacy, Czechoslovakia in reality had less of a usable past, constitutionally speaking, than did its Polish and Hungarian neighbors.[44]

Yet a comparative assessment of the status of democratic consolidation in Poland, Hungary, and the Czech and Slovak republics today, however, suggests that Ackerman's framework has limitations, at best, and is misleading, at worst, for several reasons. First, while the constitutional moment for a nation may pass in vain, the constitutional window of opportunity, so to speak, can be reopened. The trouble here is that those likely to be doing the reopening need not necessarily be the forces that catalyzed democratization in the first place. Mass cynicism about the law and its architects is a characteristic feature of authoritarian regimes, but it is an unhealthy development for countries that seek to build the rule of law. Some of this cynicism was inevitably generated by nearly fifty years of communist abuse of the legal system, but it is also one consequence of a constitution-drafting

[44] Restoring the interwar constitution of 1920 was never an option that was seriously entertained, perhaps because it was based on the notion of Czechoslovakism (its opening lines, for example, read "We the Czechoslovak people"), which in 1989 was for some Slovaks a euphemism for Czech chauvinism. See "Sbírka zákonů a nařízení státu Československého," 6. března 1920, Archives of the Center for the Study of Constitutionalism in Eastern Europe.

process that has collapsed into ordinary politics. Put another way, building on Ackerman's concept, a missed constitutional moment need not put a new constitution beyond reach, but it will result in constitutional deliberations driven by political parties rather than by the opponents of authoritarianism. While this leaves political actors with "no choice but to accept the drawbacks of a highly politicized, and that means parliamentarized, process," where "everyday politics is part of an ongoing constitutional crisis," this reality also results in a host of unintended consequences, many of them at odds with the establishment of the rule of law (Holmes and Sunstein, 1995: 288).

Although only the future may render a definitive verdict, the Hungarian exception also challenges Ackerman's conclusions about the consequences of failing to seize the constitutional moment. As the case of contemporary Hungary illustrates, when complementary organizational forms arise to stabilize political and social life, fledgling democracies may be able to initiate their self-transformations even absent long-awaited new constitutions. Hungary's activist Constitutional Court seems to serve this function. Without its stabilizing activism, which has gained the respect of the general population, Hungarian democratic development might have taken a quite different road. Put simply, when a newly democratic political system, regardless of the path it may have taken to present circumstances, is perceived to be delivering a better life for the majority of the population, voices demanding its alteration are likely to subside. Outstanding controversial constitutional issues may contribute to and indeed be constitutive of the form democratic consolidation takes in particular countries.[45] The critical question, of course, is how durable such a system might be when prosperity fades or when the international system in which a given state is embedded undergoes profound change. But that, of course, is an enduring question for all aspiring stable democracies, regardless of whether they have seized the constitutional moment when confronted with it or not. What I have argued here is that it is a question that cannot be properly addressed without a clear understanding of the origins of particular democratic institutions, which brings us face to face with Leninism's legacies.

Viewed in the light of Ackerman's framework, Czechoslovakia's successor states appear relatively fortunate; the constitutional moment may have passed for Czechoslovakia, but this had the effect of recreating opportunities for securing a clean legal break with the past in each of the member republics. In closing the regime question, new constitutions provided a firmer

[45] Anna Seleny has argued that two models of democracy have emerged in contemporary Poland and Hungary, a conflictual-pluralist model (Poland) and a compromise-corporatist model (Hungary). It is not much of a stretch for the reader to see that the trajectories of constitutional politics in these two countries, as sketched in the main body of this chapter, both reflect and reinforce these forms. See Seleny (1999: esp. 488–511).

foundation for consolidating democracy; while it may not be impossible, it is surely more difficult for old elites to retain or regain their positions under the cover of the rule of law when the rules that they created have been pronounced illegitimate. The cause of democratic consolidation is typically advanced when the rules structuring political conflict are not themselves a source of conflict.[46] By redefining the state, therefore, constitutional democracy was given a second chance in the Czech and Slovak republics. This is not to say that what Stephen Holmes has called "stopgap constitutionalism" has not served a useful function in some postcommunist transitions. As Holmes has pointed out, "if successful constitutionalism is to be judged by the speed at which a country hammers a 'definitive' constitution into place, then Bulgaria and Romania would be the most legally advanced countries in Europe" (Holmes, 1993: 22). Rather, it is to acknowledge that the costs of stopgap constitutionalism were uncommonly high in the case of the former Czechoslovakia.

A close inspection of constitutional engineering efforts in Central Europe highlights the dual sense in which both Leninist legacies and legacies of state socialism outlived communism's official collapse. In the most obvious sense, the institutions that aspiring democrats chose to inherit and that framed the arena in which transition politics played had an extended half-life that produced a host of unintended consequences, especially in the former Czechoslovakia. In a less obvious sense, the impact of nearly fifty years of Marxist-Leninist rule also shaped dissident orientations toward the law and its role in democratization in consequential ways. If anything, this study indicates that to come to terms with the constraints on democratization efforts to date, one cannot ignore the twin factors of institutional and human inertia. Attitudes toward the law forged in the crucible of Marxist-Leninist power lingered on after that power had been irreparably undermined, even in the minds of communism's fiercest adversaries. The legacy of the past, therefore, must be seen as a phenomenon of both institutions and an orientation toward those same institutions and their representatives. Put another way, it is quite difficult to account for the choices that democratic forces in each of the countries under examination made without references to the struggles that brought them to the negotiating table in the first place. Challenging communist regime legitimacy, to cite a pivotal example, required a different set of skills than bargaining with the custodians of communist power. As a result, the interaction of democratizing elites with their former torturers often did not follow the path one might expect, having abstracted away particular contexts. Thus, to explain the variation in constitutional outcomes in the cases this chapter examines, we need to consider both forms of legacy and

46 In such circumstances, a "vicious circle" of contestation and instability is circumvented. See Elster, Offe, and Preuss (1997: 34).

their interrelated interaction, the ways in which both informal and formal rules constrain and inform agency.

When we do so, we find many common features in the story of constitutional engineering in Poland, Hungary, and the former Czechoslovakia. Each tale features a multitude of unintended consequences, the largest of these being Czechoslovakia's extinction. As Douglass North has argued, "how and why [institutions] change incrementally and why even discontinuous changes (such as revolution and conquest) are never completely discontinuous are a result of the imbeddedness of informal constraints in societies" (North, 1990: 6). The method of radical continuity, in part a manifestation of the dissident code of conduct, thereby fostered forces of institutional inertia at the same time that it endeavored to actualize meaningful change. Finally, once the constitutional moment had passed in each of these countries, the existing institutional arrangements grew increasingly difficult to replace. Choices made in the early moments of postrevolutionary freedom shaped political outcomes long after those initial actions had faded from public memory.

Yet the tenor of the constitutional conversation in each of these countries over the course of the past decade was by no means uniform. In a variety of ways, external pressures or a sense of what "proper states" must do had a greater impact in the Polish, Czech, and Slovak cases than they did in the Hungarian context. This difference in part accounts for Hungary's present constitutional status, unique among its neighbors. Why was this the case? It would not be unreasonable to suggest that Budapest's status as the seat of a former empire provided a wholly different initial point of departure for thinking about state legitimacy, both at the elite and mass levels. Entering a self-proclaimed new era without a new constitution to justify recently restituted sovereignties was unthinkable in Warsaw, Prague, and Bratislava. The legitimacy of the new arrangements themselves was perceived to be at stake. In contrast, the debate over Hungary's constitutional future never displayed the same sense of urgency. The negotiated character of the Hungarian transition provides part of the explanation, the brand-new statehood of the Czech and Slovak republics another, but the weight of a glorious past was also a critical factor. In Hungary, establishing a clear link to the old empire's glory in some ways seems to have served the functional purpose of a new constitution, rendering constitutional transformation a secondary concern. Consequently, a constitutional framework that was initially presented as a stopgap measure has been treated with greater reverence over time. Precommunist contexts can have postcommunist repercussions.

In the end, the trajectory of constitutional politics in postcommunist Central Europe provides a classic example of a path-dependent sociopolitical process. By path dependence, I mean, "once a country or region has started down a track, the costs of reversal are very high... the entrenchments of certain institutional arrangements obstruct an easy reversal of the initial choice."[47] With each move down a particular path, the probability of staying on that path grows, because the costs of switching course rise commensurately. The initial reluctance of postcommunist Central Europe's democratizers to scuttle communism's constitutional framework and the obstacles to further institutional reform that arose as revolutionary gains were locked in demonstrate two different variants of path dependency, the former with its origins in informal rules of conduct, the latter in the rules of the game itself. As we have seen, in order to account for the variation across cases, careful attention must be paid to issues of timing and sequence and to those critical junctures where path-dependent processes might successfully be derailed and transcended. Because history has repeatedly shown that the immediate aftermath of regime collapse is typically a crucible in which profound change, often manifesting itself in quite unintended forms, is likely to emerge, it should not surprise us to find that the months following the fall of the wall were a critical moment in Central European political development.

References

Ackerman, Bruce. 1992. *The Future of Liberal Revolution*. New Haven: Yale University Press.

Anderson, Lisa. 1997. Introduction. *Comparative Politics* 29(3): 253–61.

Arato, Andrew. 1994. Elections, Coalitions and Constitutionalism in Hungary. *East European Constitutional Review* 3(3–4): 26–32.

1996. The Constitution-Making Endgame in Hungary. *East European Constitutional Review* 5(4): 31–39.

N.d. Constitution and Continuity in the East European Transitions. *Journal of Constitutional Law in Eastern and Central Europe* 1(1): 97–128.

Ash, Timothy Garton. 1990. *The Magic Lantern*. New York: Random House.

Bruszt, László, and David Stark. 1992. Remaking the Political Field in Hungary: From the Politics of Confrontation to the Politics of Competition. In Ivo Banac, ed., *Eastern Europe in Revolution*, pp. 13–55. Ithaca: Cornell University Press.

Brzezinski, Mark F. 1993a. The Emergence of Judicial Review in Eastern Europe: The Case of Poland. *American Journal of Comparative Law* 41(2): 153–200.

1993b. Constitutionalism within Limits. *East European Constitutional Review* 2(2): 38–43.

Čalda, Miloš. 1996. The Roundtable Talks in Czechoslovakia. In Jon Elster, ed., *The Roundtable Talks and the Breakdown of Communism*, pp. 135–77. Chicago: University of Chicago Press.

Cepl, Vojtech. 1993. Constitutional Reform in the Czech Republic. *University of San Francisco Law Review* 28: 29–35.

Cutler, Lloyd, and Herman Schwartz. 1991. Constitutional Reform in the Czech Republic. *University of San Francisco Law Review* 58: 511–53.

[47] The definition is Margaret Levi's, and it has been brilliantly deployed by Paul Pierson to argue that political scientists might profitably conceptualize path dependence as a dynamic of increasing returns. See Pierson (2000); quoted portion of Levi on p. 252.

Di Palma, Guiseppe. 1990. *To Craft Democracies: An Essay on Democratic Transitions*. Berkeley: University of California Press.

Eberts, Mirella W. 1998. The Roman Catholic Church and Democracy in Poland. *Europe-Asia Studies* 50(5): 817–42.

Elster, Jon. 1997. Ways of Constitution-Making. In Axel Hadenius, ed., *Democracy's Victory and Crisis*. Cambridge: Cambridge University Press.

1993. Constitution-Making in Eastern Europe: Rebuilding the Boat in an Open Sea. *Public Administration* 72: 169–217.

Elster, Jon, Claus Offe, and Ulrich K. Preuss. 1998. *Institutional Design in Post-Communist Societies: Rebuilding the Ship at Sea*. Cambridge: Cambridge University Press.

Ekiert, Grzegorz, and Jan Kubik. 1998. Contentious Politics in New Democracies: East Germany, Poland, Hungary, and Slovakia. *World Politics* 50(4): 547–81.

Hall, Peter A., and Rosemary C. R. Taylor. 1996. Political Science and the Three New Institutionalisms. *Political Studies* 44: 936–57.

Halmai, Gabor. 1999. No New One. In *Heti Világgazdaság*, August 21. Available: <http://folioweb.hvg.hu/cgi-bin/foliocgi.exe/hvg2.nfo/query=alkotm!E1ny++/doc/{t0,0,511,16504}/hit_headings/hits_only>.

Hanson, Stephen E. 1995. The Leninist Legacy and Institutional Change. *Comparative Political Studies* 28(2): 306–14.

Hanzel, Vladimír. 1991. *Zrychlený tep dějin*. Prague: OK Centrum.

Havel, Václav. 1989. The Power of the Powerless (1978) and Politics and Conscience (1984). In Jan Vladislav, ed., *Living in Truth*, pp. 36–122 and 136–57. London: Faber and Faber.

1990. *Projevy: leden – Červen 1990*. Prague: Vyšehrad.

Holmes, Stephen. 1993. Back to the Drawing Board: An Argument for Constitutional Postponement. *East European Constitutional Review* 2(1): 21–25.

Holmes, Stephen, and Cass Sunstein. 1995. The Politics of Constitutional Revision in Eastern Europe. In Sanford Levinson, ed., *Responding to Imperfection: The Theory and Practice of Constitutional Amendment*, pp. 275–306. Princeton: Princeton University Press.

Huntington, Samuel P. 1991. *The Third Wave: Democratization in the Late Twentieth Century*. Norman: University of Oklahoma Press.

Jasiewicz, Krzysztof. 1997. Poland: Wałęsa's Legacy to the Presidency. In Ray Taras, ed., *Postcommunist Presidents*, pp. 130–67. Cambridge: Cambridge University Press.

Karpiński, Jakub. 1995. The Constitutional Mosaic. *Transitions* 1(14): 4–9.

Kitschelt, Herbert. 1993. Comparative Historical Research and Rational Choice Theory: The Case of Transitions to Democracy. *Theory and Society* 22(3): 413–27. (Review of *Democracy and Market*, by Adam Przeworski [1991]).

Kraus, Michael. 1995. Settling Accounts: Post-Communist Czechoslovakia. In Neil J. Kritz, ed., *Transitional Justice: How Emerging Democracies Reckon with Former Regimes*, vol. 2, *Country Studies*, pp. 542–87. Washington, D.C.: United States Institute of Peace Press.

Kukorelli, István. 1992. Constitutional Changes in Hungary. *Notes et Documents*, January–August.

Linz, Juan, and Yossi Shain, eds. 1995. *Between States: Interim Governments and Democratic Transitions*. Cambridge: Cambridge University Press.

Linz, Juan, and Alfred Stepan. 1996. *Problems of Democratic Transition and Consolidation: Southern Europe, South America, and Post-Communist Europe*. Baltimore: Johns Hopkins University Press.
Lipset, Seymour Martin. 1959. Some Social Requisites of Democracy: Economic Development and Political Legitimacy. *American Political Science Review* 53(1): 69–105.
Mathernova, Katarina. 1993. Czecho?Slovakia: Constitutional Disappointments. In A. E. Dick Howard, ed., *Constitution Making in Eastern Europe*, pp. 57–92, Washington, D.C.: Woodrow Wilson Center Press.
Mihalicz, Csilla, 1999. Trench Wars with Retreats. *168 óra*, January. Available: <http://www.168ora.hu/1999/01/ketharna.htm>.
North, Douglass C. 1990. *Institutions, Institutional Change and Economic Performance*. Cambridge: Cambridge University Press.
O'Donnell, Guillermo, Philippe C. Schmitter, and Laurence Whitehead, eds. 1986. *Transitions from Authoritarian Rule*. Baltimore: Johns Hopkins University Press.
O'Neil, Patrick H. 1996. Revolution from Within: Institutional Analysis, Transitions from Authoritarianism, and the Case of Hungary. *World Politics* 48(4): 579–603.
Osiatyński, Wiktor. 1996. The Round Table Negotiations in Poland. In Jon Elster, ed., *The Round Table Talks*, pp. 21–68. Chicago: University of Chicago Press.
Paczolay, Peter. 1993. The New Hungarian Constitutional State: Challenges and Perspectives. In A. E. Dick Howard, ed., *Constitution Making in Eastern Europe*, pp. 21–56. Baltimore: Johns Hopkins University Press.
Pierson, Paul. 2000. Increasing Returns, Path Dependence, and the Study of Politics. *American Political Science Review* 94(2): 251–66.
Rapaczyński, Andrzej. 1991. Constitutional Politics in Poland: A Report on the Constitutional Committee of the Polish Parliament. *University of Chicago Law Review* 58: 595–631.
Sajó, Adrás. 1992. The Arrogance of Power. *East European Reporter* 5(May–June): 45–47.
1996. Round Tables in Hungary. In Jon Elster, ed., *The Roundtable Talks and the Breakdown of Communism*, pp. 69–98. Chicago: University of Chicago Press.
Seleny, Anna. 1999. Old Political Rationalities and New Democracies: Compromise and Confrontation in Hungary and Poland. *World Politics* 51(4): 484–519.
Stepan, Alfred, and Cindy Skach. 1993. Constitutional Frameworks and Democratic Consolidation: Parliamentarianism versus Presidentialism. *World Politics* 46(1): 1–22.
Szacki, Jerzy. 1995. *Liberalism after Communism*. Budapest: Central European University Press.
Vinton, Louisa. 1992. Poland's "Little Constitution" Clarifies Walesa's Powers. *RFE/RL Research Report* 1(35): 19–26.
Zielonka, Jan, ed. 2001. *Democratic Consolidation in Eastern Europe: Institutional Engineering*. New York: Oxford University Press.

7

Historical Legacies, Institutions, and the Politics of Social Policy in Hungary and Poland, 1989–1999

Tomasz Inglot

During the past two decades political struggles over various plans to restructure traditional social security programs in Western democracies and in Latin America have generated intense debates among social scientists and policy experts (Diamond, Lindeman, and Young, 1996; Kingson and Schulz, 1996; Torfing, 1998; Huber, 1995). Parallel developments in Eastern and Central Europe, however, have received much less attention from either specialists in comparative public policy or in postcommunist transitions.[1] Therefore, crucial questions such as "What happened to the so-called communist welfare state?"[2] and "What explains significant differences in social policy making and outcomes within the former Soviet bloc after 1989?" still await full exploration. This chapter aims to provide more-complete answers to these questions. It focuses not only on the current politics and the structural-institutional context of postcommunist social policy since the collapse of the old regimes (Müller, Ryll, and Wagener, 1999; Müller, 1999) but also uncovers and compares the distinct historical legacies that have continued to shape social policies and the social security systems of individual states for most of this century.

[1] Comparative economists and policy experts from the World Bank have conducted most comprehensive studies of contemporary social policy in East Central Europe to date (see Barr, 1994; Milanovič, 1998; and Müller, 1999).

[2] This question was posed for the first time by Castles (1986).

Research for this study was supported by a grant from the International Research and Exchanges Board (IREX), with funds provided by the U.S. Department of State (Title VIII program) and the National Endowment for the Humanities, and also by a faculty research grant from Minnesota State University at Mankato. I would like to thank Stanisława Golinowska, Michał Boni, Hanna Zalewska, Ewa Borowczyk, Małgorzata Pawlisz, Júlia Szalai, Zsuzsa Ferge, Maria Augusztinovics, Péter Bod, Péter Gedeon, István Tóth, Maria Major, Ilona Antal, Gyorgy Marosi, Gabriella Béki, Gabriella Papp, Katalin Novák, and Tünde Czinder for their assistance during my field research in Poland and Hungary. My special thanks go to Grzegorz Ekiert and David Stark for their comments on earlier versions of this work.

TABLE 7.1. *Pension Expenditure (including Old-Age, Invalidity, and Survivors) as Percentage of GDP for Selected Industrialized Countries*

Country	Year	Pension Spending
Belarus	1992	5.4
Bulgaria	1992	10.1
Chile	1989	8.9
Czech Republic	1992	8.4
Hungary	1991	10.5[a]
Italy	1993	15.5
Latvia	1991	7.8
Poland	1991	12.6[a]
Romania	1993	6.4
Russian Federation	1995	4.6
Spain	1993	10.4
Sweden	1993	12.4

[a] Other sources indicate 12.2 percent for Poland and 11.3 percent for Hungary in 1991; see Table 7.3.

Source: World Bank, Pension Primer, approximate raw data.

Since the early 1990s the countries of Eastern and Central Europe have maintained relatively high expenditure levels for pensions and other social benefits in cash, generally close to or above 10 percent of the GDP. By this measure of social spending they are more comparable with developed Western welfare states than with the former Soviet republics where in practice, even if not in theory, traditional social security benefits have been often supplanted by a rudimentary "poverty relief" structure (see Table 7.1). A smaller subgroup of Central European countries, including Hungary and Poland, have also, for the most part, sustained a reliable system of revenue collection and distribution of social payments, introduced a permanent system of indexation of benefits, and begun to implement some elements of social security reform. Because they not only preserved the preexisting social insurance systems but also made considerable efforts to enhance these benefit schemes during the period of regime transitions, I refer to these specific countries as postcommunist *entitlement states*. The two leading entitlement states, Poland and Hungary, deserve special attention for the following reasons: first, they have tended to rely heavily on social security payments as a remedy for the most urgent welfare problems of the initial stage of postcommunist transition and, second, in the late 1990s they began a long and complex process of introducing comprehensive social security reforms that now include new, partially privatized and mandatory pension plans[3] (see Table 7.2).

[3] Hungary introduced its partially privatized pension system in 1998 and Poland in 1999. For a more detailed analysis of these reforms, see Müller (1999).

TABLE 7.2. *The Dynamics of Economic Growth and the Expenditures for Major Social Insurance Benefits*

	1990	1991	1992	1993	1994	1995
GDP (% change from previous year)						
Poland	−11.6	−7.0	2.6	3.8	5.2	7.0
Hungary	−3.5	−11.9	−3.1	−0.6	2.9	1.5
Social benefits expenditure in % GDP						
Pensions						
Poland	8.1	12.2	14.7	14.6	15.2	15.6
Hungary	9.7	11.3	11.6	11.1	11.5	10.6
Family benefits						
Poland	1.4	1.8	1.9	1.3	1.0	0.7[a]
Hungary	3.8	n.a.	3.9	2.9	2.4	1.8
Unemployment benefits						
Poland	0.2	1.0	1.3	1.2	1.2	1.3
Hungary[b]	–	–	2.7	2.6	1.7	1.5

[a] Excludes benefits paid by local governments.
[b] Includes some noncash benefits.

Sources: Statistical Handbook of Hungary (1995 and *1997)* (Budapest: Central Statistical Office, 1996 and 1997); *Rocznik Statystyczny GUS 1996* (Warsaw: Głowny Urząd Statystyczny, 1996); Ministry of Welfare – Republic of Hungary, Stanisław Gomułka, "Polowiczna reforma czy antyreforma: projekt ministra Millera," *Życie Gospodarcze* 24 (November 6, 1995): 11; PlanEcon Report, Washington, D.C., September 30, 1995; and my calculations.

Although Poland and Hungary also share many other features that set both countries apart from most of the postcommunist region, such as substantial progress in political and economic stabilization since 1989, they nonetheless represent different models of democratic consolidation and policy formulation that can be linked to their individual paths of historical development under communism. As Anna Seleny argues, this kind of differentiation within the "cluster of stable and essentially consolidated [East Central European] democratic systems" enriches our understanding of the new democracies and enables us to evaluate better the long-term prospects for political stability within the postcommunist region (Seleny, 1999: 486–87). In fact, Poland and Hungary not only pursued dissimilar paths of extraction from communism and subsequent consolidation of their polities and economies (Seleny, 1999: 488) but also selected different reform strategies in the area of social policy. A comparative analysis of these strategies and their outcomes helps us explain why some postcommunist states were more successful than others in safeguarding their traditional "safety nets" in the early stage of transition (Kramer, 1997). However, it also enables us to identify, comprehend, and classify a number of specific historical legacies that continue to shape these states and their social policies in distinct ways. As Grzegorz Ekiert argues in this volume, "legacies of the past," along with different "modes of power transfers and initial outcomes of democratic competition," are most helpful in explaining the diverging outcomes of postcommunist transitions.

Analyzing the Politics of Social Policy in the Former Communist Countries: Comparative Social Policy and the Study of Democratic Transitions

Social policy constitutes a vital component of postcommunist transition in general and of democratic consolidation in particular (Cook, Orenstein, and Rueschemeyer, 1999: 246). Therefore, social insurance reforms in Poland and Hungary must be analyzed in the context of the current processes of democratization in each country. Even though these processes began in the late 1980s and early 1990s, their origins have been traced to much earlier events – political crises and pivotal periods of social change under the old regime – that shaped the subsequent trajectories or "paths" of sociopolitical development (Ekiert, 1996; see also Ekiert, Chapter 3 in this volume). I argue that the emphasis on "path dependence" is indispensable for the understanding of the dynamics of social security reform in postcommunist countries. This approach, which is also grounded in the rich tradition of historical-institutional investigation of social policy, allows us to conceive of the emergence of the new entitlement states in Central and Eastern Europe as part of a larger picture – namely, the long-term development of the welfare state in the industrialized world as a whole.

Comparative studies of Western welfare states have shown the benefits of historical analysis by revealing the major factors behind government decisions to establish, expand, or reduce various social benefit programs. For example, Hugh Heclo pointed out that the distinct origins of the first social insurance institutions could explain many crucial differences in policy among Western democracies later in the twentieth century (Heclo, 1974). Others carried this argument further by presenting powerful evidence in favor of *policy legacies* and preexisting government structures as key factors in the development of social policies in the industrialized countries of South and North America, Asia, and Western Europe (Malloy, 1979; Skocpol, 1993; Anderson, 1993; Pierson, 1994). Within this subfield of comparative inquiry, Paul Pierson's argument is especially significant since it shifts the focus of study from the *politics of expansion* to the *politics of retrenchment* of the welfare state. He points out that although in industrial democracies, following government attempts to reduce social programs, policy makers routinely seek broad consensus on social security reforms in anticipation of a political backlash, in the final analysis *structural factors* will determine whether these efforts will succeed (Pierson, 1996: 147).

I argue that the postcommunist entitlement states of East Central Europe are largely a product of the structural, institutional, and policy legacies of the communist or sometimes even precommunist past. These legacies have continued to shape opportunities for government action and especially the policies of welfare retrenchment and reform during the 1990s. Yet the transformative character of the postcommunist states compels us to revise Pierson's argument to be able to account for the different structural-institutional environments that set the stage for social policy reforms in the countries of Eastern and Central Europe. These environments consist of a specific blend of old and new structures, institutions, and policy legacies, rather than a firmly established and much more predictable pattern of democratic governance found in Western countries. As David Stark and László Bruszt argue, during the 1990s East European states have experienced not so much transitions to democracy and the market but rather transformative processes of "recombination" and "reconfiguration" of various "building blocs" inherited after the fall of state socialism. Moreover, the existence of working democratic institutions and processes, which remind us of Western models, should not obscure the fact that postcommunist countries are, and may well remain for years to come, distinct new types of capitalist democracy (Stark and Bruszt, 1998: 3–7). We may add that since 1989 these countries have also developed distinct new patterns of dealing with social policy problems and challenges; the entitlement states of East Central Europe can be viewed as *reconfigured* communist welfare states that have emerged after a series of institutional and policy adaptations of past practices to the new institutional framework of democratic governance and the incipient free-market system.

Such adaptations do not represent a totally new phenomenon linked exclusively to the postcommunist era. They had been taking place over a long period of time and continued under different political and economic regimes. Thus, these social policy adaptations should be seen, both in spatial and temporal terms, as essential components of the larger process of state development in a specific country and within a particular geographical region over a period of several decades. In fact, following each of the two world wars and under the influence of their larger and stronger neighbors, Germany, Austria, and Soviet Russia, many small Central and Eastern European countries either introduced major new social programs or initiated comprehensive reforms of the existing ones. After World War II, dissatisfaction with the less advanced Soviet model of social security, whose shortcomings became apparent during the Stalinist years of the late 1940s and early 1950s, prompted different communist states to adopt their own individual versions of "socialist social policy." Many East European nations then departed from the strict Soviet model, attempting to utilize preexisting social security traditions, which allowed them to respond better to current economic and political needs. As a result, various communist states, Poland and Hungary included, developed diverse approaches to pensions, family benefits, or work injury compensation that were not always congruous with the long-term ideological goals of the Leninist state.[4]

The actual impact of historical legacies in East Central Europe becomes much more clear once we turn our attention from a general notion of communist social policy to specific social security programs. Since the early 1980s a number of comparative studies of welfare state politics have moved away from focusing on aggregate measures of "social spending" or "welfare effort" (Wilensky, 1975; Hicks and Swank, 1992) toward an emphasis on the qualitative characteristics of individual benefit programs in different countries. Pierson, for example, has emphasized the need for disaggregating pensions and other individual programs to understand better how specific policy designs and formal political institutions interact with one another within a given institutional environment (Pierson, 1994: 175). Similarly, in the study of postcommunist social policy a combination of a broad historical-institutional perspective with a special attention to separate policies can yield meaningful comparisons of social security reforms as they affect social groups, political interests, and ideological debates within each country (Pestoff, 1995: 793; Muller et al., 1999; Muller, 1999). Even more important, examining specific policy areas of individual countries in a larger historical context enables us to treat the "Leninist legacy" or the "legacy of state socialism" as dynamic concepts, rather than as static sets of "preconditions." It shifts our attention from the frequently exaggerated similarities in *preexisting* socioeconomic circumstances among the Soviet bloc states to the actual contrasting "paths of social development" that have impacted both communist and postcommunist politics of social policy over a longer period of time. As Ekiert argues, if we want to understand the political transitions in this region and the differences among democratizing countries, we must account for their *diverging experiences* during the communist period (Ekiert, 1997: 338).

Throughout the 1990s most studies of postcommunist transitions have emphasized common, rather than distinct, legacies of the old regime, such as the closed policy-making process and excessive concentration of state power in the executive branch (Bunce and Csanadi, 1993). Detailed studies of individual cases, examining the interactions among historical legacies, traditional patterns of decision making, and new political institutions (see Comisso, 1995) still constitute rare exceptions to this general trend. Studies of postcommunist social policy, in particular, have tended to define the "communist legacy" in strictly ideological and social terms, as a uniform and widespread system of values, beliefs, and behavioral patterns. The social legacy of communism is often summarized generally as "the belief that the government is responsible not only for assuring general prosperity for the

[4] For a detailed comparison of Soviet and East European social policies under communism, see Minkoff and Turgeon (1977).

country, but also for guaranteeing employment and the basic needs of individual citizens" (Millar and Wolchik, 1994: 16). Others have argued that in the 1980s, before the start of the transition, "[w]ith minor variations, the Soviet model of social protection was the standard model of welfare in Poland and throughout other Eastern Europe [*sic*] countries" (Cain and Surdej, 1999: 152). These arguments imply that a certain common set of "initial conditions" has produced similar types of obstacles to comprehensive social policy reform across the postcommunist region.

Identification of certain common social policy legacies is a necessary first step that helps us to reclassify post-Soviet countries as a distinct category of postindustrial welfare states but, if taken too far, it can lead us to minimize or even ignore the significant historical variations in policy patterns and welfare institutions. Consequently, in the study of social policy transformations in East Central Europe the "legacies" argument is often dismissed in favor of the "new institutions" thesis, a view that treats welfare state reforms exclusively as a product of postcommunist politics and economics – that is, the structural-institutional conditions and constellations of political actors, examined almost exclusively in the short-term historical setting since 1989. Such actors include not only the powerful government agencies in charge of the reforms (Muller, 1999) but political parties as well (Cook et al., 1999).

Political parties and their ideologies have often appeared as crucial independent variables in the comparative social policy literature dealing with the expansion of Western democratic welfare states (Castles, 1978; Stephens, 1979; Korpi, 1983). When applied to Central and Eastern Europe, however, this argument often rests on two assumptions that lack sufficient empirical support. First, it takes for granted the reemergence of traditional policy differences in the newly democratized Eastern Europe along the lines of the conventional ideological split between the anticommunist, neoliberal opponents of social spending on the "right" and the pro-welfare "left." The latter group consists largely of the ex-communists and their allies, now seemingly playing the role of Western social democrats. Second, this perspective anticipates that in a short period of time the new, strengthened party organizations in Eastern and Central Europe will be willing and able to propose coherent policy agendas relying on stable constituencies (Deacon, 1992; Przeworski, 1993; Offe, 1993; Cook et al., 1999).

Given the actual political developments in the region during the past decade, it may be extremely difficult, if not impossible, to validate these assumptions empirically. As this study later demonstrates, since 1989 radical shifts in the polities, economies, and societies of East Central Europe have blurred previous ideological distinctions among numerous political groups and their constituencies. Today, even in the countries with relatively developed and stable party-systems, divisions over policy preferences constantly cut across party lines. Therefore, contemporary postcommunist governments cannot be expected to opt for any particular clear-cut model of social policy, such as, for instance, a social democratic welfare state or its neoliberal (*residual*) opposite.[5] Moreover, during the 1990s most political parties, including the ex-communist left, have been unable to propose or follow any coherent and consistent social policy program. Such a wide-ranging program would unavoidably carry a serious risk of alienating many supporters of the existing policies. In fact, during the past decade the public was reluctant to embrace any particular party as a stable guarantor of welfare benefits.[6] Instead, large segments of the population appear to have opted for what they consider to be a politically neutral relationship with particular state officials or government bureaucracies whose patronage role had been largely consolidated and expanded already under the previous regime. This situation is deeply rooted in the structural conditions of the communist past, when the basic constitutive units of the socialist state consisted of increasingly particularistic special interests that were "brought into the polity through the bureaucracy itself" (Stark and Bruszt, 1998: 112). Therefore, I argue that to explain current social policy developments in the region, we should focus not so much on formal ideology and contemporary party politics but rather on the long-term patterns of interaction between various social groups and the state institutions or, in other words, we ought to engage in a more detailed contextual analysis of "interactional time and interactional space," not only in individual countries (Ekiert and Hanson, Chapter 1 in this volume, Table 1.1) but also within specific areas of policy.

In his 1997 study of postcommunist social policy in transition, Mark Kramer points out that in East Central Europe, in contrast to other Soviet bloc states, the better-developed bureaucracies and institutional frameworks played a large role in the creation of "stable safety nets" based on the most expensive cash benefits, such as pensions and unemployment compensation. This argument, however, stems largely from the analysis of general spending data and similar social indicators, aiming primarily at explaining the perceived absence of major social protest in this cluster of former Soviet bloc countries after 1989 (Kramer, 1997: 46–123). What still needs to be understood better is *how* postcommunist social policy continues to function and evolve in the increasingly complex political and economic conditions of these emerging capitalist democracies, and *why* this process has varied so widely even among the most stable polities, such as Poland and Hungary. For this reason, we must now turn to the comparison of the historical legacies, reform strategies, and policy outcomes of these two postcommunist entitlement states.

[5] For a discussion of the traditional models of social policy, see Esping-Andersen (1989) and Golinowska (1999).

[6] During the 1990s, in several parliamentary election campaigns both the so-called "right" and the "left" parties placed heavy emphasis on redistributive policies.

Social Policy Legacies in Poland and Hungary

The first half-century of social policy development in East Central Europe differed fundamentally from the early days of the more prosperous Western welfare states, such as Great Britain or Sweden, not only because of the socioeconomic gap between the east and the west of the continent but also due to extensive foreign influence. Poland and Hungary inherited considerably well developed social insurance programs from the two former imperial powers that dominated East Central Europe until 1918, Germany and Austria-Hungary.[7] Before World War II employees in the private sector received their pensions, sick pay, and work injury benefits from separate risk-related funds financed by joint contributions of workers and employers. Civil servants, the military, and the police had their own separate entitlement programs supported by the state budget. Initially, these early developments produced considerable advantages, helping impoverished nations both to establish modern institutions and to launch ambitious social programs. However, the worldwide economic depression of the 1930s, the enormous economic devastation of World War II, and the imposition of communist rule drastically altered the shape and the overall direction of these emerging welfare systems. Most significantly, the introduction of the Soviet model after 1945 ushered in a new era of perpetual crisis and experimentation in socioeconomic policy based on a vague promise of a better future. In the late 1940s the communist authorities took over the autonomous social insurance organizations and created a new system of cash entitlements whose assets and immediate revenues were seized by the state and channeled toward economic reconstruction and industrial development. This system was based on four fundamental principles:

1. The pay-as-you-go (PAYG) method of benefit financing replaced previous insurance-based and -funded systems, and all insurance risks – old-age, sickness, work injury, and the like – were combined into one single fund within the general state budget.
2. Any person with a substantial record of employment in the state sector or government service after 1945 had a right to basic social insurance benefits, but the rules of eligibility underwent constant revision in accordance with current political and economic priorities.
3. Most pensions and other cash benefits remained at a very low level, and no permanent mechanism existed to allow for their adjustment for inflation (*indexation*).
4. Select occupations, such as miners, railroad workers, the military, and the police, were entitled to special entitlement privileges.

[7] Many studies have shown that the age of the social insurance program is the key variable in the explanation of welfare expansion and social spending over time. See Heclo (1974); Wilensky (1975); and also Castles (1986).

TABLE 7.3. *Distribution of Social Expenditures in the Soviet Bloc Countries, 1980–1982*

Country	Year	% In Cash	% In Kind
Poland	1980	47.3	52.7
	1981	49.8	50.2
	1982	57.2	42.8
Hungary	1980	59.0	41.0
Bulgaria	1980	45.2	54.8
Czechoslovakia	1980	50.4	49.6
GDR	1981	37.2	62.8
Soviet Union	1980	39.5	60.5

Source: Michał Winiewski and Helena Góralska, "Kryzys, inflacja i reforma gospodarcza a polityka społeczna," *Polityka Społeczna* 8 (1983): 4.

Thus, on the institutional level it is possible to detect common patterns of geographical diffusion of foreign models (see Kopstein and Reilly, Chapter 4 in this volume), both during the early, precommunist period of program adoption and also later, during the Stalinist era of the late 1940s and early 1950s. Still, Poland and Hungary differed in the extent to which they followed the Soviet example of the administration of social benefits, defying the standard social policy practice of most communist states that favored the expansion of collective social services such as different forms of factory-based programs for the workers and benefits in kind – for example, meals, subsidized fuel, and summer vacations – over traditional social security payments. Instead, after some initial experimentation with the Soviet model during the 1950s and the early 1960s, beginning in the 1970s and especially in the early 1980s these two countries once again began to expand the scope of the traditional core of their welfare systems – social insurance benefits in cash (see Table 7.3).

By 1975 the Hungarian social policy planners, encouraged by the successes of János Kádár's "market socialism," created a uniform pension system for the entire population with a standard low retirement age of sixty for men and fifty-five for women. Also in the late 1960s and early 1970s, the Hungarian family benefit systems and childcare payments were extended to become one of the most generous and the most extensive programs of this kind in Europe (Ferge, 1979). The communist regime in Poland, which experienced much more serious economic and political problems, pursued a considerably more cautious benefits policy. It maintained the originally established retirement age at sixty-five for men, with a slightly lower requirement of sixty years for women, and extended cash benefit coverage more gradually. In contrast to policy changes in Hungary, the expansion and reforms of the Polish social insurance system were driven not so much by economics or demography but largely by immediate political considerations. Significant changes in the social insurance schemes usually took place in the immediate aftermath of social unrest, most strikingly during the crisis of 1980–82 when the share of cash benefits in overall social spending jumped suddenly from 47 to 57 percent (see Table 7.3). In addition, following the 1970 workers' unrest under the Gierek regime, heavy pressure from traditionally influential occupational lobbies and the introduction of the new agricultural policies granting pension coverage to private farmers and their families played a crucial role in the expansion of cash benefit programs. At first, the agricultural pension scheme seemed to be just another misguided effort to coerce farmers to sell their landholdings to the state, but in the long run it produced a new type of entitlement that became incredibly resistant to reform.[8]

As Soviet-style command economies, Poland and Hungary had much less flexibility to make even small changes in the Stalinist model of social security financing, which was invented in the 1930s and adopted throughout the communist region after the war. Under this system, social insurance contributions became virtually indistinguishable from other sources of revenue and as such were absorbed into the general state budget. Technically, it was a typical "pay-as-you-go" arrangement, similar to the current social security program in the United States, where the current workers subsidize the benefits of the present-day retirees. Under state socialism, however, constant arbitrary, ad hoc regulation of both economic and social policy and obscure accounting practices made it impossible to produce any long-term estimate of the financial viability of the pension program (or any other expanding social insurance schemes for that matter). State planners frequently diverted sizable surplus funds generated by the pension insurance to direct investment in economic development and failed to construct any consistent mechanism for cost-of-living adjustments to protect the incomes of the benefit recipients. In Poland, when the economy stagnated in the late 1970s and early 1980s, such surpluses began to dwindle, leading first to a drastic increase in the social security tax and later also to the creation of an autonomous Social Insurance Fund (Fundusz Ubezpieczeń Społecznych, FUS).

In 1987, as a part of the overall economic reform program of the Jaruzelski regime, the FUS took over the responsibility for financing pensions, family benefits, sickness and maternity payments, and other smaller cash entitlements. By separating the FUS from the general budget, a group of reform-minded bureaucrats in the last communist regime hoped to make the finances of social policy more transparent and amenable to change, but in fact in the very first year of its operation significant "interest-free loans" were made to the state budget.[9] Yet, despite such problems during 1988, on the eve of

[8] For a detailed historical analysis of the politics of social policy in Poland, see Inglot (1994).

[9] In 1987 the Polish government "borrowed" 291 million złoty from the FUS to finance budget expenditures. The loan was returned in 1989 in the same exact amount (without interest).

transition the overall financial condition of the Polish social security system was still relatively sound. This appearance of stability was augmented by tight and centralized administrative controls that remained in place throughout the communist period. A single national organization, the Social Insurance Institution (Zakład Ubezpieczeń Społecznych, ZUS), supervised directly by the minister of labor and social policy, began to administer the newly integrated Polish social insurance system in 1935 and continued to do so with little interruption until the late 1990s, allowing for only token participation of the trade unions and other social organizations.[10]

In contrast to Poland, Hungary most of the time followed the decentralized Soviet-style model of social security administration that depended on the heavy involvement of the official trade unions. Only in 1989 did the Hungarian government move to streamline its control over pensions and other cash benefits, creating the so-called National Central Administration of Social Security (Orsrzágos Tarsadalombiztosítasí Föigazgatosag), and in consequence also undermining the traditional influence of the unions in this area. In the late 1980s the country began to experience serious fiscal difficulties and also attempted to solve this problem by restructuring the financing of social security and separating social insurance funds from the general state budget (Muller, 1999: 64). Yet the considerable economic improvements experienced by the Hungarian society since the late 1960s had produced significant pressures to expand the welfare state and provide better, more generous benefits. Such an expansion would require cutting subsidies to factories and raising taxes, neither of which was a feasible option in the late 1970s and early 1980s, when the economy was beginning to slow down again. The expected welfare improvements failed to materialize and many critics of the regime blamed excessive government control over policy making for the failure to reconcile the needs of social and economic policy. Social policy experts, and increasingly also the leaders of the official trade unions, lobbied the communist reformers to reinstate the independent, risk-related and self-governed insurance boards that had existed before the communist takeover in 1948.[11] These efforts were only briefly interrupted by the fall of the regime in 1989.

These attempts to create their own unique versions of Marxist-Leninist social policy collapsed before the communist rulers of Poland and Hungary managed to agree on the final shape of the "socialist welfare state." In reality, the old regimes left behind overextended social policy budgets that were economically unsustainable and a confusing legacy of programs that

See *Rocznik Statystyczny Ubezpieczeń Społecznych* (Warsaw: Zakład Ubezpieczeń Społecznych, 1992), table 1(13), 19.

[10] The Soviet-style system of social insurance administration by the trade unions was adopted in Poland for a very brief period in 1955, but the old system was quickly restored in 1960 (Borowczyk, 1991: 243).

[11] Péter Bod and Zsuzsa Ferge (Hungarian Academy of Sciences), interviews by author, Budapest, September 1996.

promised more than these states could ever possibly deliver. Several layers of legislation adopted under different political and economic systems blended together to produce the contemporary maze of laws, government regulations, and legal entitlements, creating a formidable challenge for the inexperienced policy makers of the new democratic states. In addition, the transition governments had to deal with two fundamental social problems. One of them was the widespread public expectation that the injustices of the old system, such as dismally low pensions and the pervasive lack of permanent benefit indexation, would be immediately corrected. The other, even more challenging obstacle was the deep popular resistance toward fiscally conservative ideas and any type of financial controls on social spending, which were commonly associated with the outgoing communist "reformers" and their unsuccessful efforts in this area during the late 1980s.

Social Security Policies of the Early Transition Period

The rampant inflation of the early 1990s created an immediate social policy emergency for the new democratic governments of both Poland and Hungary. However, each country chose different strategies to deal with the inflationary pressures on pensions that shaped distinct new dynamics for future reform and, more important, for the relationship between the government and the benefit recipients. Poland's first democratic government of Prime Minister Tadeusz Mazowiecki introduced regular quarterly indexation of pensions in May 1990, and later, in October 1991, the Sejm approved new permanent rules for the calculation of benefits, put more emphasis on the record of insurance contribution,[12] and, even more significant, established a ceiling for the highest pension at 250 percent of the average wage. During this time, in accordance with agreements reached with the trade unions at the famous Round Table talks in the spring of 1989, the Polish government continued to use a wage-related indexation scheme. Thus, the reform hurt mainly the higher-income groups. In Hungary, pension indexation was introduced gradually during 1991–92, following a lengthy debate and multiple previous incremental adjustments that repeatedly, since the late 1980s, had failed to compensate pensioners for the loss of purchasing power. At least in theory, beginning in the mid-1990s all Hungarian pensions had to be adjusted once a year in accordance with the increase in average wages.[13]

As a result of these changes, average nominal payments for most new pensioners increased and the replacement ratio (the relation of average pensions to average wages) quickly climbed to over 60 percent in both countries (see

[12] This record includes the actual years of employment, and the nonemployment years were counted as "years of insurance coverage" (maternity leave, school, military service, etc.) but were actually not equal in value to a regular time of employment.

[13] After the initial raise at the beginning of the year, additional corrections were usually applied in the fall (Antal et al., 1995: 202).

TABLE 7.4. *Pension Replacement Ratio in Poland and Hungary (average pension as % of average wage)*

	1990	1991	1992	1993	1994	1995	1996
Poland	55.8	64.8	61.8	60.7	63.0	63.0	n.d.
			59.4[a]	58.6[a]	60.1[a]	60.1[a]	59.0[a]
Hungary	66.1	64.4	62.4	62.5	59.7	61.9	59.9

[a] Estimate of the average old-age and disability pension paid by the Social Insurance Fund (Fundusz Ubezpieczeń Społecznych, FUS), excluding farmers' pensions and other related social security benefits paid from other funds. From <www.zus.pl/statyst/>, updated on February 13, 2000.

Sources: Zakład Ubezpieczeń Społecznych (ZUS), Warsaw, March 1996, and National Pension Insurance Administration, *Statistical Yearbook (1995* and *1996)* (Budapest, 1996 and 1997).

Table 7.4). However, the actual income of the retired population remained relatively secure only in Poland, where in 1991, for example, an average pensioner gained 13.6 percent in real terms, a move that largely offset the substantial benefit decline of the previous year (see Table 7.5). In the context of a 7 percent drop in GDP and a huge decrease in real wages, this clearly indicates a deliberate government effort to safeguard the livelihood of the social group considered likely to suffer most during economic shock therapy. Even though Polish pensioners with long employment records and higher salaries were hurt by the new restrictions on the maximum benefit amount, in general retirees fared much better in relative terms than many other groups in society. A comparison of average real household incomes (see Table 7.6) clearly shows that, in relation to the previous period, during 1989–92 the retired population was in a much better economic situation than an average working family.

Hungarians had much more reason to complain. Since 1990 the average real pension continued to decline at a fast rate, with the largest drop of as much as 11.4 percent in 1993 (see Table 7.5). In addition, various studies consistently showed a sharp decline in the purchasing power of pensions, approximately by 13–14 percent, with the survivors of pensioners suffering the highest net loses of income (Antal et al., 1995: 205).[14] A minor improvement took place in 1994, but the situation deteriorated again in the following years. Still, from a longer-term perspective, with the exception of 1994, the year of parliamentary elections and a brief economic recovery (2.6 percent growth in GDP), the overall dynamics of average real pensions changed little since the earlier period of 1992–93. Unlike their counterparts in Poland, the two consecutive postcommunist governments in Hungary failed to safeguard the real value of pensions. Furthermore, a comparison of the dynamics of

14 Also Maria Augusztinovics and András Simonovits, Institute of Economics, Hungarian Academy of Sciences, interviews by author, Budapest, September and December 1996.

TABLE 7.5. *A Comparison of Real Dynamics of Net Average Pensions and Wages in Poland and Hungary during 1989–1997 (% change over previous year)*

	1989	1990	1991	1992	1993	1994	1995	1996	1997
GDP (% change from previous year)									
Poland	n.d.	−11.6	−7.0	2.6	3.8	5.2	7.0	6.1	6.9
Hungary	n.d.	−3.5	−11.9	−3.1	−0.6	3.0	2.0	1.0	4.0
Poland									
Pensions	4.4	−14.9	13.6	−5.3	−2.5	4.1	3.8	2.2	5.5
Wages	6.3[a]	−24.4	−.3	−2.7	−2.9	0.5	3.0	n.d.	n.d.
Hungary									
Pensions	n.d.	−4.2	−6.5	−8.4	−11.4	0.7	−9.3	−8.2	n.d.
Wages	n.d.	−5.5	−6.9	−2.3	−4.8	8.5	−17.7	−5.6	n.d.

Notes: For Poland, wages are net averages, after taxes calculated according to the consumer price index (CPI); pensions are net figures, after taxes and adjusted to CPI. Since 1990 pension values do not include supplemental family benefit payments and nursing allowances paid to qualified recipients. Farmers' pensions are not included.

For Hungary, wages are annual averages, pensions are of January each year, wages are net figures, pensions are not taxed, and calculations are based on the CPI measure for each year.

[a] Based on gross amount before taxes.

Sources: Social Insurance Institution (Zakład Ubezpieczeń Społecznych), Department of Analysis and Statistics, Warsaw, February 17, 1997; *Główny Rocznik Statystyczny GUS (1993* and *1996)* (Warsaw: Główny Urząd Statystyczny, 1993 and 1996); and Tárki – The Social Research Information Center, Budapest, February 3, 1997; Central Statistical Office, Business Central Europe, Warsaw, Poland, available: <www.paiz.gov.pl>; and my own calculations.

TABLE 7.6. *A Comparison of Changes in Real Household Income in Poland during 1989 (% change)*

	1990:1989	1990:1991	1992:1991	1992:1989
Wage earner's household	−24.9	1.7	2.2	−23.2
Pensioner's household	−15.8	8.7	−6.9	−11.3

Source: Jacek Mojkowski, "Cery na łatach" (Patching it up), *Polityka* 51, December 18, 1993, 12.

average pensions and average wages during the seven-year period of economic and political transformation in both countries shows that in Poland the real value of an average pension was better protected than the average income of a wage earner. In Hungary, with the exception of the very early years of 1990–91, the situation was almost exactly opposite. It must be noted, however, that during 1995–96, following the imposition of an economic austerity plan, both pensioners and wage earners suffered an equally severe drop in their living standards (see Table 7.5).[15]

[15] These figures must be viewed in the proper context. In today's Hungary the black market sector represents 30–32 percent of the economy. See Bossanyi (1995: 94). Also, in Chapter 8

The incremental reforms of the pension system in Poland during the early 1990s solved the perpetual problem of the *old cohort of pensioners* whose benefits have always lagged behind the new group of retirees under communism. However, these changes failed to arrest the overall rate of growth of social security spending since 1990 and did little to satisfy benefit recipients, causing widespread protests and intensive lobbying of senior government bureaucrats by the trade unions and groups of Polish pensioners representing the traditionally well-paid occupations.[16] In Hungary, however, the growing impoverishment among the elderly stimulated labor leaders and the community of social policy experts to pressure the conservative government of Jozsef Antall to reform radically the administration of social insurance and to transfer decision-making power from the state bureaucrats to the representatives of society.[17] The reforms of the Polish and Hungarian social security systems, which started gradually during the early 1990s, focused primarily on three major areas: financing of benefits, rules and regulations concerning the eligibility and amount of pension paid to individuals and select occupational groups, and political and administrative oversight. If successfully implemented, these reforms would result in major shifts in the control and distribution of enormous resources, equal to one-third of the national budget or approximately 15 percent of GDP. However, they also could threaten the government's ability to support existing entitlements and social obligations to its citizens and undermine state capacity to generate revenue.

The Return of the "Left": Legacies of the Past and Policy Continuities

By the time the anticommunist parties lost power in the parliamentary elections of 1993 in Poland and 1994 in Hungary, it had already become clear that any proposal to change the existing social security system carried serious political risks. Therefore, regardless of the pro-welfare rhetoric of the new "left-wing" governments, few observers expected to see substantial progress in pension reform. Yet, by the end of the next electoral cycle, in 1997 and 1998 respectively, Hungary and Poland managed to achieve a consensus on one of the most controversial problems of postcommunist social policy – the introduction of a three-tier pension system with a mandatory funded (capitalized) component, based in part on the Latin American examples of Chile and Argentina.[18] The nature of this consensus, just like the type of policy

in this volume Phineas Baxandall gives an estimate of "informal activity" in Hungary at 28.1 percent.

16 See, for example, "Ostry protest emerytów" (Pensioners strongly protest), *Tygodnik Popularny Związkowiec* 50 (1992): 2.

17 Péter Bod, member of the Presidium of the Pension Fund, interview by author, Budapest, September 1996.

18 For more-detailed comparisons of pension systems in East Central Europe and Latin America, see Müller (1999: 18–23).

pursued by each country during the early years of the transition, was largely determined by the historical legacies that gave rise to two diverging paths of social policy development and eventually shaped the content of the final pension reform legislation.

In November 1993, Polish prime minister Waldemar Pawlak announced that his government "would not treat social expenditures as a burden on the budget,"[19] and the new coalition of the ex-communist Alliance of the Democratic Left (SLD) and the reconstituted Polish Peasant Party (PSL) blamed the former Solidarity-based governments for the lack of progress in the area of social policy reform. A high-ranking Labor Ministry official claimed that the previous cabinet of Hanna Suchocka abandoned social policy reform for political reasons on the eve of the parliamentary elections, ignoring the "years of unbearable sacrifice" imposed on the public in the early 1990s. Now, he declared, "[we will] find a less painful way to reach the same [reform] goals."[20] Contrary to such pronouncements, however, Polish social policy during 1990–93 was influenced not so much by electoral politics or policy agendas of different political parties but by preexisting structural constraints and opportunities.

All postcommunist governments inherited a centralized social security system that had been highly vulnerable to the lobbying efforts by well-entrenched insiders, allowing determined individuals within the government and numerous occupational groups to derail reforms at the very top of the administrative structure – the Ministry of Labor and Social Policy. This situation favored many special and politically powerful groups of workers, such as miners, the police, steelworkers, the military, and the farmers. Therefore no significant social pressure to "democratize," or even to restructure and decentralize, the social insurance administration existed in Poland during 1990–91. In consequence, despite the huge burden of budget deficits in the first two years of transition, joint efforts of the fiscal bureaucrats from the ZUS and the Ministry of Finance helped to preserve tight control over the financial assets of the state. By utilizing preexisting fiscal mechanisms and the extensive regulatory powers of the executive branch, including those of the minister of labor, these officials for the most part managed to control excessive spending despite increasingly hostile confrontations with their opponents in the parliament, the cabinet, and the public at large. For example, during 1992–93 the minister of labor in the Suchocka cabinet, Jacek Kuroń, initiated a series of small but significant administrative measures that prepared the ground for changing the nature of family benefits from a universal social insurance benefit to a means-tested payment financed by the budget,

[19] "Ludzki rząd" (The humane government), parliamentary address of Prime Minister Waldemar Pawlak, *Gazeta Wyborcza*, November 9, 1993, 10–11.

[20] Jerzy Hausner, an interview, "Mniej boleśnie dochodzić do celu" (Reaching the same goal with less pain), *Rzeczpospolita*, June 10, 1994, 4.

rather than by the Social Insurance Fund. The Solidarity governments suffered the brunt of the initial and the most hostile policy feedback from the interested constituencies and the parliamentary opposition throughout the early 1990s, causing the paralysis of most major reform efforts and contributing to the eventual fall of the Suchocka cabinet in the spring of 1993.[21]

In fact, in the fall of 1993 the new minister of labor and the former high-ranking communist official Leszek Miller declared his support for the pending legislation aiming at the reduction of spending on sick pay and family benefits. However, the ex-communists, just like their predecessors, refrained from making radical changes in the pension laws. In an early 1995 interview, Miller candidly defended his policy of maintaining and even extending retirement benefits and privileges to select groups of employees by claiming that "nine million pensioners who vote could not be ignored and any government coalition that does not want to provoke a large social conflict must take this fact into consideration." He also backed the efforts of his parliamentary colleagues from the SLD to secure the benefit rights of the members of the state apparatus, arguing that "in a case when the salaries in the military and the police are too low it is acceptable to use pension privileges as an incentive."[22]

Unlike their Polish counterparts, the Hungarian ex-communists, led by Prime Minister Gyula Horn, ranked social policy as a distant third item on their agenda, following other urgent needs such as balancing the budget and privatization.[23] This order of business reflected the position of the so-called pragmatic problem-solvers within the ruling establishment, including the newly appointed supporters of budgetary cuts, Finance Minister Lajos Bokros and the president of the National Bank György Surányi. Such policy preferences provoked the resentment of the "leftist faction," which insisted on more social spending, as promised in the election program of the Socialist Party (MSzP).[24] However, once the third, middle-of-the-road faction led by senior party leaders and Prime Minister Horn himself, together with the junior coalition partners from the Alliance of Free Democrats (SzDSz), endorsed the economic plans of the "pragmatists," the Ministry of Finance

[21] See Mering (1992: 4), and Jacek Kuroń, interview by author, Warsaw, April 1993.

[22] Leszek Miller, "Władza odbiera pewność siebie" (Power takes away self-confidence), an interview with Jolanta Koral and Natalia Skipiertow, *Gazeta Wyborcza*, February 15, 1995, 12.

[23] As stated by a Hungarian political scientist, "the government has no choice but to institute very *unsocialist* measures to manage the current economic crisis, even though the Socialist Party campaigned in 1994 on a platform promising increasing benefits to workers." Laszlo Vass in Daniel Langenkamp, "Inside Hungarian Politics," *Budapest Week*, September 5–11, 1996, 7.

[24] In her address to the Woodrow Wilson Center in Washington, D.C., Radio Free Europe analyst Zofia Szilagyi distinguished these three factions within the MSzP. See Smith (1996: 7).

emerged as the unquestionable leader of both economic and social policy reforms.

This development signified again the predominance of continuity rather than change in the overall dynamics of social security reform in Hungary during the 1990s. Despite the growing indication of potential deficits and the inefficiencies of the existing system of cash benefits, successive regimes, including the communist ones before 1989, did not consider social security reform as an urgent matter from either an economic or a welfare perspective. During the mid-1970s increased government attention to cash benefits created a "safety cushion" for the partial market reforms of the Kádár era. Even later in the 1980s, when the economy began to slow down considerably, the society did not experience any sudden drop in welfare that would be comparable to the situation in Poland. During the last years of the old regime, the lack of improvement in the real value of government cash payments was offset to some degree by the expansion of new opportunities to earn extra income in the growing "informal" economy (see Phineas Baxendall, Chapter 8 in this volume). Therefore, it seems that the communist leaders saw little need for radical reforms in social policy, with the exception of minor adjustments in the fiscal administration toward greater centralization and efficiency. This apparent neglect of social policy issues by the government marginalized and alienated many supporters of "welfare state" expansion, including government experts, trade-union activists, and academics who in the past often warned against the dangers of growing inequalities in the Hungarian society (Ferge, 1979).

While in Poland the postcommunist social policy reformers were eager to use the preexisting state capacities to realize their goals, in Hungary the opposite took place. A growing sense of mistrust in the state bureaucracy and its ability to consider seriously necessary changes in the social security and health systems prompted the Hungarian social policy community to emphasize administrative reforms. Proposals to shift the control of the social security administration from the state bureaucracy to social organizations resurfaced in 1992 and gained unexpected support from the right-wing government of the Hungarian Democratic Forum (MDF).

As the second postcommunist elections to the parliament drew near, the MDF government became increasingly unpopular in public opinion polls, and its leaders gladly embraced this plan as a chance to gain political support from pensioners and other social groups. Furthermore, the anticommunist parties hoped to encourage the growth of independent trade unions that would challenge the monopoly of the ex-communists in the area of social policy. When in November 1992 social and economic conditions in the country began to deteriorate, the government moved to avert social protests by signing a "new social contract" with all the major trade unions. This agreement included important social insurance provisions such as a pension raise, a tax exemption for social benefits, a temporary suspension of the proposed retirement age increase for women, and, most significant, free elections to the self-government of the Pension Fund and the Health Fund, to be organized with the participation of the labor organizations (Pataki, 1993).

These elections, held on May 21, 1993, represented a major turning point in the early process of social policy reform in postcommunist Hungary. The combined pressure of the new and old trade unions, opposition politicians, and the community of welfare experts led to the enactment of laws that substantially weakened government control over the pension and health insurance administration. The elected boards won extensive rights to advise and consult with the parliament on social insurance issues and to veto its policies – an exceptional situation even by the standards of highly developed West European welfare states. Moreover, to the great surprise of the governing party, the elections turned into a highly politicized event and an early indication of the growing influence of the ex-communists. The National Confederation of Hungarian Trade Unions (MSzOSz) won a plurality of over 45 percent of the seats on the Pension Insurance Board and a majority of over 50 percent on the Health Insurance Board.[25] Meanwhile, fearing adverse reaction from the voters, the government suspended all further efforts to reform the system of pension benefits.

Politics also undoubtedly impacted Hungary's budgetary policy in 1994. The deficit grew from the previous year's 6 percent to 8, in large measure because of a sudden surge in social spending before the parliamentary elections (Beck, 1996: 8) (see Table 7.2).[26] Hence, in contrast to Poland, the newly elected left-wing cabinet was unable to capitalize on the improved economic performance during the previous administration but instead had to contemplate immediately a major policy retrenchment. As Péter Gedeon has pointed out, "[I]t is the irony of postsocialist transition" that the conservative Antall government "internalized" the welfare expectations created by the pre-1989 regime, while the former communists began to "ease the burden of the state in financing social policy" (Gedeon, 1995: 456–57).[27] He also observed that aside from economic factors, during 1990–94 "[t]he change in social policy in Hungary has been determined by inner constraints and domestic political coalitions" (Gedeon, 1995: 441).

The same pattern apparently continued after the 1994 elections. The coalition of two center-left factions within the Socialist Party, backed by the SzDSz, easily won cabinet approval of the 1995 budget proposal, managing to avoid a lengthy parliamentary discussion and, even more important, a

25 Ibid., and Péter Bod, interview by author, Budapest, September 1996.

26 Real wages in Hungary increased dramatically before the 1994 elections; see Table 7.5, and also Mizsei (1994: 70).

27 Contrary to the predictions of the social democratic school of social policy, during 1990–94 the predominance of liberal-conservative politics did not undermine the state commitment to welfare spending and social policy institutions in Hungary (Gedeon, 1995: 44–47).

widespread public debate. Such a debate might have weakened the policy makers' resolve, could have exposed serious differences within the cabinet, and also threatened to reveal the continuous neglect of social security reform by the policy planners within the Ministry of Finance. Moreover, in contradiction to campaign promises to develop a system of tripartite negotiations on social policy issues, in early 1995 a program of economic austerity named after its main author, Finance Minister Bokros, was announced without meaningful participation of the trade unions or other social groups (Pataki, 1993).[28]

Although in Poland the newly elected government faced no such immediate economic pressure, initially the coalition of the ex-communists and the Peasant Party also failed to agree on a common course of pension reform. In fact, since 1989 an ongoing debate over welfare ideology and the direction of changes in social security had cut across political affiliations. On one side, the defenders of the existing PAYG system advocated slow, incremental change that would protect, first and foremost, the rights and benefits of current pensioners. On the other side, the proponents of reform favored a more radical transformation of the current social insurance into mandatory investment funds, liberated from monopolistic government control.

In 1991 the latter group suffered an early defeat that considerably slowed down the reform process. The short-lived window of opportunity for radical reforms created by the unprecedented social consensus on Polish "shock therapy" (Balcerowicz, 1995), and also the appearance of a serious social insurance deficit in 1990, encouraged the newly appointed president of the Social Insurance Institution (ZUS), Wojciech Topiński, and his academic collaborators to push for a swift transformation of the existing PAYG structure. This proposal, based largely on the Chilean example from the 1980s, immediately ran into a wall of opposition within the government and among most of the social policy establishment, including the ZUS itself, leading eventually to the widely publicized resignation of Topiński in the summer of 1991.[29]

Once the worst financial crisis was over, the parliament approved a new package of pension legislation that streamlined pension regulations without changing the basic tenets of the existing PAYG system. The social policy establishment believed that during this time of political instability and economic uncertainty the policy of slow, incremental reform of social security was the only available option. The ministers of labor in the Solidarity governments, Jacek Kuroń and Michał Boni, understood well that they had to balance carefully the perils and advantages of the existing social security

[28] Also Péter Bod, interview by author, Budapest, September 1996.

[29] Topiński traveled to Chile in December 1990 to study the effectiveness of the privatized pension system. Wojciech Topiński, interview by author, Warsaw, May 5, 1993. See Topiński and Wiśniewski (1991).

system in the context of the pressing socioeconomic and political challenges around them. On one hand, the continuation of the status quo created constant short-term crises, such as the one in 1991, and in the long run could presumably lead to a progressing deficit of the pension fund around the year 2025, when the "baby boom retirement" is expected to begin. On the other hand, a radical pension reform seemed to be a far more dangerous solution. This could alienate crucial constituencies and undermine government capacity to collect sufficient revenue needed to address the most immediate social problems.[30]

In the early 1990s the postcommunist governments were able to react efficiently to crisis situations not only because of the sound institutional foundation of the social security system but also through skillful utilization of the centralized executive power and the expertise, or "policy learning,"[31] acquired by the social security bureaucracy in the past. This expertise involved drawing important lessons from past periods of severe economic and political crises. For example, in 1971, 1980–81, and 1987–88 the social security agencies took over the distribution of emergency cash benefits and wage subsidies and managed to fulfill this task with admirable efficiency and speed.[32]

The policies of Jacek Kuroń, a longtime opposition leader and the minister of labor in the first Solidarity government, were greatly influenced by this legacy as he struggled to maintain his two contradictory roles, that of a leading proponent of fiscally responsible social policy reform and also an advocate for various benefit recipients. After the collapse of the communist regime in the fall of 1989, the Social Insurance Fund (FUS) began to show first signs of a looming deficit. Kuroń, his deputy Michał Boni, and the minister of finance, Leszek Balcerowicz, revealed this fact to the public in hope of gaining support for a further increase in the social security tax, and also for future reductions in the rate of spending.[33] The latter, more difficult task depended largely on the government's ability to control the growth of the pension fund and therefore had to be implemented carefully in several stages. However, the former, along with many other pension-related measures that determine the real value of benefits, could happen quietly as a part of the annual budget legislation prepared jointly by the Ministry of Finance and the Ministry of Labor and Social Policy.

In the short run, the tax increase immediately affected employers, not the working population, because enterprises (both public and private) were required to transfer all of their required payments directly from their wage funds to the ZUS. By forcing employers to carry the fiscal burden of

30 Jacek Kuroń, interview by author, April 1993.

31 For a discussion of this concept, see Heclo (1974: 315–17).

32 For a more detailed discussion of this aspect of social policy in Poland, see Inglot (1994).

33 Michał Boni, interviews by author, Warsaw, March 1993 and January 1997.

social policy, which recalled similar practices under the old regime,[34] the government created a temporary financial cushion and managed to avoid a sudden political backlash. Hence, the Solidarity ministers rejected radical calls for pension reform in large measure because of the structural opportunities offered by the existing system. Keeping the status quo allowed them better to handle social policy emergencies under the stress of postcommunist transition without undermining the essential tenets of the state as the key provider of income for large segments of the population. In essence, this policy of continuity prepared the ground for the emergence of a new type of an entitlement state in Poland.

Pension Reform Strategies of the Ex-Communist Coalitions in Poland and Hungary

By focusing extensively on maintaining state capacities in the area of social policy, the Solidarity governments helped the conservative government bureaucrats and policy experts with strong ties to the previous regime to preserve their influence within the Ministry of Labor and Social Policy. After the 1993 elections these officials "emerged from the closet" while the remaining radical reformers were purged from the Ministry of Labor and the ZUS.[35] Subsequently, an old team of policy experts was reassembled by Minister Leszek Miller to draft his government's proposal of pension reform that included a guaranteed pension for everyone (at the level of 30 percent of an average wage), wage- and insurance-based retirement benefits for persons with at least fifteen years of employment, and a *voluntary* supplementary pension for those willing to pay additional contributions. The first of these provisions was eventually dropped, but only after the finance minister, Grzegorz Kołodko, threatened his resignation. Kołodko's economic program, the *Strategy for Poland*, announced in the fall of 1994, insisted on urgent and comprehensive pension reforms that would generate long-term savings for the state budget.[36] Unlike the situation in Hungary, this conflict between the two ministers quickly became public and stimulated widespread media criticism of the proposed legislation. In consequence, the government was forced to revise its pension proposal approved by the cabinet in May 1995 and to eliminate several of its most costly provisions, especially those favoring a more generous indexation of benefits.[37]

[34] The best example of this policy has been sick-pay insurance. For details, see Inglot (1994: 217–20).

[35] Małgorzata Pawlisz, president, Social Security Foundation (former deputy director of ZUS), interview by author, Warsaw, September 1996.

[36] "Kołodko Sets Conditions for Remaining in Government," *Open Media Research Institute (OMRI) Reports*, February 24, 1995.

[37] *Program Reformy Ubezpieczeń Społecznych*, government document (Warsaw: Ministry of Labor and Social Policy, December 1995).

In Budapest, just as in Warsaw, by the mid-1990s senior ex-communist politicians and Finance Ministry technocrats began to play an important role in shaping the new social security system. Still, the central bureaucracies directly responsible for social policy in Hungary found it increasingly difficult to control the reform agenda and process.[38] The Hungarian Welfare Ministry[39] never acquired the same political significance or public influence as its counterpart in Poland. In addition, since 1993 the Ministry of Welfare formed a de facto political and ideological alliance with the Pension Fund. The fund, however, as a new and independent body no longer subject to direct government control, lacked the institutional experience of the ZUS to be able to play any significant role in shaping the direction of social security reforms in Hungary. It also found itself in an unenviable position of being a political outsider under two consecutive governments: after the 1993 board elections, won by the ex-communist trade unionists against the wishes of the MDF, and again under the Horn cabinet, when the so-called "left-wing" faction within the Socialist Party lost its internal struggle against the fiscal conservatives.

In 1994 the Pension Fund and Ministry of Welfare, in consultation with the financial lobby, jointly offered a pension reform plan that envisioned only moderate changes with minimum pensions for the poorest individuals and *voluntary* private old-age insurance schemes, treated largely as a supplement to state-funded entitlements and the traditional PAYG system.[40] This proposal followed the earlier separate law of late 1993, which permitted the creation of independent and privately run pension insurance funds but did not challenge the institutional status quo in any significant way. Paradoxically, even though the general intention of the Ministry of Welfare seems to have been to preserve the existing safety net for working people, during the difficult economic transition the main beneficiaries of this approach were actually the large employers. The endorsement of a voluntary, rather than mandatory, third pillar of pension insurance encouraged employers to seek generous tax breaks and to offer different independent retirement plans to their workers (Batty, 1997: 7). In this way substantial financial resources could be easily diverted from the Pension Fund to relatively flexible and autonomous private schemes. Clearly, until the late 1990s both the employers

[38] Mária Major (deputy state secretary for pension insurance, Ministry of Welfare), interview by author, Budapest, December 1996.

[39] In Hungary, social policy is administered by two different ministries: the Ministry of Labor, which handles labor-related issues (unemployment, disability, sick pay, etc.) and the Ministry of Welfare, which has been responsible for pensions.

[40] A joint statement to this effect was published in 1994 by a group of foreign and Hungarian economists and social policy experts, including Györgi Surányi, then a director of the Central European International Bank. See *Hungarian Welfare State in Transition: Structure, Initial Reforms and Recommendations*, Joint Hungarian-International Blue Ribbon Commission and Hudson Institute, Policy Study no. 3, February 1994

and the social policy establishment in Hungary opposed radical changes in the existing social security systems but for dramatically different reasons. On one hand, employers feared that the creation of new mandatory private pension funds would strengthen the central government as a tax collector and regulator of financial markets. On the other hand, the social policy reformers from the Ministry of Welfare, the Pension Fund, and the trade unions resisted the idea of centralized control over the administration of benefits, a trend that in their estimation threatened to replace the concept of a generous European welfare state with "American-style" neoliberalism.[41]

When the Horn government came to power in the spring of 1994, it inherited a severe budget deficit and mounting problems with revenue collection that derived in a large part from the rapid growth of social spending during the election year. At an urgent cabinet meeting on March 12, 1995, the cabinet endorsed the new austerity plan prepared by Minister of Finance Lajos Bokros. Bokros ostensibly aimed at large expenditure cuts and new sources of revenue to improve external balance of payments, but in doing so he explicitly targeted a variety of social programs. Family benefits eligibility was restricted to families with incomes below 25,000 forints per person (approximately equivalent to average net monthly earnings in 1995). Childcare benefits ceased to function as universal payments and became income-related, and home construction subsidies were cut as well. In addition, the Bokros plan included adjustments in the calculation of social insurance tax, the transfer of some of the sick-pay burden from the Health Fund to employers, and an introduction of partial fees for medical services and university tuition. The focus on family benefits, childcare, and tuition, rather than pensions, most likely stemmed from a political calculation that a diffuse action of this kind would generate less resistance both within and outside the governing coalition. Nonetheless, during the spring and summer of 1995 large protests and street demonstrations were held throughout Hungary and the conflicts within the government intensified (Kocsis, 1995: 6–7).

Initially, regardless of the growing social discontent and criticism within his own party, Prime Minister Horn decided to stand firm behind Bokros, alienating other cabinet members who advocated a more gradual and less painful approach to budget reductions. The minister of welfare, Pal Kovacs, resigned almost immediately after the March 12 meeting. The minister of labor, Maria Kosa-Kovacs, left in October, following a government decision to let the Finance Ministry negotiate a sick-pay deal with employers without prior consultation with social policy experts. The head of the largest trade union (MSzOSz) also resigned in November due to "disagreements with

[41] Péter Bod, Júlia Szalai, Zsuzsa Ferge, interviews by author, Budapest, September and December 1996.

government over leftist values and internal conflicts."[42] Despite all these problems, however, the government was determined to implement the austerity program in its entirety. Horn moved quickly to reassert his control over the Ministries of Welfare and Labor and also established better relations with the new head of the trade-union federation. By early 1996, a new political compromise emerged among the ex-communist politicians, but once again it mostly ignored the pressing problems of social policy and pension reform and focused instead on cabinet reshuffling with the intention of ensuring the continuation of economic policy.

The pragmatic wing of the MSzP became the first casualty of this compromise. Lajos Bokros, who lent his name to the most unpopular government program since 1989,[43] resigned in February, following an aborted attempt to introduce a special social insurance tax. In addition, the supporters of the finance minister had to accept the annulment of some austerity measures by the Constitutional Tribunal. The demise of Bokros caused temporary anxiety in the financial markets and among Hungary's Western allies, but skillful political maneuvering by Horn prevented a larger government crisis. He quickly nominated Péter Medgyessy, a highly respected chairman of the National Bank, to the post of minister of finance, won the parliamentary approval to continue the economic reforms, and announced that no more austerity measures would be passed in 1996. Judging from opinion polls, this cabinet reshuffle worked well for the Socialists, since Horn's popularity rose to a record 53.4 percent in May.[44] Still, the heavy-handed attitude of the leading Hungarian policy makers during 1995–96 generated serious political turmoil within the MSzP, leading eventually to the formation of a splinter political group – the Hungarian Democratic People's Party. These developments put to rest fears that social security reforms in Hungary would be shaped exclusively by the "neoliberals" and showed that any meaningful changes in social security had to involve a difficult compromise between the pragmatic reformers and the defenders of the traditional welfare state.[45]

Also in Poland by late 1995 an uneasy consensus on pension reforms had begun to emerge. Miller's pension reform was relegated to lengthy and cumbersome "social consultations," with little chance of passage before upcoming presidential elections, and the Labor and Finance Ministries agreed on a new law restricting the indexation of retirement benefits. This provision

[42] *OMRI Reports*, March 13, May 15, June 1, October 9–10, and November 10, 1995. Also see *Rzeczpospolita (Warsaw)*, October 11, 1995, 6.

[43] Public opinion polls published in February testified to the fact that most people associated the painful decisions of 1995 exclusively with the person of the finance minister. *OMRI Reports*, February 18, 1996.

[44] Ibid., February 25, 26, and 29, March 2, and May 2, 1996.

[45] Ibid., November 23, 1995.

was immediately challenged by an executive veto, overruled by the Lower House (the Sejm), and then again turned over to the Constitutional Tribunal by President Wałęsa.[46] Regardless of the final ruling, which deemed such restrictions illegal, the delay in policy implementation enabled the Finance and Labor Ministries to coordinate their positions and gave the government more time to prepare for a possible backlash. The pragmatic reformers, however, began to regain influence in the process of pension reform only after the election of the new president, ex-communist Aleksander Kwaśniewski, and the formation of the next government under Prime Minister Włodzimierz Cimoszewicz in early 1996.

State Structures and the Political Dynamics of the Pension Reform Agreements

The crucial turning point in the process of pension reform in Poland came with the departure of Leszek Miller, who was moved "upstairs" to the post of the chief of staff of the Council of Ministers, and with the arrival of the new minister of labor, Andrzej Bączkowski, the nonpartisan outsider and former Solidarity activist. Before his premature death in November 1996, Bączkowski assumed personal responsibility for social security reform and succeeded in building political momentum for a series of comprehensive pension bills adopted during the following year by the Sejm. His team undertook a major revision of the pension project introduced by Miller in 1995, inviting its critics and the advocates of more-radical approaches to propose further changes in the ministerial plan. The revised pension reform was first unveiled in February 1997, in a publication called *Security through Diversity* (Chłon, Góra, and Rutkowski, 1999: 19).

Until now, the reformers had received only partial support from a few officials of the Ministry of Finance and the Solidarity trade union, each presenting their own alternative pension proposals. Just as in Hungary, the major controversy centered on whether the partially privatized pension funds should be voluntary or mandatory. In the past, Ministry of Labor officials insisted on the former solution, whereas the Finance Ministry and Solidarity argued for a compulsory *second-tier* scheme, in addition to other voluntary individual and group pension accounts to be created in the future. They again quoted the Chilean example, claiming that this decision would generate valuable capital for future economic growth. All three proposals also envisioned different methods of transition from the old system to the new one.[47] In contrast to Hungary, however, the main structure of social security

[46] "Lech Wałęsa Sends a Bill on Pensions to Constitutional Tribunal," *OMRI Reports*, October 10, 1995.

[47] Andrzej Bączkowski, Ewa Borowczyk (deputy director of ZUS), and Michał Boni, interviews by author, August and December 1996 and January 1997.

administration remained intact throughout the 1990s.[48] In 1992 a group of Polish senators, backed by the Solidarity trade union, introduced legislation that would divide the Social Insurance Fund into three separate funds according to insurance risk and transform the ZUS into an autonomous, self-governing organization supervised directly by the parliament. This project, however, met with widespread criticism from social policy experts and government officials and never advanced beyond the early draft stage. The government, and especially the ministers of labor and finance, who had depended on the ZUS for effective collection of state revenues and implementation of social policy, were determined not to allow any such initiative to succeed. The general secretary in the Ministry of Finance commented bluntly on the Senate project: "[I]n regards to the proposed autonomy of the ZUS we need to emphasize that we cannot seriously consider any autonomy of an institution that implements the policy of the state and pays the benefits regulated by state law and guaranteed by the state."[49]

The legislative work on mandatory privatized pension funds continued under Bączkowski's successors, Jerzy Hausner and Ewa Lewicka, neither of whom advocated major changes in the structure of the ZUS, but who instead focused on keeping the momentum of reform through the time of the election campaign and change of government in 1998. The first package of legislation in this area was passed already under the ex-communist regime in 1997, but the second was approved a year later by the new Solidarity government. The legislative complexity of this undertaking, lengthy parliamentary debates, and the need to conduct consultations with the trade unions and other social organizations pushed the implementation date of the new system to January 1, 1999. The Bureau of the Special Government Representative for Social Insurance Reform (Biuro Pełnomocnika Rządu do Spraw Reformy Ubezpieczeń Społecznych), established by Bączkowski in August 1996, took the lead in coordinating efforts at reform. These efforts were officially conducted outside of the existing government structure by nonpolitical experts with the advice of the World Bank but in reality involved a carefully crafted political compromise. These difficult negotiations involved the Ministry of Finance, Ministry of Labor, and a number of powerful occupational lobbies, represented by different trade-union leaders, ex-communist politicians, and organizations of pensioners. Simultaneously, a related proposal to use the

48 Officially ZUS has been subject to "social control" by a special supervisory board that represents employers and employees, including the trade-union representatives and pensioners' delegates. During the initial period of transition this board has remained intact, staffed by the old guard, and its members traditionally have exercised very limited influence.

49 *Opinie do senackiego projektu inicjatywy ustawodawczej o ubezpieczeniach społecznych (MPiPS, MF, ZUS)* (Comments on the Senate legislative proposal on the reform of social insurance: Ministry of Labor and Social Policy, Ministry of Finance, Social Insurance Institution) (Warsaw: Biuro Studiów i Analiz Kancelarii Senatu, October 1992), 8 (manuscript for internal use). Translated by the author.

proceeds from privatization to finance the transition from the old to the new social security system was announced. Not surprisingly, as the budgetary crisis subsided and the economy continued to grow steadily at an average rate of 5 percent annually, this idea became extremely popular among the general public.[50]

The new pension scheme provides for mandatory participation in the new private pension funds by all persons born after January 1, 1969, and possible voluntary membership for employees and their families born after January 1, 1949. At the same time, the government pledged to protect the benefits and privileges of current pensioners and all those who would remain under the old system. These privileges still include some of the most popular but also most expensive entitlements, such as early retirement provisions for many professions and significantly lower retirement age for women.[51] In fact, union members working in traditionally well-paid occupations – for instance, in mining, steel industries, military, and police – have demanded a series of separate agreements that would protect their special pension rights inherited from the communist regime.[52] In addition, the authors of this reform have largely ignored the problem of the separate and heavily subsidized pension system for private farmers. This neglected aspect of the Polish social security reforms clearly shows the continuing detrimental impact of certain historical legacies, originating in the 1970s or even earlier. The institutional features of the new pension system also suggest a preference for continuity and a deep-seated anxiety about the long-term role of the state as the chief guarantor of social entitlements. The mandatory retirement funds are now subject to strict regulatory controls by the newly created government boards, granting licenses to private investment funds and watching over detailed investment guidelines. Furthermore, the ZUS not only preserved its central role as the distributor of benefits in the basic PAYG system but also was charged with the collection and recalculation of old-age benefits for the private funds.

The situation in Hungary was initially much less promising than in Poland, but to the surprise of many observers the reform breakthrough occurred relatively quickly and, according to some observers, rather unexpectedly.[53] One

[50] In the February 1996 referendum 90 percent of the voters supported the use of the proceeds from privatization to finance the new pension schemes. *Open Media Research Institute (OMRI) Daily Report*, February 20, 1996.

[51] Many female employees in Poland have continued to take advantage of early pension benefits from their state jobs while pursuing new career opportunities in the emerging private economy. See *Nowy System Emerytalny w Polsce, Pytania i Odpowiedzi* (The new pension system in Poland: Questions and answers) (Warsaw: Biuro Pełnomocnika Rządu do spraw Reformy Zabezpieczenia Społecznego, May 1998), 17–18.

[52] Ibid., 16–17.

[53] A recent World Bank report remarked that "[t]he factors that led the Government [in Hungary] to commit to a multi-pillar system in mid-1996 are not entirely clear" (Palacios and Rocha, 1997: 17).

possible reason for this change of pace in the reform process was growing pressure from foreign financial institutions. The economic stagnation of 1995 (see Table 7.2) and the conflicts within the ruling coalition caused considerable alarm among Western creditors who had long emphasized the urgency of pension reform in Hungary. For instance, in September 1995 the International Monetary Fund (IMF) delegation complained to Prime Minister Horn about the lack of progress in this crucial area. Yet, little action took place for another year, until April 1996, after the visiting vice-president of the World Bank, Johannes F. Linn, remarked publicly that by delaying a comprehensive reform of both the health and pension systems, Hungary risked a major financial disaster.[54]

Increased pressure from the international financial institutions and new disclosures of growing deficits in both the Health and Pension Funds could indeed be seen as two significant factors that finally compelled the Hungarian government to act. In mid-1996 both the Ministry of Labor and the Ministry of Finance approved the first draft of the revised pension proposals. However, the ex-communist regime had little incentive to seek immediate cooperation and approval for the social security reform from the major interest groups. The strong political position enjoyed by Horn and his new finance minister bought the MSzP/SzDSz coalition more time to delay the submission of the legislative draft to the parliament until May 1997. According to the World Bank experts, throughout this period the Hungarian policy makers continued to favor ad hoc temporary solutions that would prevent pension deficits rather than reform the social security system as a whole. Finally, in mid-1997, "some government officials and Parliamentarians realized the growing crisis of credibility facing the PAYG scheme and considered the multi-pillar solution as the one most likely to produce permanent results" (Palacios and Rocha, 1997: 17). In the light of the previous developments, we might argue that the "permanent results" meant in fact the attempt by both the pragmatists and the welfare state advocates (Kornai, 1995)[55] to institutionalize the fragile political consensus hastily put together by the most influential centrist leaders of the Socialist Party during 1996. The nature of this consensus reminds one of the uneasy truce between the economic reformers and the social policy establishment of the late 1980s and early 1990s. Moreover, the lingering institutional problems also indicate significant continuities with the past. One of these is the unresolved tension between the tendencies to decentralize and "democratize" social policy making and the legacy of tight executive controls that by design curtail both the autonomy of individual executive agencies and limit the outside input of organized lobbies.

54 *OMRI Reports*, September 21, 1995.

55 It is also interesting to note that after his dismissal from the post of finance minister Lajos Bokros went to Washington to work for the World Bank.

To a large extent the new Hungarian pension legislation reflects a rather tenuous compromise between these two opposing trends. Under this three-tier system, approximately two-thirds of the currently collected funds would function as a conventional PAYG scheme (a social assistance part plus an insurance-related part) and the remaining one-third would cover mandatory funded pensions. Many of the provisions, especially those creating new rules for the regulation of investment of these funds and protecting the present pensioners, are similar to those introduced in Poland. However, the Hungarian solution also contains many other important elements that indicate a distinct path of social policy development. One difference is the requirement of mandatory coverage only for the new entrants into the labor force, with a possibility of joining voluntarily for the rest of the working population. Also, the Hungarians opted for a more lax regulation of pension fund assets and for giving employers, rather than any government agency, the responsibility for collecting insurance contributions. This liberal policy toward employers, who also retained special privileges associated with the existing voluntary pension funds, contrasts with the rigid rules mandating state regulation of the amount of the minimum pension and advance setting of performance targets (minimum rates of return) for individual pension funds (Batty, 1997: 6–7).

These and other similar provisions testify to the fragile and often quite contradictory character of this pension reform settlement that was constructed on the basis of the two dramatically opposed positions. One of them is represented by the pragmatic politicians in the Ministry of Finance, employers, and the financial lobby eager to keep the state out of market regulation, whereas the other is favored by many social policy experts in the Ministry of Welfare, the Pension Fund, and a diverse group of union leaders and politicians with a long-standing record of resistance to both the strong state and liberal economics. In sum, even though outside forces and domestic socioeconomic considerations undoubtedly played a major role in the timing of this social security reform, country-specific legacies of the past have continued to influence the political dynamics and the final agreement on the new pension system, in effect laying the foundation for a Hungarian version of the postcommunist entitlement state that differs in many important respects from its Polish equivalent.

Conclusion

The main argument of this chapter is that the initial outcomes of social policy reforms undertaken during 1989–99 are indicative of country-specific historical experiences, before, during, and immediately after the end of communist rule. A comparative analysis of the politics of pension reform in Poland and Hungary reveals the pivotal importance of historical legacies and preexisting structures of policy making in shaping postcommunist social policy. The new democratic governments in East Central Europe inherited from their predecessors an amalgam of political, economic, and social problems and in many cases have consistently applied old, well-tested methods in trying to solve them. Poland and Hungary share four kinds of structural and institutional social policy legacies: (1) a traditional reliance on easily accessible social security benefits as a primary cure for economic inequality and/or political discontent; (2) an excessive concentration of power in the executive branch, especially in the areas of economic and social policy; (3) an effective mechanism of utilizing surplus social security funds to finance budgetary deficits and socioeconomic growth; and (4) long-standing patterns of managing social security deficits by making selective and often quite arbitrary cuts in the most vulnerable programs, such as sick or maternity pay and family benefits, rather than pensions. These common characteristics constitute necessary conditions for the emergence of the new entitlement states in East Central Europe. Their absence can help to explain the weakness of postcommunist "social safety nets" in other parts of the former Soviet bloc, as much as their presence demonstrates the apparent resilience of the Polish and Hungarian social security systems in transition (see also Kramer, 1997). At the institutional level of analysis, we can trace the first of these four legacies to the precommunist period and the second to the combined inheritance of the pre- and post-1945 era. The last two patterns of policy making mentioned earlier, however, are clearly the legacies of the "more mature" welfare system developed exclusively during the "state socialist" period. However, only by paying closer attention to the interactional level (see Ekiert and Hanson, Chapter 1 in this volume) can we actually explain why individual entitlement states in the postcommunist region have followed separate paths of development and how specific social policies have evolved in each country over a longer period of time.

Although both in Hungary and in Poland policy-making power has remained heavily concentrated in the executive branch (Bunce and Csanadi, 1993: 257) – that is, mainly in the Council of Ministers – the social policy coalitions in each country differed in their origins and composition. The Hungarian Finance Ministry and the narrow group of political leaders, most of whom had neither interest nor expertise in social security matters, became reluctant mediators in the struggle for pension reform between employers and the financial lobby on one hand and the trade unions, Ministry of Welfare, and the social policy community on the other. None of these groups, however, was powerful enough or possessed sufficient resources to assume the leadership role in the process of pension reform. Furthermore, even at the peak of their strength and popularity the most committed economic reformers, such as Prime Minister Horn, Minister of Finance Bokros, and other powerful leaders of the MSzP, continued to postpone decisive action in this area. Most likely they anticipated, with good reason, that the already weakened state apparatus would be quickly overwhelmed by the need to conduct simultaneous radical changes in economic and social policy. Because the social security administration had been traditionally decentralized and its bureaucrats lacked experience in dealing with intense emergency situations, it could not be easily relied upon to implement such a complex transition to a new pension system. Eventually, under intense outside pressure coming from the World Bank and the IMF, a small group of dedicated officials from the Ministries of Welfare and Finance began quietly to prepare the details of the compromise reform proposal.

In the absence of political resolve and in view of the institutional weakness of the main reform agents, the influence of the World Bank in Hungary became much more pronounced than in Poland, where the foreign role in creating the necessary political momentum for the reforms was limited largely to logistical and financial support. Still, the final Hungarian plan of pension reform did not adhere to all recommendations of foreign advisers. For instance, the employees and employers have retained a large degree of freedom to choose the type of old-age insurance that suits their needs, and the pension laws did little to prevent the continuing erosion of the state capacity to conduct socioeconomic policy and regulate the markets. This finding supports Ekiert's observation that "international factors should be seen as facilitating conditions, not as causes responsible for specific outcomes [of postcommunist transformations]" (Ekiert, Chapter 3 in this volume).

In Poland the efforts to reform social policy after 1989 were shaped mainly from the top of the government. The key bureaucracies and department heads, such as the ministers of labor, played the leading role in policy planning, just as they did in the past under the communist regime. Furthermore, the lines of division between the proponents and opponents of mandatory pensions often cut across not only the major political parties and the ruling coalitions, but also across the ministries and trade unions themselves, making it possible for determined reformers or policy entrepreneurs such as Minister Bączkowski to assemble a wide-ranging group of supporters. In contrast to Hungary, the Polish trade unions, and especially the representatives of powerful occupational groups, as well as employers, had little incentive to disrupt a system that had proved capable of guaranteeing generous benefits in a time of hardship. Thus, the first task of the reformers was to neutralize these highly concentrated and influential interests, as happened many times in the past, by promising generous protection of the present social payments, publicizing the benefits of reform among the increasingly influential younger generation of employees, and only then proceeding with more-fundamental changes in the system.

The Hungarian government officials faced a better situation in this respect because most of the pension rules in that country had been substantially simplified and unified under the communist regime in 1975. Also, in contrast to Poland, advancing liberalization of the economy and the emergence of a competitive party system pushed the Hungarian labor unions into defensive positions in the very early stage of transition, long before any major social security reform proposals were announced. However, even if the basic structure of decision making that minimized the influence of the outside-organized interests remained intact in Budapest, the decentralization of the pension and health administration in 1993 effectively slowed down the progress of pension reform until it was eventually phased out five years later.[56]

A successful strategy of pension reform depends not only on policy inheritances but also on existing institutional capacities (Pierson and Weaver, 1993). In Poland, government policy planners refused to tamper with centralized administrative control over social security largely because they viewed the Social Insurance Institution (ZUS) as the ideal vehicle for managing the welfare consequences of a failing economy. Actually, since 1935 all successive governments, including the left-wing coalition during 1993–97, benefited from the traditionally rigid ministerial control over the ZUS. The central social security administration had accumulated considerable experience in handling large-scale social and economic emergencies and thus was better prepared to handle social policy crises. These preexisting structures and policy legacies enabled individual reform-minded politicians, such as the two ministers of labor, Jacek Kuroń and Andrzej Bączkowski, to play an instrumental role in opening up the decision-making process and to forge a broad proreform coalition, consisting of Finance Ministry officials, independent experts, the two major trade unions, and other major social groups. Hence, the political struggle over the privatization of pensions concluded with a relatively widespread social consensus in Poland, but in Hungary the reform agreement emerged only as a result of a reluctant compromise, negotiated under intense foreign pressure mostly by a deeply divided government and relatively few outside actors.

The continuation of old institutional forms and policy patterns alongside the emerging ones have helped stabilize the new democracies in East Central Europe during the 1990s, but as the reform progresses and the old structures begin to fade away, the emerging entitlement states will most likely become much more vulnerable to sudden crises. As long as the economy performs fairly well, governments can claim credit for the anticipated success of pension reforms before any actual changes become a reality. If this trend does not continue, however, the consensus on the future of social security may not last very long. We must remember that after 1989 government policy makers, state bureaucrats, social organizations, and the community of welfare experts were forced to reexamine their traditional roles in accordance with new political and economic circumstances. The legacies of bureaucratic centralization and relatively efficient fiscal regulation helped them to survive the social and political turmoil of the first decade of transition,

56 Self-government of the Pension Board was eliminated in the summer of 1998 (Müller, 1999: 65).

but such tendencies also clashed with the growing demands for a more open and democratic system of policy management. This situation exacerbated political conflicts over the direction of social security reform and often paralyzed the government. Clearly, finding a resolution to this dilemma is essential not only for the success of pension reforms but also for the whole process of democratic consolidation in East Central Europe. Whether such a resolution is actually achieved will depend on the kind of historical legacies that remain relevant in the next stage of transition and on the extent of institutionalization of new policy patterns compatible with the rapidly changing political and socioeconomic reality.

References

Anderson, Stephen J. 1993. *Welfare Policy and Politics in Japan: Beyond the Developmental State.* New York: Paragon House.

Antal, Kálmánné, János Réri, Ádám Résmovits, and Miklós Toldi. 1995. Pension Outlay and Changes in the Pension System in the Nineties. In Péter Bod, ed., *Human Resources and Social Stability during Transition in Hungary*, pp. 200–15. Budapest: Institute for World Economics of the Hungarian Academy of Sciences; San Francisco: International Center for Economic Growth.

Balcerowicz, Leszek. 1995. Understanding Postcommunist Transitions. In Larry Diamond and Marc F. Plattner, eds., *Economic Reform and Democracy*, pp. 86–100. Baltimore: Johns Hopkins University Press.

Barr, Nicholas, ed. 1994. *Labor Markets and Social Policy in Central and Eastern Europe: The Transition and Beyond.* Washington, D.C.: World Bank; New York: Oxford University Press.

Batty, Ian. 1997. Mandatory Pension Funds in Hungary and Poland. *Benefits and Compensation International* 4: 2–7.

Beck, Ernest. 1996. What Next with the Hungarian Austerity Program? *Wall Street Journal Europe/Gazeta Wyborcza* (in Polish), March 11, 8.

Borowczyk, Ewa. 1991. Organizacja ubezpieczeń społecznych. In Czesław Jackowiak, ed., *Rozwój ubezpieczeń społecznych w Polsce*, pp. 239–53. Wrocław: Ossolineum.

Bossanyi, Katalin. 1995. Taking Stock of the Economic Transition. *Hungarian Quarterly* 36(138): 90–105.

Bunce, Valerie, and Maria Csanadi. 1993. Uncertainty in the Transition: Post-Communism in Hungary. *East European Politics and Societies* 2: 240–85.

Cain, Michael J. G., and Aleksander Surdej. 1999. Transitional Politics or Public Choice? Evaluating Stalled Pension Reforms in Poland. In Linda J. Cook, Mitchell A. Orenstein, and Marilyn Rueschemeyer, eds., *Left Parties and Social Policy in Postcommunist Europe*, pp. 145–74. Boulder, Colo.: Westview Press.

Castles, Francis G. 1978. *The Social Democratic Image of Society: A Study of the Achievements and Origins of Scandinavian Social Democracy in Comparative Perspective.* London: Routledge and Kegan Paul.

1986. Whatever Happened to the Communist Welfare State? *Studies in Comparative Communism* 3–4.

Chłoń, Agnieszka, Marek Góra, and Michał Rutkowski. 1999. *Shaping Pension Reform in Poland: Security Through Diversity*. Washington, D.C.: World Bank Report (Pension Primer manuscript).

Comisso, Ellen. 1995. Legacies of the Past or New Institutions: The Struggle over Restitution in Hungary. *Comparative Political Studies* 2: 200–38.

Cook, Linda J., Mitchell A. Orenstein, and Marilyn Rueschemeyer, eds. 1999. *Left Parties and Social Policy in Postcommunist Europe*. Boulder, Colo.: Westview Press.

Deacon, Bob, ed. 1992. *Social Policy, Social Justice, and Citizenship in Eastern Europe*. Averbury: Aldershot.

Diamond, Peter A., David C. Lindeman, and Howard Young. 1996. *Social Security: What Role for the Future?* Washington, D.C.: National Academy of Social Insurance.

Ekiert, Grzegorz. 1996. *The State against Society: Political Crises and Their Aftermath in East Central Europe*. Princeton: Princeton University Press.

1997. Rebellious Poles: Political Crises and Popular Protest under State Socialism, 1945–1989. *East European Politics and Societies* 2 (Spring): 299–338.

Esping-Andersen, Gøsta. 1989. The Three Political Economies of the Welfare State. *Canadian Review of Sociology and Anthropology* 1: 10–36.

Ferge, Zsuzsa. 1979. *A Society in the Making: Hungarian Social and Societal Policy, 1945–1975*. London: Penguin.

Gedeon, Péter. 1995. Hungary: Social Policy in Transition. *East European Politics and Societies* 3 (Fall): 433–58.

Golinowska, Stanisława. 1999. Political Actors and Reform Paradigms. In Katharina Muller, Andreas Ryll, and Hans Jurgen Wagener, eds., *Transformation of Social Security: Pensions in Central and Eastern Europe*, pp. 173–99. Heidelberg: Physica-Verlag.

Heclo, Hugh. 1974. *Modern Social Policies in Britain and Sweden: From Relief to Income Maintenance*. New Haven: Yale University Press.

Hicks, Alexander M., and Duane H. Swank. 1992. Politics, Institutions, and Welfare Spending in Industrialized Democracies, 1960–82. *American Political Science Review* 3: 658–74.

Huber, Evelyne. 1995. *Options for Social Policy in Latin America: Neo-Liberal versus Social-Democratic Models*. Geneva: United Nations Research Institute for Social Development.

Hungarian Welfare State in Transition: Structure, Initial Reforms and Recommendations. 1994. Joint Hungarian-International Blue Ribbon Commission and Hudson Institute, Policy Study no. 3, February.

Inglot, Tomasz. 1994. The Communist Legacy and the Postcommunist Politics of Welfare: The Origins, Evolution, and Transformation of Social Policy in Poland from the 1920s to 1993. Ph.D. dissertation, University of Wisconsin at Madison.

Kingson, Eric R., and James H. Schulz. 1996. *Social Security in the Twenty-first Century*. New York: Oxford University Press.

Kocsis, Györgi. 1995. Stabilization through Restriction. *Hungarian Quarterly* 138 (Summer): 6–7.

Kornai, János. 1995. A Steep Road. Interview by László Zolt Szabo. *Hungarian Quarterly* 138 (Summer): 11–20.

Korpi, Walter. 1983. *The Democratic Class Struggle*. London: Routledge and Kegan Paul.

Kramer, Mark. 1997. Social Protection Policies and Safety Nets in East-Central Europe: Dilemmas of the Postcommunist Transformation. In Ethan B. Kapstein and Michael Mandelbaum, eds., *Sustaining the Transition: The Social Safety Net in Postcommunist Europe*, pp. 46–123. New York: Council on Foreign Relations.

Langenkamp, Daniel. 1996. Inside Hungarian Politics. *Budapest Week*, September 5–11, 7.

Malloy, James. 1979. *The Politics of Social Security in Brazil*. Pittsburgh: University of Pittsburgh Press.

Mering, Wojciech. 1992. Obyś zasiłkami dzielił. *Zycie Gospodarcze* 22: 4.

Milanovic, Branko. 1998. *Income, Inequality and Poverty during the Transition from Planned to Market Economy*. Washington, D.C.: World Bank.

Millar, James R., and Sharon L. Wolchik. 1994. *The Social Legacy of Communism*. New York: Woodrow Wilson Center Press; Cambridge: Cambridge University Press.

Minkoff, Jack, and Lynn Turgeon. 1977. Income Maintenance in the Soviet Union in Eastern and Western Perspective. In Irving L. Horowitz, ed., *Equity, Income and Policy: Comparative Studies of Three Worlds of Development*. New York: Praeger.

Mizsei, Katalin. 1994. Recipes for Growth. *Hungarian Quarterly* 135 (Autumn): 68–79.

Müller, Katharina. 1999. *The Political Economy of Pension Reform in Central-Eastern Europe*. Cheltenham: Edward Elgar.

Müller, Katharina, Andreas Ryll, and Hans Jurgen Wagener, eds. 1999. *Transformation of Social Security: Pensions in Central and Eastern* Europe. Heidelberg: Physica-Verlag.

Nowy system emerytalny w Polsce, Pytania i odpowiedzi (The new pension system in Poland: Questions and answers). 1998. Warsaw: Biuro Pełnomocnika Rzadu do spraw Reformy Zabezpieczenia Społecznego.

Offe, Claus. 1993. The Politics of Social Policy in East European Transitions: Antecedents, Agents, and Agenda for Reform. *Social Research* 4: 649–84.

Opinie do senackiego projektu inicjatywy ustawodawczej o ubezpieczeniach społecznych. 1992. Warsaw: Biuro Studiów i Analiz Kancelarii Senatu (manuscript for internal use), October.

Palacios, Robert, and Roberto Rocha. 1997. *The Hungarian Pension System in Transition*. Washington, D.C.: World Bank Report, November.

Pataki, Judith. 1993. A New Era in Hungary's Social Security Administration. *RFE/RL Research Reports* 27, July 2.

Pestoff, Victor A. 1995. Reforming Social Services in Central and East Europe: Meso-Level Institutional Change after the Fall of Communism. *American Behavioral Scientist* 5 (March–April): 788–808.

Pierson, Paul. 1994. *Dismantling the Welfare State? Reagan, Thatcher, and the Politics of Retrenchment*. Cambridge: Cambridge University Press.

1996. The New Politics of Welfare State. *World Politics* 48 (January): 143–79.

Pierson, Paul, and Kent R. Weaver. 1993. Imposing Losses in Pension Policy. In R. Kent Weaver and Bert A. Rockman, eds., *Do Institutions Matter? Government Capabilities in the United States and Abroad*, pp. 110–50. Washington, D.C.: Brookings Institution.

Program reformy ubezpieczeń społecznych. 1995. Government document. Warsaw: Ministry of Labor and Social Policy, December.

Przeworski, Adam. 1993. Economic Reforms, Public Opinion, and Political Institutions: Poland in the Eastern European Perspective. In Luiz Carlos Bresser Pereira, José María Maravall, and Adam Przeworski, eds., *Economic Reforms in New Democracies: A Social Democratic Approach*. Cambridge: Cambridge University Press.

Seleny, Anna. 1999. Old Political Rationalities and New Democracies: Compromise and Confrontation in Hungary and Poland. *World Politics* 51 (July): 484–519.

Skocpol, Theda. 1993. *Protecting Soldiers and Mothers: The Political Origins of Social Policy in the United States*. Cambridge, Mass.: Harvard University Press.

Smith, Paula Bailey. 1996. Hungarian Politics and the Bokros Economic Program. *Woodrow Wilson Center for East European Studies: Meeting Report*, July–August: 7.

Stark, David, and László Bruszt. 1998. *Postsocialist Pathways: Transforming Politics and Property in East Central Europe*. Cambridge: Cambridge University Press.

Stephens, John D. 1979. *The Transition from Capitalism to Socialism*. London: Macmillan.

Topiński, Wojciech, and Marian Wiśniewski. 1991. *Projekt systemu dodatkowych ubezpieczeń emerytalno-rentowych*. Warsaw. Unpublished manuscript.

Torfing, Jacob. 1998. *Politics, Regulation and the Modern Welfare State*. New York: St. Martin's Press.

Wilensky, Harold. 1975. *The Welfare State and Equality*. Berkeley: University of California Press.

8

Postcommunist Unemployment Politics

Historical Legacies and the Curious Acceptance of Job Loss

Phineas Baxandall

Just as social scientists failed to predict the fall of communism, they did not predict the central political issues of postcommunism. Unemployment was supposed to be the great threat to postcommunist political stability. It was anticipated that unemployment might present the greatest danger to political support for the transition to liberal democracy. Scholars joined journalists and politicians to warn of the political fallout if unemployment were to increase precipitously.[1]

These were not unfounded prognostications. A long literature in political science suggests that even short-term economic hardship can erode political support, and unemployment is considered a basic benchmark for blaming the government.[2] In Eastern Europe a number of factors were thought to make the political threat of unemployment especially grave. Basic job security was taken for granted under communist rule. It was proclaimed as a fundamental right and framed as a basic criterion for government legitimacy. Newly elected governments after the fall of communism inherited social welfare institutions that not only were ill-prepared to handle mass unemployment; they also threatened to magnify the pain of job loss because many workplaces delivered social services such as childcare or housing (Rein, Friedman, and Worgotter, 1996).

Moreover, the economic downturn after the fall of communism was sharper than any had anticipated and was especially steep in industrial production where most jobs would be lost. The adoption of Western-style markets were expected to entail some unemployment; but the COMECON

[1] Evans and Whitefield (1993: 532), for instance, predicted unemployment to be first among the "formative issues" of postcommunist politics. See also Przeworski (1991); Offe (1992). The dismay is clear in Javeline's account: "They are not taking to the streets and bringing life in the country to a standstill. Russia is not becoming Indonesia" (2003: introduction).

[2] See, for example, Heclo (1974: 65); Robertson (1984); Morris (1985); Warwick (1992); Piven and Cloward (1993: 6–7); Anderson (1995: 88); Saint-Paul (1996).

trading arrangements that had previously guaranteed markets for Warsaw Pact countries were surprisingly dismantled overnight, leaving firms scrambling to find new customers and suppliers. Many firms that might have been able to navigate these problems failed because of a lack of banking infrastructure to substitute for old sources of state credit (Amsden, Kochanowicz, and Taylor, 1994; Jacoby, 2000: 133). Even firms that remained afloat tended to reduce their staffing levels to cut costs. The fall in GDP across the region was greater than the Great Depression had been in the West (Aslund, 1992).

Yet political stability survived. In fact, throughout most of the region unemployment virtually disappeared as a political issue at the same time that unemployment rates skyrocketed. The general deterioration of economic conditions certainly did contribute to the unpopularity of postcommunist governments, but unemployment was surprisingly not the focus of how people made judgments about the economy and the competency of economic rule. When the 1992 New Democracies Barometer asked citizens in nine former communist countries whether they were more worried about unemployment or inflation, unemployment lost out by a ratio of almost two to one. Over the following three years inflation generally abated throughout the region (from a median rate of 93 percent to 28 percent), while unemployment increased; yet the follow-up poll in 1995 found that the fear of inflation relative to unemployment had moved in the opposite direction, widening to almost three to one (Rose, 1997).[3] Postcommunist survey data even show that support of government responsibility for unemployment assistance is significantly weaker than for other social programs (Lipsmeyer, 2001). While any indicator of an issue's political salience is bound to be problematic, it is safe to say that across the postcommunist world unemployment has been a less politically volatile matter than other economic issues, such as privatization, pensions, and wage arrears.[4]

Don't Legacies Matter?

One conclusion that might be drawn is that historical legacies don't matter. Or perhaps postcommunist unemployment politics suggests that causal arguments about historical legacies can show merely that "things stay the same

[3] Anxiety about the relative threat of unemployment versus inflation was not a simple function of the rates of these measures in a country. In Belarus, for instance, the lowest portion of people felt inflation was the larger threat, despite the fact that unemployment was low and hyperinflation ran at 1,500 percent. Rose found that macroeconomic conditions explain a "trivial" amount of the variations in people's perceived relative threat. In a separate study using this data to examine four postcommunist elections from 1992 to 1994, Harper (2000) finds no statistically significant relationship between unemployment and voting against incumbents.

[4] For an attempt to measure and explain differences in the political salience of unemployment across the European Union, see Baxandall (2001b).

until they change" – a kind of post hoc deterministic contingency. But I will show that if we closely examine how the political taboo against unemployment was established and sustained, we then get a different kind of picture.[5] Instead of merely arguing over whether historical legacies or transitional politics are responsible for postcommunist outcomes, we can understand the interaction between these kinds of effects. We see that the communist legacy of a taboo against unemployment varies systematically across countries and that the new circumstances of postcommunist liberalization have sometimes reinforced and sometimes been at odds with the inherited taboo against unemployment.

This chapter argues that the mechanisms that dispelled the unemployment taboo can only be understood as the result of distinct counterlegacies from the late communist period. The political taboo against unemployment was not an inherent feature of communist regimes or their one-party rule, Marxist-Leninist ideology, or central economic planning. Postcommunism inherited a historical taboo against unemployment along with other, sometimes competing, legacies from different time periods. The challenge is to disentangle one such legacy from other self-reinforcing chains of causality.[6] Using the Hungarian case and extending it for comparative analysis to Poland, Russia, and East Germany (GDR), I argue that there existed under communism a political feedback loop that sustained the taboo against unemployment, but under late communism it was supplanted by an alternative feedback loop that negated much of the political salience of the unemployment taboo.

I show this by demonstrating how the taboo was based on a particular conception of unemployment that was defined against a particular model of the state employment relationship. The Communist Party's commitments to eradicate unemployment provided definite microlevel mechanisms that reinforced the inherited disapproval of unemployment.[7] The political commitment created its own microlevel "barriers to exit" because once the eradication of unemployment became an established benchmark for the competency of economic rule it then became more politically costly to reintroduce unemployment. The presumption of full employment was further embedded in new social policies that delivered benefits through employers. Employment was typically an administrative precondition for receiving most social

[5] This is not to say that arguments about historical legacies are not ripe for such post hoc abuse. See, for example, Porter (1990).

[6] Mahoney (2000) distinguishes between two kinds of path dependence in historical explanation. He distinguishes, on the one hand, "self-reinforcing sequences" where there are mechanisms in which particular social outcomes make similar patterns more likely in the future from, on the other hand, "reactive sequences" in which a chain of events depends upon previous events, perhaps from a contingent outcome at a critical juncture. This chapter focuses on the first kind of path dependence.

[7] See Pierson (2000) for a discussion of the microfoundations of path dependence in politics.

benefits, which made the prospect of job loss represent an even greater social exile. Once legitimacy had been established along particular benchmarks, this also created political "returns to scale" for individuals who subsequently sought to claim credit for their accomplishments. Once "success" had been defined in terms of eradicating unemployment, there was an incentive to claim success along the same lines. Petty officials, supreme leaders, and even aggrieved workers could justify their own ends in terms pursuant to the established goal of eradicating unemployment. In doing so, individuals both benefited from the norm against unemployment and simultaneously reinforced its perceived priority.

Such self-reinforcing patterns, however, began to erode the political threat of unemployment when entrepreneurship was officially embraced as an alternative kind of work relationship. Under post-Stalinism, the informal economy and multiple job holding began to proliferate in different countries with different timing, speed, and official recognition. The indirect effect was to create various mechanisms of self-reinforcing "returns to scale," which undermined the salience of unemployment as a political issue and as a focus of the struggles of organized labor. Once workers received incomes from a variety of sources, job loss no longer seemed so grave a threat. The self-employed might sometimes lack income, but they could not lose their means of livelihood and identity in the radically severe sense that employees could. Once workers became increasingly oriented toward the second economy as their means of opportunity and advancement, they also became less inclined toward union militancy in their official main jobs. This in turn made it easier for employers to cut wages and thereby make "main" jobs still less important. As governments had difficulty collecting taxes on secondary and informal work, they were forced to raise taxes on officially registered work and thereby created even greater incentives for people to avoid official registration. And once "entrepreneurship" was embraced as a public virtue, then individuals could claim credit or justify their own selfish goals in terms of promoting "entrepreneurship" in much the same way that they had earlier claimed to be championing universal employment in state enterprises. Framing success in terms of entrepreneurship recast unemployment as a secondary issue.

Understanding the dynamic basis for the taboo against unemployment also helps explain why unemployment has been more politically important in some postcommunist countries than others. In places where there was continuity in the old industrial factory prototype of employment (such as East Germany, parts of Poland, Hungarian steel towns, and among miners from Russia to Romania) unemployment has had greater political salience. In other places, where the distinction between employment and unemployment has been eroded, job loss had comparatively less political salience. The argument is not that Hungarians and Russians were not really suffering whereas East Germans and Poles were. On the contrary, Hungarians lost jobs in great numbers and Russians lost their paychecks, while Poles enjoyed relatively generous compensation from the state and much of East German unemployment was disguised by improvised apprenticeship programs and public works. Postcommunist citizens suffered job loss in different ways, and the challenge is to explain why some kinds of losses were more politically salient than others. For the most part, my discussion of postcommunism is restricted to the early 1990s because this is the period when unemployment was supposed to have been so politically disruptive.

Alternative Explanations for the Political Acceptance of Unemployment

Among the various hypotheses for why unemployment lost its political taboo in Eastern Europe, let us consider the most obvious explanations.

Return to Europe?

One possible explanation is that unemployment was accepted as normal in the context of the larger transition to market democracy and a broadly understood "return to Europe." Incumbent politicians undoubtedly tried to push the view that unemployment should be accepted as a necessary feature of economic restructuring. One Czechoslovak economics minister famously quipped that if unemployment failed to reach high levels, "It would be a sign that the reforms were not working."[8] Western advisers repeated this same message. In Hungary, the 1990 Blue Ribbon Commission, which included Western economists, recommended that the new government should copy the West as quickly as possible. They urged that mass unemployment should be seen as a sign of success rather than failure (Blue Ribbon Commission, 1990). East European elites, enticed by a vision of integration with Western Europe, must have also recognized that European Union unemployment was also rising into double digits during this period.

These may be accurate descriptions of how unemployment was normalized, but they do not constitute an explanation of why this occurred. A large body of research on postcommunist norms indicates persistent continuities in political values from the communist era.[9] The "return to Europe" is an

[8] *Financial Times*, February 6, 1991. The minister is Vladimir Dlouhy.

[9] As late as the end of 1993, 84 percent of Hungarians agreed that the state should be mainly responsible for employment (Miller, White, and Heywood, 1998: 114). Almost half (47 percent) of Hungarians held that "unemployment is unacceptable" and only 8 percent agreed that "unemployment is necessary" (1998: 117). When asked about societal goals in 1988, "full employment" was regarded as more important than "freedom," "democracy," "national independence," or "efficient economic reform." Other research that traces the strong legacy of communist-era norms on postcommunist political evaluations, especially regarding issues of social justice, includes Rose and Makkai (1993); Csepeli et al. (1994); Csepeli and Örkény (1994); Örkény and Csepeli (1994); Blanchflower and Freeman (1997); Miller, White, and Heywood (1998).

important feature of postcommunist transformation but, especially given the resurgence of other national particularities,[10] it could just as easily explain why Eastern postcommunist polities might cling to the job securities that had distinguished their societies. In the former GDR, for instance, the absorption into West Germany made East Germans more nostalgic for the old security.[11] The general trend toward "Europeanization" tells us nothing about *which* norms will be swept away and which will become badges of political distinction.[12]

Generous Unemployment Benefits?

Another possible explanation is that the generosity of unemployment benefits defused the political threat of the unemployment bomb. Bartlett supports this view, describing a "politically inert population of hard-core unemployed workers who were far more inclined to stay on the public dole than to undertake active opposition to market reforms" (Bartlett, 1997: 230).

This view is triply flawed. First, the unemployed generally are politically marginal and have great difficulty mobilizing collective action. The political threat posed by unemployment is posed by the discontent of employed workers who are more politically influential and who worry about losing their jobs (Saint-Paul, 1996).[13] Second, as a wide literature on voting and public opinion concludes, the political opposition arising from unemployment does not come directly from the effect it has on people's incomes, but instead results indirectly through changes in citizens' interpretations about the economy and government culpability. People tend to view the state of the economy based on "sociotropic" or collective evaluations, rather than "pocketbook" or personal ones (Fiorina, 1981; Kinder and Kiewiet, 1981; Lau and Sears, 1981; Kinder and Mebane, 1983). Indicators of *perceived* business conditions are a consistently better predictor of how people

[10] It was not the case that unemployment was lost as a political issue simply because political energies were absorbed in ethnic-nationalist crises. Popular discontent about job loss has fed the flames of ethnic separatism in less cohesive states, such as the former Soviet republics, and has fostered virulent racism and antiimmigrant violence in other places, such as East Germany. Ethnic-nationalist crises might serve as a partial explanation for why surging unemployment was not politically salient in places like Yugoslavia or Soviet Georgia but not in Hungary, where there has been no similar intensity of ethnic conflict.

[11] On societies' tendency to magnify small distinctions as a means of affirming solidarity, see Freud's discussion of "the narcissism of minor differences" (1961: 72).

[12] The "return to Europe" thesis would also suggest that political parties had no significant differences on their stances toward unemployment because they closely conformed to "European" norms. But studies of citizen perceptions of the parties on major issues at the end of 1993 shows that voters did not perceive their stances on unemployment as any less dispersed than on other issues (Karajánnisz, 1994).

[13] On the difficulties of mobilizing organizations of the unemployed in postcommunist Hungary, see Betlen (1993).

vote than are surveys of personal financial well-being (Kinder and Mebane, 1983).[14]

Finally, a closer look at the unemployment benefit system shows that benefits were not generous enough to support recipients. As a result of decades of public denigration of the jobless as social parasites, unemployment also carried a strong social stigma.[15] Postcommunist unemployment benefits across the region were generally linked to minimum wages that were not inflation-indexed and fell far below minimum subsistence levels (Standing and Vaughan-Whitehead, 1995). In Hungary in the beginning of 1994, most unemployment benefits were indexed to the minimum wage, which was only 73 percent of the minimum subsistence level (Standing and Vaughan-Whitehead, 1995: 22). Only 43 percent of Hungarian unemployment insurance recipients at the end of 1993 received benefits over the official subsistence level, and according to an International Labor Organization (ILO) study the official subsistence level actually covered only 64 percent of the most modest costs of living (Frey, 1994b). If generous benefits defused the political bomb of job loss, then we would expect unemployment to have been the least politically contentious where benefits were most generous. Polish benefits were substantially more generous than neighboring countries, but rather than defuse opposition, Poland experienced especially strong militancy against unemployment.

Rapid Job Turnover?

Similarly, it was not the case that unemployment could be ignored because people moved quickly into new jobs. The oft-voiced hope was that a booming private sector would create demand for unemployed workers and make spells of joblessness brief. If this were the case, it could account for the low political salience of even high levels of short-lived unemployment spells. But despite political rhetoric suggesting that the unemployed were necessary to provide staffing for new enterprises, unemployment spells instead tended to be long-term and lead to exit from the labor market rather than to

[14] "Only very few citizens are motivated to vote against the incumbent simply because they see their financial situation has deteriorated. In election surveys from these six nations, retrospective personal economic circumstance (no matter how it is measured) virtually always fails to register statistically significant main effects on legislative vote" (Lewis-Beck, 1988: 155). The exception is U.S. presidential elections, where there is a mild but significant effect (Kiewiet, 1983: 49; Markus, 1988). Evidence from postcommunist countries shows that individuals who suffer greater economic hardship are less likely to express support for the political system but sociotropic interpretations still dominate these effects (McIntosh and MacIver, 1992; McIntosh et al., 1994; Mishler and Rose, 1996).

[15] In a comparative study with the Netherlands, 66 percent of Hungarians said that they were ashamed of being unemployed, compared with 20 percent in the Netherlands. Only 6 and 7 percent of Hungarians agreed with the statement that unemployment was respectively a freedom or that it was good because their leisure time increased – compared with 49 and 48 percent who agreed with these statements in the Netherlands (Simon, 1997).

private employment. Where unemployment rates climbed highest in Eastern Europe, it was precisely because of the very long jobless spells that people suffered. Even with relatively modest inflows to unemployment, the stock of unemployed tended to grow rapidly because there was little outflow from unemployment (Köllö, 1995b; Koltay, 1995). The characteristic pattern of postcommunist unemployment was not one of constant job turnover but that of a stagnant pool. This pattern should, if anything, increase our expectation that political resistance would arise from layoffs.

Something else must explain why the unemployment lost its political bite. To explain the disappearance of the unemployment taboo, it is important to understand where it came from in the first place.

Origins of the Communist Unemployment Taboo

In order to understand the mechanisms for continuity and change in unemployment politics, we need to get past simple notions that automatically associate communism with the absence of unemployment. The "eradication" of unemployment is not an ineluctable systemic feature of state socialism; nor can it be read directly from Leninist ideology (Baxandall, 2000). Unskilled and undisciplined workers were not infrequently dismissed, and certain groups like gypsies or young women often had great difficulty finding employment, especially in certain subregions (Fazekas and Köllö, 1990; Cook, 1993: 54–55).[16]

The aversion to particular kinds of joblessness *became* a fundamental priority for communist regimes over time. Like the QWERTY keyboard configuration on a typewriter or other favorite examples of path-dependent arguments, the abolition of unemployment was quasi-accidental rather than prefigured in the inherited ideas themselves.[17] Once established, however, full employment became entrenched. As David Lane observes, "in the early period of Soviet power, industrialization and economic growth" became "the primary objective of the Soviet government, but once full employment had been achieved, it became a sacred element in Soviet social policy" (Lane, 1987).

The supposed eradication of Soviet unemployment was an expression of the regime's aspirations for a new prototype of labor allocation. In the 1920s the number of those recognized as employed grew steadily, but so did registered levels of unemployment.[18] The unemployed remained at about

[16] The Soviet press reported that over a million workers were dismissed from industrial enterprises in 1964, 30 to 35 percent illegally (CIA, 1967: 12).

[17] On the argument that subsequent discovery of more-efficient configurations could not alter the QWERTY configuration of typewriter keys because it was embedded in physical capital and habit, see David (1985). For a critique, see Sabel (1995).

[18] Those recognized as employed included independent workers and salaried employees.

10 percent of the labor force throughout the middle and latter part of the decade (Markus, 1936; Baykov, 1947). Unemployment was primarily caused by the migration of surplus agricultural population from the villages toward the relative affluence and job growth in towns and cities. Government policies in the end of the 1920s were aimed at industrialization and improving labor discipline and were relatively unconcerned about unemployment. As Davies argues,

> In preparing to industrialize the Soviet Union, Soviet political leaders and officials were at first pessimistic about the prospects for eliminating mass unemployment.... [T]he deliberate aim of eliminating unemployment quickly was not a decisive factor in the switch to rapid industrialization between 1927 and 1929. Unemployment was not a prominent issue in the speeches of Stalin and his associates justifying accelerated industrialization; these were primarily couched in terms of such factors as the need to overtake the capitalist countries in the interests of the defense of the USSR, and to provide the base for the industrialization of peasant agriculture. (1986: 25)

The end of unemployment was an administrative and classificatory fact that only secondarily became politically important. In late 1929 Soviet officials in the final draft of the first five-year plan had still anticipated that unemployment levels of half a million would continue through 1933 (Schwartz, 1951). But the 1930s began a campaign for labor discipline and against job turnover that accidentally eliminated unemployment. "Quitters" were denounced in newspapers and bulletin boards, and unions and Communist Party cells were urged to expel them from their ranks. Workers were urged to sign a pledge stating that they would not leave their job (Christian, 1985: 97). As part of this campaign, new administrative measures greatly restricted eligibility for unemployment benefits, which brought down the number of registered unemployed. Christian argues that "the elimination of unemployment was as big a surprise to the Soviet government as to anyone else." He explains that the liquidation of unemployment, announced in an October 1930 decree, "was in fact little more than a retrospective justification for a number of other measures designed to tighten labor discipline, one of which was the abolition of unemployment benefits" (Christian, 1985: 89).

The new regulations of 1930 corresponded chronologically with the preparation of a new model for allocating workers to jobs. Unveiled in 1931, the Soviet Orgnabor system was initiated to recruit individuals directly and place workers in specific enterprises, unlike under the previous system, which had adjusted labor flows through incentives, general directives, and quotas. Orgnabor was primarily meant to supply the industrial establishments that were clamoring for more workers with labor from collective farms that planners viewed as largely redundant. By the internal logic of this system, no workers could be without a job, because individuals were officially prohibited from seeking new jobs on their own, and the state directly placed workers into available jobs (Markus, 1936; Baykov, 1947; Davies, 1986).

Even transitory or "frictional" unemployment was thought to be eliminated since surplus workers were placed in new positions by the state before they would be laid off. Much as this model fit the ideal vision of socialist planning and "totalitarian" pictures painted by western Cold War scholars, it never came close to being the dominant form of allocating labor in the Soviet Union.[19] It was, however, the *prototype* of employment placement against which unemployment was conceived to be wholly eradicated, a legacy that persisted far longer than the push for the Orgnabor system itself.

Origins of the Unemployment Taboo in Hungary

Similarly in Hungary the period of most hard-core and doctrinaire Hungarian communism during the early 1950s paid little political attention to the eradication of unemployment per se. The early Stalinist leadership led by Mátyás Rákosi instead viewed all workers outside of state industry as underutilized and viewed displaced workers as a necessary concomitant of rapid industrialization. The eradication of unemployment emerged as an independently important claim for regime legitimacy only after the popular uprising of 1956 and the regime's subsequent attempt to establish broader public support.

Once Russian tanks had cleared the streets in 1956, the first major policy resolution of the new leadership denounced the pre-1956 "ruling clique's disregard for the rise of working people's living standards" (Berend, 1990: 31). In a 1958 speech to the Ironworkers' Congress, the new party secretary János Kádár explained, "We have learned that socialism cannot be built without the support of the masses. And raising the living standards is part and parcel of socialist construction" (*Hungarian Trade Union News* [January 1958]: 6). Party documents from this time began to refer to the state's "provisioning responsibility" (*ellátási kötelezettség*). This was a distinct break from the previous ideas of the party that had portrayed consumption as something to be nobly deferred. State wages were increased 11.4 percent in 1956 and a further 17.9 percent in 1957 – even though the existing five-year plan had originally sought average gains of less than 5 percent for those years (Adam, 1984: 234). Economic policies turned decidedly more proconsumption, including a renewed emphasis on the production of consumer durables and a steady growth in pensions and other, mostly employment-based, social benefits. The party still preferred "social consumption," but rising living standards became an end in themselves.

19 "For the majority of Soviet workers in the 1930s, the existence of a highly authoritarian government, willing to use harsh sanctions against its population to achieve its end, nonetheless did not mean the end of freedom to choose their place of work" (Barber, 1986: 63). At most a quarter of new labor entrants were ever placed by Orgnabor, and most did not remain long in their allocated jobs before seeking higher wages or benefits (Lane, 1987: 44).

The post-1956 regime restored political stability on the basis of an implicit social compromise: the party-state ensured rising living standards in exchange for popular political quiescence.[20] The class war was officially declared to be over, and the state increasingly came to tolerate informal initiatives that fell outside the law, so long as they did not threaten communist rule. Kádár replaced Stalin's stated principle that "those who are not with us are against us" with one proclaiming that: "those who are not against us are with us." Permitting citizens to retreat to their domestic life placed increased importance on the employment relationship as the nexus of political life: an ongoing connection where Hungarians received propaganda, participated in works councils, and were provided with basic benefits. Worker involvement in the factory was intended not only to boost productivity and work effort but also to foster cooperative political attitudes and an attachment to socialism (Hethy and Mako, 1979; Bielasiak, 1981). *Un*employment took on the new symbolic meaning – that of the state breaking with its side of the social bargain. The crux of the regime's commitment against unemployment was never that all Hungarians could readily find work. Employment problems persisted, especially for groups such as teenage girls and gypsies (Fazekas and Köllö, 1990). But state employees, especially in core industries, enjoyed almost complete job security.

The importance of regularized employment within this new social arrangement was apparent in Kádár's speech at the 1962 Eighth Congress of the Communist Party that initiated what came to be known as the "Alliance Policy."[21] Compared with previous militancy, the language was strikingly conciliatory in its gestures toward "normalization." Citizen normalcy was primarily anchored in employment relations: "In the Hungarian People's Republic all people who earn their living by work – and do not spend their days and nights plotting and making bombs – go to their jobs in the morning and

[20] Many have described post-Stalinist regimes in terms of a "social contract" (Cook, 1993). Social contracts are purely historical fictions even in cases where there is a strong rule of law and democratic governance. The explanatory metaphor may nonetheless have limits in a state socialist context because, whereas the notion of "contract" typically evokes a formal agreement, in Eastern Europe legitimacy was secured by informal social norms (Baxandall, 1994). It may be clearer to describe the politics of state-socialist unemployment in terms of the state's *conceded conventions* or what Kornai refers to as the state's reaction to "grumbling" and other signals that result from "the transgression of social tolerance levels" (Kornai, 1980: 278). Others describe a "moral economy" in which violation of tacit norms by the regime invited various forms of resistance (Kopstein, 1996: 394–95). There is an extensive literature on legitimacy and social contracts in Soviet-style regimes. For debates about the basis of East European legitimacy or its absence, see Lewis (1984).

[21] The timing of the "Alliance Policy" is telling with regard to employment. This implicit social compromise was premised upon the work force's transformation into more-advanced forms of socialist work. The Alliance Policy was initiated only after agriculture had been successfully collectivized – that is, only after independent farmers had been tied to state-organized collective farms.

work; they are actually with us even if perhaps this is not a conscious attitude on their part. If in the country the general policy is sound, then socialist society is being built in industry, in agriculture, in intellectual life; *everyone who works is building a socialist society*" (Gyurkó, 1985). The state had become overwhelmingly the employer of its citizens and the new regime came to view the employment relationship as the primary means for exercising power (Hankiss, 1990; Róna-Tas, 1997).

There were a number of advantages of the new strategy for the regime. The constant political mobilization and terror of the Stalinist era was no longer necessary (Zaslavsky, 1982; Róna-Tas, 1997). Political legitimacy (or at least popular quiescence) could be maintained without directly winning over the hearts and minds of the populace. State employment gave the regime the ability, with minimal use of force, to punish and reward, as well as to divide groups through internal status differences. If the gulag was the symbol of state discipline under the previous hard-line rule of Mátyás Rákosi, it was replaced by Kádár with the workbook: the document that laborers deposited with their employer when they changed jobs. Their employer entered into the workbook a detailed account of each employee's work history, punishments, and achievements.[22] "People were dependent on their bosses, who acted as representatives of the state. Many actions, from travels abroad to adult education classes, could not be undertaken without written recommendation from workplace supervisors" (Róna-Tas, 1997). Moreover, individuals depended on their status within state employment for employment-based social benefits such as pensions, sick pay, and maternity leave. These kinds of nonwage benefits grew in importance under Kádárism. Employment regulations and social policies institutionalized the Kádárist social compromise and thereby gave a heightened political meaning to "unemployment." It is in this context that we can understand how the political importance of guaranteed employment was a product of *de-Stalinization*, not Stalinism.

Eroding the Communist Taboo

Changes in the political significance of *un*employment can be explained largely as a result of changes in the political meaning of *employment*.[23] During the 1980s, many East European regimes embraced various degrees of "secondary" economic activity outside of workers' state jobs. There was ideological resistance to this change; however, in the context of stagnant economic growth and slowing wages in state employment, regimes found it expedient at least passively to permit individuals more space to pursue

[22] Similar kinds of workbooks had been introduced in the Soviet Union in 1938. I am not arguing that the workbook caused political change, only that in the new political context the workbook took on greater symbolic importance.

[23] For a general statement of this relationship, see Baxandall (2001a).

supplementary means of livelihood.[24] In Hungary the "second economy" was very extensive and had its own legal basis as an officially socialist "helper" economy (Seleny, 1994; Sík, 1996a). In the mid-1980s a highly restrictive benefit system for job losers was even introduced. But even in Hungary the government was still considered responsible for full employment. The constitution continued to proclaim "the right to work, to freely choose [a] job and occupation" (section 70/B), and all six parties that entered Parliament after the first democratic elections of 1990 pledged full employment (Frey, 1994b). In other countries such as Czechoslovakia or the Soviet Union, changes often took the form of more permissive licensing for the self-employed, toleration of open-air agricultural markets for family-grown produce, and lax enforcement of rules against informal taxis and other forms of "profiteering" (Portes and Böröcz, 1988). Regardless of the differing degrees and mechanisms, East Europeans entered the postcommunist period with an already existing trend away from sole reliance on a state job and toward reliance on wide portfolio of income sources and sustenance.[25]

Postcommunism further eroded the taboo of unemployment by diminishing the political and material importance of main jobs in traditional state employment and accelerating the growing importance of entrepreneurship. As wages in the state sector fell precipitously under the first years of postcommunism, informal work and multiple job holding were encouraged – a trend further encouraged by the demands of the tax system and a general retreat of the state from regulating the economy. New pension policies encouraged large numbers of workers to leave their official "main" jobs only to work off the books to supplement their meager social benefits. Instead of being the model of modernization, employment in state industry was viewed as the millstone around the economy's neck. Citizens became less and less reliant on their main job to be their sole source of livelihood. Rather than the number of new jobs, governments began to trumpet the number of new businesses as evidence of their success. Entrepreneurship was celebrated and institutionally encouraged as the new prototype of successful employment policy.

[24] The emergence of the "second economy" may in some sense have itself been a legacy of the party's dual commitment to eradicating unemployment and suppressing wages. Workers sought ways to supplement their meager incomes and alternative means to exercise their skills. On alternative worker strategies, see Galasi and Sziracak (1985). To avoid unemployment, the government increasingly removed workers from the formal labor force through meager pensions that were then supplemented through the informal economy.

[25] This was clearly recognized by the state in Hungary by the mid-1980s (Andorka, 1990). According to a ten-country poll of Eastern European countries in 1991, only 48 percent of families said that a regular job was their main source of income. When a 1992 poll asked Hungarians, "Do you get enough money from your regular job to buy what you really need?" only a quarter responded that they received even barely enough, compared with almost three times that amount in neighboring Austria. Only 22 percent of Hungarians relied solely on activities officially recognized as employment (Rose and Haerpfer, 1993).

Traditional state employment declined in importance both in simple terms of people's income and also in the ways in which interests were framed and institutionally mediated. In pure material terms, the meaning of employment was most eroded by sharp declines in the value of postcommunist wages. The freeing of price controls unleashed suppressed demand, and inflation was further fed by relatively expensive new Western imports. Government policies deliberately kept annual wage increases below inflation as a way to prevent upwardly spiraling prices. Governments suppressed wages most in the sectors they believed needed downsizing: the state sector and especially heavy industry. In other words, wages suffered the most in traditionally socialist jobs. Traditional jobs also lost many kinds of fringe benefits as newly profit-conscious enterprises began selling off their worker housing, health spas, vacation homes, and childcare facilities. Wages were already a smaller portion of worker incomes in communist countries than in the West (Milanovič, 1992), a feature that became more pronounced under postcommunism. In Hungary, the percentage of family income from the wages of main jobs fell from about two-thirds in the 1970s, to about half at the fall of communism, and to 42 percent in 1994 (Andorka, 1990; Kornai, 1996). As the status of "employment" became less and less capable of providing a livelihood, the distinction between employment and unemployment became increasingly blurry. Being employed no longer guaranteed protection against destitution.

There are a number of reasons for the increase in unofficial or unreported economic work outside of main jobs. For one thing, radically uncertain business conditions, such as those in the years after 1989, encouraged economic arrangements that were less formalized because people sought out parallel, personal assurances and preferred short-term arrangements with high profit margins and low sunk costs (Bunce and Csanadi, 1993). The retreat of post-communist states from regulation of the economy also eliminated many of the potential benefits from formality. In accordance with the liberalization of the market economy, the government cut back sharply on state assistance, such as development credits and export incentives. The state cut back on assistance to businesses in financial distress in order to harden budget constraints and to promote the dissolution of inefficient firms. Even when governments may have wanted to provide services and aid for businesses, they typically lacked the administrative capacities for doing so. Contrary to the view that central authorities held great power as the result of communism, an important institutional legacy of late communist plan bargaining was that there was very little of the state left to hand over.[26]

[26] Toonen (1993: 158) suggests "that the real problem is not only that there are no local authorities, but, even worse, initially there was hardly any effective central power to hand over to them." Even in terms of sheer numbers of civil servants, the image of the bloated communist state is belied by the paltry number of staff in central ministries. According to Rice (1992: 121), there were only 8,000 staff in all Hungary's central ministries in 1992. Toonen

Postcommunist administrative and legislative capacities were typically overwhelmed, underfunded, and neglected. At every level of government the administration was overloaded with a flood of new tasks for which it had little experience or resources. As Guy Standing asserts, the region suffered from "state desertion": public services deteriorated and public officials were so underpaid that "the capacity of the public administration to regulate the labour market was seriously eroded" (Standing, 1997: 136).[27] Poorly functioning postcommunist public administration reduced the benefits of formal state recognition relative to the bureaucratic hassles and incompetence involved.[28] The cost of formality in employment also increased as an indirect result of "the financial crisis of the postcommunist state" (Campbell, 1992). Governments faced increased demands for funding social benefits and modernization projects at the same time that their tax receipts declined. Declining national output and tax receipts led to a vicious cycle of governments boosting taxes and contribution rates, which in turn increased the incentive for tax evasion (Kornai, 1992). The inherited norms of regulatory evasion from the communist era (that "everybody does it") were reinforced by a postcommunist emphasis on profit seeking. The marketization of the economy and the economic retreat of the state left little capacity for tracking economic accounts to enforce tax laws. Governmental bodies typically had little idea of who was really working or how much they were earning.[29]

Postcommunist social policies also intensified the late communist penchant for using social policies in ways that blurred rather than reinforced distinctions between the employed, the unemployed, and those outside the labor force.[30] Liberalizing communist regimes defended their commitment

(1993: 158) points out that by comparison "the Netherlands has over 150,000 *national* civil servants without ever having had the ambition to be a centrally planned economy." On plan bargaining, see, for instance, Hough (1969); Winiecki (1991).

[27] In Hungary the problems were compounded because one objective of the political compromises from the Round Table talks in 1989 was to ensure an effective separation of powers by preventing any one part of the state from gaining dominant executive power over the others. According to Hungarian political scientists, this led to an overburdening of legislative competencies of the Parliament (Balázs, 1993; Verbélyi, 1993). In the initial flurry of legislation, laws were often intentionally vague to help them gain passage in a condensed schedule (Szabó, 1993).

[28] Stark (1996: 999) describes the situation as follows: "When private entrepreneurs look to government policy, they see only burdensome taxation, lack of credits, virtually no programs to encourage regional or local development, and inordinate delays in payments for orders delivered to public sector firms."

[29] Before the late 1980s, communist governments did not worry at all about major enterprises conducting activity "off the books" because virtually all payments were tallied through a central system of accounts. "When the country was under Communist rule, raising payroll taxes was merely a statistical manipulation because firms were state-owned and both their profits and expenses were part of the total state budget" (Cox, 1993: 356).

[30] Not that planners viewed the labor force under these categories. See Fajth (1993); Heynes (2001); Baxandall (2000).

against unemployment by manipulating labor market levers such as pensions and maternity leave (Timár, 1966). Government officials were accustomed to thinking of the labor supply as a planning lever, and they responded to heightened unemployment pressures with ambitious new ways to ease those at risk of losing their jobs out of the labor market altogether. Only about a third of Hungarians leaving employment became unemployed (Timár, 1998). Such individuals typically found some work to supplement their social benefits. These policies diminished the political importance of unemployment by making it less distinct from other labor force conditions. This was the effect not only of the administration of unemployment benefits but also of programs for retirement, sickness, and disability.

Unemployment programs gave low benefits and made little effort to sort out who actually worked. Means testing was impractical given the lack of administrative capacities. In the initial years of postcommunism, the regulations often explicitly permitted recipients to work while receiving their benefits, so long as they made less than a certain wage.[31] The fact that the unemployed typically worked was not just an open secret; it was an active presumption that was institutionally embedded into new social policies. The 1990 party platform of the newly reformed Socialist Party (MSzMP) acknowledged that the official unemployment numbers grossly understated the true extent of job losses as well as the number of those working. But their stated attitude regarding unreported work was that while on the one hand it was harmful, on the other hand it mitigated social conflict from unemployment and falling wages (Frey, 1994b). Policies should encourage the unemployed, they concluded, to take up extra work.

Changes made to the old-age pension system also blurred the line between employment categories by encouraging able-bodied workers to leave the official labor force. In Hungary, the official National Labor Market Center brochure, titled "The Laws and Opportunities for Those without Jobs in 1990," opened with a section called "Labor Market Services" that promised "everyone can find a solution" and then listed the eligibility requirements for preretirement pensions alongside other unemployment benefit programs and benefits (Országos Munkaeröpiaci Központ, 1990). "Preretirement" was instituted in 1988 for workers within five years of retirement.[32] Workers fearing layoffs rushed to these programs, and preretirements were twelve times more numerous in 1991 than they had been in 1989 (Széman, 1994: 12). "Anticipatory retirement," another program, was introduced in 1991 and

[31] The Hungarian Labor Inspectorate in 1996 had only 200 inspectors, 80 percent of whom were devoted to safety issues.

[32] Workers could go into preretirement if they were within five years of retirement, had been employed for twenty-five or thirty-five years (for women and men, respectively), and had worked at least five years in their current firms. Firms could take the option to retire a worker early by paying six months advance pension insurance payments.

gave pensioner status to unemployed workers who had worked the minimum service requirements and been unsuccessful finding new work. The program was a kind of subsidized early retirement for the long-term unemployed. Eleven percent of all new pensions awarded in 1993 were for anticipatory retirement (Széman, 1994). These programs were very effective at redesignating older workers who were likely to become unemployed into official retirement from the labor force. By the end of 1993, less than 2 percent of the unemployed were over fifty-five years of age (Frey, 1994b).

The disability system was similarly used as an alternative to unemployment in ways that have blurred the boundaries of the labor market. Disability pensions had been used under communism to avoid layoffs; the proportion of new disability pensions among total pensioners had already increased sixfold between 1960 and the fall of communism, with most of the jump occurring after the mid-1980s.[33] By 1989 registers indicated that 27 percent of all pensioners were on a disability pension (Ehrlich and Révész, 1993: 18). By 1995 there was approximately one disabled person for every ten healthy Hungarians above the age of fifteen (International Monetary Fund, 1998: 33).[34]

But it would be too simple to conclude that unemployment lost its special political salience purely because changing job patterns and social policies stripped it of its special economic salience. The income-reducing effects of unemployment were indeed mitigated as a result of increasing informal supplementary work, self-employment, and multiple job holding. But unemployment also lost its political threat because of the political ascendancy of "entrepreneurship" as the frame for successful employment policy. Entrepreneurial activities were typically supplements to main jobs, but in the waning years of communism the regime recognized that they had become the fastest growing source of national income, and they presented these secondary activities as a source of livelihood for those eased out of the labor force. Significantly, policy commitments and debates came to *presume* that most Hungarians held a diverse portfolio of income sources. A lack of a primary job could thereafter be acceptable so long as alternative income sources were made available. Against the backdrop of political expectations for prosperous self-employment, unemployment became less politically salient.

The embrace of the second economy as a solution to unemployment was a political assertion more than a mere reflection of existing economic realities.

[33] The number of disability pensioners per 10,000 insurees increased from 26 in 1960 to 70 in 1970, 89 in 1985, 101 in 1988, and 162 in 1993. All data are from Hungarian Social Security Yearbook 1994 (draft copy) tables 4.2.2. Some part of this increase is undoubtedly due to deteriorating health.

[34] A breakdown of national data on unemployment and new disability claims into regional data for the years 1990 to 1993 shows that new claims became increasingly correlated with unemployment as unemployment increased over time. See Baxandall (2001a).

While the second economy was increasingly portrayed as a solution to unemployment, the unemployed did not actually participate disproportionately in the "supplementary" and "helping" economy. The unemployed were no more likely to be involved in supplementary incomes than other workers.[35] On the contrary, unemployed individuals tended to be unskilled and located in depressed areas with less entrepreneurial resources and opportunities.[36] As the longtime Hungarian expert on entrepreneurship István Gábor explains, "rather than serving to decrease unemployment in regions afflicted by depression, self-employment is itself the victim of local depression" (Gábor, 1997: 163–64). The unemployed had relatively less access to second-economy income, but it was politically consequential that employment came to be generally *conceived* of in terms of multiple sources of income.

The notion that the "second economy" was a bastion of the less fortunate drew from its earlier agricultural roots. When informal work was primarily in agriculture, it had also been more prevalent among the poor and unskilled. Poor and unskilled workers continued to be overrepresented among the unemployed even after the second economy changed in the 1980s; but it does not therefore follow that they continued to be overrepresented in secondary private activities. Róna-Tas discusses a pivotal 1980 secret party memorandum that urged an expansion of the second economy, partly based on the justification that participation in the second economy was more prevalent in the lower rungs of the socioeconomic ladder. He states that, "The fact that the private sector was compensatory precisely because of the restrictions that were about to be lifted most certainly occurred to many in the leadership" (Gábor, 1997: 142). By the mid-1980s the party was publicly discussing solutions to employment difficulties in terms of providing greater opportunities for entrepreneurship (*Népszabadság*, 1988). The second economy was embraced for relieving political tensions by compensating the less well off.

But by 1986, largely as a result of reforms in the early 1980s, the second economy expanded outside of agriculture and lost its redistributive compensatory function.[37] The old theory put forward by Szelényi was that the second economy reduced the inequalities generated by state salaries and social benefits (Szelényi, 1978), but already by the mid-1980s even Szelényi agreed

35 For instance, Fazekas and Köllö (1990) found in their case study of layoffs during the mid-1980s that 28.9 percent of those dismissed reported a secondary income compared with 43.8 percent of the elite workers.

36 On the correlates of entrepreneurship, see Fazekas, Koltay, and Köllö (1994). On how social connections diminish the duration of unemployment, see Csoba (1993).

37 The unemployed lack the skills, contacts, and equipment and are too often concentrated among depressed areas to have much opportunity for moonlighting income. Tax evasion is more the province of the self-employed than the unemployed (Pahl, 1987). See also Róna-Tas (1994); E. Szalai (1997).

this was no longer the case (Szelényi and Manchin, 1987).[38] One reason was that relatively affluent party members were vastly overrepresented in new after-hours subcontracting partnerships instituted by new policies in 1982 (Róna-Tas, 1997: 160). Regardless of whether the net effect of the second economy ever lived up to its redistributive reputation, with the reforms of 1982 "[t]he private sector was now the economy of the strong, the domain of dominant groups. To discontinue the reforms would have required the leadership to turn against its own cadres" (Róna-Tas, 1997: 162).[39] Secondary labor incomes in 1989 were more than twice as important a component of income for the richest 20 percent of the population than such income was for the poorest quartile (Ehrlich and Révész, 1993: 253).

The unemployed rarely started their own businesses, but entrepreneurship nonetheless became the benchmark of success in employment policy. Gábor describes "the exaggerated and one-sided propaganda campaign advertising entrepreneurship as a wide and preferable alternative path to success in life" (Gábor, 1997: 166). Surveys showed that the proportion of Hungarian adults who saw themselves as prospective entrepreneurs shot up from previous years to over 40 percent, among the world's highest (Lengyel and Tóth, 1993). Stark notes how for postcommunist governments eager to show their success in fostering capitalism on the international stage their accomplishment was often measured by the number of new private firms. International pressures encouraged "the ever more excited and breathless tones" of assertions about the percent of GDP that postcommunist governments claimed were generated from their budding private sectors.[40] Stark makes direct comparison to the previous pressures to conform to communist prototypes of employment in an earlier era:

> [P]olitical pressures [exist] to show higher and higher levels of "private sector" activity in order to represent better the government's case to international lending institutions, potential foreign investors, and the domestic electorate. The race among Hungary, Poland, and the Czech Republic to show the highest private sector statistics to the IMF recalls, of course, an earlier race.... when the parties and governments of these countries competed for the right to claim the highest proportion of collectivized or state property in their national statistics. Indeed, it is an open secret in Budapest that high government officials urged the use of different statistical cut-offs and measures upon returning from international conferences where Polish officials proudly displayed figures showing that the Hungarians no longer deserved the yellow jersey as first place in the statistical race to capitalism. (1995: 7–8)

[38] Andorka (1990: 110–11) shows how second-economy income was much less egalitarian in 1987 than 1977.

[39] Manchin (1988: 88–89) found that in 1982–83 Communist Party membership was already associated with higher levels of nonagricultural second income and multiple-income strategies in general (including overtime).

[40] Stark (1995: 7) points especially to the special section of the *Economist*, March 13, 1993. On international ideological pressures on postcommunist governments, see also Cox (1993); Deacon and Hulse (1997); Jacoby (1998).

Such pressures to conform to a particular metric of successful transition gave postcommunist governments even greater incentive to recognize the large numbers of new "firms" created by would-be entrepreneurs. It mattered little that these start-ups very often had no employees and little business activity. Some governments, such as in Hungary, passed laws that greatly encouraged citizens to start their own businesses, if only to write off their taxes on their apartment and telephone (Gábor, 1991). In 1995 firms with fifty people or fewer accounted for 56 percent of employment yet only 26 percent of employee income (my calculations based upon data in Köhegyi, 1998: 399, 404).[41]

Even the unemployment insurance system encouraged entrepreneurship by giving those who qualified for unemployment the opportunity for below-market loans meant explicitly for starting up new companies. This program, a kind of regional development policy folded within active labor market policy, had no equivalent in any other OECD nation (Frey, 1994a: 61–62).[42] Spending on these start-up loans for the unemployed increased more dramatically than other active labor market measures in its first years of postcommunism (Láng and Bonifert, 1994: 28).[43] The program was discontinued when the government realized that many people were simply recycling these low-interest loans into higher-interest-bearing bank accounts (Braun, Kendra, and Matoricz, 1993). Postcommunism accelerated the late communist trend toward small proprietorships and reinscribed the privileged place of entrepreneurship in Hungarian policy, discourse, and statistics.[44] By the beginning of 1998 as many as 97 percent of all operating businesses employed fewer than ten people, and more than half of Hungary's economic organizations, a full 54 percent, were self-employed "entrepreneurs" (*Népszabadság*, July 29, 1998, 5).

The entrepreneurial prototype also undermined union militancy. Organized labor is ordinarily predisposed to oppose unemployment because

41 By 1996 there were more than 1 million registered private ventures, three-quarters of which were individuals. Ninety-seven percent of all enterprises employed fewer than ten people and an estimated 30 percent of all registered companies were completely dormant (Köhegyi, 1998 #782: 399).

42 On entrepreneurial start-up loans, see Munkaügyi Minisérium (Labor Ministry), Budapest, Interest Reconciliation Council Labor Market-Board, government draft memorandum, March 26, 1991 (*Népszabadság*, 1988; Braun et al., 1993).

43 Spending for start-up loans for the unemployed to become entrepreneurs rose from 1.2 percent of all active labor market spending in 1991 to a peak of 6.2 percent in 1993 (Frey, 1995: appendix). In addition to financial support equal to up to six months of lump-sum unemployment benefits, the program reimbursed or covered up to 50 percent of professional counseling, training, or credit insurance costs (Frey, 1994a: 1).

44 According to Köllö's studies of firm behavior before 1990, paid employment fell 11 percent in the five years before 1990 despite the fact that total GDP increased 5.8 percent over this time period. This decrease occurred all within the large enterprise sector where surveyed firms cut employment an average of 20 percent. Self-employment took up the slack (Köllö, 1995a).

layoffs harm workers and diminish their bargaining power with management (Golden, 1997). In Hungary, the official organization of unions became more independent from the Communist Party during the 1980s and tried to fashion itself as more of a movement defending the interests of those who were threatened by economic reform. Yet, despite high unionization rates[45] and the unprecedented advent of mass layoffs, unions did not try to mobilize collective action or take strong political stands against rising unemployment.[46] First, union leadership was preoccupied with how the new forms of work organization undermined their bureaucratic power (Neumann, 1997). Second, workers largely shifted their concerns and aspirations about their livelihood to supplementary work and entrepreneurship, which made it easier for the state to buy off the unions with additional income-supplementing schemes such as severance packages and pensions. Severance payments were especially attractive because they could be collected simultaneously with other income so long as income was not reported to the state.[47] When the new Labor Code was debated before Parliament in 1991, the unions agreed to support it if it mandated seniority-based severance payments.[48] It was already well established by the time communist rule ended in 1990 that unions would not militantly resist layoffs the way they had in Poland. Hungarian unions in the 1990s would have been more militant against unemployment if they had seen themselves as protecting traditional good jobs rather than engaged in backdoor deals to secure entrepreneurship and subcontracting ventures.

Postcommunist unemployment may have spread rapidly, but it became less and less distinct from other forms of socioeconomic deprivation. Household panel data in the early 1990s show that no significant differences existed

[45] At the fall of communism Hungary inherited unionization rates that were as high as 70 percent. More-recent estimates place the unionization of the work force at 25–30 percent (Neumann, 1997).

[46] Hungarian officials granted greater autonomy to their official unions in the 1980s because they feared the rise of unofficial unions such as Solidarity in Poland. Unions exhibited some militancy around other kinds of economic issues. In 1988 and 1989 the communist trade-union council (SzOT) was involved in unprecedentedly confrontational wage negotiations with the government (Bartlett, 1995). In 1989 May Day demonstrations were able to rescind utility price hikes and institute wage increases; during the Round Table talks the union also challenged hikes in the price of meat (Bartlett, 1995). After 1989 SzOT reorganized itself into a new body (MSzOSz) that had no formal links to the government or the Communist Party; it still eschewed confrontation or even sustained attention regarding unemployment.

[47] Interview with Labor Ministry deputy László Hercogh, Budapest, January 1997.

[48] The 1991 Labor Code made severance pay up to six months of salary compulsory for dismissals due to economic reasons and obliged negotiations with employee representatives if there were more than fifty redundancies over six months. Enterprises could largely get around these regulations by claiming that the layoffs were due to individual performance problems rather than "economic reasons." According to Köllö (1995a), only about 40 percent of redundancy qualified for severance pay. Maximum compensation paid six months salary to workers who had been at a firm for twenty-five years or more.

in the level of consumption between Hungarian households with unemployed members and those without (Keszthelyiné, 1995). Galasi shows instead that the best predictors of poverty are whether the head of household was a woman, elderly, or poorly educated (Galasi, 1995). Sík similarly finds that once the statistical incidence of poverty is controlled for age, gypsy origin, education, and rural location, the independent effect of unemployment as a predictor of poverty becomes quite weak. In other words, the unemployed were more likely to be impoverished than other Hungarians, but not necessarily more likely than other Hungarians who shared the low education, remote location, and other characteristics that typified the unemployed (Sík, 1996b). As Julia Szalai argues, poverty was not associated with unemployment as strongly as it was with the lack of supplementary economic activities. Postcommunist poverty struck hardest at the kind of families that exemplified the communist worker: former peasants who had been mobilized into socialist industry in search of higher living standards (Szalai, 1996: 73).

The general deterioration of economic conditions certainly did contribute to the unpopularity of postcommunist governments, but field research on the years since 1990 found little public record of politicians talking about the issue.[49] In Hungary no major new initiatives or commissions were established. Benefits were extended for the long-term jobless, but no "War on Unemployment" was declared.[50] The height of public concern was, if anything, the period before unemployment skyrocketed in 1991 to 1992, when intervention funds were created and politicians spoke more about the issue.[51] The overall political effect was, as Bartlett states, that "[f]ar from intensifying political opposition to economic transition, rising unemployment diminished it" (Bartlett, 1997). Comparisons of electoral outcomes between counties also seem to reveal much independent political effect from unemployment.[52]

[49] Congresses of major parties held special sessions on health care and pensions but not unemployment. Parliamentary debates arose about reducing the costs of unemployment benefits but not about the human costs that only recently before would have been regarded as scandalous and intolerable.

[50] One study found that unemployment was included in the themes of the nightly news less than 1 percent of the time during the time that unemployment rose most precipitously (Bartók and Terestyéni, 1995).

[51] Interview with Károly Fazekás, labor economist, governmental expert advisor, and participant in national tripartite bargaining meetings for the academic workers' union LIGA, Budapest, February 1997.

[52] Tucker's in-depth statistical analysis of the 1990 and 1994 Hungarian national elections using ecological inference methods shows that, once controlled for other independent effects (from income change, GDP/capita, urban population, agriculture, and industry), the only party that received statistically higher levels of votes in high-unemployment counties was the unreconstructed hard-line Workers Party. This was the only party that absolutely opposed plant closures and Western-style unemployment. This party narrowly failed to gain the minimum threshold of 3 percent to enter Parliament in 1990 and then fell in popularity in

Insofar as the issue of postcommunist unemployment has been politically salient in Hungary, it was most so in places where *employment* more closely resembled the patterns of the early post-Stalinist era. The former steel town of Ózd is a telling exception that helps prove the general rule that the changing characteristics of employment diminished the political salience of unemployment. In an interview with the labor minister in 1996, she distinguished between "*real* unemployment like that in Ózd, and other kinds" (Mária Kovács interview, Budapest, 1997). Almost half of spending budgeted to "crisis areas" in the 1992 budget went to Ózd.[53] Unlike other places, the workers in Ózd protested repeatedly and even came to Budapest to stage prominent demonstrations in front of Parliament.

Unemployment rates in Ózd grew to almost 40 percent in the early 1990s, but terrible though this situation was, unemployment rates were often worse in other more rural towns and former cooperatives.[54] When government attention turned to particularly severe pockets of unemployment, the devastated villages and cooperatives were largely overlooked in the budget while places like Ózd were showered with special initiatives. This was despite the fact that poor rural areas also had only a small tax base to pay for the unemployment assistance benefits of workers who exhausted their unemployment insurance.

Thus, we cannot simply conclude that unemployment lost political salience wherever the relative suffering of unemployment was not especially severe.[55] The exceptional political charge attached to unemployment in Ózd makes sense in the context of how the Ózd steel mill jobs exemplified the old communist idea of generous paternalism with the factory providing workers with cultural events, housing, and childcare (Károly Fazekás interview, Budapest, February 1997). Ózd had even been a showcase for the Stalinist

1994 (Tucker, 2000: tables AIII.2 and AIII.3). Tucker's results do not contradict the finding that the unemployed voted disproportionately for leftist parties. Opinion polls indicate they did; but only in proportion to what we would otherwise expect due to the fact that these unemployed voters tended disproportionately to live outside Budapest and were more likely to be poor (Simon, 1994).

[53] About 80 percent of what remained went to two other classically socialist enterprises: the railways and a metalworks plant in Diósgyör (Budget and Social Policy Project, 1990: 27).

[54] Unemployment rates above 33 percent could be found in 10 of the 176 labor placement districts in 1992 (Koltay, 1995).

[55] Bánfalvi and Gere (1994) describe how in the most blighted areas workers generally combined agricultural and industrial pursuits on the cooperatives and that these were both hit simultaneously by postcommunist depression. Fazekás shows how between 1990 and 1992 agricultural employment was eliminated far more than industrial employment. Moreover, industrial companies first laid off their commuting work force from rural regions or closed down their plants established in rural regions (Fazekás, Koltay, et al., 1994). "In industrial regions, those fallen victim to mass layoffs stood a much greater chance to find employment immediately or only after a short time out of work, than those who sought new employment in rural regions" (Fazekás et al., 1994: 6).

industrialization drive.[56] Jobs had been relatively high paying, and workers had less need to rely on supplementary work arrangements than in most places.[57] By contrast to Ózd, the character of employment in most of the other high-unemployment areas was irregular and nonindustrial. Politicians feared that the Ózd steelworks might become the Hungarian version of the Gdansk shipyards in Poland (Fazekás interview, February 1997). Postcommunism led to a proliferation of blurred forms of quasi-unemployment, but not in Ózd, where employment resembled the old communist prototype and carried with it the earlier expectations and state commitments.

Cross-National Comparisons

Just as Ózd was an exception within Hungary, there are also exceptions across East Europe more generally. In Hungary we have shown how the politics of postcommunist transformation greatly amplified the existing legacies of entrepreneurship and multiple job holding. But in other countries the dominant trends sometimes reinforced traditional prototypes of employment. Observers of the region are familiar with scenes of Polish labor militancy against proposed layoffs or with the great importance attached to unemployment in the former East Germany. Scholars note that the degree of popular anxiety about postcommunist unemployment does not seem to reflect the differences in macroeconomic conditions (Rose, 1997). How might we explain these cross-national differences in the political salience of postcommunist unemployment?

Because the political salience of unemployment depends on the distinctiveness of unemployment from the category of employment, we should predict greater militancy about unemployment in those exceptional places where employment remained a status that was distinct from work more generally. Unemployment should be politically most salient in the early 1990s, when there were extensive layoffs of workers whose employment had been a protected category ensuring minimum livelihood and security with institutional supports that were not accorded to other forms of work. Where new systems of industrial relations or prior labor militancy existed (i.e., the GDR or Poland), there could be positive feedback between the strong

[56] Shortly after the war the communist government had nationalized the steelworks. It flourished, churning out the basic materials for industrialization such as steel reinforcing bar, wire and rod, and structural steel. The steelworks were expanded, and communist propaganda of the period depicted the steelworkers as shock troops in the building of a new society in a "country of iron and steel." At its peak the town's huge foundry, steel mill, and mines employed 22,000 workers, producing 1.5 million tons of steel a year, much of it for export. Nearly a third of Hungary's iron ore and over a third of its steel came from Ózd.

[57] Wages of workers in the Ózd steel plant averaged in 1987 a monthly 7,311 forints, compared with 5,889 forints in other machine industry and compared with a mere 4,593 forints for light industrial workers in the area (Kormos and Munkácsy, 1989: 41).

employment-unemployment distinction on the one hand and the strong political salience of unemployment on the other.

These differences in the political salience of unemployment match what Sík found to be the cross-national relationship between unemployment and poverty. Comparing similar data in Hungary, Poland, and the former East Germany, he concludes that "[a]lthough the factors that cause poverty in [these other countries in] Central Europe and Hungary are more or less the same, the role of unemployment in Hungary seems to be less significant" (Sík, 1996b: 367). Let us very briefly consider these cases and that of Russia.[58] Figure 8.1 is necessarily schematic and would ideally be more accurate if each country was disaggregated into subregions, but it nevertheless illustrates the general comparative differences.[59]

In Poland, unemployment has been a particularly contentious issue. When the Polish polling agency CBOS asked Poles in 1992 what were the most important problems facing the country, two-thirds mentioned unemployment, a proportion that rose to 69 percent in 1993 and fell to 65 percent in 1994. In second place was "low wages and high prices," which received 59 percent in 1992, 49 percent in 1993, and 54 percent in 1994. Bell (1997) shows that in Polish elections in 1990, 1991, 1993, and 1995, regional differences in unemployment corresponded to less support for free-market candidates. In high-unemployment areas support was generally higher for populist and former communist candidates. Przeworski similarly concludes that anxiety about unemployment was a crucial factor that eroded popular support for Poland's "shock therapy" program in 1990. Four months into the program 85 percent of respondents deemed unemployment "despicable." "And those threatened with unemployment were willing to resist it: 65 percent of them said ... that they were willing to strike in defense of their jobs" (Przeworski, 1993: 181). Polish unions continue to hold major protest marches against unemployment, and opposition leaders proclaim that unemployment is the nation's number one problem.[60]

[58] Another familiar example is the miners in Romania. They were also a relatively privileged group of workers under communism who maintained high wages and lived in economic conditions where few other income opportunities for work existed. For miners, in other words, there was little other work than their employment, and their employment meant a good deal in terms of livelihood, security, and prestige. The loss of such jobs was particularly politically salient. A 1998 study conducted by the Institute of Sociology of the Romanian Academy and financed by the World Bank clearly showed that the main concern of the population in the Jiu mining valley was unemployment (followed closely by the high cost of living) (Larionescu et al., 1999: 57). On unemployment, political upheaval, and policy responses in Romanian mining, see Köllö and Vincze (1999); Boboc and SOCO (2000): 1; Chiribuca et al., (2000).

[59] On the advantages of regional analysis of the politics of labor markets, see Locke (1995).

[60] These days Polish unemployment is nearly triple the Hungarian rate, so its greater political salience seems less in need of explanation. But in the early years of the transition the Polish and Hungarian rates were almost as high but never became a politically central issue.

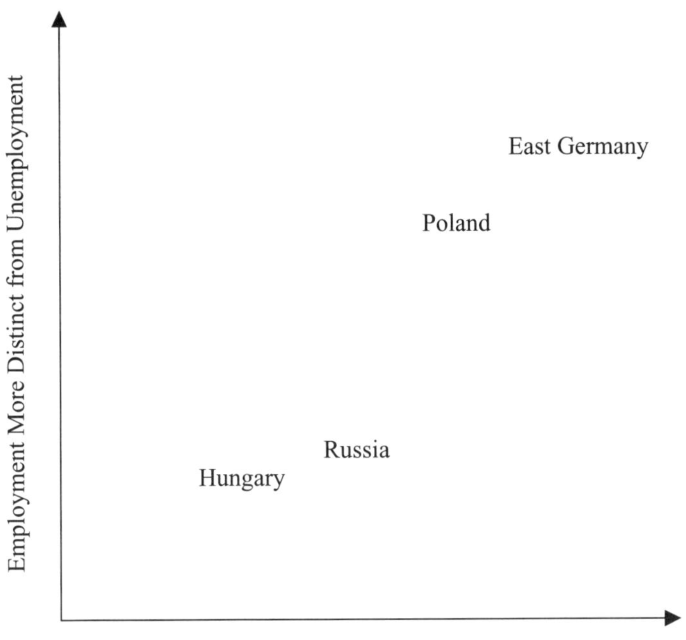

FIGURE 8.1. Political salience of unemployment in Eastern Europe.

Unemployment is a bigger political issue in Poland than places like Hungary or Russia because the exceptional militancy of industrial labor during late communism kept wages among heavy industrial workers at levels that continued to pay a family wage. Polish wages did fall after communism, and multiple job holding surely increased somewhat, but industrial workers (who were hit hardest with the threat of job loss) still regarded their jobs as a solid source of livelihood. In a 1991 New Democracies Barometer, Poles were more than 50 percent more likely than Hungarians to say that their regular job provided them with the money to buy what they needed (Rose and Haerpfer, 1993). The size of the informal, unreported economy in Poland was estimated at 15.8 percent in 1993–94. This figure, though sizable, was about half the estimated extent of informal activity in Hungary (28.1 percent) or Russia (36.8 percent) at that time (Rosser et al., 2000: 164). Poland also did not have the strong legacy of multiple job holding that had emerged out of the agricultural cooperatives in Hungary because the Polish peasantry instead kept its independent farms and generally worked solely in farming. Polish employment also maintained exceptional distinctness as a labor force category because it was the only postcommunist country where postcommunist minimum wages rose as a portion of the average wage (Standing and

Vaughan-Whitehead, 1995: 21). In most other countries, sharp declines in the real value of the minimum wage meant that a job no longer guaranteed subsistence.

Thus, in Poland the legacy of labor militancy meant that the politics of transition did not erode the political salience of unemployment as greatly. Unions were able to defend the distinctiveness of employment vis-à-vis nonemployment, largely through ensuring relatively high minimum wages. Poland had a strong tradition of entrepreneurial farming, but, unlike Hungary, the fact that this occurred through a continuation of the peasantry rather than through collectivization meant that it generally did not erode the distinctiveness of citizens' main jobs.[61] Overall, the interaction of late communist political legacies and postcommunist transition politics reinforced much about the previous character of (at least industrial) employment and thereby partially reinforced previous taboos against unemployment.

On the face of it, East German unemployment should have been less politically contentious than in other postcommunist countries. Although unemployment reached high levels, there was an initial moratorium period on layoffs and tremendous efforts and resources were dedicated to making the process of transition humane and efficient.[62] Huge sums of money were spent to cushion the effects of displacement from restructuring the East German economy.[63] Half or more of the unemployed were placed in training or make-work programs without large drops in pay (Jacoby, 2000: 21). There were generous early retirement programs (*Vorruhestand*) and "further training programs" (*Fortbildungsmaßnahmen*). The latter program had limited success at relocating workers into the private sector because unemployment was chiefly the result of a general oversupply of labor rather than a mismatch of skills; but these workers were placed into job creation programs (*Arbeitsbeschaffungsmaßnahmen*) to perform production for which no private demand existed (Pohl, 1999: 18–19).

Yet far from exemplifying quiescence about unemployment, East Germany saw some of the most contentious unemployment politics in the

[61] Again, there is great regional variation underlying this general claim. In agricultural areas around major cities there may have been far more mixing of agricultural and industrial employment. In eastern areas where the land had been controlled by Russia and private farmers had been forced to give their land to state farms, postcommunist unemployment has even greater political salience. This is partly because large plants such as those in Ózd were located disproportionately in these areas. My thanks to Grzegorz Ekiert for pointing this out.

[62] From 1989 to 1991, the national product of East Germany fell by about a third and industrial production by around two-thirds. About 4 million East Germans were out of work or in make-work positions (Maier, 1997: 290). Employment in industry dropped from 8 million at the fall of communism to 3.7 million in 1992 (Maier, 1997: 300).

[63] An estimated 750 billion Deutschemarks were transferred between 1990 and 1995 (Jacoby, 2000: 133).

region. The most publicized examples were the metalworkers strike in spring 1993 and the hunger strike by potassium miners protesting the closing of their mine. As case studies by Turner make clear, East German militancy was the norm despite the inauspicious circumstances of a weakened bargaining position and an economy that had declined in real GDP terms by 42 percent from 1989 to 1992 (Turner, 1999: 43).[64] In Leipzig the weekly protests that had helped bring down the communist regime were repeated in 1991, with unemployment as a central grievance and as many as 80,000 people shouting slogans such as "close down the closer-downers." The head of the Treuhandanstalt privatization agency was assassinated in 1991. East German voters in 1990 elections had voted overwhelmingly for the party most closely affiliated with the center-right Christian Democratic Union (CDU), but after the Kohl government was perceived as caring more about inflation than unemployment, Eastern voters subsequently turned their votes to the Social Democrats and even the reconstituted communists (Party of Democratic Socialism).[65]

A critical part of explaining the high political salience of unemployment must be the nature of East German *employment* and the changes that took place in the employment model during this time. First of all, the GDR was the most industrialized country in the former Soviet bloc, which made layoffs particularly difficult and dramatic. Postcommunist protests were concentrated in industrial centers such as Dresden, Leipzig, and Chemnitz. But more important is the fact that the changes that took place in employment were the opposite of that in other postcommunist countries. Rather than falling wages and a relaxation of the distinction between employment and other forms of work, the distinct status of employment was maintained and even bolstered by the adoption of the West German industrial relations system. There was an almost wholesale institutional transfer of West German industrial relations and social policy institutions.[66] These institutions are the quintessential example of an employment-based, insurance-style model with strong restrictions on the nature of employment and relatively few opportunities for casual work (Esping-Andersen, 1990). German welfare state institutions

[64] The large number of postcommunist strikes contrasts starkly with the more general tendency of strikes to decrease during times of loose labor markets. During economic collapse, striking workers have less bargaining leverage because employers need workers less and workers face more competition from others willing to take their jobs with lower pay, lesser benefits, and worse conditions. See Soskice (1978); Kennan (1986).

[65] Through the mid-1990s the PDS had significantly higher party membership than any of the major parties from the West (Eith, 1999: 13). In 1994 in the state of Brandenberg that surrounds Berlin the PDS finished second in regional elections, leaving the CDU in third place.

[66] As Jacoby (2000) shows, in the process of implementing this transfer many innovations and accommodations of the German model resulted. For more on industrial restructuring in Eastern Germany, see Locke and Jacoby (1997).

have been designed to discourage downward pressures on employment standards. This encouraged workers to fight for their jobs. For example, during the 1993 metalworkers strike, "Leaders also reminded eastern workers that if unemployment came, it would be better to be laid off at a higher wage than a lower one, since unemployment benefits were based on the last monthly wage" (Jacoby, 1998: 159). Wages did not fall. In fact, in manufacturing and construction wages increased almost 60 percent from April 1990 to April 1991 (Pohl, 1999: fig. 4). Nominal wages for East Germany as a whole increased from 47 percent of West German wages in 1991 to 71 percent in 1994 (Pohl, 1999: 7). In the simplest terms, unemployment meant more in postcommunist Germany because the jobs people lost meant more.

Russia has been almost the diametric opposite of East Germany: "It has often been assumed that the greatest tension would come from rising unemployment, but there are many other social discontents," such as low pensions or late wages that have been the focus of political discontent (Roxburgh and Shapiro, 1996: 19).[67] Opinion surveys confirm that Russian grievances over unemployment are overshadowed by disaffection over wage arrears, which they identify as a more pressing social issue.[68] Outright layoffs were relatively rare up until the financial crisis in August 1998 sent scores of businesses over the brink.[69] Under the Soviet regime, production was so centralized that the least efficient firms slotted for downsizing were often one-company towns. This geographic concentration of labor in huge enterprises made mass layoffs and plant closures politically infeasible. Even in smaller enterprises, Russian managers tried to avoid outright layoffs because of tax penalties and mandated severance payments of two to three months of salary. Because Russian firms paid taxes on their average wage levels, they could bring down their tax liability by retaining surplus workers and paying them minimal wages. The excess-wages tax indirectly functioned as a subsidy to retain surplus workers (Roxburgh and Shapiro, 1996). Instead of layoffs, managers often tried to get workers to quit by delaying their wages or placing them on extended leave.[70]

[67] Crowley (1994: 589–90) poses the question with regard to the former Soviet Union: "The miners have since continued their militancy and strike activity, while steelworkers and almost every other category of industrial worker have hardly made a sound."

[68] According to Javeline (2003: introduction), "In the spring of 1997, wage arrears was named by more Russians as the most serious problem facing Russia than any other single issue (18 percent) and unemployment (14 percent). These surveys were commissioned by USIA's Office of Research. The findings are similar to those from other surveys. For example, according to a fall 1998 survey of 2,400 respondents by the All-Russian Center for the Study of Public Opinion (VtsIOM), a majority of Russians (55 percent) named the back payment of wages, pensions, and student stipends as the top priority for the Primakov government (*Interfax*, 28 September 1998)."

[69] Russian unemployment stood at 10 percent at the end of 2000, as measured by the International Labor Organization (ILO).

[70] Lehmann et al. (1999) argue that the dominant form of labor market adjustment in the Russian transition process has been delayed receipt of wages. There were also 4.6 million

Wage arrears were most acute in heavy industries that would otherwise be prone to layoffs, such as ferrous metals, where 62 percent of companies had wage arrears, or oil production where 86 percent did.[71] In 1994 almost half of Russian enterprises owed their workers back wages (Javeline, 2003). Because of high inflation, deferred wages had often lost much of their value by the time they were finally paid. Workers would often be paid "in kind" in goods produced by the enterprise itself.

Enterprise directors could afford to retain surplus workers as a way to avoid taxes or severance payments because the minimum wage in Russia was kept very low, insufficient even to buy a daily loaf of bread and liter of milk. It fell from about a quarter of the average wage in 1990 and 1991 to less than an eighth of the average wage in 1992 and subsequent years (Roxburgh and Shapiro, 1996). Wages in 1995 comprised only 40 percent of Russians' total money income, down from 46 percent the year before.[72] Only a mere 7 percent of workers in state enterprises said they earned enough from their first job to live on. Among all Russian workers, only 13 percent earned enough from their regular job to get by; 54 percent did not earn enough from regular job but could scrape by with additional incomes; and 33 percent did not earn enough and had to borrow or sell household goods. Russians turned to secondary informal jobs and household work so much that the typical (mean) Russian participated in 3.7 different forms of activities for income or food (Rose and Haerpfer, 1993). Wages and salaries by the end of 1999 accounted for only 42 percent of people's incomes, with the difference mainly filled by unofficial sources, according to Labor Minister Sergei Kalashnikov. Official jobs posted through state labor offices paid so little that there were more vacancies than registered jobless, a situation from which the labor minister curiously concluded that "There is no unemployment in Russia."[73]

Russian workers often were kept nominally employed but paid only part of their wages and permitted to continue to enjoy nonwage amenities such as factory housing, kindergartens, medical treatments, and subsidized cafeterias (Crowley, 1994).[74] It is hard to know whether to regard such

workers simply placed on "administrative leave" at the end of 1995 (*Interfax*, May 28, 1996, cited in Penny Morvant and Peter Rutland, "Russian Workers Face the Market," *Transition* 2[13] [1996]: 7).

71 Cited in Penny Morvant and Peter Rutland, "Russian Workers Face the Market," *Transition* 2(13) (1996): 7.

72 Goskomstat (1995), cited in Penny Morvant and Peter Rutland, "Russian Workers Face the Market," *Transition* 2(13) (1996): 7.

73 FBIS Daily Report, "Russia: Labour Minister Denies Unemployment in Russia," Central Eurasia, November 23, 1999, from ITAR-TASS.

74 In state enterprises workers received the following free or very cheap as part of compensation from the firm: meals (22 percent), medical care (50 percent), housing (11 percent), holiday facilities (43 percent), kindergarten (42 percent), and food (12 percent) (Rose, 1996a).

workers as unemployed. The diminished meaning of employment was clear from the 1995 New Russia Barometer (Rose, 1996b) in which 56 percent of Russian workers said their wages had been paid late the previous year (82 percent of whom by three months or more), and 9 percent said their wages were not paid at all. The Russian statistical agency Goskomstat even started keeping track of wages-actually-paid as a separate statistical category from wages-formally-allotted. The use of sham employment to lower taxes is such common knowledge in Russia that the St. Petersburg booklet for new Russian taxpayers, *47 Legal Ways of Lowering Your Taxes*, recommends hiring casual workers to "wash windows, sit at telephones, courier duty, etc." (cited in Roxburgh and Shapiro, 1996).

Conclusions and Reflections on the Methodology of Studying Historical Legacies

Thus, we have seen that the inherited norm of no unemployment was an institutional legacy of state socialism, but not of Leninism per se (see Ekiert and Hanson, Chapter 1 in this volume). Nothing in Leninist ideology necessitated the institutionalization of such a norm, but it did become part of the lived experience and implicit social contract of state socialism in practice. This "institutional legacy" provides one critical context within which contemporary debates about employment are conducted in Eastern Europe; but it interacted in differing ways in different places with the particular interactional contexts of postcommunism. The fall of communism greatly eroded remaining norms against unemployment, but in ways that were entirely consistent with the specific historical basis of the norm itself. The unemployment taboo was premised on a particular kind of state employment relationship as a near-universal guarantee of livelihood and as a cornerstone of the post-Stalinist political order. To varying degrees epitomized by Hungary on one extreme and East Germany on the other, postcommunism eroded the political importance of the employment relationship. Economic circumstances and new social policies encouraged individuals to get by with a broader portfolio of income sources. This undermined the previous political salience that employment held when individuals had a single long-term job that guaranteed their livelihood, provided a wide array of social benefits, and represented the chief nexus of citizenship. Postcommunism eroded the old norm of full employment through purely economic mechanisms, such as the declining wages of "main jobs," through institutional factors that partially subsidized withdrawal from old-style jobs, and ideologically through the embrace of "entrepreneurship" as part of the hegemonic discourse of postcommunist elites.

Two conclusions can also be drawn from the foregoing discussion for the study of historical legacies more generally. The first is a cautionary reminder that the emergence of historical legacies does not always correspond to the periodization we attach to historical change more broadly. Analysis of historical legacies in Eastern Europe tends to view the Stalinist period as the "ideal type" for examining state socialism;[75] but this convention can obscure as much as it reveals. We run the risk of making historical analysis ironically ahistorical.[76] The problem is not just that "reform" periods typically extended far longer than classical Stalinism. More important, many of the postcommunist legacies we observe may be generated from these post-Stalinist political feedback loops.

The second conclusion concerns how much comparative-historical analysis can distinguish arguments based on microlevel interests as opposed to legacies based on the symbolic and ideological meanings that do not reside in specific individuals. Kathleen Thelen (2002) distinguishes two strains of comparative historical analysis:

1. "*Path dependence as increasing returns*" perspectives examine how specific historical turning points result in institutional configurations that constrain subsequent political developments. Moments of contingency, innovation, and exogenous shocks are followed by "periods of institutional reproduction." Initial contingent events determine subsequent developments by locking in certain political patterns through specific mechanisms such as positive feedback, returns to scale, and costs to exit. A central insight of this approach is that political actors adjust their strategies to accommodate prevailing political patterns in ways that may reinforce those same patterns.
2. *Political constructionists* "emphasize the causal and especially constitutive relevance of specific historical events." This approach emphasizes the importance of background scripts, norms, or ideas as critical for facilitating new institutional configurations that structure politics while remaining open to contestation.

One implication that can be drawn from the preceding discussion is that, at least with well-structured and institutionalized categories such as unemployment, social constructions can themselves be mechanisms for returns to scale. Commitments to legitimacy, such as the commitment to eradicate some prescribed notion of unemployment, are social constructions; but they also provide definite microlevel mechanisms for path dependency. They present "barriers to exit" because once benchmarks for evaluating the competency of rule have been defined, individuals then find it politically costly to betray

[75] The "classical" period began at different times in different countries and ended everywhere but Albania in the early 1950s.

[76] Keyssar (1987: 201) makes a similar criticism of a singular focus among Western historical studies of unemployment on the Great Depression: "Most modern scholarship dealing with the problem of the unemployment possesses the peculiar distinction of being both ahistorical and haunted by memories of a single historical period."

or defect from these goals. Such ideological commitments also create "returns to scale" because once legitimacy has been established along particular benchmarks there is both an incentive to claim credit in terms of the same definition of "success" and an incentive for various actors, from petty officials to supreme leaders to aggrieved workers, to use the established goal of eradicating certain forms of joblessness as a way to justify their own ends. The same is true of counterlegacies against the political importance of unemployment based on the emergence of entrepreneurship as a strategy and benchmark for postcommunist economic achievement.

References

Adam, Jan. 1984. *Employment and Wage Policies in Poland, Czechoslovakia and Hungary since 1950*. London: Macmillan.

Amsden, Alice H., Jacek Kochaniwicz, and Lance Taylor. 1994. *The Market Meets Its Match*. Cambridge, Mass.: Harvard University Press.

Anderson, Christopher. 1995. *Blaming the Government: Citizens and the Economy in Five European Democracies*. Armonk, N.Y.: M. E. Sharpe.

Andorka, Rudolf. 1990. The Importance and the Role of the Second Economy for Hungarian Economy and Society. *Society and Economy* 12(2): 95–113.

Aslund, Anders. 1992. Post-Communist Economic Revolutions: How Big a Bang? Washington, D.C.: Center for Strategic and International Studies.

Balázs, István. 1993. The Transformation of Hungarian Public Administation. *Public Administration* 71(1–2): 75–88.

Bánfalvi, István, and Ilona Gere. 1994. The Social Cost of Restructuring Agrarian Organizations. Vienna, Institut für die Wissenschaften vom Menschen, No. 18.

Barber, John. 1986. The Development of Soviet Employment and Labour Policy, 1930–41. In David Lane, ed., *Labour and Employment in the USSR*, pp. 50–65. Sussex: Wheatsheaf Books.

Bartlett, David. 1995. Losing the Political Initiative: The Impact of Financial Liberalization in Hungary. In Andrew Walder, ed., *The Waning of the Communist State: Economic Origins of Political Decline in China and Hungary*, pp. 114–50. Berkeley: University of California Press.

1997. *The Political Economy of Dual Transformations: Market Reform and Democratization in Hungary*. Ann Arbor: University of Michigan Press.

Bartók, János, and Tamás Terestyéni. 1995. A Televízívós Tájékoztatás és a Közönség a Válaszást Követö Idöszakban (The TV news and the public after the elections). *Jel-Kép* (2): 13–20.

Baxandall, Phineas. 1994. Social Rights under State Socialism/Pensions and Housing in Hungarian Welfare State Development. Cambridge, Mass., Center for European Studies, Harvard University.

2000. The Communist Taboo against Unemployment: Ideology, Soft-Budget Constraints, or the Politics of De-Stalinization? *East European Politics and Societies* 14(3): 597–635.

2001a. Reinventing Unemployment: Hungarian Joblessness in Comparative Perspective. Ph.D. dissertation, Massachusetts Institute of Technology.

2001b. When Is Unemployment Politically Important? Explaining Differences in Political Salience across European Countries. *West European Politics* 24(1): 75–98.

Baykov, Alexander. 1947. *The Development of the Soviet Economic System*. Cambridge: Cambridge University Press.

Bell, Janice. 1997. Unemployment Matters: Voting Patterns during the Economic Transition in Poland, 1990–1995. *Europe-Asia Studies* 49(7): 1263–91.

Berend, Iván. 1990. *The Hungarian Economic Reforms, 1953–1988*. Cambridge: Cambridge University Press.

Betlen, Anna. 1993. Érdekvédelem, Vállalkozás, Nagypolitika: Önsegítö Egyesületek a Munkanélküliség Ellen (Interest protection, enterprise, and large politics: Self-help organizations against unemployment). *Esely* (4): 48–63.

Bielasiak, Jack. 1981. Workers and Mass Participation in "Socialist Democracy." In Jan Triska and Charles Gati, eds., *Blue-Collar Workers in Eastern Europe*, pp. 88–107. London: George Allen and Unwin.

Blanchflower, David G., and Richard Freeman. 1997. The Attitudinal Legacy of Communist Labor Regulations. *Industrial and Labor Relations Review* 50(3): 438–59.

Blue Ribbon Commission. 1990. Hungary in Transformation to Freedom and Prosperity. Indianapolis: Hudson Institute.

Boboc, Ion, and SOCO Project Paper No. 72. 2000. The Social Costs of Restructuring the Coal Mining Industry in Romania. Vienna, Institut für die Wissenschaften vom Menschen, No. 19.

Braun, Judit, Károly Kendra, and Anna Matoricz. 1993. A munknélküli járadék folyósitás anomáliái, valamint az ujrakezdök-pályakezdök vállalkozói kölcsöne müködésének értékelése (Ongoing anomalies of unemployment, evaluation of the operation of entrepreneurial loans for new workers). Budapest.

Budget and Social Policy Project. 1990. Unemployment and Unemployment-Related Expenditures. Budapest, Blue Ribbon Commission.

Bunce, Valerie, and Maria Csanadi. 1993. Uncertainty in the Transition: Postcommunism in Hungary. *East European Politics and Society* 7(Spring): 32–50.

Campbell, John L. 1992. The Fiscal Crisis of Post-Communist States. *Telos* 93: 89–110.

Chiribuca, Dan, Mircea Comsa, Vasile Dîncu, and Traian Rotariv. 2000. The Impact of Economic Restructuring in Mono-Industrial Areas: Strategies and Alternatives for the Labor Reconversion of the Formerly Redundant in the Jiu Valley, Romania. Vienna, Institut für die Wissenschaften vom Menschen, No. 16.

Christian, David. 1985. Labour in a Non-Capitalist Economy: The Soviet Counter-Example. In J. Roe, ed., *Unemployment: Are There Lessons from History?* pp. 85–104. Sydney: Hale and Iremonger.

CIA Directorate of Intelligence. 1967. Unemployment in the Soviet Union: Fact or Fiction? Report number RR ER 66-5. Washington, D.C.: Central Intelligence Agency, Office of Research and Reports.

Cook, Linda J. 1993. *The Soviet Social Contract and Why It Failed: Welfare Policy and Workers' Politics from Brezhnev to Yeltsin*. Cambridge, Mass.: Harvard University Press.

Cox, Robert Henry. 1993. Creating Welfare States in Czechoslovakia and Hungary: Why Policymakers Borrow Ideas from the West. *Government and Policy* 11: 349–64.

Crowley, Stephen. 1994. Barriers to Collective Action: Steelworkers and Mutual Dependence in the Former Soviet Union. *World Politics* 46: 589–615.

Csepeli, György, I. Kolosi, M. Neményi, and A. Örkény. 1994. Our Futureless Values: The Forms of Justice and Injustice Perception in Hungary in 1991. *Social Research* 60(4): 865–92.

Csepeli, György, and A. Örkény. 1994. Cognitive Walls in Europe. Budapest.

Csoba, Judit. 1993. Munkanélküliek Kapcsolatainkak Alakulása A Munkanélküliség Ideje Alatt (The relationship of connections among the unemployed and variation in the duration of unemployment). *Esely* (4): 64–73.

David, Paul A. 1985. Clio and the Economics of QWERTY. *American Economics Association Papers and Proceedings* 75: 332–37.

Davies, R. W. 1986. The Ending of Mass Unemployment in the USSR. In David Lane, ed., *Labour and Employment in the USSR*, pp. 19–35. Sussex: Wheatsheaf Books.

Deacon, Bob, and Michelle Hulse. 1997. The Making of Post-Communist Social Policy: The Role of International Agencies. *Journal of Social Policy* 26(1): 43–62.

Ehrlich, Éva, and Gábor Révész. 1993. Present and Feasible Future in Hungary. Budapest.

Eith, Ulrich. 1999. Political Behavior in Eastern Germany since 1989. The German Road from Socialism to Capitalism: Eastern Germany Ten Years after the Collapse of the GDR. Harvard University.

Esping-Andersen, Gøsta. 1990. *The Three Worlds of Welfare Capitalism*. Princeton: Princeton University Press.

Evans, Geoffrey, and Stephen Whitefield. 1993. Identifying the Bases of Party Competition in Eastern Europe. *British Journal of Political Science* 23: 521–48.

Fajth, Gaspar. 1993. Measuring Unemployment in Central and Eastern European Countries. In *OECD, Employment and Unemployment in Economies in Transition: Conceptual and Measurement Issues*, pp. 87–99. Paris: OECD, Centre for Cooperation with the European Economies in Transition.

Fazekas, Károly, and János Köllö. 1990. *Munkaerõpiac Tõkepiac Nélkül* (Labor market without capital market). Budapest, Közgazdági és Jogi Könyvkiadó.

Fazekas, Károly, Jenö Koltay, and János Köllö. 1994. Unemployment – Causes and Cures in Regions of Crisis in Hungary. Vienna, Institut für die Wissenschaften vom Menschen, No. 19.

Fiorina, Morris P. 1981. Short-Term and Long-Term Effects of Economic Conditions on Individual Voting Decisions. In Douglas A. Hibbs Jr. and Heino Fassbender, eds., *Contemporary Political Economy: Studies on the Interdependence of Politics and Economics*, pp. 73–100. Amsterdam: North-Holland.

Freud, Sigmund. 1961. *Civilization and Its Discontents*. New York: W. W. Norton.

Frey, Mária. 1994a. Formerly Unemployed as Entrepreneurs. Budapest, ILO/Japan Project, Employment Policies for Transition in Hungary.

1994b. The Role of the State in Employment Policy and Labour Market Programmes: The Hungarian Case in International Comparison. Budapest, ILO.

1995. New Job Creating Initiatives Outside the Mainstream Labour Market in Hungary. Budapest, Labor Research Institute.

Gábor, István R. 1991. Prospects and Limits to the Second Economy. *Acta Oeconomica* 43(3–4): 349–52.

1997. Too Many, Too Small: Small Entrepreneurship in Hungary – Ailing or Prospering? In Gernot Grabher and David Stark, eds., *Restructuring Networks in Post-Socialism: Legacies, Linkages, and Localities*, pp. 158–75. Oxford: Oxford University Press.

Galasi, Péter. 1995. *Szegények és Gazdagok* (Wealthy and poor). Paper for the Project on the Impact of the Reform of the State Budget on the Distribution of Income, TÁRKI, Budapest.

Galasi, Péter, and György Sziráeak, eds. 1985. *Labour Market and Second Economy in Hungary*. Socio-Economic Labour Market Research. New York and Frankfurt: Campus Verlag.

Golden, Miriam A. 1997. *Heroic Defeats: The Politics of Job Loss*. Cambridge: Cambridge University Press.

Gyurkó, L. 1985. Introductory Biography. In *János Kádár, Selected Speeches and Interviews*. Budapest, Akadémai Kiadó.

Hankiss, Elemér. 1990. *East European Alternatives*. New York: Oxford University Press.

Harper, Marcus A. G. 2000. Economic Voting in Postcommunist Eastern Europe. *Comparative Political Studies* 33(9): 1191–1227.

Heclo, Hugh. 1974. *Modern Social Politics in Britain and Sweden: From Relief to Income Maintenance*. New Haven: Yale University Press.

Hethy, Lajos, and Csabo Mako. 1979. Worker Participation and the Socialist Enterprise: A Hungarian Case Study. In Cary L. Cooper and Enid Mumford, eds., *The Quality of Working Life in Western and Eastern Europe*, pp. 296–326. Westport, Conn.: Greenwood.

Heynes, Barbara. 2001. Meaning and Measurement in the Post-Communist Labor Market: Employment and Unemployment in Poland, 1992–1996. In Fatos Tafira, ed., *The Breakdown of Socialism and the Emergence of the Post-Socialist Order*, pp. 149–78. The Hague: Centre for the Study of Transition and Development.

Hough, Jerry. 1969. *The Soviet Prefects: The Local Party Organs in Industrial Decision-Making*. Cambridge, Mass.: Harvard University Press.

International Monetary Fund. 1998. Hungary: Economic Policies for Sustainable Growth. Washington, D.C.: IMF.

Jacoby, Wade. 1998. Tutors and Pupils: International Organizations, CEE Elites, and Western Models. Paper presented at the annual meeting of the American Political Science Association, Boston, September 3.

2000. *Imitation and Politics: Redesigning Modern Germany*. Ithaca: Cornell University Press.

Javeline, Debra. 2003. *Protest and the Politics of Blame: The Russian Response to Unpaid Wages*. Ann Arbor: University of Michigan Press.

Karajánnisz, Manolisz. 1994. 5 × 5 Kérdés a gazdaságról: A pártok gazdasási elképzelései a választások elõtt (5 times 5 questions about the economy: The parties' economic thinking in the run-up to elections). In S. P. Sándor Kurtán and Vass László, eds., *Magyarország politikai évkönyve* (Hungarian political yearbook), pp. 688–97. Budapest, Demokrácia Kutatások Magyar Központja Alapítvány.

Kennan, John. 1986. The Economics of Strikes. In Orley Ashenfelter and Richard Layard, eds., *Handbook of Labor Economics*, 2: 1091–1137. Amsterdam: Elsevier Science Publishers.

Keszthelyiné, R. M. 1995. *Az indirekt adók újrelosztó hatásai* (The redistributional effects of indirect taxes). Paper for the Project on the Impact of the Reform of the State Budget on the Distribution of Income, TÁRKI, Budapest.

Keyssar, Alexander. 1987. Unemployment before and after the Great Depression. *Social Research* 5(2): 201–21.

Kinder, Donald R., and Roderick D. Kiewiet. 1981. Sociotropic Politics. *British Journal of Political Science* 11(April): 129–41.

Kinder, Donald R., and Walter R. Mebane Jr. 1983. Politics and Economics in Everyday Life. In K. Monroe, ed., *The Political Process and Economic Change*, pp. 141–80. New York: Agathon Press.

Köhegyi, Kálmán. 1998. Small Ventures in the 1990's. *Acta Oeconomica* 49(3–4): 397–414.

Köllö, János. 1995a. Transformation before the "Transition": Employment and Wage Setting in Hungarian Firms 1986–1989. Budapest. Unpublished manuscript.

1995b. Unemployment and the Prospects for Employment Policy in Hungary. In Jenö Koltay, ed., *Unemployment and Evolving Labor Markets in Central and Eastern Europe*, pp. 183–227. Aldershot: Avebury.

Köllö, János, and Mária Vincze. 1999. Self-employment, Unemployment and Wages: Regional Evidence from Hungary and Romania. Budapest, Institute of Economics, Hungarian Academy of Sciences, No. 7.

Koltay, Jenö. 1995. Unemployment and Employment Policy in Central and Eastern Europe: Similarities and Differences. In Jenö Koltay, ed., *Unemployment and Evolving Labor Markets in Central and Eastern Europe*, pp. 1–30. Aldershot: Avebury.

Kopstein, Jeffrey. 1996. Chipping Away at the State: Workers' Resistance and the Demise of East Germany. *World Politics* 48(3): 391–423.

Kormos, Imre, and Ference Munkácsy. 1989. *Foglalkotatáspolitika válságos helyzetben* (Ózdi tanulságok) (Employment politics in critical areas [lessons from Ozd]). Budapest: Közgazdasági és Jogi Könyvkiadó.

Kornai, János. 1980. *Economics of Shortage*. Amsterdam: North Holland.

1992. The Post-Socialist Transition and the State: Reflections in the Light of Hungarian Fiscal Policy. *American Economic Review* 82(2): 1–21.

1996. Paying the Bill for Goulash Communism: Hungarian Development and Macro Stabilization in a Political Economy Perspective. Harvard Institute for Economic Research Discussion Papers, No. 1748.

Lane, David. 1987. *Soviet Labour and the Ethic of Communism*. Boulder, Colo.: Westview Press.

Láng, Zsanna, and Donát Bonifert. 1994. A Vállalkozások, Válamint a Rugalmas Foglalkoztatási Formák Szerpe a Munkanélküliég Csökkentésésben (The role played by enterprises in forms of flexible employment for reducing unemployment). Budapest: Piacgazdaság Alapítvány.

Larionescu, Maria, Cosima Rughinis, and Sorin Radvlescu. 1999. *With the Eyes of the Miners: The Mining Reform in Romania*. Bucharest: Gnosis Publishing House.

Lau, Richard R., and David O. Sears. 1981. Cognitive Links between Economic Grievances and Political Responses. *Political Behavior* 4: 92–111.

Lehmann, Hartmut, Jonathan Wadsworth, and Allesandro Acquisiti. 1999. Grime and Punishment: Job Insecurity and Wage Arrears in the Russian Federation. *Journal of Comparative Economics* 27(4): 595–617.

Lengyel, György, and István Tóth. 1993. A vállalkozói hajlandóság terjedése (A growing willingness to venture). *Szociólogiai Szemle* 97(1).
Lewis, Paul, ed. 1984. *Eastern Europe: Political Crisis and Legitimacy*. New York: St. Martin's Press.
Lewis-Beck, Michael. 1988. *Economics and Elections: The Major European Democracies*. Ann Arbor: University of Michigan Press.
Lipsmeyer, Christine S. 2001. Welfare and the Discriminating Public: Explaining Entitlement Attitudes in Post Communist Europe. Paper presented at the annual meeting of the American Political Science Association, August 30–September 2, San Francisco.
Locke, Richard M. 1995. *Remaking the Italian Economy*. Ithaca: Cornell University Press.
Locke, Richard M., and Wade Jacoby. 1997. The Dilemmas of Diffusion: Social Embeddedness and the Problems of Institutional Change in Eastern Germany. *Politics and Society* 25(1): 34–65.
Mahoney, James. 2000. Path Dependence in Historical Sociology. *Theory and Society* 29: 507–48.
Maier, Charles S. 1997. *Dissolution: The Crisis of Communism and the End of East Germany*. Princeton: Princeton University Press.
Manchin, Robert. 1988. Individual Economic Strategies and Social Consciousness. *Social Research* 65(1–2): 77–95.
Markus, Boris. 1936. The Abolition of Unemployment in the U.S.S.R. *International Labour Review* 33(3): 356–90.
Markus, Gregory. 1988. The Impact of Personal and National Economic Conditions on the Presidential Vote: A Pooled Cross-Sectional Analysis. *American Journal of Political Science* 32: 137–54.
McIntosh, Mary, and Martha Abele MacIver. 1992. Coping with Freedom and Uncertainty: Public Opinion in Hungary, Poland and Czechoslovakia 1989–1992. *International Journal of Public Opinion Research* 4(4): 375–91.
McIntosh, Mary, Martha Abele MacIver, Daniel G. Abele, and Kina Smeltz. 1994. Publics Meet Market Democracy in Central and East Europe, 1991–1993. *Slavic Review* 53(2): 483–512.
Milanovič, Branko. 1992. Income Distribution in Late Socialism: Poland, Hungary, Czechoslovakia, Yugoslavia and Bulgaria Compared, Second Draft. Socialist Economics Unit, World Bank.
Miller, William L., Stephen White, and Paul Heywood. 1998. *Values and Political Change in Post-Communist Europe*. New York: St. Martin's Press.
Mishler, William, and Richard Rose. 1996. Trajectories of Fear and Hope: Support for Democracy in Post-Communist Europe. *Comparative Political Studies* 28(4): 553–81.
Morris, Michael. 1985. Are Poverty and Unemployment Social Problems? The Dynamics of Public Definitions. *Sociology and Social Research* 69(3): 396–411.
Népszabadság. 1988. Munkanélküliség és Kisvállalkozás (Unemployment and small business). Budapest: 3.
Neumann, László. 1997. Circumventing Trade Unions in Hungary: Old and New Channels of Wage Bargaining. *European Journal of Industrial Relations* 3(2): 183–202.

Offe, Claus. 1992. Capitalism by Democratic Design? Democratic Theory Facing the Triple Transition in East-Central Europe. *Social Research* 58(4): 865–92.

Örkeny, Antal, and György Csepeli. 1994. Perceptions of Social Inequality in Hungarian Society. *Comparative Social Research* 14: 173–92.

Országos Munkaeröpiaci Központ. 1990. Állásnélküliek Jogai, Lehetöségei 1990–ben (The laws and opportunities for those without jobs in 1990). Budapest: OMK.

Pahl, Raymond E. 1987. Does Jobless Mean Workless? Unemployment and Infernal Work. *Annals of the American Academy of the Political and Social Sciences* 493: 36–46.

Pierson, Paul. 2000. Increasing Returns, Path Dependence, and the Study of Politics. *American Political Science Review* 94(2): 251–67.

Piven, Francis Fox, and Richard Cloward. 1993. *Regulating the Poor: The Function of Public Welfare.* New York: Vintage Books.

Pohl, Rüdiger. 1999. The Macroeconomics of Transformation: The Case of East Germany. The German Road from Socialism to Capitalism: Eastern Germany Ten Years after the Collapse of the GDR. Harvard University.

Porter, Michael. 1990. *Competitive Advantage of Nations.* New York: Free Press.

Portes, Alejandro, and József Böröcz. 1988. The Informal Sector under Capitalism and State Socialism: A Preliminary Comparison. *Social Justice* 15(3–4): 17–28.

Przeworski, Adam. 1991. *Democracy and the Market.* Cambridge: Cambridge University Press.

1993. Economic Reforms, Public Opinion, and Political Institutions: Poland in the Eastern European Perspective. In J. M. Maravall, L. C. B. Pereira, and A. Przeworski, eds., *Economic Reforms in New Democracies: A Social-Democratic Approach*, pp. 132–98. Cambridge: Cambridge University Press.

Rein, Martin, Barry L. Friedman, and Andreas Wargotter, eds. 1996. *Enterprise and Social Benefits after Communism.* Cambridge: Cambridge University Press.

Rice, Eric M. 1992. Public Administration in Post-Socialist Eastern Europe. *Public Administration Review* 52(2): 116–25.

Robertson, John D. 1984. Toward a Political-Economic Accounting of the Endurance of Cabinet Administrations: An Empirical Assessment of Eight European Democracies. *American Journal of Political Science* 28(4): 693–709.

Róna-Tas, Ákos. 1994. The First Shall Be Last? Entrepreneurship and Communist Cadres in the Transition from Socialism. *American Journal of Sociology* (100): 40–69.

1997. *The Great Surprise of the Small Transformation: The Demise of Communism and the Rise of the Private Sector in Hungary.* Ann Arbor: University of Michigan Press.

Rose, Richard. 1996a. Comparing Workers in Russian Enterprises. Glasgow, Scotland, Center for the Study of Public Policy, University of Strathclyde, Working Paper No. 258.

1996b. New Russia Barometer V: Between Two Elections. Glasgow, Scotland, Center for the Study of Public Policy, University of Strathclyde, Working Paper No. 260.

1997. What Is the Demand for Price Stability in Post-Communist Countries? Glasgow, Scotland, Center for the Study of Public Policy, University of Strathclyde, Working Paper No. 282.

Rose, Richard, and Christian Haerpfer. 1993. New Democracies Barometer II: Adapting to Transformation in Eastern Europe. University of Strathclyde, University of Strathclyde, Glasgow, Working Paper No. 212.

Rose, Richard, and Toni Makkai. 1993. Consensus or Dissensus in Welfare Values in Post-Communist Societies? Glasgow, University of Strathclyde Center for the Study of Public Policy, Working Paper No. 219.

Rosser, J. Barkley, Jr., Marian V. Rosser, and Ehsan Ahmed. 2000. Income Inequality and the Informal Economy in Transition Economies. *Journal of Comparative Politics* 28(1): 156–71.

Roxburgh, Ian, and Judith Shapiro. 1996. Russian Unemployment and the Excess Wages Tax. *Communist Economics and Economic Transformation* 8(1): 5–27.

Sabel, Charles. 1995. Intelligible Differences: On Deliberate Strategy and the Exploration of Possibility in Economic Life. 36th annual meeting of the Societá Italiana degli Economisti, Florence.

Saint-Paul, Gilles. 1996. Exploring the Political Economy of Labour Market Institutions. *Economic Policy* 23(October): 263–306.

Schwartz, Solomon M. 1951. *Labour in the Soviet Union.* London: Cresset Press.

Seleny, Anna. 1994. Constructing the Discourse of Transformation: Hungary 1979–82. *East European Politics and Society* 8(3): 439–66.

Sík, Endre. 1996a. Egy ló-öszvér a lovakról és a szmarakról; Adalék a második gazdaság hazai eszmetörténetéhez (About a horse-mule and horses: A contribution to the theoretical history of the Second Economy). *Közgzdasági Szemle* 48(7–8): 704–25.

1996b. The Social Consequences of Unemployment in Hungary – A Household Perspective. *Innovation* 9(3): 355–69.

Simon, János. 1994. Politika alulnézetböl: avagy hogan politizálnak a munkanélküliek? (The view from below: Or how the unemployed see politics). In S. P. Sándor Kurtán and Vass László, eds., *Magyarország politikai évkönyve* (Hungarian political yearbook), pp. 653–64. Budapest: Demokrácia Kutatások Magyar Központja.

1997. The Culture of Unemployment in Hungary. Budapest, Institute for Political Science of the Hungarian Academy of Sciences.

Soskice, David. 1978. Strike Waves and Wage Explosions, 1968–1970. In Colin Crouch and Allesandro Pizzorno, eds., *The Resurgence of Class Conflict in Western Europe*, 2:221–46. London: Macmillan.

Standing, Guy. 1997. Labour Market Governance in Eastern Europe. *European Journal of Industrial Relations* 3(2): 133–59.

Standing, Guy, and Guy Vaughan-Whitehead, eds. 1995. *Minimum Wages in Central and Eastern Europe: From Protection to Destitution.* New York: Central European University Press.

Stark, David. 1995. Recombinant Property in East European Capitalism. Unpublished manuscript.

1996. Recombinant Property in East European Capitalism. *American Journal of Sociology* 101(4): 993–1027.

Szabó, Gábor. 1993. Administrative Transition in a Post-Communist Society: The Case of Hungary. *Public Administration* 71(1–2): 89–103.

Szalai, Julia. 1996. Why the Poor Are Poor. *New Hungarian Quarterly* 37(144): 70–78.

Szelényi, Iván. 1978. Social Inequalities under State Socialist Redistributive Economics. *International Journal of Comparative Sociology* 19(1–2): 63–87.
Szelényi, Iván, and Robert Manchin. 1987. Social Policy under State Socialism. In Gøsta Esping-Anderson, Lee Rainwater, and Martin Rein, eds., *Stagnation and Renewal in Social Policy*. White Plains, N.Y.: M. E. Sharpe.
Széman, Zsuzsa. 1994. The Elderly in the Labour Market in a Time of Social Transition in Hungary. Budapest, Active Society Foundation.
Thelen, Kathleen. 2002. How Institutions Evolve: Insights from Comparative Historical Analysis. In James Mahoney and Dietrich Rueschemeyer, eds., *Comparative Historical Analysis in the Social Sciences*. Cambridge: Cambridge University Press.
Timár, János. 1966. *Planning the Labor Force in Hungary*. White Plains, N.Y.: International Arts and Sciences.
1998. Particular Features of Employment and Unemployment in the Present Stage of Transformation of the Post-Socialist Countries. Budapest.
Toonen, Theo. 1993. Analyzing Institutional Change and Administrative Transformation: A Comparative View. *Public Administration* 71(1–2): 151–68.
Tucker, Joshua A. 2000. It's the Economy, Comrade! Economic Conditions and Election Results in the Czech Republic, Hungary, Poland, Russia, and Slovakia, 1990–1996. Ph.D. dissertation, Harvard University.
Turner, Lowell. 1998. *Fighting for Partnership: Labor and Politics in United Germany*. Ithaca: Cornell University Press.
Verbélyi, Imre. 1993. Options for Administrative Reform in Hungary. *Public Administration* 71(1–2): 105–20.
Warwick, Paul. 1992. Economic Trends and Government Survival in West European Parliamentary Democracies. *American Political Science Review* 86(4): 875–87.
Winiecki, Jan. 1991. Large Industrial Enterprises in Soviet-Type Economies: The Ruling Stratum's Main Rent-Seeking Area. *Communist Economies* 1(4): 363–83.
Zaslavsky, Victor. 1982. *The Neo-Stalinist State*. New York: M. E. Sharpe.

9

"Past" Dependence or Path Contingency?

Institutional Design in Postcommunist Financial Systems

Juliet Johnson

> Life has proved to be richer and more complex than the theoretical notions that all of us were guided by.
>
> Russian central banker Aleksandr Khandruev

The surprisingly peaceful revolutions that swept the Soviet Union and East Europe in the late 1980s and early 1990s seemed to present a golden opportunity for institutional design. The economic and political institutions of state socialism had been discredited, and having discarded the past, these countries sought to create a new set of institutions to underpin their emerging market democracies. Indeed, institutional change does not simply describe an aspect of the postcommunist transformation process but is the essence of transformation itself. Putting old institutions at work to serve new ends, creating market-oriented institutions where none existed before, and redirecting institutions to act as links between state and society rather than as instruments with which to oppress society define the attempt to break with the Soviet era.

Yet the way in which institutional change has actually taken place in postcommunist states remains poorly understood. Our now-cautious use of the word "transition" illustrates this uncertainty. These countries may have made a transition *from* communism, but what are they making a transition *to*? Most observers no longer assume that they will all inevitably transform themselves into Western-style free-market democracies. While significant change has indeed occurred, many old institutional forms and practices have persisted in postcommunist countries far longer than most would-be reformers had initially expected. These lasting Soviet-era legacies have also been joined by new and sometimes disturbing institutional phenomena that arose as unexpected consequences of well-meaning reformist policies. Moreover, as Bunce has stated bluntly, "the dominant pattern of postsocialism has been one of variation, not uniformity ... what is striking is the intraregional contrast in postsocialist economic and political pathways" (Bunce, 1999: 759; Ekiert and Hanson, Chapter 1 in this volume).

Consequently, scholars have sought to assign blame for the rocky, uneven nature of these transformations and to determine what, if anything, could have been done differently. The controversy typically boils down to a single question: did these failures result from postcommunist leaders' insufficient "political will" to carry out effective reforms, or should persistent Soviet-era institutional legacies bear the primary responsibility?

Scholars' answers to this question depend upon their implicit or explicit theories of institutional change. These theories fall roughly into two groups: agency-centered and structure-based.[1] Agency-centered theorists express optimism that correct policy choices can overcome the legacies of the past, whereas structure-based theorists believe that legacies trump choice and bar radical change from occurring. Agency-centered approaches, advocated primarily by neoclassical economists and rational choice theorists, emphasize the role of political elites, bargaining, and incentives in the institutional design process.[2] These scholars typically minimize the uniqueness, tenacity, and usefulness of old institutional forms and stress the importance of rapid economic and political change. In this view, existing institutions and networks break down under conditions of extreme uncertainty, and policy entrepreneurs can then replace them with new, market-oriented ones. Accordingly, these theorists place primary responsibility for institutional design outcomes on the shoulders of policy elites. Proponents would argue, for example, that Leszek Balcerowicz boldly guided market-oriented institutional reform policies in Poland, whereas Boris Yeltsin failed to carry through with similar policies in Russia. This approach has been widely criticized for its voluntaristic, ahistorical nature, particularly in light of postcommunist states' unexpected difficulties in shedding many patterns and predilections of the past. Moreover, arguing that radical policy breaks typically fail because policy makers do not implement them with enough enthusiasm sidesteps the more interesting question of what underlying institutional features may be enabling or impeding such change.

In contrast, structure-based theories, advanced primarily by evolutionary economists and sociological institutionalists, emphasize the path-dependent

[1] The terms "agency-centered" and "structure-based" come from Clark (1998), who in turn credits Nancy Bermeo with coining them.

[2] Stephen Hanson persuasively makes this same point in his critical review of five influential books on the postcommunist economic reform process, arguing that "the central role of political elites in promoting postcommunist reform emerges as implicitly crucial to the arguments of all five books examined here" (Hanson, 1998). Hanson reviewed Sachs (1993); Aslund (1995); Goldman (1994); Porket (1995); and Bresser et al. (1993). Other important works in this vein include Przeworski (1991); O'Donnell, Schmitter, and Whitehead (1986); Nelson (1993); Sachs (1990); and Berg (1994). As Sachs (1990: 246) states, "It is up to politicians with vision and daring to create the conditions for Eastern Europe's economic transformation."

nature of institutional change (see Poznánski, 1997; Murrell and Wang, 1993; Murrell, 1995; Millar, 1996; Burawoy and Krotov, 1992; Nelson and Kuzes, 1995). They turn to institutional legacies, initial conditions, and cultural patterns to explain the difficulties behind institutional design; in this view, particular policy choices and political will are relatively unimportant because existing institutional structures strongly constrain the path of development. Evolutionary economics analogizes this path dependent process with a branching tree, where choices made at critical junctures ("forks" in the tree) lock in future choices and development. This is commonly referred to as the QWERTY model, named after the inefficient typewriter keyboard design that maintained its market dominance long after the original, functionalist reasons for its use had passed.[3] Similarly, sociological path dependence approaches argue both that the wider social and cultural environment constrains policy choices and institutional changes, and that conditions of uncertainty typically reinforce old networks and patterns as people turn back toward the familiar and the safe. According to this perspective, Balcerowicz "succeeded" where Yeltsin failed not because of superior leadership, but because Poland began the transformation race much closer to the finish line. Indeed, these theorists commonly condemn the kind of rapid economic reform program espoused by Balcerowicz. Structure-based theories argue that insufficient attention to the unique institutional legacies of particular states leads to policy failure and that the natural, evolutionary process of institutional change inevitably causes numerous unexpected consequences during attempts at institutional design.

Such structure-based approaches also have explanatory limitations. Stark and Bruszt characterize this strand of theory as "past dependency," in which the heavy hand of the past weighs in on all decisions and institutional outcomes (Stark and Bruszt, 1998). As Thelen writes, "both the economic-technological and the sociological-institutional perspectives provide strong tools for understanding continuity, but ... they are not particularly helpful in talking about change" (Thelen, 1999: 387). This built-in theoretical determinism is, not surprisingly, especially problematic when applied to periods of extraordinary politics. Yet how can we acknowledge the central role that choice and chance play in postcommunist transformations without discounting the importance of past "paths" as well?

In this chapter, I attempt to reconcile this dichotomous debate by using the "disciplined-contextual" approach to understanding postcommunist institutional change outlined by Ekiert and Hanson at the beginning of this volume. By examining the factors that enable or disrupt state-led institutional design in postcommunist states, I explicitly explore the issue of when and how Leninist institutional legacies matter in the postcommunist transformation process. In doing so, I examine the conditions under which "backward

[3] For a critique of the QWERTY model, see Leibowitz and Margolis (1990).

linkages" can and cannot occur. Elster, Offe, and Preuss define backward linkages as "cases in which choices put agents and institutional rules in their place, and these new arrangements alter or nullify the determining force of structural legacies or replace them with newly created legacies" (1998: 296). In short, when can conscious design create new institutional arrangements during periods of extraordinary politics?

I argue that the effectiveness of such institutional design depends on the interaction among policy choice, institutional legacies, state capacity, and policy sequencing. In this conceptual framework, policy choice is the independent variable, and institutional outcomes are the dependent variable. State capacity and institutional legacies are intervening variables, whose relative role in affecting outcomes depends on the type of policy choice adopted, either passive or active. Sequencing incorporates a temporal dimension to the analysis, demonstrating how the institutional outcomes engendered by particular policy choices can build upon each other, constraining policy-making effectiveness in the future. This approach, which I call path contingency, addresses Hellman's concern that Elster et al. "present a more complete and more compelling explanation of the obstacles to institutional consolidation than one of conditions for success" (Hellman, 1998: 72).

In the next section of this chapter I briefly explain the path contingency framework in theoretical terms, delineating the conditions under which policy choices may be more or less successfully translated into predictable, desirable institutional outcomes. I then employ two case studies of financial-sector reform in East Europe and Eurasia to further illuminate the concepts of passive and active institutional design. The first, highlighting passive institutional design, employs the logic of path contingency to explain the distorted evolution of the Russian commercial banking system. The second, emphasizing active institutional design, discusses the surprisingly successful evolution of Western-style central banks in postcommunist states. Finally, the conclusion suggests ways in which the concept of path contingency might be refined and expanded upon in subsequent research.

Designer Institutions

Path contingency has its origins in historical institutionalist theory. Institutions themselves can be characterized as the "glue of society," writ large. On one level, they allow us to deal with our limited capacity to absorb and process information by routinizing numerous tasks and lowering transaction costs. On another level, institutions reinforce, justify, and perpetuate political, economic, and social orders. Historical institutionalists argue that institutions are legacies of political struggles and that they can shape preferences as well as reflect them. Thus, institutions are usually treated as forces of stability in maintaining routine, predictable political and social outcomes. Path contingency extends this basic interpretation to periods of extraordinary politics, in which states experience immediate and intense political and economic uncertainty. Moreover, it avoids the imprecise use of the phrase "path dependence" that, as Ekiert and Hanson observe, has been employed to describe a wide range of postcommunist developmental patterns.

The path contingency approach differs from path dependence in two important ways: it consistently treats policy choice as an independent variable, and it argues that the relative importance of institutional legacies is contingent on the type of policy choices made by state actors. Instead of positing the primacy of either agency or structure, the theory focuses on the dynamic interaction between the two by analytically separating the voluntaristic choice of an institutional design policy from that policy's subsequent implementation. By doing so, we can begin to understand when institutional legacies will matter most in postcommunist transformations.

Institutional legacies do not play a central, causal role in determining policy choice under these conditions for two reasons.[4] First, with few exceptions (such as nationalist movements in federal states), the rapid breakdown of repressive, centralized regimes across East Europe and Eurasia briefly freed subsequent state leaders from the influence of strong, organized rivals or pressure groups that might have effectively challenged these states' right to choose policies relatively autonomously. In this atmosphere of extraordinary politics, political parties, economic interest groups, and other associations embodying civil society had little time in which to coalesce and make organized demands on the state. On the contrary, these states often developed what Fish (1995) has termed "movement societies," in which hastily assembled groups calling themselves "parties" and "associations" more closely resembled temporary political campaigns than effective institutions linking state and society. The near-total absence of strong organized labor groups at the moment of collapse is particularly notable in this context (with the exception of Poland's Solidarity), as the vast majority of research on development patterns in Western Europe, Latin America, and East Asia argues that state-labor relationships present vital constraints and opportunities for economic policy choice.

Furthermore, the near-simultaneous collapse of these self-defined communist polities undermined four fundamental bases on which these states had made policy choices in the past. First, it ended the leading role of the

[4] Treating policy choice as an independent variable departs from most historical institutionalist work, which views policies as outcomes influenced by institutional factors. For example, both Immergut (1992) and Maioni (1997) argue that country-specific institutional constraints led to the adoption of differing health care policies in advanced industrial countries. During periods of extraordinary politics, however, policy choice can neither be predicted nor determined by examining existing institutional structures. Mikhail Gorbachev's introduction of perestroika and Boris Yeltsin's decision to embark upon shock therapy can be explained post hoc, but nothing in the institutional repertoire of the USSR or Russia necessitated these choices.

Communist Party and legitimized the search for new forms of political organization. Second, it exploded the perceived right of the state to direct the economy, control property, and employ most citizens engaged in commercial transactions. Third, it forced postcommunist states to reconceptualize and redefine themselves as nations, resulting in intense political turmoil, the breakup of three states, and the reunification of another with its capitalist twin. Finally, the end of the Cold War destroyed the context in which these states had interacted with the West, forcing each state to adjust and react to a new, individual, and sometimes unsettling place in the international system. When historical circumstances call into question an entire world view around which politics has previously been constructed, the possibilities for state policy choice are vastly expanded. Institutional design policies adopted in such situations often attempt to do more than lower discrete transaction costs or redistribute political power. These policies may aim to create structures reflecting radically altered world views – policies that, at least at the beginning, naturally impose a much higher burden of institutional uncertainty on both state and society. As a result, the breakdown of communist rule can be seen as a "critical juncture" that opened a window for expanded policy choice.

Freedom of choice, however, does not necessarily mean freedom of outcome.[5] While policy choice itself breaks free of institutional shackles during periods of extraordinary politics, the implementation and outcomes of policy may still be affected by institutional variables. After all, policy makers whose countries enter critical junctures in their developmental histories still ultimately share the same basic preferences for political stability, security of incumbency, and rapid economic development, preferences that they want to translate into policy (Waldner, 1999). Yet even similar policy choices, when made in transforming states with different institutional endowments and state capacities, can yield different results. When will a particular policy choice trigger development along a particular institutional path? Why do some policies emerge stillborn or lead to unintended consequences, whereas others achieve the desired effects? In short, when do backward linkages actually occur during periods of extraordinary politics? I argue that policy choices aimed at designing postcommunist institutions can be characterized as either passive or active and that this distinction is fundamental to understanding institutional outcomes.

In passive institutional design, policy makers do not attempt to change institutional frameworks directly. Instead, they introduce broad measures designed to alter the behavior of institutional actors – for example, by privatizing enterprises, by granting bankers more freedom to set interest rates, or by liberalizing prices. Therefore, I label this approach "passive" not because

[5] It is on this point that path contingency takes issue with the literature on punctuated equilibrium and critical junctures. See Krasner (1984); Collier and Collier (1991).

these design policies lack radical elements, but because the state itself acts as an indirect agent of change. Perhaps the most important passive strategy involves the withdrawal of explicit state ownership and regulation, rescinding powers the central government had previously reserved for itself or granting greater autonomy to institutional actors. Passive policies directly attack the "tight coupling" among institutional spheres that Elster et al. (1998: 31) identify as characteristic of state socialism. Passive design works through the effects of the aggregate decisions of individual actors. In this "trickle-down" approach, market-oriented institutional frameworks emerge spontaneously from the bottom up once elites present the relevant individuals with the correct incentives to build them. In active institutional design, by contrast, a policy choice aims to replace, create, or alter an institutional framework through direct state efforts – for example, by establishing a development bank, a tax authority, or a deposit insurance system. Active institutional design affects not only the formal structure of an institution but also its practices and values. Such active institutional design will, in theory, change the incentive structures of institutional actors and yield predictable, desirable outcomes. In this "state-as-architect" approach, states create an improved institutional framework to which actors will then adapt. A normative understanding of the proper role of the state in the economy often underlies preferences for one kind of policy over the other. Should the state itself change institutions or merely provide incentives for others to do so?

It is important to differentiate between passive and active design because the efficacy of passive policies depends largely on underlying institutional conditions, whereas the efficacy of active policies depends largely on state capacity; embedded institutional legacies matter more to the outcome of passive policies than active ones. Active policies demand a strong state role. In the absence of state capacity, active design attempts will fizzle out or remain on the drawing board. Initial conditions do matter to the outcome of active design, because the greater the institutional change desired, the more state effort must be expended to bring it about.[6] To be successful, however, passive institutional design absolutely *requires* a hospitable institutional context. The more alien the environment to the desired result, the more likely that passive policies will have perverse and unexpected consequences.

Moreover, the sequencing of passive and active institutional design policies strongly affects the ultimate institutional outcomes. Purposefully sequencing policies is both more important and more difficult in postcommunist transformations. Sequencing is especially important because individual institutional design efforts take place in the broader context of rapid, fundamental, and simultaneous reconfiguration of a state's political and economic environment. Yet the difficulty of the design process increases exponentially

[6] This echoes Gerschenkron's (1962) observation that the later a state develops its industrial base, the more state intervention in the economy it will need in order to catch up.

because of the ongoing and self-referential nature of postcommunist institutional change.[7] Therefore, the more inhospitable the initial institutional framework is to the introduction of market-oriented, democratic institutions, the sooner active institutional designs will be needed and the greater the state capacity that will be required to bring about change. If passive institutional design, as a rule, precedes active design in such states, it is a near certainty that the outcomes will not only be unexpected but undesirable.

Worse, states that succumb to the rapid decentralization inherent in passive design without building the state's own regulatory institutions through active design may increasingly lose the capacity necessary to carry out active designs in the future as their authority becomes dispersed. For this reason, an overreliance on passive institutional design measures in states with inhospitable institutional environments can lead to what I call an irony of autonomy. Although the decentralization of political and economic power characteristic of passive design leaves institutions with far more autonomy from the central government than they enjoyed in the past, inhospitable institutional legacies can encourage institutional actors privileged by the old system to use this autonomy in pursuit of detrimental, short-term political and economic gains. The wider institutional context in many postcommunist states – with its absence of secure property rights, legal and judicial protections, adequate payments, taxation, and accounting systems, and so forth – provided a positive disincentive for institutional actors to invest in and develop the economy for the long term. As a result, as the following example demonstrates, inappropriately sequenced passive design policies often undermined the transformation process.

Passive Design and Bank Liberalization

Unlike active institutional design, passive design does not, in itself, cause institutional change. Instead, it attempts to provoke others to create or adapt institutions in ways intended by policy makers. Privatization of already existing economic structures represents a straightforward passive design measure that lessens state control over institutions without reconfiguring them. For example, simple privatization of industrial and agricultural enterprises changes only their ownership, not their form. Such privatization aims to provide owners with incentives to restructure these enterprises and make them profitable. That is, altering the status of institutional actors either by introducing new owners or transforming old managers into owners

[7] This distinguishes postcommunist transformations from the Latin American and Southern European experiences. Although economic and political decentralization represented the overarching goal in both cases, the rapidity and simultaneity of the postcommunist transformations yields a qualitatively higher level of uncertainty. This serves both to increase the autonomy of individual actors within existing institutions and to diminish the power of the reconstituted state to control the process.

should encourage them to fire unneeded employees, alter production strategies, and find new markets for their products if necessary (Boyko, Schleifer, and Vishny, 1995; Andreev, 1992). Privatization programs in postcommunist states may employ active design elements such as preprivatization debt restructuring and demonopolization, but this should be distinguished from the act of privatization itself. Spontaneous privatization and voucher privatization, in which states essentially give away property "as is," represent the purest forms of passive privatization.

Furthermore, passive institutional design encompasses broad macroeconomic policies such as price liberalization, fiscal restraint, currency convertibility, and free trade. Although such measures often have purposes and importance beyond institutional design, as design policies they rest on the assumption that macroeconomic changes can predictably produce certain microeconomic ones. As Aslund (1995) has argued, "the introduction of an adequate economic system should lead to structural changes, raising economic efficiency." The reform approach known as shock therapy prescribes a number of passive institutional design policies. Shock therapy advocates like Jeffrey Sachs (1993) argued that rapid, promarket institutional change could be achieved in postcommunist countries by quickly implementing certain passive policy measures such as price, trade, financial liberalization, and privatization. The shock therapists explicitly advised postcommunist states to use such methods to destroy their old command-oriented institutions in a "big bang," evoking a metaphorical destruction and rebirth of the economic universe.

Postcommunist policy makers relied more heavily on passive than on active institutional designs. Western advisors typically characterized passive policies as efficient, faster, and more controllable, arguing in particular that the broadest passive institutional design measures (like price liberalization) could serve to change a large number of institutions simultaneously. In addition, by using passive measures, political elites themselves did not have to replace or refurbish old institutional frameworks, which requires money, power, and time. As scholars interested both in East Asian developmental states and in postcommunist gradualist reform programs have observed, though, the massive decentralization of political and economic power inherent in such passive design policies does not necessarily create more efficient, dynamic economies. Nor does state intervention inevitably distort economies; while intervention can encourage rent seeking, it can also concentrate and target investment. Therefore, determining the potential efficacy of passive institutional design policies in postcommunist states requires an examination of the initial institutional context. The more inhospitable the institutional context is to the changes the state envisions, the more likely that unintended consequences will result. Conversely, the more the desired institutional change can build on and be supported by the existing institutional context, the more appropriate and successful passive design policies will be.

The emergence of a distorted, unsound, investment-shy financial system in Russia represents one of the most dramatic and unexpected developments of the postcommunist experience. Using the path contingency framework to analyze this outcome reveals the role of institutional legacies in foiling three separate passive design policies aimed at reforming the Russian commercial banking sector. These passive design attempts included the liberalization of the banking system under Gorbachev, the failed attempt at shock therapy in 1992, and cash privatization in 1995. Adopting these sequential, passive policies in an inhospitable institutional environment led to an irony of autonomy. In each case, reformers believed that these decentralizing policies would result in the spontaneous generation of market-oriented financial institutions. Sadly, they had precisely the opposite effect, driving the banks ever more firmly into the arms of the state in a sometimes symbiotic, but more often parasitic, relationship. Indeed, the particular sequence of these policies allowed their damaging results to build on each other, producing the structural weaknesses that underlay the financial crash of 1998.

Liberalization

The Soviet-era command economy, whose ideal form aimed to abolish private ownership of the means of production, represented the antithesis of the market system. The banking system itself served simply as an administrative means of channeling money to state enterprises and financing the government. When Mikhail Gorbachev came to power, he chose to restructure this command economy. As he later observed, "we came to realize that the country was living beyond its means. That holes in the budget were being covered through the Savings Bank, through credits. That we were heading for the abyss" (Gorbachev, 1990). As a result, the USSR significantly liberated its banking system in three phases between 1988 and 1992, with the goal of promoting profit-oriented behavior. Importantly, this reform process began in an institutional context where few laws governed market relations, private property barely existed, the ruble was nonconvertible, enterprises fulfilled the plan rather than seeking profit, and the Soviet financial system had a nominally federal structure mirroring the political-territorial boundaries in the USSR.

First, in January 1988 the USSR dismantled its monobank, Gosbank, to create a two-tiered banking system. Gosbank itself became a true central bank, while the reform sheared three new banks (called specialized banks) off of the old Gosbank structure. These included Agroprombank, which dealt with agriculture; Promstroibank, which dealt with industry; and Zhilsotsbank, which handled small enterprise, trade, and municipal finances. Gosbank retained control over the state savings bank (Sberbank) and the foreign trade bank (Vneshtorgbank). This increased the size of the banking bureaucracy and the opportunities for corruption without giving these specialized banks the freedom to set their own interest rates or choose their own customers.

Second, in 1988 the USSR passed legislation allowing the formation of cooperative and commercial banks, unaccompanied by active institutional design policies that would bolster Gosbank's ability to regulate them. This led to the creation of two new kinds of banks: zero banks and industry banks. Most so-called zero banks – created primarily by the Communist Party and its affiliated groups, specialized banks, and other "nonproductive" organizations – arose in Moscow. These banks, and the bankers who ran them, would loom large over Russia's political and economic landscape after 1991. Most industry banks, on the other hand, remained closely tied to their enterprise founders. Such banks came to be known as pocket banks, because they were kept in the pockets of enterprise directors and created in order to feed off of the loopholes in the old system. The legalization of commercial banking under these freewheeling conditions led to an almost uncontrollable proliferation of undercapitalized, poorly regulated, less-than-professional banks.

Finally, beginning in September 1990 the Russian state encouraged the specialized banks on its territory to "commercialize" themselves. This was a rapid passive design process that allowed bankers to break up the highly centralized system and transfer the state's shares in the hundreds of resulting banks to their enterprise customers. By the end of 1991, Russia alone boasted 1,360 operating credit institutions. This kind of decentralization encouraged banks to strengthen their ability to use state connections for profit. During this period, these banks acquired as much freedom as possible while still carrying out their traditional economic mission of channeling state credits to industrial enterprises and agriculture. In short, they sought and attained autonomy in their endeavors without bearing responsibility for the consequences.

The banking system prospered and evolved through 1991 because both old and new bankers used and adapted the Soviet-era institutional framework to exploit the decline in central political power, even as nationalist politicians used the federalized banking system as a tool with which to pry apart the USSR. Soviet-era banks were poorly suited to evaluating borrowers and making small loans but, once liberalized, provided ample opportunity to siphon money from the government into private hands. Using their Soviet-era connections, bankers redefined their ties with state enterprises and state and local bureaucracies. These ties gave the banks access to central bank credits, enterprise resources, and other lucrative (but not productive) sources of income. In short, these banks facilitated spontaneous privatization. Usually called nomenklatura privatization in Russia, this refers to the way in which those in positions of economic and political influence in the Soviet system (called the nomenklatura) took advantage of economic decentralization by appropriating state resources for themselves. The banks formed a bridge with which to safely cross the "abyss" separating a command and a market economy. As a result of passive liberalization, therefore, commercial banks in Russia – whatever their formal, legal origins and status – were born tightly wedded to the state.

Shock Therapy

After the USSR disintegrated, in early 1992 Yeltsin and his government adopted another set of passive design policies – shock therapy. Although they immediately undertook major price liberalization and mass privatization, institutional legacies prevented macroeconomic stabilization from beginning to take hold until late 1993. As a result, unexpectedly high inflation wiped out people's life savings, cash became scarce, capital flight and dollarization both skyrocketed, the ruble's value fell, and mutual debt among enterprises reached billions of rubles.

The Central Bank of Russia (CBR) played an important role in thwarting the Russian shock therapy attempt, epitomizing the institutional barriers to such a policy at that time. When Yeltsin and Gaidar tried to introduce shock therapy, they had no choice but to implement their monetary policies through the CBR. Success depended on the CBR's ability to restrict the money supply in order to control inflation after price liberalization. The CBR, however, was not willing or able to control cash and credit emissions. At this time, Russia's central bankers had a different conception of the proper role of a central bank, preferring to support production rather than price stability. Indeed, some central bankers, especially in the early years of reform, saw no inherent incompatibility between controlling inflation and supporting enterprises with subsidized credits. Moreover, as a result of the Gorbachev-era passive decentralization policies that had given the CBR greater autonomy from the central government, CBR leaders had the ability to refuse to cooperate with the shock therapy attempt. More important, though, the CBR lacked the ability to control the money supply. Up to that point, the state had not used active institutional design policies to increase the CBR's technical capabilities, and actors within the CBR had not made these changes on their own. The inefficient interbank payments system, the CBR's inadequate tools of monetary policy, and the persistence of the credit-hungry ruble zone left the CBR technically unable to control the levels of cash and credit in the economy. The ruble zone in particular, with its fifteen nominally sovereign central banks in each of the former Soviet republics, proved to be an uncontrollable source of credit emissions. Liberalizing prices before the CBR had the ability to restrict the money supply made an inflationary trend all but inevitable.

The high inflation and interenterprise debt engendered by the failed shock therapy attempt crippled the productivity of Russian industry and agriculture, while simultaneously allowing Russia's already established banks to earn hyperprofits on centralized loans granted at negative real interest rates, wide interest rate spreads between deposits and loans, and on currency speculation. While the Russian economy as a whole declined by 32 percent between 1992 and 1995, the financial sector alone grew by 43 percent (Warner, 1998). This paved the way for the continued acquisition of political power and state economic resources by the most prominent bankers, despite their unpopularity in the emerging democratic political system. Banks, for example, provided extensive financing for Russia's political campaigns and therefore influenced the development of the party system in Russia. They also developed strong lobbying organizations, which successfully thwarted Tatiana Paramonova's nomination as CBR director in 1995 and ensured that foreign banks gained only limited access to the Russian market. Rather than bringing economic prosperity to Russia, the abortive shock therapy attempt accelerated the decline in production, legitimized the results of earlier nomenklatura privatization, contributed to the spiraling chain of nonpayments, enriched the commercial banks, and touched off a political firestorm. This cannot be blamed on shock therapy policies per se (which proved more successful in other states) but on their poor timing and on the inhospitable institutional environment in Russia for such passive, market-oriented design measures.

Cash Privatization

In 1995 the Russian government adopted a third passive design policy – cash privatization. Cash privatization involved selling shares of large state-owned enterprises by auction to the highest bidder. The state expected that privatization would improve corporate governance in these enterprises, as the new owners restructured them and made them more profitable. Instead, after acquiring these companies Russian banks often engaged in asset stripping and used them as pawns in their broader battle for political and economic influence in Russia. Immediately before the parliamentary elections in late 1995, the Russian government sanctioned a series of cash privatization auctions now known as loans for shares. In these auctions, leading banks acquired significant stakes in key Russian export companies, including metallurgical enterprises (e.g., Norilsk Nickel and the Novolipetsk Metallurgical Combine) and oil companies (e.g., Sidanko, Yukos, and Sibneft), in exchange for relatively small loans to the government. After the government decided not to repay these loans, further questionable tenders in 1997 gave the winning banks free-and-clear ownership of the shares, again without significant financial gain for their nominal state owners. While bank-led financial-industrial groups (FIGs) had begun to emerge in the early 1990s, the loans-for-shares auctions catalyzed the bank-led FIGs' leap from important economic players to dominant financial-industrial conglomerates and discredited the privatization process in the eyes of the Russian public.[8]

[8] For a detailed analysis of FIG development, see Johnson (1997).

The Russian government undertook cash privatization both because the International Monetary Fund (IMF) had been pushing it to privatize the rest of its state enterprises and because the state desperately needed a new source of revenue. Although the initial round of privatization and liberalization had cut it off from much of the command economy's revenue sources, Russia lacked the immense state capacity necessary to design and implement an efficient, fair, and lucrative taxation system. It attempted to fill the gaps after 1993 by developing a treasury bill (GKO) market and accumulating foreign loans, but the situation continued to worsen as capital flight drained the monetary economy while more and more of Russia's economic transactions took place through the use of barter or surrogate currencies (Woodruff, 1998). The distorted way in which the government implemented the cash privatization policy, however, resulted directly from the earlier politicization and relative financial power of the banks. By 1993 the largest banks had became central political players in Russia due to their ownership of media outlets, their financial support for political parties and candidates, and their close ties to the Yeltsin government. The government, in turn, depended on the banks not only for campaign finance but also for operating capital at all levels, from local to national organs of power. Bankers used this power to advance their own economic, political, and legal agendas. This intermixing of political and financial clout reached its height in the 1996 presidential election campaign, as influential Moscow bankers used every means at their disposal to ensure Yeltsin's ultimate victory in July despite his single-digit public approval ratings in February.

Commercial banks, focused on politics, made few comparable efforts to reorient their economic activities in market-oriented ways. They engaged in only minimal restructuring of the enterprises they had acquired in the auctions, while a broader lack of institutional development in the industrial and agricultural sectors meant that granting long-term loans remained unprofitable for banks. Meanwhile, Sberbank's near-monopoly over household deposits and the persistent public distrust of commercial banks made it difficult for these banks to profit from the retail market. As a result, the largest banks survived in this period of increasing state fiscal restraint by buying government GKOs, playing the stock market, acting as "authorized" banks for the state, accumulating loans from Western banks, and drawing up so-called "dollar-forward" contracts with Western GKO investors (in effect covering the foreigners' currency risk by locking in a ruble-dollar exchange rate three to six months in advance). By 1998, debts to foreign banks represented over 20 percent of the liabilities of half of Russia's twenty largest banks. More than twenty banks, including all of the largest bank-led FIGs except Alfa Bank, held over 15 billion rubles' worth of dollar-forward contracts (Inkombank alone held over 138 billion).[9] From 1995 to 1997,

[9] "Virtual Banking," *Russia Review*, November 1998, 27 and 31.

the percentage of securities in Russian banks' asset structures rose from 5.7 to 18 percent (OECD, 1997). In short, the largest banks remained heavily reliant on politically contingent, speculative means of making money.

Unfortunately, so did the state, whose dependence on high-yielding GKOs and on international capital markets became more and more untenable after the Asian financial crisis and the continuing fall in international oil prices. A last-minute IMF loan in July 1998 failed to avert the crisis, as Russian banks and enterprises used the capital influx to desperately convert ruble holdings to dollars. On August 17, the Russian government's GKO default, ruble devaluation, and subsequent moratorium on foreign-debt payments laid bare this glaring structural weakness in the banking system as Russia's biggest banks suddenly found themselves irreparably bleeding red ink.

Designing Disaster

These three decentralizing, passive institutional design policies, which progressively relinquished the state's power over the Russian financial system, each led to similar, unexpected, and undesirable institutional outcomes, even though they were introduced under two different leaderships, two separate regime types, and in different international contexts. By implementing a sequence of passive institutional design measures, Soviet and then Russian reformers asked command-era economic institutions to adapt themselves to the rapidly changing political and economic situation. The initial, prereform institutional structures, practices, and values set the framework for what followed, both by providing the institutional "raw material" and by privileging certain actors in the transformation process. Defying expectations, the interaction of institutional legacies and state capacity with policy choices yielded hybrid institutional forms. Granting greater economic autonomy to individual institutions did not ensure that these institutions would then undertake the desired changes on their own. Instead, an irony of autonomy resulted, in which economic institutions given more freedom from central control used that freedom to the detriment of Russia's long-term economic development.

The Russian case reveals that rapid financial liberalization, rather than accelerating the pace of institutional change, may actually postpone the development of a market-oriented financial system because such liberalization can reinforce command-era economic ties, permit spontaneous privatization of state resources, and promote the entanglement of state and financial interests. Ironically, although supporters of both shock therapy and gradualism "suggest that the gross distortions of economic restructuring in Russia were largely avoidable," by 1992 neither alternative held much promise for engendering comprehensive change in post-Soviet Russia (Roberts and Sherlock, 1999). Inhospitable initial institutional conditions waylaid the shock therapists' passive design policies, while Russia's minimal state capacity, exacerbated by Soviet-era financial liberalization, limited its ability to carry out policies requiring active means.

As McKinnon (1991) and Rostowski (1993) have argued, in order for commercial banks to function there must be a market economic environment in which they can operate. Liberalizing financial institutions leads to unanticipated, nonmarket-oriented outcomes if the country lacks both a supporting external infrastructure (such as enterprises with hard budget constraints and effective bank regulatory bodies) and a supporting internal institutional framework (computer technology, the ability to evaluate borrowers, and a functioning payments system). Without private enterprises, to whom could banks make loans? Without effectively enforced laws to protect contracts and ensure property rights, how could potential borrowers legitimately provide collateral? Under such circumstances, banks cannot act like banks. As a result, it should not be surprising that relatively successful postcommunist countries such as Hungary, Poland, and the Czech Republic refrained from relinquishing significant control over their financial sectors before undertaking enterprise privatization and restructuring. This further illustrates the central importance of sequencing in the institutional design process.

More broadly, in states with entrenched, barely altered command economies, passive institutional design often renders resource redistribution more profitable than investment activities for both state-owned and emerging private enterprises. Russia's initial voucher privatization program caused widespread bewilderment and served only to cede power over most large enterprises to their Soviet-era managers. These managers, in turn, did not find that private ownership encouraged them to fire "unnecessary" workers or seek profits in expected ways, because the institutional context that would make such decisions rational had not appeared. Instead, Russian industry spiraled further downward in a cycle of barter, corruption, interenterprise debt, and wage arrears. Similarly, poorly developed Kyrgyzstan's early and extensive Western-supported liberalization and privatization programs did little to encourage enterprise restructuring and foreign investment; however, Hungary, with its history of "goulash communism" and quasi-capitalist institutions, became one of the most dynamic economies in Eastern Europe in spite of its comparatively slow liberalization, privatization, and stabilization after 1989.

The interaction of passive policies with institutional legacies does much to explain the relatively greater efficacy of shock therapy methods in countries with economies that had already been marketized (e.g., Latin American states) or partially marketized (e.g., Poland). In addition, as Ekiert and Hanson observe, institutional legacies have important spatial as well as temporal characteristics. In the case of Leninist financial systems, for example, the contrast between the institutional structures of the unitary Eastern European banking systems and the federalized Soviet banking system meant that similar, passive financial liberalization policies in these two contexts would yield strikingly different outcomes. For these reasons, one must analyze initial institutional conditions when choosing design strategies or when comparing the results of reform efforts in different countries. Under the wrong conditions, passive institutional design, instead of engendering improved institutional frameworks, founders on the rocky shoals of the old ones.

Active Design and Central Bank Development

Despite the prevalence of passive design policies, postcommunist states attempted to implement a variety of active institutional designs as well. Most so-called gradualist economic reform programs called for active design policies to alter legal, financial, and other institutional frameworks, and the founding of state-owned consolidation banks (charged with appropriating and resolving command-era bank debts) and central tax authorities are just two of many examples of active design (Murrell and Wang, 1993; Murrell, 1993; Stark, 1992; Pickel, 1992). Active policies can aim either to create new institutions or to adapt old institutions to new purposes in a process Thelen (2000) calls "institutional conversion." Either process entails significant effort. Creating new institutions requires the state to design, staff, fund, and then interact with a wholly fresh entity, whereas actively converting existing institutions in a short period of time typically requires extensive personnel training, technical adaptations, and administrative reconfigurations that may meet with resistance.

The success of active institutional design, therefore, depends upon sufficient state capacity. It is important in this context to recognize that state capacity and institutional legacies cannot be neatly pried apart. Indeed, Roberts and Sherlock (1999) argue that state capacity should be measured along three dimensions: political, administrative, and institutional.[10] However, institutional legacies are only one of many factors that affect a postcommunist state's capacity to implement active design policies. Elite polarization and conflict, the mode of transformation, financial resources, the extent of democratization, and international influences, among other factors, may all affect state capacity. Democratization, for example, can increase the legitimacy and consistency of a state's policy making because it regularizes the policy-making process and makes elites accountable for their policy choices. As Stark and Bruszt (1998) found in their study of postcommunist economic development, the capacity of elites to implement reform programs improves with their level of democratic accountability because this leads to increased coordination and legitimacy of the reforms.

States with high capacity can achieve three goals in policy implementation: consensus, consistency, and credibility. *Consensus* means that the relevant elites broadly agree on the need for a particular institutional design policy.

[10] On state autonomy and capacity more generally, see Nordlinger (1981); Migdal (1988).

Without consensus, policy makers may undercut and sabotage each others' attempts at institutional design. *Consistency* means that this policy will be unlikely to change in the short term and will not overtly contradict the aims of other relevant state policies. Without consistency, institutional actors will not treat the policy seriously and, in fact, will often do their utmost to bypass it or twist it to their own short-term advantage. *Credibility* means that relevant outside observers believe that the state has the means with which to implement this policy. Without credibility, the policy remains merely words on paper. Finally, the more dramatically the active design policy aims to alter the existing institutional repertoire, the more state capacity will be needed to bring it about.

Importantly, international actors can, in some cases, "artificially" enhance state capacity. For example, the lure of the European Union and NATO helped postcommunist states in East Europe to implement policies with consensus and consistency; the long-term goal of political, economic, and military unification with Western Europe, with its prescribed standards and clear, attractive path, lengthened the time horizons of institutional actors and gave them a ready-made set of institutional frameworks toward which to aspire.[11] As Kopstein and Reilly point out in Chapter 4 of this volume, spatial proximity to Western Europe intensifies the diffusion of political democracy and market institutions through changing incentive structures and enabling more-rapid expansion of informal cross-national networks. Carefully targeted technical assistance programs may also help to bridge the credibility gap, with external agencies providing the resources to implement an active institutional design plan. International influences cannot perfectly substitute for domestic state capacity (after all, the domestic government must still both cooperate and then maintain the institutions), but they can significantly jump-start active design programs.

Postcommunist central bank development presents a particularly interesting case of both domestically and internationally driven active institutional design. In the first years of transformation, postcommunist central banks exhibited large differences in their legal independence and technical capabilities, reflecting both initial conditions and the varying (in)ability of these states to carry out institutional conversion on their own. Yet within a decade, most postcommunist states had developed technically sophisticated central banks that approached Western standards in a variety of areas. This transformation occurred because of the intensive involvement of the transnational central banking community in active institutional design within these central

[11] Post-Soviet states (with the exception of the Baltics) do not enjoy this advantage. In fact, the perception that NATO and EU expansion is exclusionary and directed *against* them may actually be decreasing state capacity in these countries, inasmuch as it reinvigorates the ongoing, polarizing debates among liberal Westernizers, communists, extremist nationalists, and nationalistic centrists.

banks, which in effect allowed the postcommunist states to "import" capacity from the West.[12] The few states left behind in this process, such as Belarus, Turkmenistan, and Azerbaijan, failed to reach an elite consensus on the desirability of central bank reform and so remained relatively closed to the Western central bankers.

Stage One: Institutional Transformation from Within

Although all of the central banks in formerly command economies had inauspicious starting points from which to launch their massive transformation efforts, important differences arose among them in the first years of this process. Those states that entered the postcommunist period with the least capacity to carry out active design also, as a rule, had the most difficult initial conditions to deal with in the central banking realm. Therefore, the ever increasing divergence in postcommunist central bank development during this period should not have been surprising.

The initial differences divided the states into roughly eight groups. The first included only Hungary, which began in the most advantageous position. Before 1989 it already had its own currency and central bank, a comparatively open economy (including IMF membership), and a relatively recent history of capitalism. Not only did it have potential European Union (EU) membership to look forward to, but it began its transformation earlier than other postcommunist states. The second group included Poland and the Czech Republic, which enjoyed all of Hungary's advantages except its comparatively open economy at the start of the transition. The third group comprised Slovenia and Slovakia, legitimate EU hopefuls that began the transition a bit later and had to create their own currencies and central banks after the breakup of Yugoslavia and Czechoslovakia (the Czechs inherited the Czechoslovak central bank in Prague).

The fourth group included Bulgaria, Romania, and Albania, which had their own central banks and currencies but began the transition later and with less realistic hopes of near-term EU membership. The fifth group included Croatia, Macedonia, Latvia, Lithuania, and Estonia, which began the transition late, had to create their own central banks and currencies, and appeared to be less likely EU candidates at that time. Russia itself composed the sixth group. While it took over the Soviet central bank and controlled the printing of rubles, it also began its significant economic transition later than the East European states and with the legacy of over seventy years of a command economy. The seventh group encompassed the post-Soviet states of Armenia, Georgia, Kyrgyzstan, Moldova, and Ukraine. These countries began the separation and transformation late, with no advantages, and, at least in the Kyrgyz case, unwillingly. Finally, the eighth group included

[12] See Johnson (2001) for an extended discussion of this issue.

those former Soviet states such as Belarus, Azerbaijan, Uzbekistan, and Turkmenistan, as well as Serbia in East Europe, which were burdened not only by economic legacies but also by a lack of political liberalization.

Furthermore, a brief comparison of the initial, state-led efforts at central bank development in Russia, Estonia, and Hungary reveals the differing capacities of these various governments to undertake institutional conversion. In the Russian case, the government acted to increase the central bank's legal independence and to redefine its duties, but in the context of a wider political struggle that diminished the consensus and consistency of the reforms. In August 1990 the Russian government turned the Moscow branch of Gosbank into the Central Bank of Russia (CBR) in order to provide a counterweight to Gosbank in Russia's struggle for sovereignty. Both the Soviet and Russian governments took numerous measures, especially legal ones, to increase the political autonomy of their respective central banks during this period as a way of increasing their power in the battle for control over Russia's financial resources. This struggle for sovereignty provided no incentives for the central bankers to increase their technical capabilities or to cease funneling cheap credits to state enterprises, and the Soviet state took few active measures to promote this. As a result, this partial reform created a Russian central bank with enormous political autonomy vis-à-vis both the Russian government and the commercial banks but with little technical capacity to carry out market-oriented central banking tasks. This, as we have seen, wreaked havoc when the Yeltsin government attempted to implement shock therapy in 1992.

This same process occurred simultaneously in the other Soviet republics, a design legacy that put post-Soviet central banks in especially difficult positions when compared with the central banks of East Europe. In 1992 the main branches of Gosbank in the other post-Soviet states immediately became their countries' central banks. These central banks had enhanced legal statuses and had been partially separated from the specialized banks, yet further, highly technical and politically contentious development typically proved to be too difficult for these new governments. In the Estonian case, the government had reached a consensus on the need for conservative macroeconomic policy, but recognized its inability to quickly forge a credible, independent central bank. This led to the 1992 introduction of a currency board in Estonia, a much more easily created, temporary monetary institution. Under a currency board, any domestic currency in circulation must be backed by foreign reserves, and the domestic currency is exchangeable with a chosen anchor currency at a fixed rate. The Estonian central bank operated the currency board and, by relinquishing control over monetary policy, bought itself more time for its own institutional development. This gave Estonian monetary policy instant credibility but at the expense of economic flexibility, a real trade-off in a state undergoing a fundamental economic transformation.

Finally, in the Hungarian case, a firm state consensus on the desirability of a Western-style central bank and a consistent, early start in central banking reform led to the rapid evolution of a relatively independent, respected central bank. Hungary broke up its monobank in 1987 (far earlier than the other East European states) but, unlike the USSR, it did so in the context of a mixed economy with partially liberalized prices. Legislation modeled after the Bundesbank gave the National Bank of Hungary formal legal independence in 1990, and it quickly moved to issue bonds and raise interest rates to positive levels. Hungary's previous interactions with Western Europe (especially through its IMF membership), its comparatively progressive economics training, and the prestige of the central bank allowed it to attract competent economists with the basic knowledge necessary to begin internal reforms. Even Hungary, however, faced serious problems in dealing with accumulated debt in the financial system, poor transmission mechanisms for monetary policy, and an internal central banking culture and structure better suited to a command than a market economy. Further rapid central bank development across the postcommunist world, development that would occur far more quickly than in other domestic institutions, required a jolt from outside.

Stage Two: Institutional Transformation from Without

Only a decade later, postcommunist central banks across East Europe and Eurasia had made surprisingly rapid strides toward Western-oriented development, in marked contrast to the varied cross-national institutional development patterns in other arenas and to the initial developmental differences among the central banks themselves. This transformation involved changing both the preferences of postcommunist central bankers and the structure of their central banks to conform to an accepted Western model.

These structures included legal frameworks, tools of monetary policy, payments systems, statistical bureaus, banking supervision and regulation frameworks, accounting systems, and frameworks for foreign exchange operations. As an indication of this structural change, consider six internationally accepted measures of central bank development: the central bank's main goal, codified in law, is to defend "price stability" or "currency stability"; the central bank enjoys formal legal independence from the government; the central bank has maintained positive real interest rates for a full year;[13] the central bank has introduced current account convertibility for the currency; the central bank can employ open market operations as a tool of monetary policy;[14] and the central bank abides by International Accounting Standards

[13] I looked at positive real interest rates rather than inflation rates because, while the central bank cannot control government spending and external borrowing, it can control the interest rate at which money enters the banking system. Positive real interest rates express the central bank's intention to restrain excessive borrowing.

[14] Although Bulgaria (1997) and Lithuania (1994) became currency board states, their central

(IAS). None of these conditions obtained in the era of the command economy, and none is absolutely necessary for a central bank in a market economy. Yet, by 2001, eighteen of the nineteen central banks in groups one through seven had fulfilled at least five of these conditions, reflecting deep, convergent structural changes within these central banks.

Similarly, the values underpinning these structures had changed considerably, embracing the two ideological pillars of Western central banking in the 1990s: price stability and political autonomy. My survey of 250 central bankers in Hungary, the Czech Republic, and Kyrgyzstan in 2000–1 illustrated this ideological transformation. When asked to evaluate statements about the proper roles of a central bank, the postcommunist central bankers replicated Western patterns of beliefs in every case, even though these directly opposed the beliefs that had guided central banks in command economies. For example, the postcommunist central bankers strongly agreed with the statements that "Central banks should be independent from the executive" and "Price stability should be the primary goal of the central bank," while disagreeing with the statement that "Central banks should be allowed to loan money to the government." The belief pattern did not vary significantly by age or tenure at the bank, indicating that in many cases command-era central bankers changed their beliefs (and/or that those not willing to change were no longer employed as central bankers). In short, central bankers in the East came to think much like central bankers in the West.

How did this relatively successful transformation take place? By the late 1980s Western central bankers (both from individual central banks in Western Europe and North America and from the international financial institutions) had effectively coalesced into a transnational community with consensual principles and extensive resources, allowing them to promote the institution of independent central banks around the world. As a result, beginning in the early 1990s, the transnational central banking community began an expensive, concerted, hands-on effort to remold the central banks of East Europe and Eurasia. Their efforts went far beyond ideational and institutional "diffusion." Rather, the transnational central banking community played a major role in actively designing postcommunist central banks. They did this through a combination of technical assistance (designed to create a Western-style central banking infrastructure) and personnel training (designed to give postcommunist central bankers the skills to use these new tools).

Technical assistance programs focused both on introducing Western-style central banking legislation and on developing the organization and infrastructure of the central banks. In the legal arena, Western central bankers suggested legal changes, encouraged borrowing from Western models, and in many cases participated in the writing of the new laws. Technical

banks developed open market capabilities as well. The third currency board state in the region, Estonia (1992), did not.

assistance programs to develop central bank organization and infrastructure came in the form of short-term missions (often IMF-sponsored) and long-term advisors ("resident experts") in individual central banks. These technical assistance programs allowed the central banks to gain technical capacity far earlier than they would have been able to manage on their own.

Training programs sponsored by the transnational central banking community included conducting seminars either at the donor's or at the recipient's central bank, founding training centers designed to teach specialized banking skills, and accepting East European and Eurasian central bankers for residential internships. Over twenty-five different central banks regularly provided such specialized training courses and internship opportunities. These programs not only aimed to pass on the knowledge necessary to run a Western-style central bank but to inculcate postcommunist central bankers with the culture of the central banking community. Both donor and recipient central banks found these programs to be extremely successful in fostering a culture of professionalism and shared expertise in East European and Eurasian central banks. In interview after interview, central bankers told me that training programs had been vital to their work and that they developed important, lasting contacts with other central bankers during these courses. Such courses served to expand the transnational network of individual central bankers, in effect reducing the perceived spatial distance among these widely dispersed professionals and accelerating isomorphic institutional development. In short, the transnational central banking community played the key role in actively designing central banks in postcommunist states, which led to these postcommunist central banks changing far more quickly than other governmental institutions around them.

Ironically, however, in many ways this example reveals the inherent limitations of internationally driven active institutional design. Although the transnational central banking community achieved remarkable success in transforming postcommunist central banks, this success stemmed from advantages enjoyed by very few transnational actors. On the supply side, the transnational central banking community had an attractive, unchallenged ideology, a strong existing network, and the extensive financial and personnel resources necessary to embark on such a significant institutional development project. In addition, it had the international power, legitimacy, and perceived independence and objectivity required to engage in this kind of intense interference in the domestic politics of the postcommunist states.

On the demand side, postcommunist central bankers had strong incentives to welcome this international assistance. For these central bankers, effective integration into the transnational central banking community promised a new kind of independence both for their states and their institutions. Postcommunist states felt that establishing Western-style central banks would help them to establish monetary sovereignty within their own countries and represented an important step in disaggregating the cross-regional command economic structures. Conditionality and credibility played a role as well, because international financial institutions and capital markets viewed independent central banks as important signals of a state's commitment to economic reform. Moreover, the fall of communism had wiped out the old paradigm under which these central bankers operated, and the introduction of market relations required them to carry out new tasks for which they were ill-trained and ill-equipped. Western central bankers presented them with both a widely accepted set of principles and techniques under which they could operate and an attractive, powerful community that they could join if they adapted to this model. The desire for sovereignty, financial necessity, and ideological conviction all came together in the institution of the Western-style central bank. Therefore, it is no surprise that this relatively small group of East European and Eurasian central bankers, employed in specialized organizations, embraced the integration process. In short, this internationally driven active design effort required both a unified, powerful transnational community of donors and receptive, malleable domestic institutions. For this reason, it is difficult to imagine such intensive, ongoing foreign involvement occurring in, for example, postcommunist defense ministries, judiciaries, or parliaments.

It is also important to conclude this section with a more general word of caution. Merely creating Western-style institutions in East Europe and Eurasia does not mean either that they will persist over time or that their policies will have similar, desirable, or predictable effects in each country. International training and technical assistance programs can lay the intellectual and organizational groundwork for change, but they cannot ensure that externally generated institutions will be able to develop further on their own, contribute to economic growth, or build domestic constituencies for their policies. External support cannot perfectly substitute for domestic state capacity. Postcommunist states can borrow credibility from international actors, while international actors can work to forge policy consensus among domestic elites. Consistency, however, depends upon deeper domestic political and economic developments that international actors cannot (and arguably should not) guide over the long term.

Path Contingency and Institutional Design

This exploration of postcommunist financial development during an era of extraordinary politics illustrates the potential power of the path contingency approach. By moving beyond the debate over agency-centered and structure-based theories, path contingency encourages scholars to investigate the specific conditions under which state-led institutional design policies will meet with relative success or failure. The next task is to develop, extend, and further test this analytical framework. Are some kinds of institutions more amenable to change by design than others? In active design, when is it easier or more desirable to create new institutions rather than convert existing ones to new purposes? To what extent do different active policies require different kinds and levels of state capacity? What specific institutional conditions inhibit or promote the efficacy of particular kinds of passive design policies? Detailed case studies that explore relatively successful and unsuccessful active and passive design policies (especially where similar policy choices across postcommunist states have led to different institutional outcomes) will answer such questions. The framework can also be tested on institutional change processes during other periods of extraordinary politics, keeping in mind that true instances of extraordinary politics, in which policy choice can fairly serve as an independent variable, are rare. Whereas revolutions, simultaneous political and economic transformations from communism, and rapid upheavals such as the Protestant Reformation introduce periods of extraordinary politics where entire world views come into question, comparatively less dramatic events such as the gradual incorporation of labor interests into politics, decolonization, and international economic crises arguably do not.

What happens to new institutions when the era of extraordinary politics ends? No sharp break occurs that delimits "extraordinary" from "ordinary" politics; institutional consolidation, when feedback loops engage and institutions again start framing and constraining policy choices, may begin sooner for some institutions and states than others. But, at a certain point, institutions that have been created or altered need to develop mechanisms by which to reproduce themselves. Thelen (1999) argues persuasively that identifying such institutional reproduction mechanisms should represent a central theoretical concern for historical institutionalists, especially since historical institutionalists take issue with functionalist arguments that infer past institutional origins from the coordination tasks they perform in the present.[15] Postcommunist states present ideal cases for identifying and analyzing institutional reproduction, inasmuch as extensive institutional creation and change have taken place across numerous countries in a relatively short period of time. If institutions were created by active state design, for example, can they then build a public constituency? If international actors and forces played a significant role in determining initial institutional outcomes, can these institutions then forge domestic bases of support? Do institutions that clearly solve collective action problems or serve the interests of powerful political constituencies exhibit more staying power than others? Alternately, can the state restrain and regulate economic institutions that emerged through passive means?

In closing, we are well reminded that history forces humility upon all theorists. When Yegor Gaidar became Russian finance minister in 1991, he

[15] In addition, see Nelson and Winter (1982: 13) for an economics-based critique of equilibrium arguments.

observed that it was like "traveling in a jet and you go into the cockpit and you discover there's no one at the controls" (quoted by Daniel Yergin and Thane Gustafson, *Washington Post*, August 2, 1998, C3). This attitude assumed that postcommunist development could be guided precisely, like a jet, if only the right pilots could be found. Unfortunately, the task at hand more closely resembled converting the plane from propeller to jet power in midair – an insanely difficult procedure, with extremely high stakes. The path-contingent process of institutional change in postcommunist states defies many efforts at guidance from above. As Josef Brada (1993: 109) cogently observes in the final paragraph of his article defending "big bang" economic reform: "I, and everyone else involved in the debate have proceeded ... as if some rational calculus, working its way through a process of historical inevitability, would, or could, guide events in East Europe and the ex-USSR, and as if such a rational calculus could really dictate the pace of events." Unfortunately, no single path to democracy and the market exists; likewise, no single theory can explain a state's ability to travel that illusory path.

References

Andreev, Vladimir. 1992. The Privatization of State Enterprises in Russia. *Review of Central and East European Law* 3: 265–75.

Åslund, Anders. 1995. *How Russia Became a Market Economy*. Washington, D.C.: Brookings.

Berg, Andrew. 1994. Does Macroeconomic Reform Cause Structural Adjustment? *Journal of Comparative Economics* 18: 376–409.

Boyko, Maxim, Andrei Shleifer, and Robert Vishny. 1995. *Privatizing Russia*. Cambridge, Mass.: MIT Press.

Brada, Josef. 1993. The Transformation from Communism to Capitalism: How Far? How Fast? *Post-Soviet Affairs* 9(2): 87–109

Bresser Pereira, Luiz Carlos, José María Maravall, and Adam Przeworski. 1993. *Economic Reforms in New Democracies: A Social Democratic Approach*. Cambridge: Cambridge University Press.

Bunce, Valerie. 1999. The Political Economy of Postsocialism. *Slavic Review* 58(4): 756–93.

Burawoy, Michael, and Pavel Krotov. 1992. The Soviet Transition from Socialism to Capitalism. *American Sociological Review* 57(1): 16–38.

Clark, William Robert. 1998. Agents and Structures: Two Views of Preferences, Two Views of Institutions. *International Studies Quarterly* 42(2): 245–70.

Collier, David, and Ruth Berins Collier. 1991. *Shaping the Political Arena: Critical Junctures, the Labor Movement, and Regime Dynamics in Latin America*. Princeton: Princeton University Press.

Elster, Jon, Claus Offe, and Ulrich Preuss. 1998. *Institutional Design in Post-Communist Societies: Rebuilding the Ship at Sea*. Cambridge: Cambridge University Press.

Fish, M. Steven. 1995. *Democracy from Scratch: Opposition and Regime in the New Russian Revolution*. Princeton: Princeton University Press.

Gerschenkron, Alexander. 1962. *Economic Backwardness in Historical Perspective*. Cambridge, Mass.: Belknap Press of Harvard University Press.

Goldman, Marshall. 1994. *Lost Opportunity: What Has Made Economic Reform in Russia So Difficult*. New York: W. W. Norton.

Gorbachev, Mikhail. 1990. Strengthen the Key Element of the Economy. *Pravda and Izvestiia*, December 10, 1–2. Translated in *Current Digest of the Soviet Press* 42(49): 9.

Hanson, Stephen E. 1998. Analyzing Post-Communist Economic Change: A Review Essay. *East European Politics and Societies* 12(1): 145–70.

Hellman, Joel. 1998. Review of *Institutional Design in Post-Communist Societies*. *East European Constitutional Review* 7(3): 71–74.

Immergut, Ellen. 1992. *Health Politics: Interests and Institutions in Western Europe*. Cambridge: Cambridge University Press.

Johnson, Juliet. 1997. Russia's Emerging Financial-Industrial Groups. *Post-Soviet Affairs* 13(4): 333–65.

2001. Agents of Transformation: The Role of the West in Post-Communist Central Bank Development. National Council on Eurasian and East European Research (NCEEER) Working Paper, October.

Krasner, Stephen. 1984. Approaches to the State. *Comparative Politics* 16: 223–46.

Liebowitz, Stan, and Stephen Margolis. 1990. The Fable of the Keys. *Journal of Law and Economics* 33: 1–26.

Maioni, Antonia. 1997. Parting at the Crossroads: The Development of Health Insurance in Canada and the United States, 1940–1965. *Comparative Politics* 29(4): 411–31.

McKinnon, Ronald. 1991. Financial Control in the Transition from Classical Socialism to a Market Economy. *Journal of Economic Perspectives* 5(4): 107–22.

Migdal, Joel. 1988. *Strong Societies and Weak States: State-Society Relations and State Capabilities in the Third World*. Princeton: Princeton University Press.

Millar, James. 1996. From Utopian Socialism to Utopian Capitalism. *George Washington University 175th Annual Papers*, Paper 2.

Murphy, Kevin, Andrei Shleifer, and Robert Vishny. 1992. The Transition to a Market Economy: Pitfalls of Partial Reform. *Quarterly Journal of Economics* 107: 889–906.

Murrell, Peter. 1993. What Is Shock Therapy? What Did It Do in Poland and Russia? *Post-Soviet Affairs* 9(2): 111–40.

1995. The Transition according to Cambridge, Mass. *Journal of Economic Literature* 33: 164–78.

Murrell, Peter, and Yijiang Wang. 1993. When Privatization Should Be Delayed: The Effect of Communist Legacies on Organizational and Institutional Reforms. *Journal of Comparative Economics* 17: 385–406.

Nelson, Joan. 1993. The Politics of Economic Transformation: Is Third-World Experience Relevant in Eastern Europe? *World Politics* 45: 433–63.

Nelson, Lynn, and Irina Kuzes, 1995. *Radical Reform in Yeltsin's Russia*. Armonk, N.Y.: M. E. Sharpe.

Nelson, Richard, and Sidney Winter. 1982. *An Evolutionary Theory of Economic Change*. Cambridge, Mass.: Harvard University Press.

Nordlinger, Eric. 1981. *On the Autonomy of the Democratic State*. Cambridge, Mass.: Harvard University Press.

O'Donnell, Guillermo, Philippe Schmitter, and Laurence Whitehead, eds. 1986. *Transitions from Authoritarian Rule*. Baltimore: Johns Hopkins University Press.

Organization for Economic Cooperation and Development. 1997. *OECD Economic Surveys: Russian Federation*, 1997–1998. Paris: OECD.

Pickel, Andreas. 1992. Jump-Starting a Market Economy: A Critique of the Radical Strategy for Economic Reform in Light of the East German Experience. *Studies in Comparative Communism* 25(2): 177–91.

Porket, J. L. 1995. *Unemployment in Capitalist, Communist and Post-Communist Economies*. New York: St. Martin's Press.

Poznański, Kazimierz. 1997. *Poland's Protracted Transition*. Cambridge: Cambridge University Press.

Przeworski, Adam. 1991. *Democracy and the Market*. Cambridge: Cambridge University Press.

Roberts, Cynthia, and Thomas Sherlock. 1999. Bringing the Russian State Back In: Explanations of the Derailed Transition to Market Democracy. *Comparative Politics* 31(4): 477–98.

Rostowski, Jacek. 1993. Problems of Creating Stable Monetary Systems in Post-Communist Economies. *Europe-Asia Studies* 45(3): 445–61.

Sachs, Jeffrey. 1990. Poland and Eastern Europe: What Is to Be Done? In Andras Koves and Paul Marer, eds., *Foreign Economic Liberalization: Transformations in Socialist and Market Economies*, pp. 235–46. Boulder, Colo.: Westview.

1993. *Poland's Jump to the Market Economy*. Cambridge, Mass.: MIT Press.

Stark, David. 1992. Path-Dependence and Privatization Strategies in East Central Europe. *East European Politics and Society* 6(1): 17–53.

Stark, David, and László Bruszt. 1998. *Postsocialist Pathways: Transforming Politics and Property in East Central Europe*. Cambridge: Cambridge University Press.

Thelen, Kathleen. 1999. Historical Institutionalism in Comparative Politics. *Annual Review of Political Science* 2: 387.

2000. Timing and Temporality in the Analysis of Institutional Evolution and Change. *Studies in American Political Development* 14(1): 101–8.

Voprosy ekonomiki. 1993. Rossiiskaia reforma: vzgliad iz kommercheskogo banka (Russian reform: View from a commercial bank), 2: 136.

Waldner, David. 1999. *State Building and Late Development*. Ithaca: Cornell University Press.

Warner, Andrew. 1998. The Emerging Russian Banking System. *Economics of Transition* 6(2): 333–47.

Woodruff, David. 1998. *Money Unmade: Barter and the Fate of Russian Capitalism*. Ithaca: Cornell University Press.

10

Cultural Legacies of State Socialism

History Making and Cultural-Political Entrepreneurship in Postcommunist Poland and Russia

Jan Kubik

> The kind of history that has most influence upon the life of the community and the course of events is the history that common people carry around in their heads.
>
> Becker, 1958: 61

> Whether the general run of people read history books or not, they inevitably picture the past in some fashion or another, and this picture, however little it corresponds to the real past, helps to determine their ideas about politics and society.
>
> Zerubavel, 1995: 3

My task in this essay is to analyze cultural legacies of state socialism. I have to deal, therefore, with two sets of questions:

1. What are cultural legacies? How can we understand the process of legacy formation and maintenance?
2. What do we have in mind when we speak of cultural legacies of communism or state socialism? How have cultural patterns, engendered under state socialism or even earlier, been transmitted and influenced postcommunist political and economic transformations? Are those patterns limited only to the products of communist states and their cultural policies? Are cultural scenarios, engendered under state socialism, still operational? How strongly?

For their invaluable critical thoughts on this essay, I would like to thank the editors and reviewers of this volume; participants of the original Harvard conference; Rutgers's Workshop on Culture, History, Institutions, particularly Leela Fernandez, Dan Tichenor, Dennis Bathory, and Bob Kaufman; my students in New Brunswick, Warsaw, and Riga, particularly Svetlozar Ivanov; and also Mike Aronoff, Val Bunce, Consuelo Cruz, Anna Seleny, and Magda Środa.

What Are Cultural Legacies? The Logic of Cultural Explanations

According to the *Merriam-Webster Dictionary*, a legacy is "something transmitted by or received from an ancestor or predecessor or from the past." This sentence quite accurately reflects basic intuitions related to the term. We tend to accept without reflection the proposition that a legacy of communism is something "received from" communists or the communist past. For some types of legacies, this proposition holds true. A dilapidated and polluted environment has been "received from" the communists as well as a run-down state-controlled economy and a set of nondemocratic political institutions. There is not much one can do to avoid working among, within, or against such material or institutional legacies while attempting to implement new, postcommunist designs.

Prevalent analyses of cultural legacies follow the same logic. Researchers assume that cultural legacies are patterns of behavior or thought "received" from the past that "stick" and thus make the life of reformers miserable because they prevent people from becoming proper "democrats" or "capitalists" in an expedient fashion.

In this chapter I argue that cultural legacies differ from material or institutional legacies. I insist that in order to understand how they work we have to ground our analysis in another verb used in the definition quoted previously: not "received from" but rather "transmitted." Whereas material legacies – and, to a large extent, institutional legacies as well – exist independently of the will and designs of most postcommunist actors, cultural legacies must be transmitted and the cultural scenarios embedded in them must be enacted by at least some actors. In short, cultural legacies are "real" only insomuch as they inform (cause) postcommunist actors' behavior.

Cultural legacies should be then defined as patterns (scenarios) of behavior or thought that are transmitted from the past and enacted in the present. They are either transmitted and enacted unreflectively (implicitly) and thus serve as habitual "ways of doing things" or are explicitly and deliberately invoked as models (blueprints) for current actions by cultural entrepreneurs. Among such entrepreneurs, the state's political and cultural elites are of particular significance. Thus, there are two basic kinds of legacies: implicit and explicit. Implicit legacies are at work when we observe unreflective (habitual) replication of an earlier pattern of behavior or thought. Such a pattern, or model, is encoded in everyday life, and its replication is often attributed to "inertia," "(cultural) inheritance," or "natural proclivities" of the actors. It can be distilled from the flow of social interactions by "natives" or outside observers; it is often accessed through survey research or participant observation. Historians also try to recover such patterns, conceptualizing them as "memory," which they then oppose to "history" (Nora, 1989: 8). Explicit legacies are perhaps best understood as deliberately propagated representations of selected fragments of the group's past. Such representations offer models of or for behavior and thinking. They are usually studied through content analysis of various texts, stories, narratives, or statements. This is, according to Nora, the domain of history proper.

There is a tendency among researchers to assume that in order to demonstrate legacies' causal power all they need to do is to point to a past cultural pattern and proclaim its causal relevance for the present behavior. Obviously, in such an argument, mechanisms through which past patterns are reproduced and made causative in the present remain unspecified. As a result, many cultural arguments have come under increasingly refined criticism.[1] For example, in an important article Stephen Holmes presents a critique of a popular view that locates the main source of postcommunist problems in cultural legacies of communism. Tellingly, Holmes is critical of the logic of cultural explanation that underlies this view. According to him, the main weakness of such explanations is contained in an assumption that "the best indicator of the future is the past" (1996: 27). Holmes is right: a cultural explanation proposed by this phrase locates the causative power of culture in an undefined "past" and leaves unspecified why some cultural patterns are replicated and others are not, and how past models of behavior (encoded in habits and explicit ideologies) are transmitted to the present.

This "pick-your-past-and-assert-its-relevance-for-the-present" way of constructing cultural causation is, however, not only defective but also quite obsolete. Newer strands of cultural theory emphasize the desirability (if not necessity) of decoupling three tasks: the identification and description of *past cultural patterns* (cultural scenarios); the reconstruction of various social mechanisms of their *selective transmission* to the present (actions of the present-day "cultural entrepreneurs");[2] and the modeling of mechanisms that (selectively) turn such patterns into *cultural scenarios informing current behavior*.[3] Cultural causation – undergirding legacy formation – must be seen as a sequence of these three mechanisms; the abused and misleading metaphor of the "weight" of "something received from an ancestor or predecessor or from the past" should be avoided.

A rationale for such a shift of focus is simple: "The past" (understood as a reservoir of cultural scenarios) does not exist for us – in the past. It exists, if it exists at all, and influences human thoughts and actions in the present, now. More specifically, the past exists in historical narratives that are told and retold in the present mostly (though not exclusively) by today's cultural-historical entrepreneurs. Interestingly, these entrepreneurs cannot

[1] See, for example, Kitschelt on Putnam (1993) in chapter 2 in this volume.

[2] For an incisive introduction to the sociology of cognitive traditions, see Zerubavel (1997).

[3] Cognitive sociology and cognitive anthropology have recently made tremendous progress in theorizing and studying such mechanisms. See, for example, Zerubavel (1997) and Strauss and Quinn (1997).

tell just any story if they want to preserve their credibility; the repertoire from which they can choose is limited. Nonetheless, they have a choice, and cultural analysis should focus on the mechanisms that enable or constrain this choice.

Significantly, cultural entrepreneurs may choose not to "transmit" certain types of cultural narratives built upon certain key historical events, thereby muting or even eliminating their impact on current political behavior. For example, it has been persuasively argued (Edles, 1998; Moran, 2000: 329–32) that after Franco's death some key members of the Spanish cultural, political, and religious elites made a conscious choice to "diffuse" the memory of the civil war, which was potentially devastating for the nascent democracy. This was achieved by a skillful reinterpretation of the war itself and the symbols it generated. Another example comes from my own research: during the 1989 Round Table negotiations in Poland, both the communist negotiators and their Solidarity counterparts made conscious efforts to interpret recent Polish history and the history of their own conflict in such a way that the crafting of a compromise became feasible (Kubik, 2000).

Holmes is therefore right to criticize cultural explanations that concentrate on "habits and expectations, which perversely constrict freedom of choice [and] can be handed down from generation to generation and survive for centuries by sheer inertia" (1996: 26). As I suggest here, one way of avoiding such faulty explanations is to problematize "inertia" and offer a more complex and complete model of cultural causation. To do so, the researcher must – inter alia – refocus her gaze from the past to the present and analyze the social, political, and cultural mechanisms of cultural transmission, beginning with the most recent ones. Before I present a strategy for such an analysis, I propose a typology of legacies, which I derive from a brief discussion of the political culture field.

Psychosocial versus Semiotic Conceptualizations of Culture: A Typology of Legacies

As many critics have observed, there is a theoretically flawed tendency within the political culture approach to reduce culture to psychological or psychosocial variables.[4] These critics sometimes argue that culture is a reality sui generis, as *real* as social (structural) or psychological realities and separate from (though interdependent with) them.[5] Somers makes this point

[4] See Dittmer (1977: 556); Gamson (1988: 220); Lijphart on the individualistic fallacy in Almond and Verba (1980: 45–47).

[5] "I suggest that political culture may best be understood as a *semiological system*" (Dittmer 1977: 566). See Geertz (1973) for the most recent influential articulation of this position. See also Aronoff (1989) and Hirschman (1991).

forcefully: "In sum, the most dramatic distinguishing quality of the rejuvenated political culture concept is definitional: rather than a collection of internalized expressions of subjective values or externalized expressions of social interests, a political culture is now defined as a configuration of representations and practices that exists as a contentious structural social *phenomenon in its own right*" (1995: 134; emphasis added). Nothing seems to be inherently wrong with the reduction of political culture to a syndrome of attitudes; it is, however, necessary to realize what kinds of conceptualizations are usually suggested by a reductionist framework, and what kinds of conceptualizations are made possible by reductionism's adversary, emergentism. Within the latter, culture is conceptualized as an emergent phenomenon irreducible to its individual (psychological) concretizations or manifestations.[6] Such a conceptualization allows for a type of analysis inconceivable within the reductionist framework. The "emergent" definition of culture (as a "web of meanings," a "system of signs," etc.) allows one to describe and analyze its components (signs, symbols, values, discourses) and their meanings, and *systematically to investigate* their relationships with social (e.g., classes, professions, communities), political (e.g., elites, interest groups, authority), economic (productivity, entrepreneurship), and psychological (personal convictions, attitudes) variables.[7]

Construed in an emergent-semiotic, rather than psychosocial, fashion, culture is a more or less loosely structured "'tool kit' of symbols, stories, rituals, and world-views, which people may use in varying configurations to solve different kinds of problems" (Swidler, 1986: 273).[8] Culture is usefully construed not as "values to be upheld but rather *points of concern* to be debated" (Laitin, 1988: 589; emphasis added). Furthermore, following recent theorizing, I assume that culture is intimately intertwined with both social practice and power games (Dirks, Eley, and Ortner, 1994; Sewell, 1999; Bonnell and Hunt, 1999). This means that cultural representations are constantly used and reused, and in this process their meanings shift and evolve. They are also used to stake positions in power struggles and to exercise power over others by redefining (or attempting to redefine) the world for them. Culture thus provides a tool kit or a repertoire of potential scenarios according to which humans may conduct their affairs. It needs to be emphasized again, though, that this repertoire is limited; the range of options available to actors who want to play within the

6 See discussions on the Popperian "third world" (Popper, 1979); Somers's (1995) idea of "dual autonomy"; and also Biernacki (1999: 65–68).

7 Somers (1995: 118) credits Talcott Parsons with introducing such an "emergent" (or "normative," as she puts it) concept of culture to sociological theory.

8 In another formulation, Swidler (1986: 273) defines culture as a set of "symbolic vehicles of meaning, including beliefs, ritual practices, art forms, and ceremonies, as well as informal cultural practices such as language, gossip, stories, and rituals of daily life."

limits of a given cultural setting (or limits of understandability) is usually finite.[9]

There is a complex discussion concerning the "source" of culture's causative import. It is variously located either within culture itself (semiotic logic) or in social and political mechanisms of cultural reproduction. For example, some clusters of cultural elements are rendered more "credible" or "hegemonic" than others by (meta)cultural rules of interpretation, however loosely articulated and enforced. Most theoreticians nowadays would agree that hegemony is achieved through a combination of cultural and sociopolitical mechanisms (Sewell, 1999: 56–57; Bourdieu, 1991: 170). A story (narrative) becomes an element of the group's cultural legacy not just on the strength of its intrinsic merit (semiotic or aesthetic). For example, a powerful sociopolitical mechanism of legacy formation is to be found in repetition. As Plummer noted, "stories once told become more tellable, more likely to assume an autonomy of their own, irrespective of their original experience.... Their significance may lie in the repeated telling of the story" (1994: 41; see also Rose, 1999, and Somers, 1995). It is therefore imperative to study social and political conditions that impede or facilitate the (re)telling of certain stories.

There is no need to claim the superiority of psychosocial or semiotic approaches. It is more productive to assume that building blocks of political culture are basically of two kinds: psychosocial (attitudes) or semiotic (symbols, signs, texts).[10] Within the "psychosocial" tradition, political culture is defined as "a people's predominant beliefs, attitudes, values, ideals,

[9] Sewell (1999: 49) introduces here a concept of "semiotic community" whose members "recognize the same set of oppositions and therefore [are] capable of engaging in mutually meaningful symbolic action." There is no room here to discuss the thorny problem of "unsettled periods" (Swidler, 1986; Goldstone, 1991) when cultural creativity is often intensified and cultural breakthroughs are more likely.

[10] For the sake of simplicity, in the remainder of this chapter I do not offer any analysis of the axiological dimension of culture. I concentrate mostly on the semiotic conception of culture and merely hint at its relationship with the psychosocial model. An almost identical distinction has been offered by Joseph Schull (1992), who writes about *ideology as a belief system* and *ideology as a discourse*, and applies these two concepts in his analysis of the Soviet-type societies. An echo of this distinction can be found in Pye's differentiation of elite political culture, whose study "involves skill in *interpreting* ideologies, in characterizing operational codes," and mass political culture, "which depends upon the advanced techniques of *survey research and modern methods of measuring public opinion*" (quoted in Putnam, 1971: 652; emphasis added). A similar analysis of the political culture approach is given by Brint, who discusses the "new textualism" and "social constructionism" in addition to more-traditional studies of attitudes and orientations (mostly through public opinion surveys): "Social constructionism can be described as based on the interpretation of public texts but adjoined to a political power analysis of cultural creation and a reader-response theory of cultural consumption and use" (Brint, 1994: 15). See also Walicki (following Lucien Goldman) on the distinction between structured *Weltanschauungen* and looser "empirical consciousness" (1975: 2–3).

sentiments, and evaluations about the political system of its country, and the role of the self in that system" (Almond and Verba, 1963: 15). By contrast, writing within the "semiotic" orientation, Gamson submits that "A nonredundant concept of political culture refers to the meaning systems that are culturally available for talking, writing, and thinking about political objects: the myths and metaphors, the language and idea elements, the frames, ideologies, values, and condensing symbols" (1988: 220).[11] Schull contrasts these two approaches sharply: "A discourse is not located in people's minds; it is a set of linguistic events and the conventions they embody, which exist in a social space shared by the members of an ideological community. A discourse, unlike a belief system, is shared not aggregatively but intersubjectively; the sharing is itself a collective action" (1922: 731).

An important corollary of the acceptance of a double – psychosocial and semiotic – character of political culture is the proposition that the analysis of the relationship between culture and politics should not need to be limited to examining the continuity or discontinuity of certain *syndromes of attitudes (implicit legacies)* and their impact on other areas of social, economic, or political life. The reconstruction and interpretation of *discourses (explicit legacies)*, as well as explanation of their genealogies, logics, and functions is an equally important task. Discourses developed by the elites are addressed to wider audiences; their explicit or implicit aim is to shape attitudes in order to achieve politically desired results (to generate support, to mask political failures, etc.). Thus, it has been recently postulated that a cultural analysis of politics must focus on the dynamic interplay among attitudes (the psychosocial dimension), discourses (the semiotic dimension), and institutional settings within which this interplay transpires (the social dimension) and where power is actualized (the political-power dimension).

Implicit legacies, reflected in attitudes accessed through surveys, are relatively easy to diagnose, but their fluctuations are difficult to explain. The tremendous complexity of the socialization process cannot be easily captured in the parsimonious explanatory models preferred by modern social science. It seems that only careful longitudinal (or even panel) studies of family-centered primary political socialization and school- and church(es)-dominated secondary political socialization would provide us with more systematic knowledge of causes lying behind the (dis)continuity of politically relevant attitudes and, by extension, implicit legacies.[12] In this essay I use survey data only as proxy indicators of the level of popular acceptance of certain cultural scenarios (embedded in certain explicit legacies).

[11] Baker (1990: 4–5) offers a similar definition. For him, political culture is the "set of discourses or symbolic practices" by which "individuals and groups in any society articulate, negotiate, implement, and enforce the competing claims they make upon each other."

[12] For an excellent example of the work that focuses on the role of family socialization in the transmission of political attitudes in postcommunism, see Mach (1998).

Explicit legacies, reconstructed through content analysis of texts (discourses), are somewhat easier to study. In particular, it seems easy (though time consuming) first to map out ideological positions of influential elite social and political actors and then to capture *the intensity of repetition* of certain cultural themes and the direction of change in the ways these themes are presented. In studying explicit legacies, researchers usually concentrate on such tertiary institutions of political socialization as political parties, social movements, civic organizations, or state agencies and attempt to determine their influence on people's attitudes (and thus implicit legacies).

In this essay I focus mostly though not exclusively on the *explicit* cultural legacies of state socialism in Poland and Russia. The basic question I am trying to answer is, How have cultural patterns, engendered under communism or even earlier, influenced postcommunist political and economic transformations? Accordingly, I try to determine whether certain cultural scenarios that inform the political actions of key political actors in post-1989 Poland and Russia are to be found in (important) past narratives, and whether those narratives are being cultivated by today's cultural entrepreneurs. In particular, I have chosen for consideration the formation of the nationalist-communist (socialist) hybrid, its role in defining the dominant polarizing cleavage in elite discourse, and its competition with Western-style liberalism.

I am, therefore, taking some preliminary steps toward developing a falsifiable cultural argument, although specifying actual conditions for falsifiability in historical research is, of course, fraught with tremendous difficulties. My argument hinges on a simple idea: if it turns out that a certain cultural scenario (surmised to constitute a "legacy"), detected in the behavior of a key political group in Russia or Poland, (1) is not cultivated (actively transmitted from the past) by cultural-political elites or/and (2) was not developed or cultivated under communism, it cannot be classified as "legacy." This, in turn, will mean the weakening of the kind of historical-cultural argument proposed in this chapter: if the cultural scenarios that inform influential politicians' behavior are proved not to be legacies, my argument that (cultural) legacies, or history, matter must be reconsidered or abandoned. In turn, the weaker the cultural-historical argument, the stronger the case for "presentism" and the model of the unconstrained, freely strategizing political actor.

During its post-totalitarian phase, state socialism diversified. One of the main sources of this diversification was the emergence of unofficial subcultures (formations, discourses) that challenged the monopoly of the official discourse organized around the principles of Marxism-Leninism. In such countries as Czechoslovakia, Yugoslavia, Hungary, Poland, and even the Soviet Union, some people (later referred to as dissidents) began producing philosophical texts, prose, poetry, essays, works of visual art and music – as well as innovative scenarios of everyday survival – that had little or nothing to do with the official culture propagated and guarded (through preventive censorship) by the state.

This diversification of cultural production is central to any discussion of the legacies of the state socialist period. Cultural formations of this period were not limited to "communist" culture; "anti-communist" (counter)cultures, wherever they emerged, must be studied as "usable pasts," that is, as important elements of the cultural "tool kit" available to postcommunist actors.

I limit my attention here to a specific cultural formation playing a prominent role in postcommunist politics: the hybrid of socialism-nationalism. First, I assess this hybrid's relative influence on politics in postcommunist Russia and Poland and try to determine its role in combating Western-style liberalism through erecting a cultural barrier between "us" (often defined as the East) and "them" (the West). Specifically, I try to determine whether the national-socialist hybrid is actively and deliberately cultivated by influential cultural-political entrepreneurs (elites). Second, I reconstruct the pre-1989 "past" of the national-socialist hybrid and its relative impact on the political culture of each country before 1989. By doing so, I can determine whether this hybrid is indeed a "legacy."

Postcommunism: Cultural Polarization, the Hybrid of Nationalism and Socialism, and the Poverty of Liberalism

One of the most significant ideological constructs that emerged from the ruins of state socialism has been the hybrid of communism and nationalism, founded on a profound distrust or outright rejection of Western-style liberalism. Shot through with threads of populism and collectivism, both ideologies provide postcommunist politicians with discursive tools to oppose the cosmopolitan individualism associated with liberal thought (Tismaneanu, 1998).

Post-1991 Russia

Postcommunist politics produced a plethora of formerly unimaginable alliances. One of the most striking is the one formed by former dissident neo-Slavophiles, national Bolsheviks, and some neocommunists in Russia. Its most successful institutional embodiment emerged under the leadership of Gennady Zyuganov, who turned the Communist Party of the Russian Federation (CPRF) into a formidable political machine and significant sociocultural phenomenon.[13] To what degree the national-communist hybrid program contributes to Zyuganov's staying power is not easy to determine; it is, however, well documented that the support for him personally and

[13] For details, see Paramonov (1996). See also Zyuganov (1995); Allensworth (1998); Urban (1998); Tolz (1998); and Bratkiewicz (1998).

TABLE 10.1. *Political Types in Postcommunist Russia*

Political Type	% of Respondents
Soviet patriot	14.7
Alienated liberal	11.6
Autarkic leveler	25.4[a]
Liberal-patriot	10.0
Rigid law-abiding citizen	22.9[b]
Authoritarian supporter of the market	15.3

[a] The clearest "communist" legacy.
[b] Strong elements of "communist" authoritarianism.

his party during the late 1990s has been very high: about one-third of the Russian populace has been ready to rally behind him and the Communist Party of the Russian Federation during the last several years.[14] In the 1996 presidential election (first round), Zyuganov received 32 percent of the valid votes; in the 2000 presidential election (first round), his support waned only marginally to 29.44 percent of the valid votes.[15]

Sociological studies reveal the distribution of attitudinal patterns that underlie such electoral results. For example, a ROMIR study offers a typology of six basic political types in postcommunist Russia (Table 10.1).[16] In another study, White, Rose, and McAllister (1997: 45) show that about one-third of the populace are "reactionaries" who are "positive about the communist regime and negative about the current system."

It is clear from these numbers that in the postcommunist Russia about one-fourth to one-third of the population is sympathetic to the "communist cultural syndrome," and its thinking is influenced, if not dominated, by its various elements.[17] What is critical is the fact that this syndrome, in its most articulate and successful incarnation, is indelibly intertwined with nationalistic themes and motifs. Urban, for example, observes that the Communist Party of the Russian Federation, "having constructed for themselves a new identity shorn of all traces of internationalism and heavily larded with patriotic and religious sentiments... achieve[d] a stunning victory in the December 1995 parliamentary elections, apparently thanks to its ability

[14] Various polls by VTSIOM, for example, Dinamika partiynykh elektoratov (October 1999). See <wciom.ru/EDITION/PrDyn10.htm> for data from August 1999 through March 2000.

[15] Vybory 2000, available at <izbircom.ru/2217/preres>.

[16] ROMIR, Tipologia politicheskikh tsennostey (Typology of political values), August 1999, available at <www.romir.ru/politics/august/tipology>.

[17] In December 2000, 24.7 percent of the ROMIR (Rossiyskoye Obshchestvennoye Mneniye i Issledovanye Rynka [Russian Public Opinion and Market Research]) respondents said they would vote for the CPRF; available at <www.romir.ru/socpolit/socio/12–2000/parties/htm>.

to speak to the country's 'national-patriotic' constituency and thus to win votes otherwise destined for non-Communist nationalists such as Vladimir Zhirinovskii" (1996: 150–51). This political success must be at least partially attributed to the deliberate actions of several influential cultural entrepreneurs, most prominently Zyuganov himself and some leading members of the cultural elite and the Orthodox hierarchy.

By contrast, during the first postcommunist decade, political-cultural entrepreneurs who espoused and cultivated liberalism in Russia were fewer in number and less influential. In general, liberalism has not become a dominant discourse in Russia.[18] Marcia A. Weigle concludes her comprehensive study of Russia's post-1991 liberal project with a somber assessment. While acknowledging the significance of this project for the policies attempted during the initial years of Yeltsin's rule, she nonetheless concludes that "[s]teeped partly in the Soviet era yet slowly responding to postcommunist changes, political culture is still clearly incapable of defining the direction of Russia's postcommunist liberal project" (2000: 461).

Most observers agree also that the liberal project gained some impetus already under Gorbachev, but it was heavily dominated by the state's actions; what began emerging was a form of state liberalism rather than social liberalism, whose essence is a widespread acceptance and practical utilization of liberal models by the populace. Fish, for example, observed that "[w]hile some organizations demonstrated progress toward developing capacities for interest representation, their abilities to articulate interests, to open channels of access to the state, and to control the process of interest intermediation with state institutions remained severely limited" (1995: 57). At the same time, Gorbachev's efforts to articulate and implement a liberal reform communism engendered an increasingly articulate national-communist countertrend whose social visibility, organizational entrenchment, and social influence soon proved to be stronger and more durable than the ideas and practices of perestroika (Brudny, 1998).

Two clear trends that emerged during the 1990s in Russia are important for my analysis. First, liberalism, initially associated with such visible names as Sakharov, Gaidar, and Starovoitova, and in 2001 represented most prominently by Yavlinsky and Nemtsov, has remained a viable albeit marginal political force. Liberal discourse's impact on the course of postcommunist transformations in Russia, never dominant, seems to have been slowly dwindling. Second, several political entrepreneurs, most prominently Zyuganov, succeeded in articulating a complex hybrid of communism and nationalism; Zyuganov attracted to his platform about one-third of the Russian society. The Communist Party of the Russian Federation's influence on governmental

[18] Following Weigle, I define liberalism broadly: "Liberalism can be identified by a basic set of principles, such as the protection of individual and civil liberties, the juridical recognition of private property, and the role of law in protecting basics human rights" (2000: 4–5).

policies has not been decisive either under Yeltsin or Putin, yet the robust articulation and propagation of the national-communist discourse has definitely contributed to the relative underdevelopment of the liberal option in Russia (see Figure 10.1).

Postcommunist Poland

Both qualitative analyses and quantitative studies reveal that such powerful cultural cleavages as secularism versus religiosity, on the one hand, and communism versus anticommunism, on the other, had at least as much influence on Polish postcommunist politics as the more "normal" economic cleavage separating liberals from social democrats. Analyzing the 1992–97 period, Markowski concludes that in the Polish party system there was an *increase of polarization* on two dimensions, both salient since 1989: economic (liberal vs. social-democratic) and cultural (religious vs. secular) (2001: 71). He also finds that polarization on the latter dimension intensified more rapidly than polarization on the former. Jasiewicz (1999a; 1999b) reminds us that the religious-secular and the communist-anticommunist cleavages *strongly overlap*; he demonstrates that the polarization of the electorate along these dimensions increased during the campaign preceding the 1995 presidential election and culminated in the strongly bipolar results of the 1997 parliamentary elections. Czyżewski, on the basis of his careful analysis of political discourse, concluded that "[s]ince 1993 the political polarization of the society increased, reflecting the polarization of the political scene: on the one side, the Solidarity camp, still strong though internally conflicted, on the other side the postcommunist camp, energized by its electoral victory" (1997: 52). Importantly, a public opinion poll conducted by CBOS in 1999 revealed that 62 percent of the respondents perceived the main social cleavage as being between "ex-communists" and "post-Solidarity" forces.

Ex-communists became the most powerful and best organized political force in Polish postcommunist politics due to several factors, including considerable resources inherited from the communist system, a loyal cadre of well-trained activists, and the chronic fragmentation of their opponents – the post-Solidarity camp.[19] But they also managed to forge an attractive, coherent, and – most importantly – convincing political discourse founded on the principles of modern, European-cosmopolitan, secular social democracy. They eventually came to dominate completely the left segment of the Polish ideological spectrum, gradually swallowing almost all significant left-leaning

[19] For example, from February 1999 to February 2000, the SLD systematically received 28 to 40 percent support from the populace; the ruling AWS (Solidarity Electoral Action) was polling within the 16 to 24 percent range. Data available at <CBOS.pl/Pref partii w lutym 2000.htm>. In June 2001, SLD was by far the most powerful party in Poland; it won the September 2001 parliamentary elections (in coalition with the much smaller Union of Labor) by a large margin (41.04 percent).

post-Solidarity groups and personages. Significantly, their platform included many elements of modern liberalism and rejected more-militant, exclusivistic forms of nationalism. In short, while Russian communists under Zyuganov went national, Polish ex-communists under Kwaśniewski went left-liberal.

As a result, they became attractive as a political partner to at least some politicians and public intellectuals representing the liberal-leaning wing of the former Solidarity movement. A tedious and still unfinished process of forming a liberal center of Polish politics commenced, to some degree above the continuously salient "ex-Solidarity versus ex-communists" cleavage. This process has been facilitated by the fact that the ex-communist SLD developed a very strong pro-European discourse, unwaveringly supported Polish membership in the European Union, and boasted a predominantly pro-European electorate (Kucharczyk, 1999: 222).

Somewhat paradoxically, then, Polish ex-communists, by undergoing a proliberal metamorphosis, helped to articulate and institutionalize a relatively robust set of liberal discourses and practices. In this project they were, of course, assisted by the liberal wing of the Solidarity movement, which during the early years of transition became very influential politically and injected into the reform process its own version of an elaborately articulated (by East European standards) liberal discourse. Together, these two groups succeeded in creating a visible and politically well-connected liberal semiotic community – or, in Wuthnow's (1989) terminology, community of discourse – that produced and successfully promulgated many key tenets of liberalism.[20]

Jerzy Szacki, the author of the most comprehensive study of postcommunist liberalism in Poland, is very cautious in his assessment of its impact on Polish politics. He distinguishes between economic and political liberalisms and concludes that while the former enjoyed tremendous success, at least during the early postcommunist years, the latter can only claim "a partial success" (1995: 212). But I would rather agree with Janine Holz, in whose view "conservative liberalism was the naturalized discourse that became most authorized in reorganizing government, economy, and society in Poland after the collapse of communism" (1997: 419). And, although its influence dwindled over the years, "*its limiting effects on the range of ways to pursue citizenship endured*" (1997: 411; emphasis added). Holz's observations are confirmed by a Polish philosopher, Miłowit Kuniński, who closes his analysis of Polish postcommunist liberalism with a strong opinion: "Even if the Polish civil society is not as liberal as the German or Swiss ones . . . it is much more liberal on the practical level than might be imagined" (1999: 242).[21]

[20] For Sewell's definition of semiotic community, see note 9.

[21] According to Harsanyi and Kennedy, "Liberalism's eutopic dimension is more apparent in Poland [compared with, say, that in Romania or Ukraine–J.K.]. Solidarity helped to generate

The analyses presented in this section lead to two general conclusions. First, while the national-communist hybrid has become very robust and influential in postcommunist Russia, in Poland it has not been propounded by any major political force and its social appeal has been negligible. Second, while pro-Western liberalism has emerged as a permanent, formative discourse in Polish postcommunist politics, in Russia during the 1990s it was relegated to the margins of political life. Moreover, a cleavage separating the national-communist option from the pro-Western liberals acquired a definitional role in the Russian politics of the 1990s,[22] whereas in Poland the liberal-minded ex-communists and post-Solidarity liberals have begun drifting toward each other, separated from the conservative-religious-nationalistic right by a deepening cultural-political cleavage (see Figure 10.1). Throughout the 1990s, this cleavage continued to generate extremely heated debates and symbolic confrontations that did not, however, transcend the boundaries of institutionalized, moderate, "liberal" political practice.[23]

Do the Hybrid of Nationalism and Socialism and the Cultural-Political Polarization Constitute Cultural Legacies of the State Socialist and/or Earlier Periods?

Communists consolidating their power had to come to terms with existing intellectual and cultural formations – first of all, with nationalism. One possible strategy was the eradication of all traces of nationalism in the name of internationalism. This was sometimes attempted, but for a variety of reasons nationalism proved resilient and ineradicable, perhaps mostly due to its astounding *opportunism*. As Bunce observes, "the nationalist message can be... easily combined with other messages, liberal and illiberal, centrist and decentralist, state-serving and state-destroying" (1999: 109). Many "socialist" cultural-political entrepreneurs decided to weave a tapestry of ideologies using both nationalist and socialist threads; they found that this was a relatively easy task.

Verdery (1993) and many others have convincingly demonstrated that nationalism is not a primordial, "ancient" identity in Eastern Europe. Rather,

not only a political class with liberal views, but also a wider Polish culture that was more tolerant and insistent on democracy" (1994: 175).

[22] Of course, there are other cleavages in Russian politics, the one separating the "étatist" option (e.g., Chernomyrdin's "Our Home Is Russia" or the pro-Putin "*Edinstvo-Otechestvo*") from the communists being perhaps most significant.

[23] Wesołowski (2000) introduces to Polish debates a useful, Sartorian distinction between (ideological) polarization and the emergence of a two-party political system. In his view, Polish postcommunist political practice oscillates between these two models of bipolarity (78–81).

Russia post-1991

	EX-COMMUNISTS	FORMER OPPOSITION
NATIONALISM		
COMMUNISM		
LIBERALISM		Isolated

Poland post-1989

	EX-COMMUNISTS	FORMER OPPOSITION
NATIONALISM		
COMMUNISM		
LIBERALISM		

Russia pre-1991

	COMMUNIST STATE	OPPOSITION
NATIONALISM		Strong
COMMUNISM		
LIBERALISM		Weak

Poland pre-1989

	COMMUNIST STATE	OPPOSITION
NATIONALISM		Weak
COMMUNISM		
LIBERALISM		Strong

FIGURE 10.1. Russian and Polish politics: Basic logic of reconfiguration in discursive cleavages and alliance building. Shaded cells represent salient political discourses; thick lines represent dominant cleavages.

it developed slowly during the eighteenth, nineteenth, and early twentieth centuries.[24] By the time of the communist takeover in the 1940s, nationalism was one of the forms of cultural capital most intensely exploited by various cultural-political entrepreneurs; it was increasingly entrenched in the public mind as an obvious, if not "natural," way of thinking. As a result, it became an attractive ideological weapon for politicians of almost every persuasion. Even communists could not refuse its charms. As Verdery (1993) argues, in communist federal states nationalism was fostered, perhaps inadvertently, by the very logic of the system: the republican elites would engage the center in the name of "their 'national' populace." On the other hand, national or ethnic discourses became very effective as tools producing trust and efficiency throughout informal networks engendered by the inefficiency of the economy of shortage. Finally, ethnically (or nationally) grounded trust proved useful in organizing anticommunist resistance or dissidence.

Pre-1991 Russia

During the Soviet period, Russian nationalists were to be found both among the influential party ideologues and among the leading dissidents (most prominently Solzhenitsyn). The former have been usually characterized as exponents of national Bolshevism; the latter have been dubbed by Dunlop the *vozrozhdentsy* (from the Russian for revival or "renaissance").[25] Most if not all of the *vozrozhdentsy* were exponents of neo-Slavophilism. As such, they shared common themes (such as anti-Westernism and patriotism) with the official communist doctrine, but, of course, most of them were highly critical of the Soviet system (Paramonov, 1996: 26).

This opposition between Slavophiles and Westernizers has been seen by many observers as the most salient, concrete manifestation of the powerful and tragic (for ineradicable, in Besançon's view) *dualism* that lies at Russian culture's foundation.[26] Mesmerized by the grand, "cursed questions" of "What's to be done?" and "What is the Russian idea?" at least since the beginning of the nineteenth century, Russian cultural entrepreneurs (artists, writers, philosophers) have tended to frame answers in terms of binary oppositions.[27] And here resides the dominant "curse" of Russian culture, for as Yuri Lotman argues in his last book, the mechanism of change in binary structures is by necessity volatile and revolutionary. By contrast, the Western culture – tertiary (as Lotman calls it) in its nature – is far more open to change through evolution, made possible by the mediating influence

[24] For an excellent reconstruction of the evolution of Polish nationalism, see Porter (2000).

[25] For a succinct presentation of both versions of the nationalistic doctrine, see Dunlop (1983: 242–73).

[26] Andrzej Walicki analyzed this debate in great detail. See, for example, Walicki (1975).

[27] There is a huge literature on this topic. For a glimpse of the most recent round of disputes on the "perennial" dualism of Russian culture, see Urban (1994: 8); Rutland (1997); Chubais (1998).

of the middle term. Lotman is very skeptical in his assessment of Russia's chances of overcoming the legacy of cultural polarization:

> A transition from thinking oriented toward explosion to evolutionary consciousness becomes very urgent today [i.e., the late 1980s], because the whole [Russian] culture, as we know it, gravitated toward polarization and maximalism. Yet, [this] self-understanding is not adequate to reality. In the realm of reality, explosions cannot disappear; the point, however, is to overcome the fatal choice between inertia and catastrophe. Additionally, maximalism is so deeply rooted at the very basis of Russian culture, that it is difficult to talk about a "danger" of the absolute domination by a golden middle or to worry that the leveling of the contradictions will stop the creative, explosive processes. (1992: 265)[28]

The (anti-Western) maximalism and polarization diagnosed by Lotman were deliberately cultivated and eventually facilitated the nationalist-socialist rapprochement that evolved in post-1917 Russia and the Soviet Union.[29] Almost since the beginning of the Soviet Union, the on-again, off-again contest between communist internationalism and national political and philosophical traditions came to dominate the official public discourse, eventually leading to the emergence of a nationalist-socialist hybrid (national Bolshevism; see Allensworth, 1998: 145–64). Lenin definitely rejected the "nationalistic" tradition of *narodnichestvo* (narrowly defined populism), but he unreservedly embraced the critique of the Western institutions so characteristic for the "generic" populist mind-set (Walicki, 1995: 282–83), which was partially indebted, in turn, to earlier Slavophilism.[30] Later, under Stalin and Brezhnev, nationalism was deliberately cultivated by the official propaganda machine (Brudny, 1998). Particularly during crises, Soviet rulers intensified the propagation of nationalism (Lasswell et al., 1949). As Bonnell shows, during World War II and its immediate aftermath, "[p]atriotism and an imperial ethos replaced class as the primary allegiances cultivated by the Soviet regime among the citizens" (1997: 255). But even during the "era of stagnation" in the 1960s, Andrei Amalrik observed that "[t]he need for an ideological underpinning forces the regime to look toward a new ideology, namely, Great Russian nationalism, with its characteristic cult of strength and expansionist ambitions" (1970: 38).[31]

[28] In my translation (from both Russian and Polish versions) I tried to preserve Lotman's specific (and at times opaque) phrasing.

[29] For a succinct analysis of this phenomenon, see Khrushcheva (2000).

[30] On this link and, particularly, Herzen's role in it, see Walicki (1975: 580–601); Besançon (1981: 74–77). Venturi observes: "The Populists shared with the nationalistic Russian Slavophiles (with whose political ideas they had otherwise little in common) a loathing for the rigidly class-conscious social pyramid of the West that was complacently accepted, or fervently believed in, by the conformist bourgeoisie and the bureaucracy" (1960: 9).

[31] There is no room here to introduce the important distinction between two versions of Russian nationalism: Russkiy (ethnic) and Rossiyskiy (comprehensive, imperial). This distinction is not crucial for my analysis.

For some thinkers, such as Solzhenitsyn, the idea that Russian nationalism, closely intertwined with Orthodoxy, could have anything in common with the programmatically secular "communist ideology" was repulsive. But, as I already observed, since Lenin, communism and Russian nationalism (nourished by various strands of Slavophilism and populism) shared at least two common ideological tenets: scornful anti-Occidentalism and a notion of "Russian uniqueness" (or the "Russian idea"), elaborated in a complex and often internally contradictory fashion (McDaniel, 1996; Rancour-Laferriere, 2000). These two commonalities presaged an intellectual bridge between the discourses of nationalism and communism and thus made it possible for some cultural entrepreneurs to propose a hybrid of nationalism-communism, often taking a concrete cultural form of neo-Slavophilism. During the waning years of the Soviet Union, neo-Slavophilism was best expressed in the writings of a group of writers called *derevenshchiki* (village prose writers), who were by and large critical of the Soviet regime but were equally ill predisposed toward "Western Europe."[32] Their novels, essays, and plays not only enjoyed the official imprimatur but were also immensely popular (Brudny, 1998: 191–94). A prescient observer noted that already in the late 1960s neo-Slavophilism circulated not only in intellectual discourse:

> The need for a viable nationalist ideology is not only acutely felt by the regime, but nationalist feelings also appear to be taking hold in Soviet society, primarily in official literary and artistic circles (where they have evidently developed as a reaction to the considerable role of Jews in official Soviet art).... This ideology can perhaps be called "neo-Slavophile." ... Its central features are an interest in Russianness, a belief in the messianic role of Russia and an extreme scorn and hostility toward everything non-Russian. (Amalrik, 1970: 38–9)

This neo-Slavophile cultural syndrome was inimical to such Western political inventions as liberal democracy or civil society. As a Russian political scientist observes, "the major aspects of the dominant political culture of Soviet society seemed not to correspond at all to a civic culture. In addition to being clearly 'Soviet' in basic value orientations (i.e. influenced by the ideology of the Soviet variety of communism), this dominant political culture has very deep Russian roots and demonstrates some continuity with basic traditional values and beliefs" (Melville, 1993: 59). Philosopher Igor Chubais shows, for example, that bridges between certain elements of the communist creed and "the Russian idea" were constructed both inside and outside of the Communist Party. Chubais separates "communist ideology" from "the communist idea" construed as "a collection of deeply positive values, among them social justice, the withering away of the state, 'he who doesn't not work doesn't eat,' 'land to the peasants'" (1998: 16) and claims that the latter is perfectly compatible with "the Russian idea."

[32] On this topic, see Paramonov (1996: 23–27); Brudny (1998).

During the 1970s and early 1980s, the intellectual milieu (semiotic community) that articulated and propagated national and national-communist discourses was "the best organized group of the Russian intelligentsia" (Brudny, 1998: 193). The same cannot be said about the proponents of Western-style liberalism. They were not only numerically weaker, but also had problems articulating a set of clear-cut liberal precepts: "What was once called the 'democratic movement' contained many different values and was united only by its opposition to the old regime; in Russia the stark opposition between state and civil society typical of east European (especially Polish) thinking was never dominant" (Sakwa, 1995: 962).

This weak and labile articulation of liberalism in itself is a cultural legacy with considerable historical depth. Writing about the late nineteenth- and early twentieth-century Russian liberals' ambivalence toward the West, Laura Engelstein observes that, "Even to the best Russian liberal, individualism was both an ardently desired prize and a threat to cultural values that distinguished their world from the 'out there,' a place that often seemed better, but also spiritually impoverished" (1994: 235).

On the other hand, the Russian dissident movement was not exclusively nationalistic; the tenor of Russian dissidence was more complex. While Solzhenitsyn and his "followers" espoused a nationalistic political philosophy, a circle of people around Sakharov cultivated an increasingly "pro-Western," liberal program (Prizel, 1998: 196–201). Such a program was more or less deliberately grounded in the domestic tradition of liberal thought that had considerable achievements (Petro, 1995; Morson, 1998). Yet liberalism in Russia, despite some noteworthy successes among the intelligentsia, has never acquired the status of a socially influential discourse.

The main contours of the discursive field in the Russian pre-1991 politics can be thus summarized as follows (see Figure 10.1): (1) various strands of nationalism were developed and cultivated on both sides of the barricade, both among the dissidents and within the officially sanctioned domain of cultural production; (2) some of those strands were built on an explicit merger of nationalistic and "communist" motifs; (3) nationalism, sometimes hybridized by the admixture of communism, emerged as a potential discursive bridge among the adversaries (Prizel, 1998: 201–11). At the same time, (4) liberalism was advanced only by a much smaller group of cultural entrepreneurs, achieved some influence only under Gorbachev, but was weakly disseminated in the society at large and eventually was marginalized.[33]

33 "...shortly after the collapse of the USSR there was a mass exodus from the liberal-democratic camp, with many former members either defecting to the nationalists or joining the reborn communist parties" (Prizel, 1998: 221).

Pre-1989 Poland

Polish communists flirted with nationalism as well, but well-articulated nationalist-communist hybrids never achieved such prominence in pre-1989 Polish public discourse as they did in the pre-1991 Russian political culture. Władysław Gomułka (the Communist Party's first secretary in 1956–70) was clearly more "nationalistic" than his Stalinist predecessor, Bolesław Bierut, yet his nationalism was quite modest compared with the aggressive exclusivistic version of nationalism (nationalist-communism) of his archenemy Mieczysław Moczar. Moczar's nationalism was, however, relegated to the backstage of Polish public life in the early 1970s, when he lost his contest for power with Edward Gierek, who espoused and aggressively propagated a more inclusive and liberal version of Polish nationalism, *socialist patriotism.*

Gierek's socialist patriotism was carefully designed and promulgated through the official communist media to the very end of the 1970s (Kubik, 1994). The general organizing principle of this discourse of power was indeed similar to Soviet nationalist-Bolshevism; it was designed as a multivalent hybrid of nationalism and internationalist socialist principles. Yet it differed from the Soviet model in several important respects. First, the version of national identity it espoused was relatively open, tolerant, and devoid of negative images of other nations (particularly anti-Semitism). Second, although it promoted a version of Polishness that was associated with socialism, it also emphasized the European roots of Polish culture. Third, it was developed in a country that enjoyed the least repressive censorship in the communist camp; it was therefore exposed to a limited yet at times robust debate, in which nationalistic and liberal motifs often clashed but also interpenetrated each other.[34]

Most important, the official socialist patriotism was not developed in an ideological vacuum. Although Poland had a well-developed apparatus of preventive censorship, the official version of patriotism was challenged by an increasingly influential and clearly articulated Christian patriotism, championed both by the Catholic Church and the increasingly vocal organized opposition (Kubik, 1994). In contrast to all other state socialist countries, in Poland cultural revolution preceded the political revolution by several years, and later they became intricately interwoven. As I have demonstrated elsewhere (1994), the Polish "refolution" of 1980–81 was a *cultural-political* phenomenon of massive proportions. During the 1970s and early 1980s, a substantial number of people engaged in the formulation, development, and defense of a counterhegemonic vision, which served to delegitimize the state-socialist system and, eventually, allowed these people to constitute themselves as an "oppositional" *cultural-class* of Solidarity. This vision was articulated and promulgated in underground publications and through relatively frequent independent public ceremonies.

[34] Walicki (1988); Harsanyi and Kennedy (1994: 172–73).

These ceremonies, especially John Paul II's first visit to Poland, aimed at the reconstruction of a public domain independent of the state. They (re)invented different traditions, invoked different values, and reached for different symbols than the state's ceremonial. In the case of nominally identical principles, such as patriotism or democracy, the state on the one hand and the church and opposition on the other offered contrasting interpretations and embedded these principles in diametrically different traditions and mythologies. By observing May 3, people invoked a tradition of democracy radically different from the official socialist democracy based on the principle of democratic centralism. When oppositional groups observed November 11, they brought back to the public discourse a form of sovereignty very different from the limited sovereignty propagated by the party-state and epitomized in the hybrid of internationalism-patriotism. By developing the tradition of "December 1970" and reclaiming May Day from the state in 1981, Gdańsk workers, students, and intellectuals demonstrated that the struggle for social justice (the routine activity of the "socialist" state, according to the official discourse) could be undertaken outside of "legality" as defined by the party-state.

Several students of the 1981–89 period in Poland have concluded that the cultural vitality and political significance of the polarized frame setting apart "the society" and "the state" during the 1970s not only did not decline but instead seems to have increased.[35] The events that helped the "opposition" to construct this hegemonic bipolar cleavage included two papal visits, the murder of Father Jerzy Popiełuszko in 1984 and the immediate emergence of his cult, countless street demonstrations and clashes with the police, and large industrial strikes in 1988. Not everybody, of course, participated in this ongoing political and symbolic confrontation with the regime, and not everybody accepted the bipolar vision of the conflict. In fact, the actual numbers of those who supported Solidarity kept declining throughout the 1980s and rebounded only after Solidarity's spectacular electoral victory in 1989 (Jasiewicz, 1993: 390). Yet it seems to be indisputable that during the waning years of state socialism in Poland (1976–89) the extreme, bipolar conceptualization of the public space ("we" versus "they") was a crucial weapon in the society's struggle against the regime.[36] This bipolar conceptualization ([di]vision) was not shared by everybody, yet it served as a mobilizing frame

[35] Anna Uhlig, the author of an excellent study of political symbolism during the 1980s, wrote: "After December 13, 1981, the opposition's drive to make a distinction between 'our Poland' (the Solidarity Republic) from 'their Poland' (the Polish People's Republic) intensifies" (1989: 61).

[36] Jasiewicz and Adamski summarized a longitudinal study of Polish attitudes in the following fashion: "Spontaneous answers show that in 1988 somewhat fewer respondents than in 1984 perceive the presence of conflict in Polish society, which is, however, perceived by almost half the respondents. The great majority of those who perceive conflict define it as between the authorities and society" (1993: 55).

for the most active individuals and groups. A very powerful symbolic cleavage was thus formed, separating "the society" from the unwanted regime.

The oppositional discourse that served to constitute this "independent" society was founded not only on nonsocialist patriotism and Catholicism; it was also based on a powerfully articulated civic-liberal component, framed in the language of civic, individual, and political rights (Harsanyi and Kennedy, 1994; Cirtautas, 1997; Glenn, 2001: 50–51). This generic liberalism (or protoliberalism, as Szacki calls it), organized by such concepts as "civil society," "antipolitics," "autonomy of the individual," "civic rights," and so on, became an integral part of the dominant dissident ideology that was developed and disseminated by the Workers' Defense Committee (KOR)[37] and several other dissident groups. Szacki usefully distinguishes three different "circles of liberal ideas": protoliberalism, economic liberalism, and integral liberalism (1995: 41); he observes that while the latter two were always relatively weak in Eastern Europe, protoliberalism was quite widely disseminated in pre-1989 Poland.

Liberal elements were also prominent in the programmatic statements of the Solidarity movement, although they were never fully and comprehensively articulated as a liberal ideology tout court. This is, of course, related to the fact that liberalism has historically never been influential in Eastern Europe. Yet, quite clearly, in Poland it was stronger than in Russia, for it merged in a characteristic fashion with Polish nationalism. As Weigle perceptively notes, *state-building nationalism* (as in nineteenth-century Poland) can be easily combined with at least some elements of liberalism (on the basis of the commonly shared principle of liberty), whereas *imperial*, conservative nationalisms are sharply antagonistic to any liberal idea (as in Russia).[38] And although during the course of the nineteenth century and in the interwar Poland (1918–39) this liberal version of Polish nationalism was overshadowed by its more chauvinistic relatives (Porter, 2000), it was never completely extinct and was partially revived – I would argue – by Gierek and the opposition in the 1970s.

The dissident movement was, however, never monolithic. Traces of ideological divisions between two major strands of political philosophy – individualistic-cosmopolitan and collectivistic-nationalistic – are detectable in the late 1970s, when two major dissident formations, KOR and ROPCiO, parted ways.[39] As Lipski has explained,

> [A] typical associate of *KOR* would be farther to the left than a participant in *ROPCiO*....If being on the left is understood as an attitude that emphasizes the possibility and the necessity of reconciling human liberty with human equality, while

[37] See, for example, Bernhard (1993); Zuzowski (1992: 105).

[38] On a similar point, see Szacki (1995: 56). See also Wandycz (1992).

[39] KOR, the Workers' Defense Committee; ROPCiO, the Movement in Defense of Human and Civil Rights. See, for example, Zuzowski (1992: 105–7).

being on the right is understood as an attitude that may mean sacrificing the postulate of human freedom in favor of various kinds of social collectives and structures [I presume that Lipski has in mind such collectives as the nation and the Catholic Church – J.K.], or foregoing the postulate of equality in the name of laissez-faire, then the above statement about the differences between an average *KOR* associate and an average *ROPCiO* participant will be understandable. (1985: 121)

These initial ideological differences between KOR and ROPCiO foretold the story of future political battles. The collectivistic and individualistic strands within Polish opposition became more pronounced during the 1970s and 1980s, developed into major programmatic disagreements, and after 1989 solidified into two major visions of the postcommunist order.

The collectivistic, organic identity – whether in "nationalistic," "socialist-egalitarian," or even combined "populist-nationalistic-egalitarian" versions – had two sources: one ideological, the other organizational. The ideological source can be located in certain elements of the ROPCiO "independence" program and, quite clearly, in the political thought of the strongly nationalistic Confederation of Independent Poland (KPN) or in "Solidarity's" organic, national-socialist vision (ethos). The organizational source was the Solidarity movement itself. Solidarity's unity resulted mostly from the unifying power of its symbolic superstructure; it was not a carefully negotiated alliance of various self-conscious and autonomous units, but rather an unreasoned, emotional, "organic community" (cultural class), which for several years united a large segment of the Polish population.[40]

Individualistic and pluralistic identities had their own ideological and organizational sources. Their ideological roots reach back to certain elements of the KOR political philosophy and the programs of Polish liberals that were elaborated in the second half of the 1980s.[41] Its organizational source was the multitude of oppositional groups, acting separately during the 1976–80 period and forming the decentralized network of the "underground civil society" of the 1981–89 period.

In a simplifying summary that emphasizes only the dominant trends in the formation of public discourses, the Polish situation prior to 1989 can be construed as a mirror image of the Russian situation before 1991. First, the hybrid of nationalism-communism in the official discourse emerged, but it was founded on a milder, less exclusivistic version of nationalism than in Russia. Second, the discourse of the Communist Party, particularly in the 1970s, was not devoid of pro-European elements (Gierek's flirtation with

40 On this point, see also Staniszkis (1989) and Kowalski (1990). Szacki writes: "[T]he idea of the autonomy of the individual, lying at the foundation of dissidentism, simply disappeared, the idea of civil society was however modified – it was adapted to the new situation, different social milieu with different mentality and traditions" (1995: 139).

41 On Polish liberalism, see Szacki (1995); Kuniński (1999); Holz (1997); Skarzynski (1994); Turek (1995).

Eurocommunism);[42] its socialist patriotism was much more liberal than most of the then dominant forms of Russian nationalism. Third, the dominant oppositional discourse was based on broadly understood liberal principles, whereas the nationalistic alternative in the dissident movement was less influential, both organizationally and intellectually (see Figure 10.1).

Conclusion

The analyses presented in this essay (summarized schematically in Figure 10.1) suggests that when after 1989–91 the main cultural-political cleavage lines in Poland and Russia were redrawn, some principal cultural-political entrepreneurs who did the redrawing relied in this task on the combinations of cultural discourses that had been developed earlier, many with clear roots in the cultural and political developments of the nineteenth century. The postcommunist transformations were certainly driven by considerable conceptual innovation, but at the same time some important cultural trends from earlier epochs were continued. It is hard, for example, to understand post-1991 Russian politics without realizing that one of its dominant political parties (the CPRF) successfully cultivates an old discourse whose essence is a powerful, gnostic, and bipolar vision of the world (East versus West) and the hybrid of nationalism-communism. In forming this discourse, Zyuganov and his allies followed the line of least resistance from the available tool kit of cultural materials; they build their political program and vision as a deliberately chosen legacy of one of the most important trends in Russian cultural and political history. This suggests a strongly path-dependent formation of at least some of the post-1989–91 cultural-political visions. They are built through the deliberate transmission of certain cultural-political schemas articulated in the identifiable past. This is the process of (explicit) legacy formation at work.

It is difficult, if not impossible, to study legacy formation at a highly abstract level. An analyst must be tuned to the concrete developments within specific discursive fields that – at least until recently – have been largely contained within the boundaries of the existing nation-states. For example, my analyses indicate that a legacy of polarization was formed and that it came to dominate both Polish and Russian postcommunist politics. This domination is not a product of some mysterious "inertia." Polarizing discourses were deliberately chosen as a political weapon by many Polish and Russian politicians, who used them with abandon throughout the 1990s. Yet, a closer examination reveals that Polish and Russian polarizations were quite different from each other, and, accordingly, their political functions varied.

A comparison with Russia reveals perhaps the most politically significant feature of Polish polarization: its nonfoundational and "democratic"

[42] See Rolicki (1990).

character. In Russia, "a democratic project" needs to be articulated within one of the basic cultural syndromes of the grand, foundational dualism, Westernism or Slavophilism. Obviously, this task can be easily accomplished within the former, but it becomes almost impossible within the latter. But as democracy is (inescapably?) linked with Westernism, the whole considerable cultural power of neo-Slavophilism (including its specifically Russian concept of "collectivism," *sobornost'*) can be turned against it, polarizing the political discourse in a truly profound manner.[43]

By contrast, in Poland – whose dominant intellectuals never cultivated Slavophilism or any other Occident-phobic discourse – "democracy," a welcome Western product, provides a foundational frame of the polity. Granted, there is a trend in Polish intellectual life that is highly critical of the historical trajectory the West has traveled, particularly since the advent of modernity (Jackowski, 1993; 1994). But this criticism is not based on the rejection of "the West" in the name of some other, superior, civilization. It is rather founded on a conviction that Poland managed to preserve and cultivate the "truer" and "purer" version of Western civilization (inescapably embedded in the Western variant of Christianity), whereas in the western part of the continent this civilization has been corrupted perhaps beyond repair.[44] As a result, Polish cultural-political (ideological) (di)visions are not easily articulatable *outside* of an Occident-centric frame, usually including a Western concept of democracy. In this sense, Polish bipolarization (Catholic–post-Solidarity versus secular-postcommunist) is nonfoundational; it does not tear the polity apart to the degree that Russian dualism does. It does, though, contribute to the incompatibility of discourses coming from both camps and a low level of communicative consensus, dubbed by a group of researchers "ritual chaos" (Czyżewski, Kowalski, and Piotrowski, 1997).

Another question I tried to answer was whether the nationalist-communist (socialist) hybrid was a newly invented cultural schema or rather a legacy of the past. I summarize my argument with the help of the concepts of *dehybridization* of the socialist-communist-nationalist discourse (dominant in Poland) and its *rehybridization* (dominant in Russia). In both countries, nationalist-communist hybrids were formed well before the fall of state socialism. They were, however, different, both in terms of their internal features and the contexts within which they were formed. The Russian variant was based on a strong, often militant, version of nationalism that was elaborated by both officially supported intellectuals and some influential dissidents, and did not face any serious competition from other visions of nationalism proposed by nonstate institutions or actors.

[43] On the difficulties of expressing the concepts of parliamentary plurality and the separation of powers within a discourse encompassing *sobornost*, see Urban (1994: 8); Biryukov and Sergeyev (1994); Sergeyev and Biryukov (1993: 112–51).

[44] See, for example, Jackowski (1997: particularly volume 2, *The Sentenced God*).

In communist Poland, such a hybrid was proposed by a political faction (led by Mieczysław Moczar) that was marginalized at the beginning of the 1970s, when Polish communists entered a path of *social-democratization*.[45] Discursively, this strategic turn was accompanied by the articulation of a *socialist patriotism* that was founded on a mild version of Polish nationalism and opened the way for the more decisive dehybridization of socialist-nationalism after 1989. It should be emphasized that Polish communists could not "appropriate" Polish nationalism and mold it any way they might have envisioned, because it was already "controlled" by the Catholic Church and certain segments of the organized opposition. Russian (Soviet) communists did not face such obstacles. After the fall of communism in Poland, the reformed communists (SLD) simply *continued* this dehybridization of the official socialist-nationalism through the complete "social-democratization" of their discourse. By contrast, in postcommunist Russia the nationalist-communist discourse, somewhat weakened under Gorbachev, was rehybridized by Zyuganov and several other cultural-political entrepreneurs. This was a successful strategy, for it proved to resonate with a large portion of the Russian electorate. Again, Zyuganov did not need to invent this hybrid; he simply used a ready-made product, concocted much earlier. In brief, Polish ex-communists continued dehybridizing nationalism and socialism and engaged in a very vigorous rehybridization of socialism and liberalism (such a hybrid constitutes the foundation of Western-style social democracy). In Russia, communists chose exactly the opposite strategy, albeit a strategy strongly suggested to them by history. They rehybridized nationalism and socialism, and they decisively dehybridized socialism and liberalism.

To generalize, the dehybridization of nationalism and socialism (as in Poland) helped to marginalize nationalism as a usable past and to strengthen pro-European, cosmopolitan social democracy. Rehybridization of nationalism and socialism (as in Russia) helped to cultivate "national Bolshevism"; it was based on a discursive strategy of amalgamating the "collectivistic" creeds of nationalism and socialism, thus facilitating the formation of a powerful "hybrid" weapon against liberalism.[46] Rehybridization also contributed to the weakening of the pro-European, social-democratic left.

In this chapter I focused on certain *explicit* cultural legacies of state socialism in Poland and Russia. My question was, How have cultural patterns, engendered under communism or even earlier, influenced postcommunist political and economic transformations? I concluded that certain past cultural scenarios informed political actions of key political actors in the post-1989

45 Rolicki (1990); Rakowski (1991).

46 "The polarization of Russian politics is thus the direct consequence of a failure to reinforce the linkage between patriotism and democracy and to create, through this linkage, a moderate, enlightened patriotism that could provide a coherent concept of the Russian national interest" (Petro, 1995: 172).

Poland and Russia. Those scenarios were found in (important) past narratives that have been cultivated by today's cultural entrepreneurs. In particular, a large and influential group of Russian political-cultural entrepreneurs formed and propagated a cultural legacy of the nationalist-communist (socialist) hybrid, used it to define the dominant polarizing cleavage in the elite discourse, and employed it successfully in combating Western-style liberalism. Polish postcommunist cultural-political entrepreneurs formed different legacies, strongly suggested by the trajectory of Polish elite political culture, at least since 1956. Those actions contributed to a tremendous divergence between Polish and Russian attitudes toward democracy. For example, in the late 1990s, when asked to express their opinion concerning the statement "Democracy may have problems but it is better than any other form of government," 29.7 percent of Poles and only 9.8 percent of Russians strongly agreed with this declaration. Additionally, 58.7 percent of Poles and 49.1 percent of Russians "agreed."[47]

Given these findings, a possible way to close this essay would be to disagree with Holmes and claim that, indeed, "the best indicator of the future is the past" – or at least to assert that legacies of the past are relevant for current politics. But given my initial theoretical argument on cultural causation in general and on the formation of cultural legacies in particular, my final conclusions are couched in that new analytical idiom. Most important, they reflect the initial observation that cultural legacies are "transmitted," not "received from."

1. *Past cultural scenarios* are relevant, because they constitute a limited repertoire of "usable pasts" and models of or for political behavior for today's cultural-political entrepreneurs. From time to time, some of these entrepreneurs will forge new ideas and cultural scenarios of action; but more often they will try to recycle the scenarios suggested to them by their national histories. This conclusion is confirmed by mainstream survey research (the psychosocial tradition). Although many researchers remain skeptical of Huntington's (1996) broad generalizations, they nonetheless confirm the persistence of certain attitudinal syndromes, dominant within specific cultural areas (see, e.g., Inglehart and Baker, 2000; Fuchs and Klingemann, 2002; Reisinger et al., 1994).

2. Past cultural scenarios, if they are to become *legacies*, must be transmitted from the past by cultural entrepreneurs. They create and sustain cultural fields (communities of discourse) constituted by discourses that are available

[47] These numbers come from the World Values Survey. For Poland, see "Poland: Democratic Consolidation in Central and Eastern Europe: Civil Society and Democratic Orientation," Conference, Robert Schuman Center of the European University Institute, Florence, June 28–29, 1999, organized by Hans-Dieter Klingemann, Dieter Fuchs, Ronald Inglehart, and Jan Zielonka. For Russia, see ROMIR (Rossiyskoye Obshchestvennye Mnenie i Issledovanye Rynka), available at <www.romir.ru>.

to and eventually accepted by politicians. These discourses, in turn, influence (if not form) politicians' thinking about what is (the social world), what is desirable (goals), what is doable (pragmatic constraints), and what methods are legitimate (ethical constraints). They thus have an impact on the policy-making process. The choices of the postcommunist Polish elites were made within a different cultural field than the choices of the Russian elites, and this helps explain the divergent paths of Polish and Russian postcommunist polities. Thus, the *choices* of today's cultural-political entrepreneurs are relevant. They may downplay or deemphasize certain "pasts," as was the case of the Spanish elites who deliberately "discharged" the potentially divisive memory of the civil war. Or they may choose continuation, that is, a *conservative strategy of legacy formation.*

3. The (non)existence of (several) competing channels of social transmission of the past patterns (cultural scenarios) is relevant, for it determines whether a cultural field, available to and cultivated by the politicians, is more or less diverse. From 1956 to 1989, the Polish cultural field was much more open, and consequently more diverse, than the Russian-Soviet one.

4. The dilemma Holmes posed in his essay – which factor is responsible for the sorry state of the Russian polity at the beginning of the twenty-first century: (the collapse of) the state or (the "faulty") political culture? – is overstated. Cultural schemas, transmitted by political entrepreneurs from the past to the present, influence the project of state building.[48] It is politically very relevant how the elites picture the new state's architecture, how they apprehend the system of rights and obligations with which people should be endowed as citizens, how they conceptualize the relationship of "their" state with the outside world, and how they visualize the "outside" world.

References

Allensworth, Wayne. 1998. *The Russian Question: Nationalism, Modernization, and Post-Communist Russia.* Lanham, Md.: Rowman and Littlefield.

Almond, Gabriel, and Sidney Verba. 1963. *The Civic Culture: Political Attitudes and Democracy in Five Nations.* Princeton: Princeton University Press.

Amalrik, Andrei. 1970. *Will the Soviet Union Survive until 1984?* New York: Harper and Row.

Aronoff, Myron J. 1989. *Israeli Visions and Divisions.* New Brunswick, N.J.: Transaction Press.

Baker, Keith Michael. 1990. *Inventing the French Revolution: Essays on French Political Culture in the Eighteenth Century.* Cambridge: Cambridge University Press.

[48] See, for example, Scott (1998) or Steinmetz (1999). Schochet analyzes the modern state, its political theory, and politics, "especially in its English-speaking form," by treating "the state as something of a linguistic construct that is maintained by a continuous commentary on its tradition, a kind of political hermeneutics" (1994: 321).

Becker, Carl L. 1958. What Are Historical Facts? In Phil L. Snyder, ed., *Detachment and the Writing of History: Essays and Letters of Carl L. Becker*, pp. 41–64. Ithaca: Cornell University Press.

Bernhard, Michael. 1993. *The Origin of Democratization in Poland.* New York: Columbia University Press.

Besançon, Alain. 1981. *The Rise of Gulag: Intellectual Origins of Leninism.* New York: Continuum.

Biernacki, Richard. 1999. Method and Metaphor after the New Cultural History. In Victoria Bonnell and Lynn Hunt, eds., *Beyond the Cultural Turn: New Directions in the Study of Society and Culture*, pp. 62–92. Berkeley: University of California Press.

Biryukov, Nikolai, and Victor Sergeyev. 1994. The Idea of Democracy in the West and in the East. In David Beetham, ed., *Defining and Measuring Democracy*, pp. 182–98. London: Sage Publications.

Bonnell, Victoria E. 1997. *Iconography of Power: Soviet Political Posters under Lenin and Stalin.* Berkeley: University of California Press.

Bonnell, Victoria E., and Lynn Hunt, eds. 1999. *Beyond the Cultural Turn: New Directions in the Study of Society and Culture.* Berkeley: University of California Press.

Bourdieu, Pierre. 1991. On Symbolic Power. In *Language and Symbolic Power*, pp. 163–70. Cambridge, Mass.: Harvard University Press.

Bratkiewicz, Jarosław. 1998. *Rosyjscy nacjonaliści w latach 1992–1996.* Warsaw: ISP PAN.

Brint, Steven. 1994. Sociological Analysis of Political Culture: An Introductory Assessment. In Frederick D. Weil and Mary Gautier, eds., *Political Culture and Political Structure: Theoretical and Empirical Studies. Research on Democracy and Society*, 2:3–41. Greenwich, Conn.: JAI Press.

Brudny, Yitzhak M. 1998. *Reinventing Russia: Russian Nationalism and the Soviet State, 1953–1991.* Cambridge, Mass.: Harvard University Press.

Bunce, Valerie. 1999. *Subversive Institutions: The Design and the Destruction of Socialism and the State.* Cambridge: Cambridge University Press.

Chinayeva, Elena. 2000. The Search for the "Russian Idea." *Transitions.* Available: <www.ijt.cz/transitions/thesear1.html>, accessed on October 2, 2000.

Chubais, Igor. 1998. From the Russian Idea to the Idea of a New Russia: How We Must Overcome the Crisis of Ideas. Strengthening Democratic Institutions Occasional Paper. John F. Kennedy School of Government, Harvard University, Cambridge, Mass.

Cirtautas, Arista Maria. 1997. *The Polish Solidarity Movement: Revolution, Democracy and Natural Rights.* London: Routledge.

Czyżewski, Marek. 1997. W strone teorii dyskursu publicznego. In M. Czyżewski, Sergiusz Kowalski, and Andrzej Piotrowski, eds., *Rytualny chaos: Studium dyskursu publicznego*, pp. 42–115. Crakow: Aureus.

Czyżewski, Marek, Sergiusz Kowalski, and Andrzej Piotrowski, eds. 1997. *Rytualny chaos. Studium dyskursu publicznego.* Crakow: Aureus.

Dirks, Nicholas B., Geoff Eley, and Sherry B. Ortner. 1994. Introduction. In Nicholas B. Dirks, Geoff Eley, and Sherry B. Ortner, eds., *Culture/Power/History: A Reader in Contemporary Social Theory.* Princeton: Princeton University Press.

Dittmer, Lowell. 1977. Political Culture and Political Symbolism: Toward a Theoretical Synthesis. *World Politics* 29(4): 552–83.

Dunlop, John B. 1983. *The Faces of Contemporary Russian Nationalism*. Princeton: Princeton University Press.

Edles, Laura Desfor. 1998. *Symbol and Ritual in the New Spain: The Transition to Democracy after Franco*. Cambridge: Cambridge University Press.

Engelstein, Laura. 1994. Combined Underdevelopment: Discipline and the Law in Imperial and Soviet Russia. In Jan Goldstein, ed., *Foucault and the Writing of History*, pp. 220–36. Oxford: Blackwell.

Fish, M. Steven. 1995. *Democracy from Scratch: Opposition and Regime in the New Russian Revolution*. Princeton: Princeton University Press.

Fuchs, Dieter, and Hans-Dieter Klingemann. 2002. Eastward Enlargement of the European Union and the Identity of Europe. *West European Politics* 25(2): 19–54.

Gamson, William A. 1988. Political Discourse and Collective Action. In Bert Klandermans, Hanspeter Kriesi, and Sidney Tarrow, eds., *International Social Movement Research*, vol. 1, *From Structure to Action: Comparing Social Movement Research across Cultures*, pp. 219–44. Greenwich, Conn.: JAI Press.

Geertz, Clifford. 1973. *The Interpretation of Cultures*. New York: Basic Books.

Glenn, John K. 2001. *Framing Democracy: Civil Society and Civic Movements in Eastern Europe*. Stanford: Stanford University Press.

Goldstone, Jack A. 1991. Ideology, Cultural Frameworks, and the Process of Revolution. *Theory and Society* 20: 405–53.

Harsanyi, Nicolae, and Michael D. Kennedy. 1994. Between Utopia and Dystopia: The Labilities of Nationalism in Eastern Europe. In M. D. Kennedy, ed., *Envisioning Eastern Europe: Postcommunist Cultural Studies*, pp. 149–79. Ann Arbor: University of Michigan Press.

Hirschman, Albert O. 1991. *The Rhetorics of Reaction*. Cambridge, Mass.: Belknap Press of Harvard University Press.

Holmes, Stephen. 1996. Cultural Legacies or State Collapse? Probing the Postcommunist Dilemma. In Michael Mandelbaum, ed., *Postcommunism: Four Perspectives*, pp. 22–76. New York: Council on Foreign Relations.

Holz, Janine. 1997. Liberalism and the Construction of the Democratic Subject in Postcommunism: The Case of Poland. *Slavic Review* 56(3): 401–27.

Huntington, Samuel P. 1996. *The Clash of Civilizations and the Remaking of World Order*. New York: Simon and Schuster.

Inglehart, Ronald, and Wayne E. Baker. 2000. Modernization, Cultural Change and the Persistence of Traditional Values. *American Sociological Review* 65 (February): 19–51.

Jackowski, Jan Maria. 1993. *Bitwa o Polskę* (A battle for Poland). Warsaw: "ad astra."

1997. *Bitwa o Prawdę* (A battle for truth). Warsaw: "ad astra."

Jasiewicz, Krzysztof. 1993. Polish Politics on the Eve of the 1993 Elections: Towards Fragmentation or Pluralism? *Communist and Postcommunist Studies* 26(4): 387–411.

1999a. Portfel czy rożaniec? Ekonomiczne i aksjologiczne determinanty zachowań wyborczych. In R. Markowski, ed., *Wybory parlamentarne 1997 roku*. Warsaw: Ebert Foundation/ISP PAN.

1999b. Polish Politics after the 1997 Parliamentary Election: Polarization or Pluralism? *Soviet and Post-Soviet Review* 26(1): 97–126.

Jasiewicz, Krzysztof, and Władysław Adamski. 1993. Evolution of the Oppositional Consciousness. In Władysław W. Adamski, ed., *Societal Conflict and Systemic Change: The Case of Poland, 1980–1992*, pp. 35–56. Warsaw: IFiS Publishers.

Jawłowska, Aldona, Marian Kempny, and Elżbieta Tarkowska, eds. 1993. *Kulturowy wymiar przemian społecznych*. Warsaw: IFiS PAN.

Jowitt, Ken. 1990. Survey of Opinion on the East European Revolution. *East European Politics and Society* 4(2): 193–97.

1992. *New World Disorder: The Leninist Extinction*. Berkeley: University of California Press.

Kennedy, Michael, ed. 1994. *Envisioning Eastern Europe: Postcommunist Cultural Studies*. Ann Arbor: University of Michigan Press.

Khrushcheva, Nina L. 2000. Cultural Contradictions of Post-Communism: Why Liberal Reforms Did Not Succeed in Russia. Available: <www.cfr.org/p/pubs/khurshcheva Russia paper.html>.

Kowalski, Sergiusz. 1990. *Krytyka solidarnościowego rozumu*. Warsaw: PEN.

Kubik, Jan. 1994. *The Power of Symbols against the Symbols of Power: The Rise of Solidarity and Fall of State-Socialism in Poland*. University Park: Pennsylvania State University Press.

2000. The Polish Round Table of 1989: The Cultural Dimension(s) of the Negotiated Regime Change. In Michael D. Kennedy and Brian Porter, eds., *Negotiating Radical Change: Understanding and Extending the Lessons of the Polish Round Table Talks*, pp. 87–109. Ann Arbor: Center for Russian and East European Studies, University of Michigan.

Kucharczyk Jacek. 1999. "Za a Nawet Przeciw": Partie polityczne wobec perspektywy integraeji evropejskiej w wyborach '97. In Lena Kolarska-Bobińska, ed., *Polska Eurodebata*, pp. 219–45. Warsaw: ISP.

Kuniński, Miłowit. 1999. Liberalism in Poland: What Is Left? In Ewa Hauser and Jacek Wasilewski, eds., *Lessons in Democracy*, pp. 229–43. Cracow: Jagiellonian University Press; Rochester: University of Rochester Press.

Laitin, David D. 1986. *Hegemony and Culture*. Chicago: University of Chicago Press.

1988. Political Culture and Political Preferences. *American Political Science Review* 82(2): 589–93.

Lasswell, Harold, Nathon Leites, et al. 1949. *Language of Politics: Studies in Quantitative Semantics*. New York: George Stewart.

Lipski, Jan. 1985. *KOR: A History of the Workers' Defense Committee in Poland, 1976–1981*. Trans. Olga Amsterdamska and Gene Moore. Berkeley: University of California Press.

Lotman, Yuri. 1992. *Kultura i Vzriv* (Culture and rebellion). Moscow: Gnosis. Polish edition: *Kultura i eksplozja* (Culture and explosion).Warsaw: PIW, 1998.

Mach, Bogdan W. 1998. *Transformacja ustrojowa a mentalne dziedzictwo socjalizmu*. Warsaw: ISP PAN.

Markowski, Radosław. 2001. Party System Institutionalization in New Democracies: Poland – A Trend-Setter with No Followers. In P. G. Lewis, ed., *Party Development and Democratic Change in Post-Communist Europe: The First Decade*, pp. 55–77. London: Frank Cass.

McDaniel, Tim. 1996. *The Agony of the Russian Idea*. Princeton: Princeton University Press.

Melville, Andrei Yu. 1993. An Emerging Civic Culture? Ideology, Public Attitudes, and Political Culture in the Early 1990s. In Arthur H. Miller, William M. Reisinger, and Vicki L. Hesli, eds., *Public Opinion and Regime Change: The New Politics of Post-Soviet Societies*, pp. 56–68. Boulder, Colo.: Westview.

Michnik, Adam. 1977. *Kosciół, lewica, dialog* (The church, the left, a dialogue). Paris: Instytut Literacki.

Millar, James R., and Sharon L. Wolchik, eds. 1994. *The Social Legacy of Communism*. Cambridge: Woodrow Wilson Center Press and Cambridge University Press.

Moran, Maria Luz. 2000. "Civil Society" and Political Change in Spain. In Gerhard Mangott, Harald Waldrauch, and Stephen Day, eds., *Democratic Consolidation: The International Dimension: Hungary, Poland, and Spain*, pp. 317–34. Baden-Baden: Nomos.

Morson, Gary Saul. 1998. Foreword: Why Read Chicherin? In G. M. Hamburg, trans. and ed., *Liberty, Equality, and the Market: Essays by B. N. Chicherin*, pp. ix–xxv. New Haven: Yale University Press.

Nora, Pierre. 1989. Between Memory and History: Les Lieux de Mémoire. *Representations* 26: 7–25.

Ortner, Sherry. 1989. *High Religion: A Cultural and Political History of Sherpa Buddhism*. Princeton: Princeton University Press.

Paramonov, Boris M. 1996. Historical Culture. In D. N. Shalin, ed., *Russian Culture at the Crossroads: Paradoxes of Postcommunist Consciousness*, pp. 11–40. Boulder, Colo.: Westview.

Perry, Elizabeth J. 1994. Introduction: Chinese Political Culture Revisited. In Elizabeth J. Perry and Jeffrey N. Wasserstrom, eds., *Popular Protest and Political Culture in Modern China*. Boulder, Colo.: Westview.

Petro, Nicolai N. 1995. *The Rebirth of Russian Democracy: An Interpretation of Political Culture*. Cambridge, Mass.: Harvard University Press.

Plummer, Ken. 1994. *Telling Sexual Stories: Power, Change, and Social Worlds*. London: Routledge.

Popper, Karl R. 1979. *Objective Knowledge: An Evolutionary Approach*. New York: Oxford University Press.

Porter, Brian. 2000. *When Nationalism Began to Hate: Imagining Modern Politics in Nineteenth Century Poland*. New York: Oxford University Press.

Powell, Walter W., and Paul J. DiMaggio, eds. 1991. *The New Institutionalism in Organizational Analysis*. Chicago: University of Chicago Press.

Prizel, Ilya. 1998. *National Identity and Foreign Policy: Nationalism and Leadership in Poland, Russia, and Ukraine*. Cambridge: Cambridge University Press.

Putnam, Robert. 1971. Studying Elite Political Culture: The Case of "Ideology." *American Political Science Review* 65(3): 651–81.

Putnam, Robert D., with R. Leonardi and R. Y. Nanetti. 1993. *Making Democracy Work: Civic Traditions in Modern Italy*. Princeton: Princeton University Press.

Rakowski, Mieczysław F. 1991. *Jak to się stało*. Warsaw: BGW.

Rancour-Laferriere. 2000. *Imagining Russia: Ethnic Identity and the Nationalist Mind*. Internet version (excerpts). Available: <www.panorama.ru:8101/works/patr/ir/index.html>, accessed on July 13, 2001.

Reisinger, William M., A. H. Miller, V. L. Hesli, and K. Hill Maher. 1994. Political Values in Russia, Ukraine, and Lithuania: Sources and Implications for Democracy. *British Journal of Political Science* 24: 183–223.

Reisinger, William M., and Alexander I. Nikitin. 1993. Public Opinion and the Emergence of a Multi-Party System. In Arthur H. Miller, William M. Reisinger, and Vicki L. Hesli, eds., *Public Opinion and Regime Change: The New Politics of Post-Soviet Societies*, pp. 168–96. Boulder, Colo.: Westview.

Rolicki, Janusz. 1990. *Edward Gierek: Przerwana Dekada.* Warsaw: BGW.

Rose, Sonya O. 1999. Cultural Analysis and Moral Discourse: Episodes, Continuities, and Transformations. In Victoria Bonnell and Lynn Hunt, eds., *Beyond the Cultural Turn: New Directions in the Study of Society and Culture*, pp. 217–38. Berkeley: University of California Press.

Rutland, Peter. 1997. Russia's Broken "Wheel of Ideologies." *Transition* 4(1): 47–55.

Sakwa, Richard. 1995. Subjectivity, Politics and Order in Russian Political Evolution. *Slavic Review* 54(4): 943–68.

Schochet, Gordon J. 1994. Why Should History Matter? Political Theory and the History of Discourse. In J. G. A. Pocock, Gordon J. Schochet, and Lois G. Schwoerer, eds., *The Varieties of British Political Thought, 1500–1800*, pp. 321–57. Cambridge: Cambridge University Press.

Schull, Joseph. 1992. What Is Ideology? Theoretical Problems and Lessons from Soviet-Type Societies. *Political Studies* 40: 728–41.

Scott, James C. 1998. *Seeing Like a State: How Certain Schemes to Improve the Human Condition Failed.* New Haven: Yale University Press.

Seleny, Anna. 1994. Constructing the Discourse of Transformation: Hungary, 1979–82. *East European Politics and Societies* 8(3): 439–66.

1999. Old Political Rationalities and New Democracies: Compromise and Confrontation in Hungary and Poland. *World Politics* 51(July): 484–519.

Sergeyev, Victor, and Nikolai Biryukov. 1993. *Russia's Road to Democracy: Parliament, Communism and Traditional Culture.* Brookfield, Vt.: Edward Elgar.

Sewell, William H., Jr. 1982. A Theory of Structure: Duality, Agency, and Transformation. *American Journal of Sociology* 91: 1–29.

1999. The Concept(s) of Culture. In Victoria Bonnell and Lynn Hunt, eds., *Beyond the Cultural Turn: New Directions in the Study of Society and Culture*, pp. 35–61. Berkeley: University of California Press.

Shalin, Dmitri N. 1996. Introduction: Continuity and Change in Russian Culture. In D. N. Shalin, ed., *Russian Culture at the Crossroads: Paradoxes of Postcommunist Consciousness*, pp. 1–10. Boulder, Colo.: Westview.

Sider, Gerald M. 1986. *Culture and Class in Anthropology and History: A Newfoundland Illustration.* Cambridge: Cambridge University Press.

Skarzyński, Ryszard. 1994. Pomiędzy radykalizmem i konserwatyzmem. Główne idęe polityczne gdańskich liberałów i Kongresu Liberalno-Demokratycznego w latach 1983–1992. *Studia Polityczne* 3: 59–71.

Snow, David A., and Robert D. Benford. 1988. Ideology, Frame Resonance, and Participant Mobilization. In Bert Klandermans, Hanspeter Kriesi, and Sidney Tarrow, eds., *International Social Movement Research*, vol. 1, *From Structure to Action: Comparing Social Movement Research across Cultures*, pp. 197–217. Greenwich: JAI Press.

Somers, Margaret R. 1995. What's Political or Cultural about Political Culture and the Public Sphere? Toward an Historical Sociology of Concept Formation. *Sociological Theory* 13(2): 113–44.

Staniszkis, Jadwiga. 1989. *Ontologia Socjalizmu*. Warsaw: In Plus.

Steinmetz, George, ed. 1999. *State/Culture: State-Formation after the Cultural Turn*. Ithaca: Cornell University Press.

Strauss, Claudia, and Naomi Quinn. 1997. *A Cognitive Theory of Cultural Meaning*. Cambridge: Cambridge University Press.

Swidler, Ann. 1986. Culture in Action: Symbols and Strategies. *American Sociological Review* 51: 273–86.

Szacki, Jerzy. 1995. *Liberalism after Communism*. Budapest: Central European University Press.

Tismaneanu, Vladimir. 1998. *Fantasies of Salvation: Democracy, Nationalism, and Myth in Post-Communist Europe*. Princeton: Princeton University Press.

Tismaneanu, Vladimir, and Michael Turner. 1995. Understanding Post-Sovietism: Between Residual Leninism and Uncertain Pluralism. In Vladimir Tismaneanu, ed., *Political Culture and Civil Society in Russia and the New States of Eurasia*, pp. 3–24. Armonk, N.Y.: M. E. Sharpe.

Tolz, Vera. 1998. Forging the Nation: National Identity and Nation Building in Post-Communist Russia. *Europe-Asia Studies* 50(6): 993–1022.

Turek, Wojciech. 1995. Gdańscy liberałowie przed upadkiem komunizmu. In *Solidarność i opozycja antykomunistyczna w Gdańsku (1980–1989)*. Gdańsk: Instytut Konserwatywny Burke'a.

Tworzecki, Hubert. 1996. *Parties and Politics in Post-1989 Poland*. Boulder, Colo.: Westview.

Uhlig, Anna. 1989. *W kręgu symbolu. O polskiej kulturze politycznej lat Osiemdziesiątych*. Warsaw: Uniwersytet Warszawski, Instytut Nauk Politycznych.

Urban, Michael. 1994. The Politics of Identity in Russia's Postcommunist Transition: The Nation against Itself. *Slavic Studies* 53(3): 733–65.

1996. Stages of Political Identity Formation in Late Soviet and Post-Soviet Russia. In Victoria E. Bonnell, ed., *Identities in Transition: Eastern Europe and Russia after the Collapse of Communism*, pp. 140–54. Berkeley: Center for Slavic and East European Studies, University of California at Berkeley.

1998. Remythologizing the Russian State. *Europe-Asia Studies* 50(6): 969–92.

Vainshtein, Grigory. 1994. Totalitarian Public Consciousness in a Post-Totalitarian Society: The Russian Case in the General Context of Post-Communist Developments. *Communist and Post-Communist Studies* 27(3): 247–59.

Venturi, Franco. 1960. *Roots of the Revolution: A History of the Populist and Socialist Movements in Nineteenth Century Russia*. New York: Alfred A. Knopf.

Verdery, Katherine. 1991. *National Ideology under Socialism: Identity and Cultural Politics in Ceausescu's Romania*. Berkeley: University of California Press.

1993. Nationalism and National Sentiment in Post-Socialist Romania. *Slavic Review* 52(2): 179–203.

Walicki, Andrzej. 1975. *The Slavophile Controversy: History of a Conservative Utopia in Nineteenth-Century Russian Thought*. Oxford: Clarendon Press.

1988. The Three Traditions of Polish Patriotism and Their Contemporary Relevance. Paper presented at Indiana University, Polish Studies Center.

1995. *Marxism and the Leap to the Kingdom of Freedom*. Stanford: Stanford University Press.
Wandycz, Piotr. 1992. *The Price of Freedom: A History of East Central Europe from the Middle Ages to the Present*. London: Routledge.
Weigle, Marcia. 2000. *Russia's Liberal Project: State-Society Relations in the Transition from Communism*. University Park: Pennsylvania State University Press.
Wesołowski, Włodzimierz. 2000. *Partie: Nieustanne Kłopoty*. Warsaw: IFiS PAN.
White, Stephen, Richard Rose, and Ian McAllister. 1997. *How Russia Votes*. Chatham, N.J.: Chatham House.
Wilson, Richard W. 1992. *Compliance Ideologies: Rethinking Political Culture*. Cambridge: Cambridge University Press.
Wnuk-Lipiński, Edmund. 1994. Fundamentalizm a Pragmatyzm: Dwa Typy Reakcji na Radykalną Zmianę Spoleczną. *Kultura i Społeczeństwo* 37(1): 1–12.
Wuthnow, Robert. 1989. *Communities of Discourse: Ideology and Social Structure in the Reformation, the Enlightenment, and European Socialism*. Cambridge, Mass.: Harvard University Press.
Yanowitch, Murray. 1991. *Controversies in Soviet Social Thought*. Armonk, N.Y.: M. E. Sharpe.
Zerubavel, Eviatar. 1997. *Social Mindscapes: An Invitation to Cognitive Sociology*. Cambridge, Mass.: Harvard University Press.
Zerubavel, Yael. 1995. *Recovered Roots: Collective Memory and the Making of Israeli National Tradition*. Chicago: University of Chicago Press.
Zuzowski, Robert. 1992. *Political Dissent and Opposition in Poland: The Workers' Defense Committee "KOR."* Westport, Conn.: Praeger.
Zyuganov, Gennady. 1995. *Veryu v Rossiyu*. Voronezh: "Voronezh."
1997. *My Russia: The Political Autobiography of Gennady Zyuganov*. Armonk, N.Y.: M. E. Sharpe.

Epilogue

From Area Studies to Contextualized Comparisons

Paul Pierson

Historically, the rise of comparative politics as a distinct subfield with an interest in understanding political processes in highly diverse settings was also the rise of "area studies." Investigations of different polities were largely oriented around specific regions of the world. Analysts either specialized on one or two countries in those regions or (less often) on the region as a whole.

In many respects this remains the case. An organizational analysis of the subfield (its thematic centers, fellowships, and professional associations) as well as an analysis of careers within the profession (patterns of graduate training, the definition of faculty positions, and procedures for evaluation and promotion) would reveal that area studies continues to be a central organizing principle for research in comparative politics. To many observers, however, this demonstrates the power of inertia rather than the currency of the animating ideas behind area studies as a framework for organizing inquiry. Intellectually, social scientists with an interest in "area studies" have been caught in a pincers movement for the past few decades.

On one side has been the rise of what might be called the "variable mindset" – the expanding (if incomplete) consensus that multiple regression constitutes the preferred, if not exclusive, method for testing hypotheses about the social world.[1] In principle, such techniques may be employed in a manner that allows analysts to consider significant degrees of causal complexity and contextuality (Braumoeller, 2002). In practice, however, this is usually not the case. The rise of regression analysis helped fuel a broader shift in thinking, which emphasized the extent to which analysts should think in terms of "variables" that can be easily abstracted from widely different contexts and treated as similar in composition and effects. As Andrew Abbott

[1] For excellent discussions of this trend in sociology and its implications, see Abbott (1988; 1997). Hall (2003) provides a thoughtful analysis of similar developments in the field of comparative politics.

I appreciate the helpful comments of the editors, as well as Allison Stanger, on an earlier draft.

(1988) has nicely described this, quantitative scholars developed a "general linear model," loaded with simplifying assumptions about the social world required to make their statistical analyses work. They gradually and unconsciously shifted from these modeling conventions to a view of "general linear reality" in which the heroic assumptions became taken-for-granted features of the social world.

This approach, of course, runs counter to the implicit or explicit justifications for area studies, which emphasize precisely the extent to which ostensibly similar "variables" in different settings are likely to mean quite different things. From this perspective, analysts need to pay much more attention to contextual effects on "variables." If so, it may make a great deal more sense to situate comparative analyses within temporally and/or spatially proximate settings.

The other side of the pincers movement has been theoretical rather than methodological: the rise of rational choice analyses within political science.[2] In most respects, the starting point for rational choice analyses is fundamentally different from the "variable mind-set," which is often atheoretical if not antitheoretical. Yet the two share one crucial commonality. Like regression analysis, typical choice-theoretic accounts are radically decontextualizing.[3] The building blocks for theory are maximizing individuals. The emphasis on combining the greatest degree of parsimony and the greatest capacity for generalization leads to a presumption that compelling hypotheses involve little in the way of "local" information. Rational choice analyses in political science typically focus on variable entities like "voters," "interest groups," and a whole range of institutions (central banks, legislatures, federalism, courts, and so on) that are taken to be similar units, with similar effects, in widely divergent settings. Theorizing grounded in rational choice analysis typically has an ambitious agenda of establishing claims that should apply, at least on average, across a wide range of settings whenever a few crucial conditions hold.

The rise of rational choice and the variable mind-set within political science have interacted to produce a decontextual revolution. They have joined to create a disciplinary environment in which "context" is for many a bad

[2] Conventionally one would say here "rational choice theory" rather than "rational choice analyses," but this is a rhetorical move that should be avoided. It implies a degree of internal coherence that no social science framework with such broad aspirations has come close to achieving. At the same time, it seems to suggest that one either has to accept or reject "rational choice theory" in its entirety – something that has fueled a very unhelpful degree of feudal jousting within the social sciences. Jepperson (2000), following Stinchcombe (1968), has usefully suggested that we should think of rational choice (as well as other broad frameworks such as sociological institutionalism or historical institutionalism) as a "theoretical imagery" rather than a theory.

[3] There are, of course, many exceptions. It is essential in discussions such as this, however, to focus on tendencies – what particular kinds of analysis *typically* do, even if there is no logical requirement that they do so.

word – a synonym for thick description and an obstacle to social scientific analysis. "Area studies" is often targeted as a particularly egregious instance of backward thinking, preoccupied with contexts that are taken to be unique and thus antithetical to the identification of patterns and the development of generalizations.

Yet there is, as Andrew Abbott has argued eloquently, another way to think about it:

> "Context" has two senses.... The strict sense ... denotes those things that environ and thereby define a thing of interest. The loose sense simply denotes detail. The acute reader will note that these correspond nicely to the two judgments of the scientific worth of contextual information. If decontextualization is merely the removal of excess detail, then it's a fine thing, scientifically. On the other hand, if it is the removal of defining locational information, it is a scientific disaster. (1997: 1171)

It is Abbott's strict sense of context that animates the current volume. Particular social contexts constrain and enable political actors and indeed shape those actors' very understandings of who they are and what they want to do. For Ekiert, Hanson, and their collaborators, a viable effort to explain key features of the remarkable and highly varied transformations of Eastern Europe requires an appreciation of how social activities are embedded in time and space.

Yet if the authors reject the decontextual revolution, they are equally unwilling to fall back on thick descriptions of single cases. They seek more than "just-so" accounts, or what Jack Goldstone terms Dr. Seuss-style explanations: "[It] just happened that this happened first, then this, then that, and is not likely to happen that way again" (1998: 833). Nor do the authors wish to rely on simple paired comparisons of complex cases that raise potentially insuperable methodological difficulties. The present volume constitutes part of a wave of recent work in comparative politics – methodological, theoretical, and empirical – that seeks to advance the case for contextualized comparisons.[4] This movement seeks to combine sensitivity to causal complexity and contextual effects with aspirations to draw out implications about social processes that transcend a single social setting.

It is an exciting and challenging agenda, raising the prospect of social analyses that capture more of the richness of actually lived histories, while still speaking to the social scientific goal of generating usable knowledge. In this short conclusion I can only single out a few of the main lines of argument that contribute to this emerging program of research. Most of these, as I point out, are ably represented in this collection.

[4] This literature is vast, but a good point of entry is the collection of essays in Mahoney and Rueschemeyer (2003). On the methodological issues involved, see Mahoney (2000b); Bennett and George (1997); and Hall (2003). On recent theoretical developments, especially focused on the temporal dimensions of social processes, see Abbott (2001); Mahoney (2000a); Pierson (2000a); and Thelen (1999). For excellent empirical analyses, see Carpenter (2001); Huber and Stephens (2001); and Waldner (1999).

Two distinct but compatible analytical moves exemplify the core orientations of contextualized comparisons. The first and most straightforward is the introduction of explicit temporal or spatial boundary conditions on the hypotheses that are entertained. This move represents a strategic retreat from the universalist aspirations of large segments of the social sciences. To establish such boundary conditions forgoes, or at least postpones, the search for relationships among variables that one would expect to hold across a wide range of settings. Instead, the expectation is that strong contextual effects (if you will, background variables that strongly influence the effects of other factors) will play a major role in determining how particular features are related to each other in a particular setting. "Ceteris paribus" clauses are considered plausible only across a restricted range of time or space.

One can see the character of the position being adopted here by contrasting it with a methodological technique that has become increasingly popular in variable-oriented comparative research: regression analysis based on pooled time-series (Shalev, 1999). Pooling has gained prominence because it hurdles the biggest obstacle to statistical analysis in much of comparative politics: the limited number of available observations. If each "country-year" can be treated as a separate observation, time series can be used to vastly expand the relatively small number of "country-cases." The "n" for statistical analysis can be increased twenty- or thirty-fold, allowing the investigator to consider more-complex hypotheses and generate more-reliable results.

For those who question the decontextual revolution, however, the assumptions underpinning the move to pooled time series elicit tremendous skepticism. Can we really assume that the causal relationship between two variables – say, economic openness and labor-union density – was the same in 1965 as it was in 1995? Pooling represents an attempt to deal with one kind of causal complexity by wishing away another – namely, the fact that relationships among variables of interest are likely to change as contexts change over time.

The presumption that such contextual effects are likely to be strong leads to the organization of research around more-bounded social entities. Typically, the boundaries are temporal, spatial, or both.[5] The powerful comparative historical analyses of state building by Anderson, Tilly, Ertman, Mann, Downing, and others did not seek to present general propositions about state building but focused on developing explanations applicable to European experiences during a particular historical period. Gregory Luebbert's impressive study of the development of liberal, fascist, and social democratic regimes fashioned explanations applicable to *interwar Europe* (Luebbert, 1991). He did not claim that the same factors could account,

[5] At least initially. As Thelen (2002) has argued, one can and arguably should strive to replace boundary conditions defined in temporal or spatial terms with ones that are defined analytically.

without modification, for regime outcomes in, say, contemporary South America.[6]

This volume, focusing on the extraordinary transformations under way in Central and Eastern Europe, provides a clear example of the rationale for contextualized comparisons within a temporally and spatially bounded setting. The countries examined here share a host of economic, social, and political experiences unlike those encountered elsewhere. Dropping these "cases" into a large-n statistical analysis of, say, transitions to democracy, is certain to miss a great deal. At the same time, these shared experiences provide a backdrop within which differences in both the processes and outcomes can meaningfully be identified, compared, and explained.

Analytical and methodological choices in the social sciences inevitably involve trade-offs, and it is important to make these explicit whenever we can. The setting of temporal and spatial scope conditions, like other choices, comes at a price. The first cost, as critics have forcefully argued, is that restricting our arguments to a small number of cases raises major problems of causal inference (Geddes, 1991; King, Keohane, and Verba, 1994). Limited samples raise the dangers of selection bias and increase the likelihood that we will end up with more variables under consideration than we have empirical observations to use in assessing causal claims. The second is that the application of such scope conditions seems to surrender one of the chief aspirations of most social scientists – namely, to identify causal factors that can "travel" across a range of settings.

It is precisely these weaknesses that suggest why the decision to bound empirical inquiries is increasingly coupled with a second analytical strategy: the development of theory and methods that are explicitly tailored to address key aspects of context. The option of setting boundary conditions seems a cautious one, embracing a strategic retreat in the face of causal complexity. It becomes much less of a retreat, however, when combined with this second strategy. Analysts seek to explore which aspects of context, or the "embeddedness" of social interactions, can be specified in terms that can potentially be applied in multiple settings. To employ Abbott's language, the goal is to identify the features of a particular setting that "environ and thus define a thing of interest." The beauty of this strategy is that it simultaneously copes with many of the weaknesses of the decontextual revolution and addresses the concern of many social scientists that relatively narrow spatial and temporal boundary conditions make powerful social science impossible.

The emphasis on context implies that we should be thinking about relationships. Indeed, the focus of recent theoretical work has been on the

[6] It should be noted that comparative historical work typically employs scope conditions for an additional reason. The motivation for these analyses has typically been a concern with specific real-world outcomes. Luebbert, for instance, was particularly interested in understanding the replacement of democracy with fascism in some, but not all, European cases. On the role of this problem-driven focus in comparative historical analysis, see Pierson and Skocpol (2002).

character of spatial and temporal relationships. Particular actors, organizations, or institutions are shaped in part by their spatial relationships to other aspects of a social setting. Similarly, a particular moment in time is part of broader temporal processes. Events are parts of various sequences of events, and their place in those sequences may play a critical role in determining their meaning. Thus these theoretical works explore the spatial and temporal settings that provide context for any object of social inquiry.

In the following discussion I focus primarily on issues related to temporal processes, but the same basic theoretical orientation could be applied equally well to issues of space. A simple analogy can start us off.[7] Imagine that you are preparing to bake a cake. Working from a recipe, you first carefully assemble and measure the necessary ingredients, and then follow the instructions for both the sequence and the specific manner in which these ingredients are to be combined. Now imagine an alternative setting, where the chef claims that as long as the ingredients are correctly measured, how and in what order they are combined *makes no difference*. Few would patronize a restaurant with such a philosophy of cooking, but many social scientists work in this kind of kitchen. The decontextual revolution makes variables the equivalent of this chef's ingredients.

By contrast, there has been a flurry of recent work that seeks to explore the theoretical dimensions of temporal processes. Work on *path dependence* has focused on chains of events or processes stemming from some initial "critical" juncture (Mahoney, 2000a; Pierson, 2000a), emphasizing, for instance, the potentially self-reinforcing effects of early outcomes.[8] Discussions of *sequencing* (Abbott, 2001; Pierson, 2000b) have explored the consequences of differences in the temporal ordering of both macroprocesses and micro-interactions. Inquiries into the significance of *long-term processes* (Pierson, 2003) emphasize the significance of the highly different rates at which distinct causal processes and outcomes in the social world may unfold – the fact that, as Abbott puts it, "events of equivalent causal importance just don't always take the same amount of time to happen" (Abbott, 1988: 174). Finally, recent work on *institutional development* (Schickler, 2001; Thelen, 2002a) has stressed the necessity of looking beyond moments of institutional selection that are the standard focus of choice-theoretic analyses. Efforts to account for institutional outcomes must also explore the factors that affect how institutional arrangements adapt, or fail to adapt, to a variety of pressures for amendment or replacement occurring over an extended period of time.

[7] Thanks to James Caporaso for this suggestion.

[8] Here and in the other areas I discuss, recent scholarship builds on a wide range of earlier research. On critical junctures, for instance, one would want to cite Collier and Collier (1991), Krasner (1989), and Stinchcombe (1968), to mention only a few. A full literature review is impossible here, but interested readers may consult the bibliographies of the recent articles I cite, as well as the extensive bibliography in Mahoney and Rueschemeyer (2003).

The goal of this body of research, as Kathleen Thelen has nicely put it, is to "capture the impact of time in as timeless a way as possible" (2000: 101n). That is, it seeks to specify common characteristics of temporal relationships that would allow one to use more-general analytical tools to make sense of particular historical contexts. All of these recent themes about temporal processes are prominent in the current volume.

Ekiert, for example, emphasizes the importance of positive feedback in the transition process, where early advantages generate a range of effects that reinforce a virtuous cycle of liberalizing reforms. Baxandall, too, points to the role of path dependence resulting from positive feedback; he eloquently demonstrates how an understanding of such mechanisms can help one to understand discontinuities as well as continuities. As Thelen (1999) has argued, a clear understanding of the mechanisms that reproduce a particular arrangement can generate insights into institutional disruption. In Baxandall's account, the strong taboo against unemployment in Central and Eastern Europe was heavily dependent on arrangements that linked social protection to the continuity of a particular employment relationship. With change in these arrangements, rising unemployment failed to produce the anticipated political outcry.

Ekiert's analysis also draws out the importance of sequencing – the order in which particular developments occur can make an important difference to the eventual outcome. As in Ekiert's argument, Anna Grzymała-Busse's research on communist successor parties suggests that early steps were crucial in determining eventual success and failure. The crucial matter of sequence is whether reformist party elites focused attention first on the goal of organizational transformation. If this strategy was not employed vigorously during a brief window of opportunity, the prospects for dislodging traditional party elites worsened rapidly. As she puts it, "attempts to transform the parties' organizations or behavior *after* 1989–91 would make little difference" (emphasis added).

In Grzymała-Busse's account, as well as Johnson's discussion of "active" and "passive" institutional reforms, sequencing refers primarily to the temporal order of strategic choices by actors. For instance, Johnson argues that it mattered a great deal whether key actors chose to pursue institutional or policy reforms first. Yet sequencing may also be a matter of the temporal ordering of different processes that are not strategically selected but rather forced on actors by circumstances or external events. In Stanger's analysis, for example, the emergence of the Czech-Slovak conflict led to a sequence of constitution building in which the issue of confederation or separation had to be dealt with first, followed only with a lag by many of the key constitutional issues facing the now separate Czech Republic and Slovakia. This sequence, she argues, was hugely consequential for the constitutional structures eventually developed in both countries.

For most of the authors, outcomes of interest can best be understood as the result of processes that unfold over significant stretches of time. Ekiert's inquiry into the diversity of transition outcomes argues for the importance of crucial legacies from earlier junctures of social conflict – especially the inherited social resources that allowed a strong, liberalizing counterelite to emerge in the early phases of the postsocialist transition. Similarly, Kitschelt provides a powerful critique of explanatory accounts that are biased toward temporally proximate factors. These may yield impressive statistical associations but run a high risk of degenerating into tautology. Richer theories will often focus on features of a social environment that are somewhat more distant in time from the outcomes of interest but that reveal more about what is decisive in influencing the contours of political development. Again, choice-theoretic accounts, with their focus on explicating strategic action, have a strong bias toward very short-term explanations of social outcomes. Recent work on transitions to democracy, structured around elite bargaining models, provide a good example of the bias this imparts to causal accounts (Collier, 1999). As Charles Tilly puts it, "recent theorists have accelerated the tempo so that at times the transition to democracy looks almost instantaneous: put the pact in gear and go" (Tilly, 1995: 365). Of course, research in the current volume emphasizes what is likely to be lost from such an approach to understanding transitions.

Indeed, my view is that Kitschelt is, if anything, too critical of what he calls excessively deep (temporally remote) explanations. As Ekiert and Hanson argue in Chapter 1, different aspects of society change at varied rates. Furthermore, there may often be considerable lags between key events or processes and the outcomes of interest, and outcomes themselves may emerge only slowly. Under these common circumstances, "deep" explanations of social phenomena may prove to be compelling.[9] All of these features suggest why the analysts in the current volume typically find a focus on "legacies" appealing.

Finally, there are compelling arguments in the current volume concerning the importance of studying institutional evolution or development rather than simply focusing on particular moments of institutional choice. Because many theories in the social sciences have recently emphasized the enormous consequences of institutions, there has been growing interest in exploring the sources of institutions (Knight, 1992; Boix, 1999; Thelen, 2003). Much of this research, particularly in the rational choice tradition, focuses on explaining institutional selection – why rational actors would select a particular institutional arrangement. In practice, these analyses often work backward from institutional outcomes, which are perceived to have particular benefits for powerful actors. These "functions" are then seen as the probable explanations for the institutional outcome.

[9] These issues are explored at length in Pierson (2003).

Explaining institutional outcomes has, unsurprisingly, been of substantial interest to students of the newly emergent political systems in Eastern Europe. As Allison Stanger argues in her detailed comparison of constitutional reforms, however, there are important limitations to functional explanations of these outcomes. Political reform movements in Eastern Europe carried powerful preconceptions about the character of political life and political activism. These preconceptions, she demonstrates, had profound effects on their approaches to questions of institutional design. Although strategic, goal-oriented behavior is evident, none of the cases she studies exemplify a logic of institutional design in which powerful actors simply incorporate those constitutional features that consolidate their political advantages. Initial results combine rationalist, instrumental elements, as well as those reflecting the significance of political symbolism. Unintended consequences are manifest – most profoundly in the unraveling of Czechoslovakia, which the constitutional design process greatly accelerated. Ongoing political and social events shaped the reform process in idiosyncratic ways. "Designers" often exhibited short-term orientations rather than long-term visions for mastering these constitutional moments. For all these reasons, as Stanger demonstrates, the downstream process of institutional development becomes just as important a focus of social science inquiry as the initial moment of institutional "selection."

Just as all these lines of argument demonstrate the compelling case for investigating temporal contexts, the same possibilities exist for exploring issues of space. As Ekiert and Hanson argue, spatial as well as temporal relationships powerfully structure the character of social interactions. Again, this is a subject that has been heavily deemphasized as a result of the decontextual revolution. Yet, just as recent work on temporal processes has moved beyond the assertion that "history matters" to develop stronger theory about the kinds of relationships we should expect to see in different settings, there are significant opportunities to say more than that "space matters." As Kopstein and Reilly argue persuasively, thinking in spatial terms about East European transitions highlights the role of diffusion and contagion processes. This has been an issue of considerable interest to sociologists (Strang and Soule, 1998; Jepperson, 2002). Sensitivity to spatial relationships has increased the sophistication with which analysts in that discipline have thought about the character of social networks. Sewell (2001), for instance, has recently argued that the study of protest and social movements – a topic of obvious importance to students of Eastern Europe and comparativists more generally – can gain considerable insight from attending to aspects of spatial context. Similarly, Herbst's investigation of state formation in Africa has argued that in this particular geopolitical context one can greatly illuminate state building by focusing attention on the highly varied spatial distributions of populations in different parts of Africa (Herbst, 2000). Control over people in this particular spatial context was the central organizing principle behind efforts to construct viable states. In turn, different spatial patterns of population distribution profoundly shaped the prospects for successful state-building projects.

Thus, "context" in this volume, and in the broader movement toward contextualized comparisons, takes on a particular meaning. It becomes a point of entry for thinking about how events and processes are related to each other in social dynamics that unfold over extended periods of time and occur in particular spatial settings. It is not a matter of treating each social setting as unique and infinitely complex. Instead, contextualized comparisons start from the recognition that any event or process is environed by its spatial location, its place within a sequence of occurrences, and its interactions with various processes unfolding at different rates. Especially when we are attempting to understand broad social transformations of the kind that motivate the current volume, these relationships constitute a central subject of social scientific inquiry. We need to know not just "what" (i.e., the value on some variable), but "when" and "where."

It is important to stress that this developing response to the decontextual revolution need not involve a wholesale rejection of either rational choice frameworks or the typical methods of variable-centered analysis. As both Kitschelt and Kopstein and Reilly demonstrate in their contributions, hypotheses about spatial and temporal relations, if clearly specified, may be translated into the language of variables. If appropriate data are available, they may be subjected to statistical testing. For example, claims about path dependence are often grounded in the scale and character of commitments resulting from previous institutional, organizational, or policy outcomes, and these commitments may be specified and measured. Again, the point is not that statistical analyses cannot consider such arguments. It is that the relevant hypotheses are unlikely to receive scrutiny absent the development of theories explicitly oriented toward the examination of these contextualized relationships.

Moreover, the appropriate data for statistical testing are not always available. Scholars pursuing contextualized comparisons are generally suspicious of the often heroic assumptions about causal relationships required to increase the number of observations available for scrutiny. Fortunately, the richer theories of causal process connected to recent work on temporal and spatial effects provide a substantial advantage for the rigorous investigation of hypotheses. "Thin" theories prevalent in decontextualized research are relatively silent about the processes or mechanisms that connect their variables to outcomes. By contrast, because these emerging approaches are far more attentive to mechanisms, they are likely to generate far more observable implications within each broad "case" subjected to empirical scrutiny. These approaches thus lend themselves to the techniques of sophisticated process tracing that have recently been championed from a variety of perspectives (Bennett and George, 1997; Hall, 2003; King et al., 1994). Recent advances in theorizing thus provide one important answer to the methodological concerns that have been raised about spatially and temporally bounded inquiry. Richer theories increase the prospects for surmounting the "many variables, few cases" problem.

So do opportunities created by collaborative research, or by a more decentralized research program involving the overlapping efforts of numerous scholars. *Multiple* research efforts, if properly coordinated, can enhance the prospects for substantial cumulation of findings. This is a central theme in Mahoney and Rueschemeyer (2003); it highlights the importance of developing coherent, clearly specified research programs involving a substantial community of scholars. Thus the current volume's contributions to knowledge reflect not just the observations contained in individual chapters but the cumulative implications of linked efforts by a number of researchers. In this case, the editors have usefully combined the broader comparative investigations of Parts I and II with the complementary insights to be gleaned from the more intensive investigation of specific social processes in Part III.

The move to contextualized comparisons also helps address the second concern about bounded comparisons – the desire of social scientists for portability. Our improving understanding of spatial and temporal relationships has involved a shift from a focus on "causal laws," which imply highly consistent relationships among particular variables across a wide range of settings to the explication of particular social mechanisms – "frequently observed ways in which things happen," as Jon Elster has put it (1989: viii). Analysts working on many of the theoretical issues outlined here have sought to explore when such mechanisms are more likely to operate and with what implications. These insights are likely to be portable across a range of contexts, as, for instance, in the recent applications of arguments about positive feedback processes to social phenomena as diverse as the development of American social welfare policies (Hacker, 2002), emerging patterns of Latin American federalism (Faletti, in progress), and the distinctive national profiles of sports culture (Markovits and Hellerman, 2001).

Contextualized comparisons thus strike a fruitful balance between the particular and the general. To a greater degree than traditional area studies, they both draw on and contribute to the broader social scientific enterprise of generating usable, portable knowledge. Yet they do so precisely by embracing and exploring the specific spatial and temporal contexts that environ and thus define particular processes that are of interest. Extraordinary, unprecedented processes have been unfolding in Central and Eastern Europe. Yet one can benefit enormously from reading the chapters in this volume even if one is interested primarily in examining politics in other settings.

References

Abbott, Andrew. 1988. Transcending General Linear Reality. *Sociological Theory* 6: 169–86.

1997. Of Time and Space: The Contemporary Relevance of the Chicago School. *Social Forces* 75(4): 1149–82.

2001. *Time Matters: On Theory and Method*. Chicago: University of Chicago Press.

Bennett, Andrew, and Alexander L. George. 1997. Process Tracing and Case Study Research. Paper presented at the MacArthur Foundation Workshop on Case Study Methods, Harvard University, October 17–19.

Boix, Carles. 1999. Setting the Rules of the Game: The Choice of Electoral Systems in Advanced Democracies. *American Political Science Review*, September.

Braumoeller, Bear. 2002. Causal Complexity and the Study of Politics. Harvard University. Unpublished manuscript.

Carpenter, Daniel. 2001. *Forging Bureaucratic Autonomy: Reputations, Networks, and Policy Innovation in Executive Agencies, 1862–1928*. Princeton: Princeton University Press.

Collier, David, and Ruth Berins Collier. 1991. *Shaping the Political Arena: Critical Junctures, the Labor Movement, and Regime Dynamics in Latin America*. Princeton: Princeton University Press.

Collier, Ruth Berins. 1999. *Paths toward Democracy: The Working Class and Elites in Western Europe and South America*. Cambridge: Cambridge University Press.

Elster, Jon. 1989. *The Cement of Society: A Study of Social Order*. Cambridge: Cambridge University Press.

Faletti, Tulia. In progress. Not Just What but *When* and *By Whom*: Decentralization Trajectories and Balance of Power in Argentina, Mexico and Colombia, 1982–1999. Ph.D. dissertation, Northwestern University.

Geddes, Barbara. 1991. How the Cases You Choose Affect the Answers You Get: Selection Bias in Comparative Politics. In James Stimson, ed., *Political Analysis*, 2:131–49. Ann Arbor: University of Michigan Press.

Goldstone, Jack A. 1998. Initial Conditions, General Laws, Path Dependence, and Explanation in Historical Sociology. *American Journal of Sociology* 104(3): 829–45.

Hacker, Jacob. 2002. *The Divided Welfare State: The Battle over Public and Private Social Benefits in the United States*. Cambridge: Cambridge University Press.

Hall, Peter. 2003. Aligning Methodology and Ontology in Comparative Politics. In James Mahoney and Dietrich Rueschemeyer, eds., *Comparative Historical Analysis in the Social Sciences*. Cambridge: Cambridge University Press.

Herbst, Jeffrey. 2000. *States and Power in Africa: Comparative Lessons in Authority and Control*. Princeton: Princeton University Press.

Huber, Evelyne, and John D. Stephens. 2001. *Development and Crisis of the Welfare State*. Chicago: University of Chicago Press.

Jepperson, Ronald L. 2000. Relations among Different Theoretical Imageries. European University Institute. Unpublished manuscript.

2002. The Development and Application of Sociological Neoinstitutionalism. In Joseph Berger and Morris Zelditch Jr., eds., *New Directions in Sociological Theory: The Growth of Contemporary Theories*. Lanham, Md.: Rowman and Littlefield.

King, Gary, Robert O. Keohane, and Sidney Verba. 1994. *Designing Social Inquiry: Scientific Inference in Qualitative Research*. Princeton: Princeton University Press.
Knight, Jack. 1992. *Institutions and Social Conflict*. Cambridge: Cambridge University Press.
Krasner, Stephen. 1989. Sovereignty: An Institutional Perspective. In James A. Caporaso, ed., *The Elusive State: International and Comparative Perspectives*. Newbury Park, Calif.: Sage.
Luebbert, Gregory M. 1991. *Liberalism, Fascism, or Social Democracy: Social Classes and the Political Origins of Regimes in Interwar Europe*. Oxford: Oxford University Press.
Mahoney, James. 2000a. Path Dependence in Historical Sociology. *Theory and Society* 29: 507–48.
2000b. Strategies of Causal Inference in Small-N Analysis. *Sociological Methods and Research* 28(4): 387–424.
Mahoney, James, and Dietrich Rueschemeyer, eds. 2003. *Comparative Historical Analysis: Achievements and Agendas*. Cambridge: Cambridge University Press.
Markovits, Andrei S., and Steven L. Hellerman. 2001. *Offside: Soccer and American Exceptionalism*. Princeton: Princeton University Press.
Pierson, Paul. 2000a. Increasing Returns, Path Dependence, and the Study of Politics. *American Political Science Review* 94(2): 251–68.
2000b. Not Just What, but *When*: Timing and Sequence in Political Processes. *Studies in American Political Development* 14: 72–92.
2003. Big, Slow, and ... Invisible: Macro-Social Processes and Contemporary Political Science. In James Mahoney and Dietrich Rueschemeyer, eds., *Comparative Historical Analysis in the Social Sciences*. Cambridge: Cambridge University Press.
Pierson, Paul, and Theda Skocpol. 2002. Historical Institutionalism and Contemporary Political Science. In Ira Katznelson and Helen Milner, eds., *The State of the Discipline*, pp. 693–721. New York: W. W. Norton.
Schickler, Eric. 2001. *Disjointed Pluralism: Institutional Innovation and the Development of the U.S. Congress*. Cambridge: Cambridge University Press.
Sewell, William. 2001. Space in Contentious Politics. In Ronald Aminzade et al., *Silence and Voice in the Study of Contentious Politics*, pp. 51–88. Cambridge: Cambridge University Press.
Shalev, Michael. 1999. Limits of and Alternatives to Multiple Regression in Macro-Comparative Research. Unpublished manuscript, Hebrew University, Jerusalem.
Stinchcombe, Arthur. 1968. *Constructing Social Theories*. Chicago: University of Chicago Press.
Strang, David, and Sarah A. Soule. 1998. Diffusion in Organizations and Social Movements: From Hybrid Corn to Poison Pills. *Annual Review of Sociology* 24: 265–90.
Thelen, Kathleen. 1999. Historical Institutionalism in Comparative Politics. *Annual Review of Political Science* 2: 369–404.
2000. Timing and Temporality in the Analysis of Institutional Evolution and Change. *Studies in American Political Development* 14: 101–8.
2002. The Explanatory Power of Historical Institutionalism. In Renate Mayntz, ed., *Akteure, Mechanismen, Modelle*, pp. 91–106. Frankfurt am Main: Campus Verlag.

2003. How Institutions Evolve. In James Mahoney and Dietrich Rueschemeyer, eds., *Comparative Historical Analysis: Achievements and Agendas*. Cambridge: Cambridge University Press.

Tilly, Charles. 1995. Democracy Is a Lake. In George Reid Andrews and Herrick Chapman, eds., *The Social Construction of Democracy*, pp. 365–87. New York: New York University Press.

Waldner, David. 1999. *State Building and Late Development*. Ithaca: Cornell University Press.

Index